Wild Ones

アラクレ

Vol. 5

Story & Art by
Kiyo Fujiwara

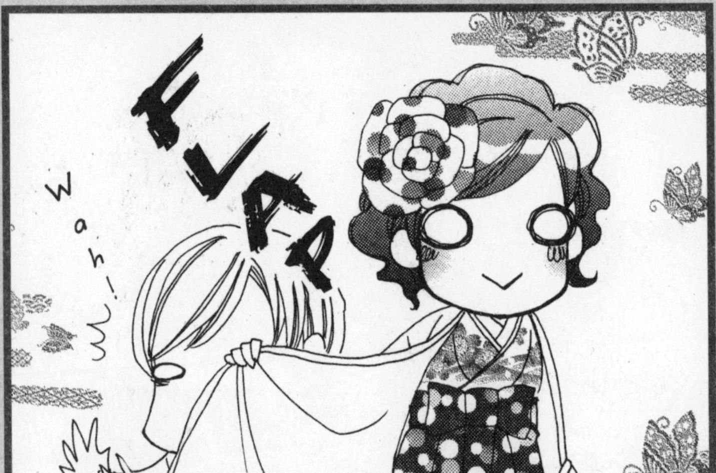
FLAP
Wah!

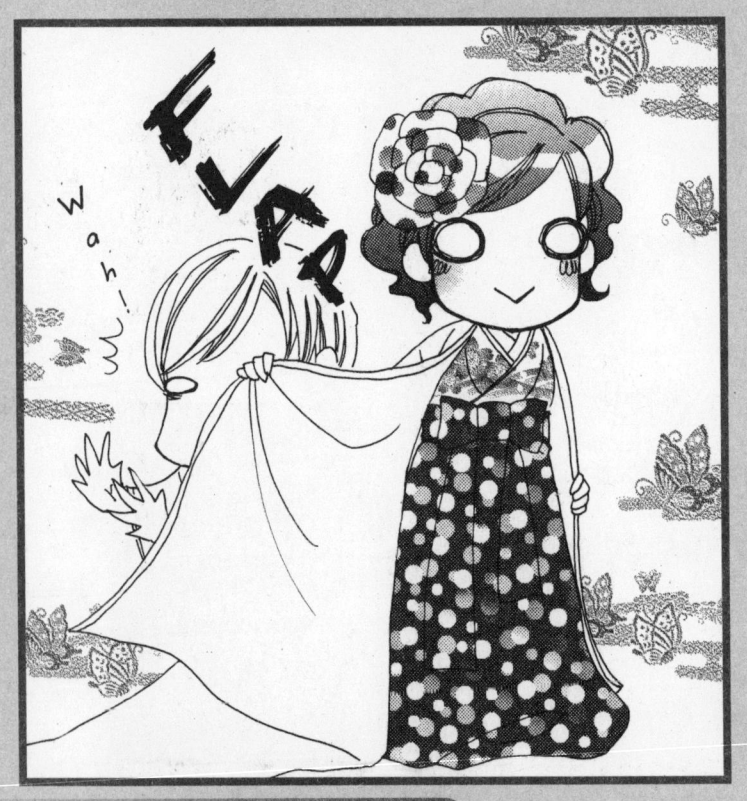

Wild Ones アラクレ

Volume 5

CONTENTS

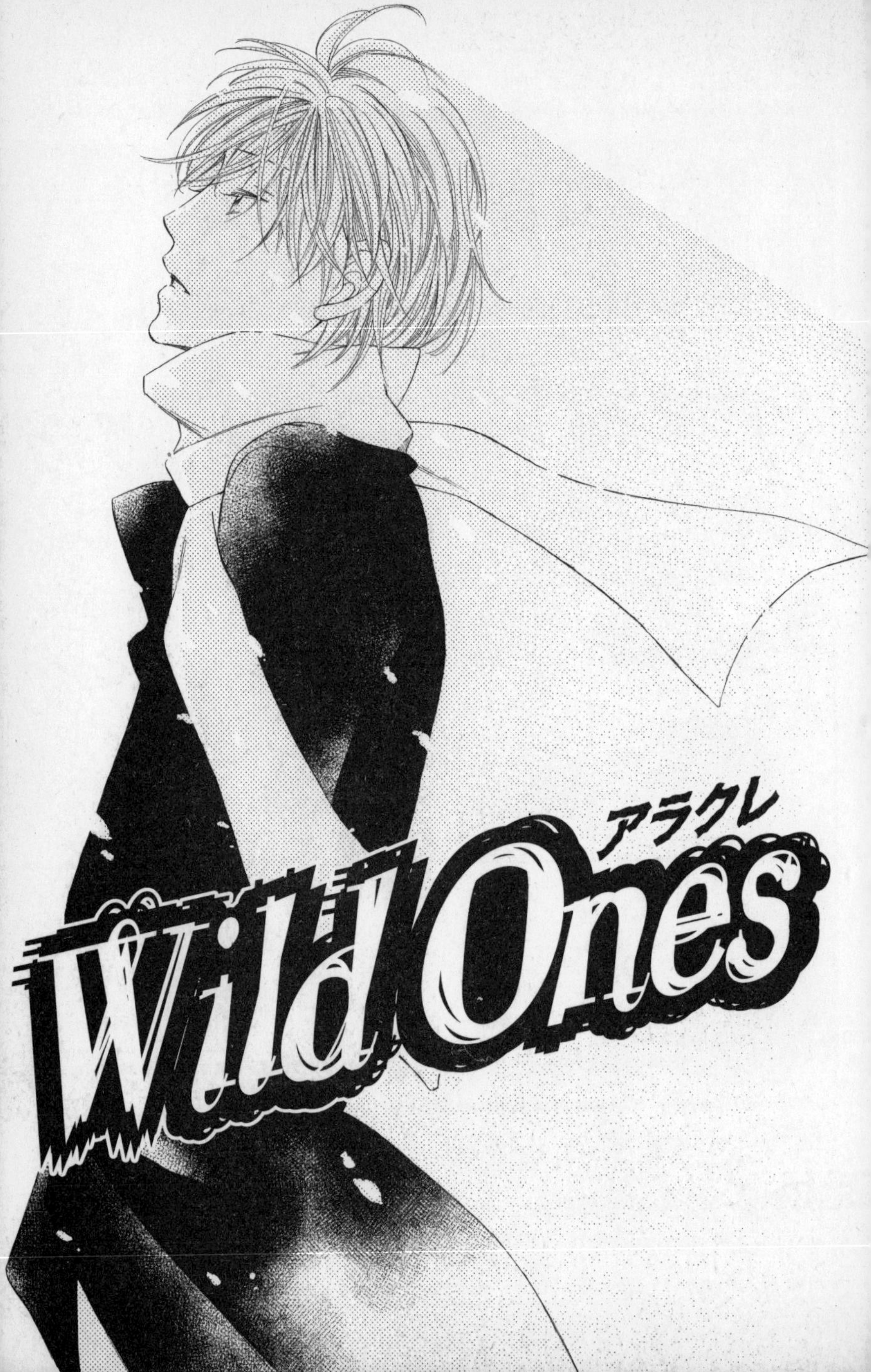
アラクレ
Wild Ones

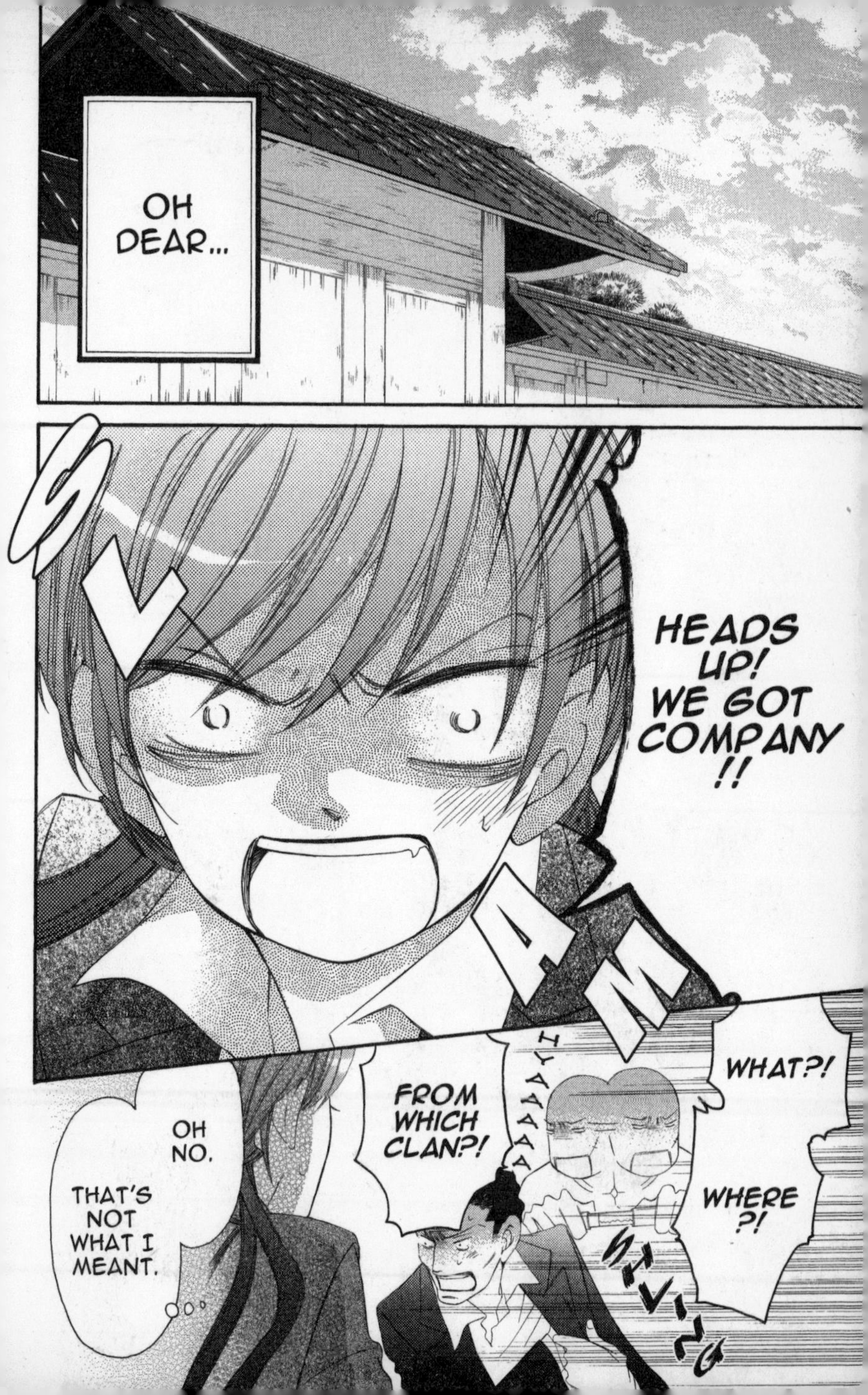
OH DEAR...
SLAM
HEADS UP! WE GOT COMPANY!!
WHAT?!
WHERE?!
SHING
HYAAAAA
FROM WHICH CLAN?!
OH NO.
THAT'S NOT WHAT I MEANT.

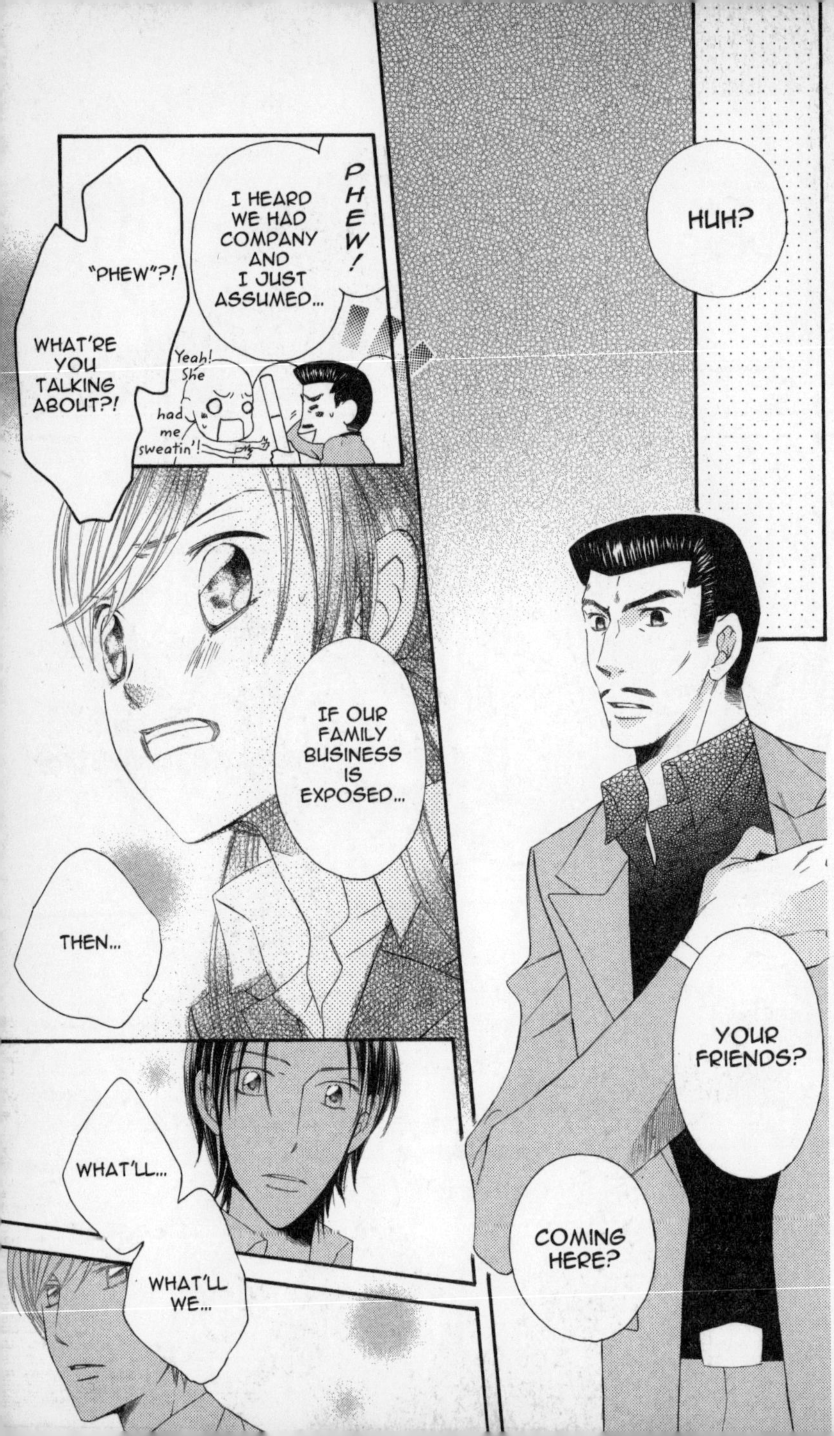
HUH?
YOUR FRIENDS?
COMING HERE?
I HEARD WE HAD COMPANY AND I JUST ASSUMED...
PHEW!
"PHEW"?!
WHAT'RE YOU TALKING ABOUT?!
Yeah! She had me sweatin'!
IF OUR FAMILY BUSINESS IS EXPOSED...
THEN...
WHAT'LL...
WHAT'LL WE...

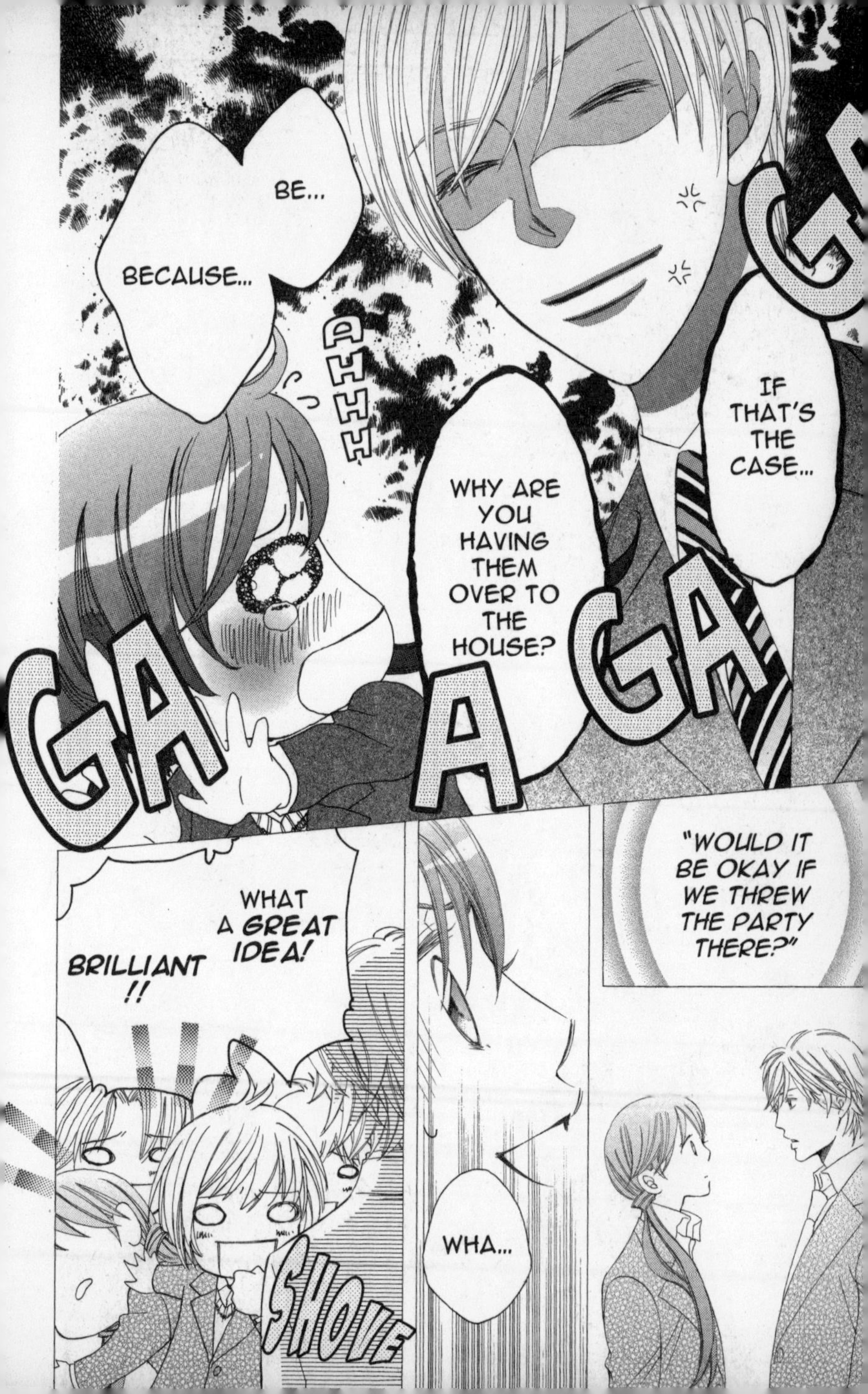
IF THAT'S THE CASE...
WHY ARE YOU HAVING THEM OVER TO THE HOUSE?
GA GA A GA
AHHH
BE...
BECAUSE...
"WOULD IT BE OKAY IF WE THREW THE PARTY THERE?"
WHA...
WHAT A GREAT IDEA!
BRILLIANT !!
SHOVE

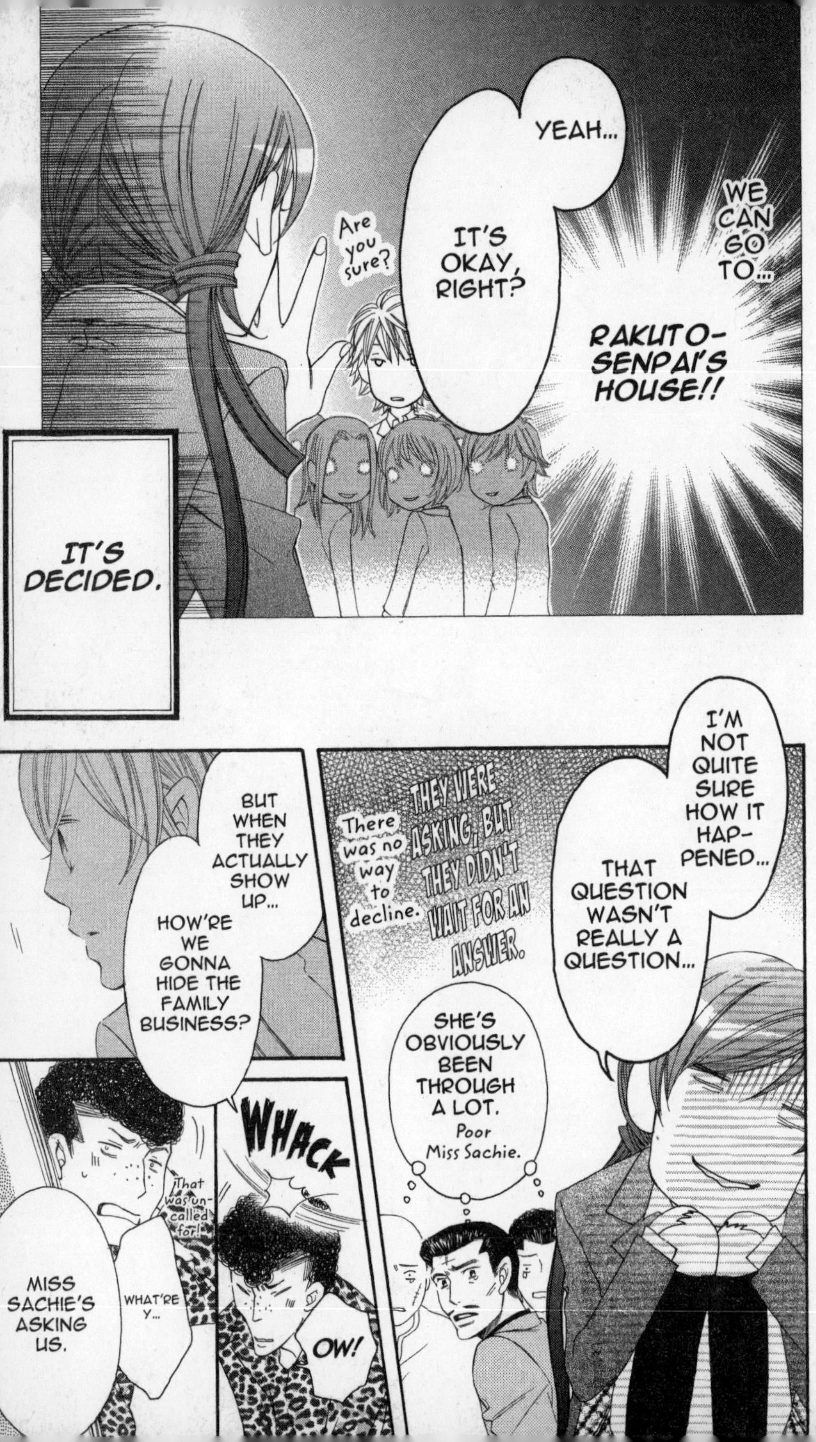
YEAH...
IT'S OKAY, RIGHT?
Are you sure?
WE CAN GO TO...
RAKUTO-SENPAI'S HOUSE!!
IT'S DECIDED.
I'M NOT QUITE SURE HOW IT HAPPENED...
THAT QUESTION WASN'T REALLY A QUESTION...
THEY WERE ASKING, BUT THEY DIDN'T WAIT FOR AN ANSWER.
There was no way to decline.
SHE'S OBVIOUSLY BEEN THROUGH A LOT.
Poor Miss Sachie.
BUT WHEN THEY ACTUALLY SHOW UP...
HOW'RE WE GONNA HIDE THE FAMILY BUSINESS?
WHACK
OW!
That was uncalled for!
WHAT'RE Y...
MISS SACHIE'S ASKING US.

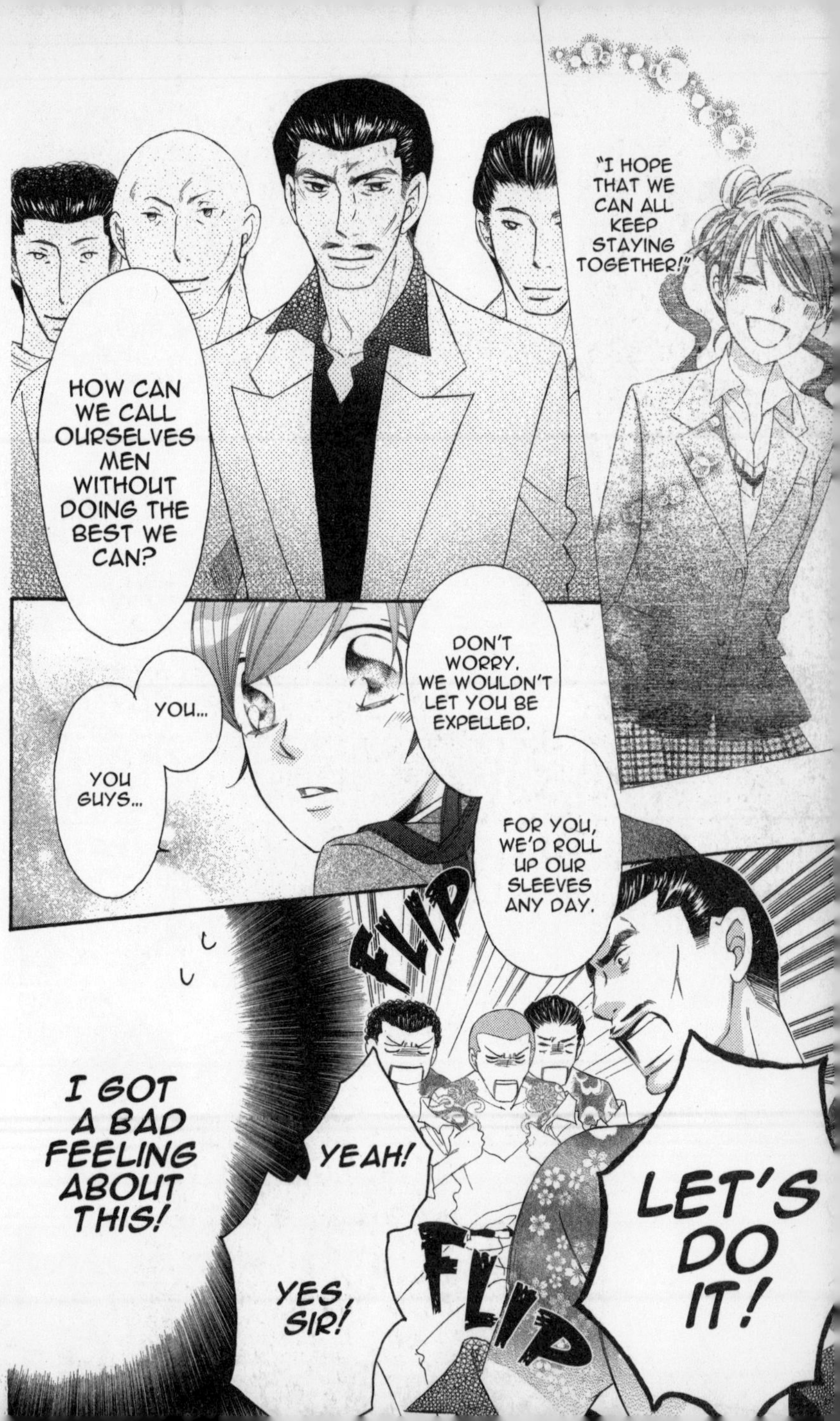
"I HOPE THAT WE CAN ALL KEEP STAYING TOGETHER!"
HOW CAN WE CALL OURSELVES MEN WITHOUT DOING THE BEST WE CAN?
DON'T WORRY. WE WOULDN'T LET YOU BE EXPELLED.
FOR YOU, WE'D ROLL UP OUR SLEEVES ANY DAY.
YOU...
YOU GUYS...
FLIP
LET'S DO IT!
FLIP
YEAH!
YES, SIR!
I GOT A BAD FEELING ABOUT THIS!

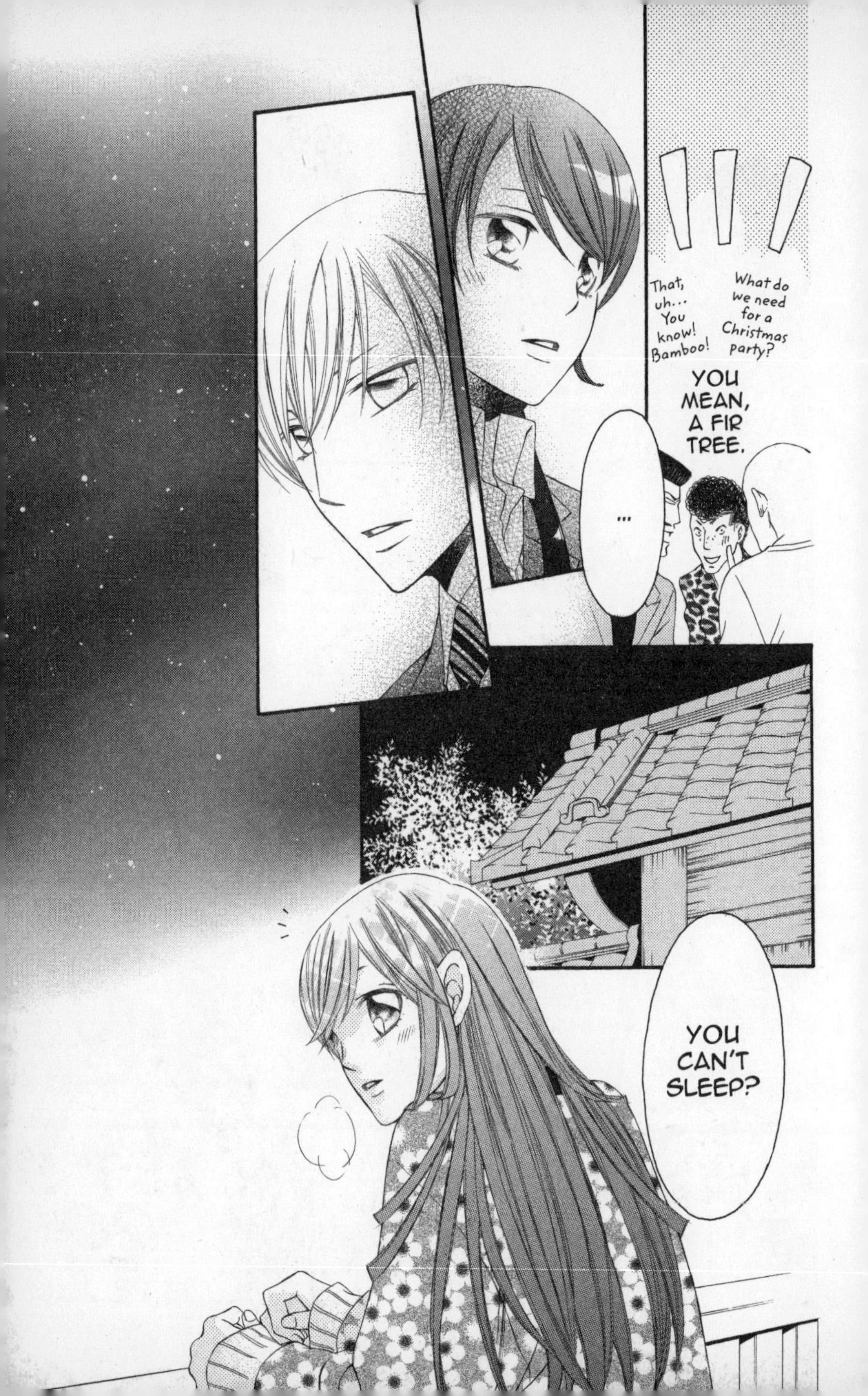
What do we need for a Christmas party?
That, uh... You know! Bamboo!
YOU MEAN, A FIR TREE.
...
YOU CAN'T SLEEP?

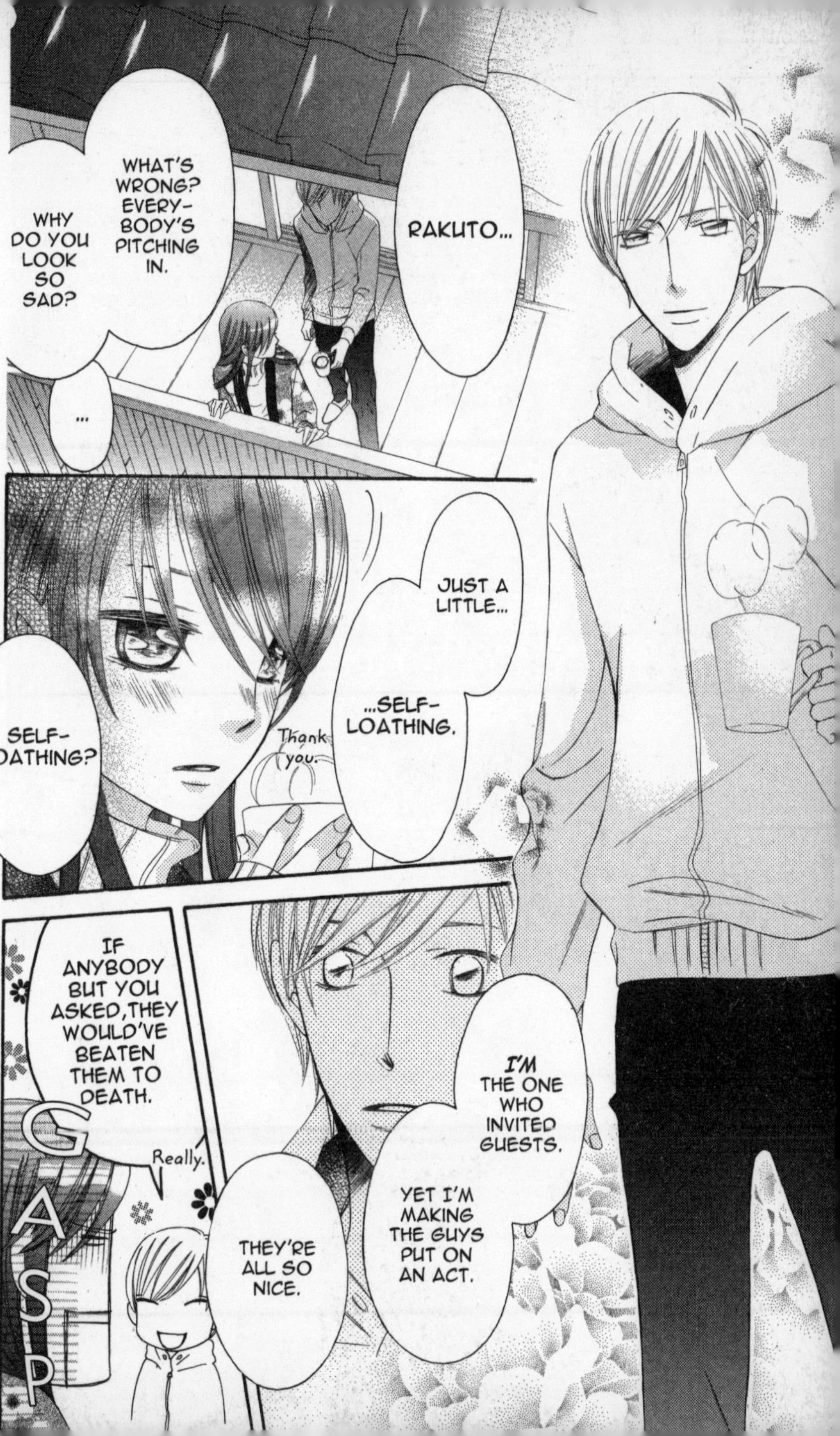
RAKUTO...
WHAT'S WRONG? EVERY-BODY'S PITCHING IN.
WHY DO YOU LOOK SO SAD?
...
JUST A LITTLE...
...SELF-LOATHING.
Thank you.
SELF-LOATHING?
I'M THE ONE WHO INVITED GUESTS.
YET I'M MAKING THE GUYS PUT ON AN ACT.
THEY'RE ALL SO NICE.
IF ANYBODY BUT YOU ASKED, THEY WOULD'VE BEATEN THEM TO DEATH.
Really.
GASP

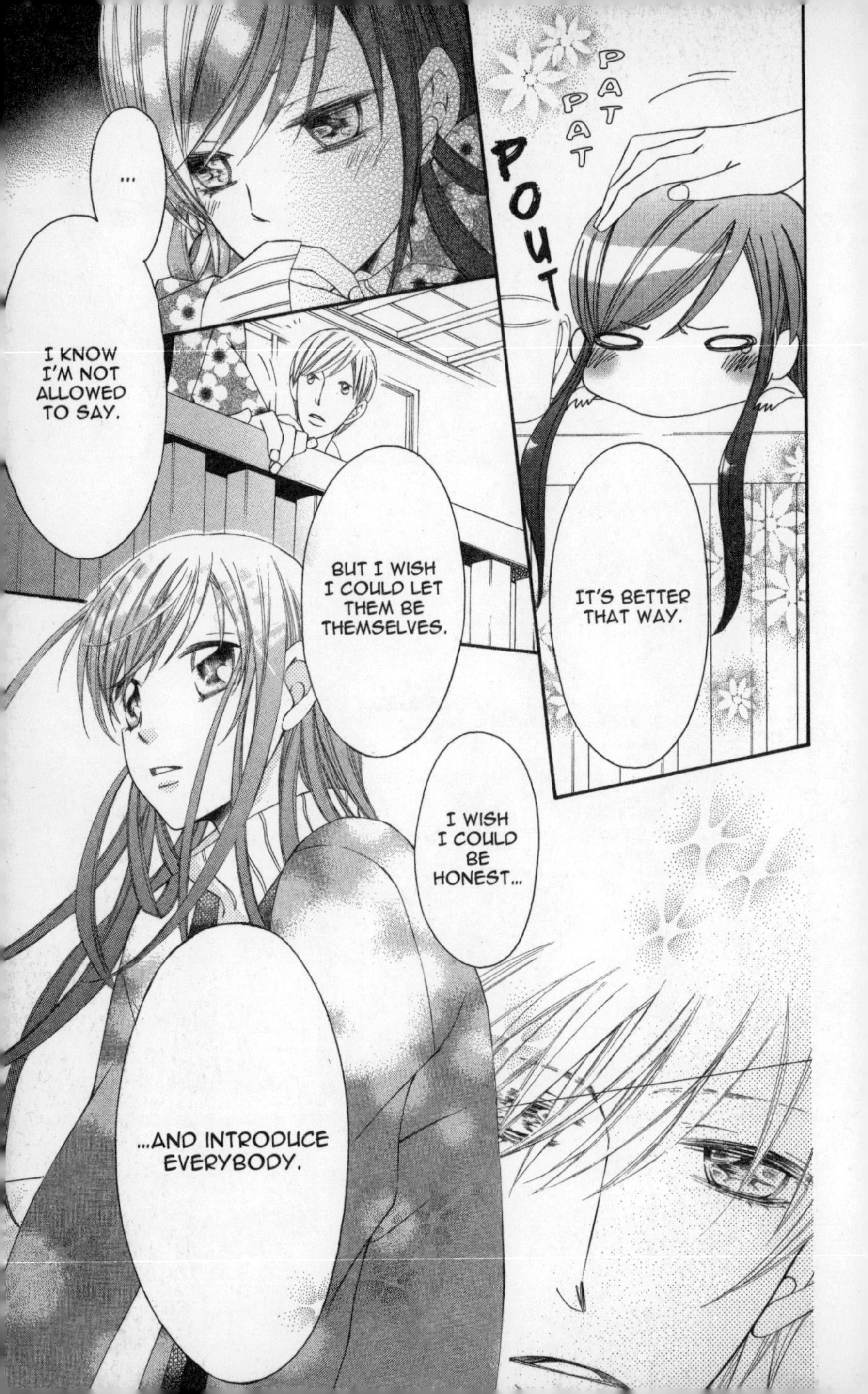
PAT PAT
POUT
IT'S BETTER THAT WAY.
...
I KNOW I'M NOT ALLOWED TO SAY.
BUT I WISH I COULD LET THEM BE THEMSELVES.
I WISH I COULD BE HONEST...
...AND INTRODUCE EVERYBODY.

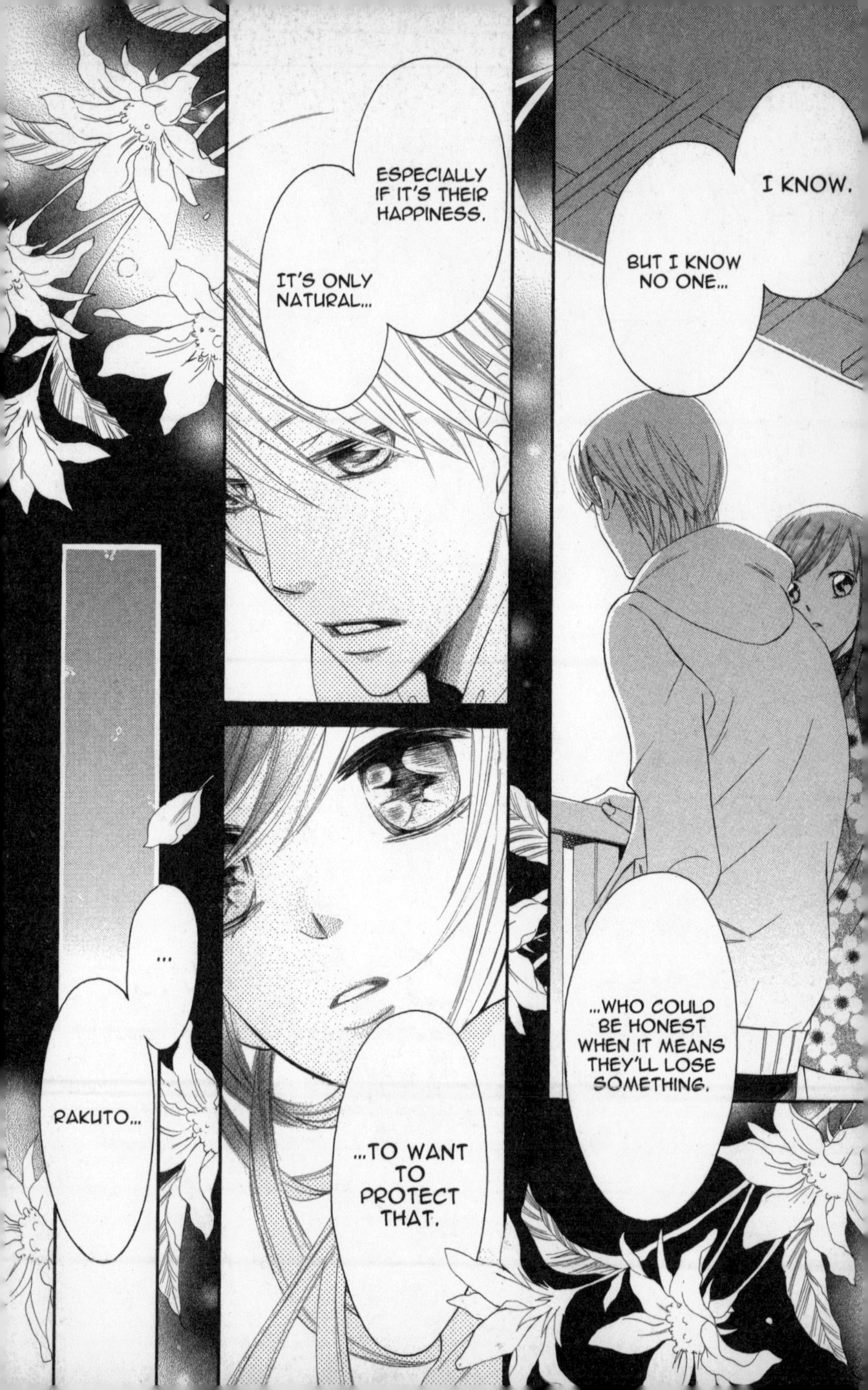
I KNOW.
BUT I KNOW NO ONE...
...WHO COULD BE HONEST WHEN IT MEANS THEY'LL LOSE SOMETHING.
ESPECIALLY IF IT'S THEIR HAPPINESS.
IT'S ONLY NATURAL...
...TO WANT TO PROTECT THAT.
...
RAKUTO...

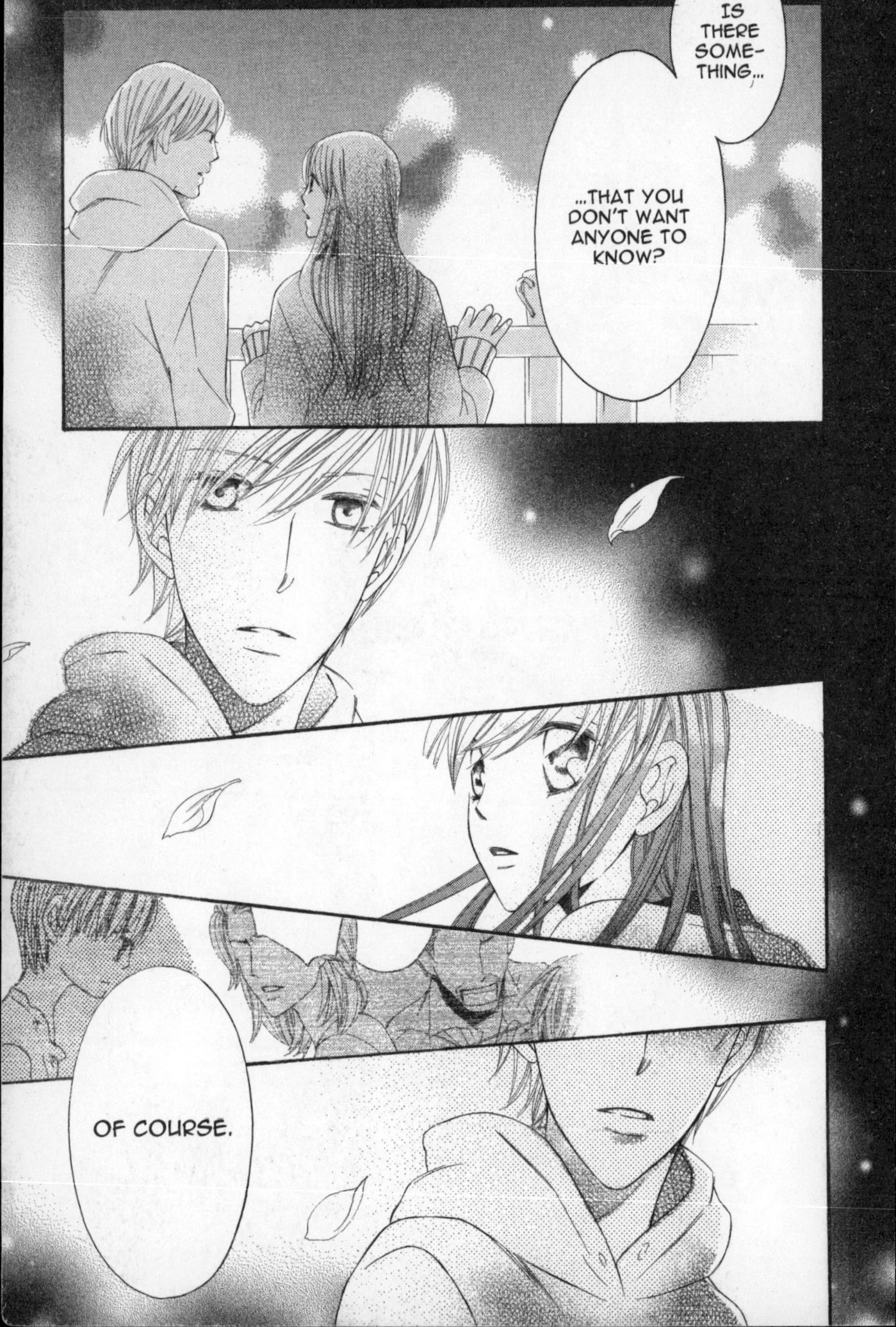
IS THERE SOME-THING...
...THAT YOU DON'T WANT ANYONE TO KNOW?
OF COURSE.

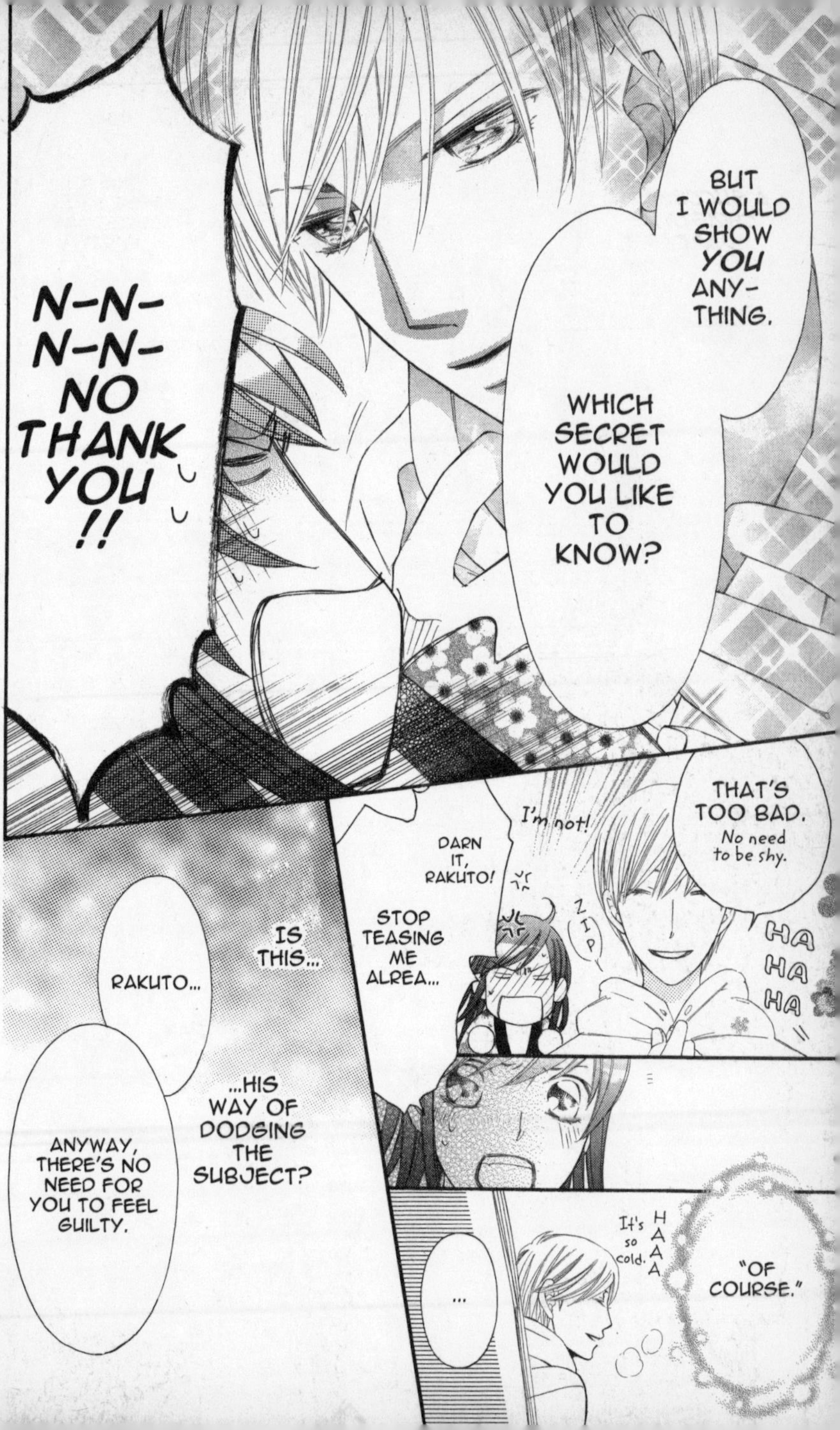
BUT I WOULD SHOW *YOU* ANY-THING.
WHICH SECRET WOULD YOU LIKE TO KNOW?
N-N-N-N-NO THANK YOU!!
THAT'S TOO BAD. No need to be shy.
HA HA HA
ZIP
I'm not!
DARN IT, RAKUTO!
STOP TEASING ME ALREA...
IS THIS...
RAKUTO...
...HIS WAY OF DODGING THE SUBJECT?
ANYWAY, THERE'S NO NEED FOR YOU TO FEEL GUILTY.
"OF COURSE."
HAAA
It's so cold.
...

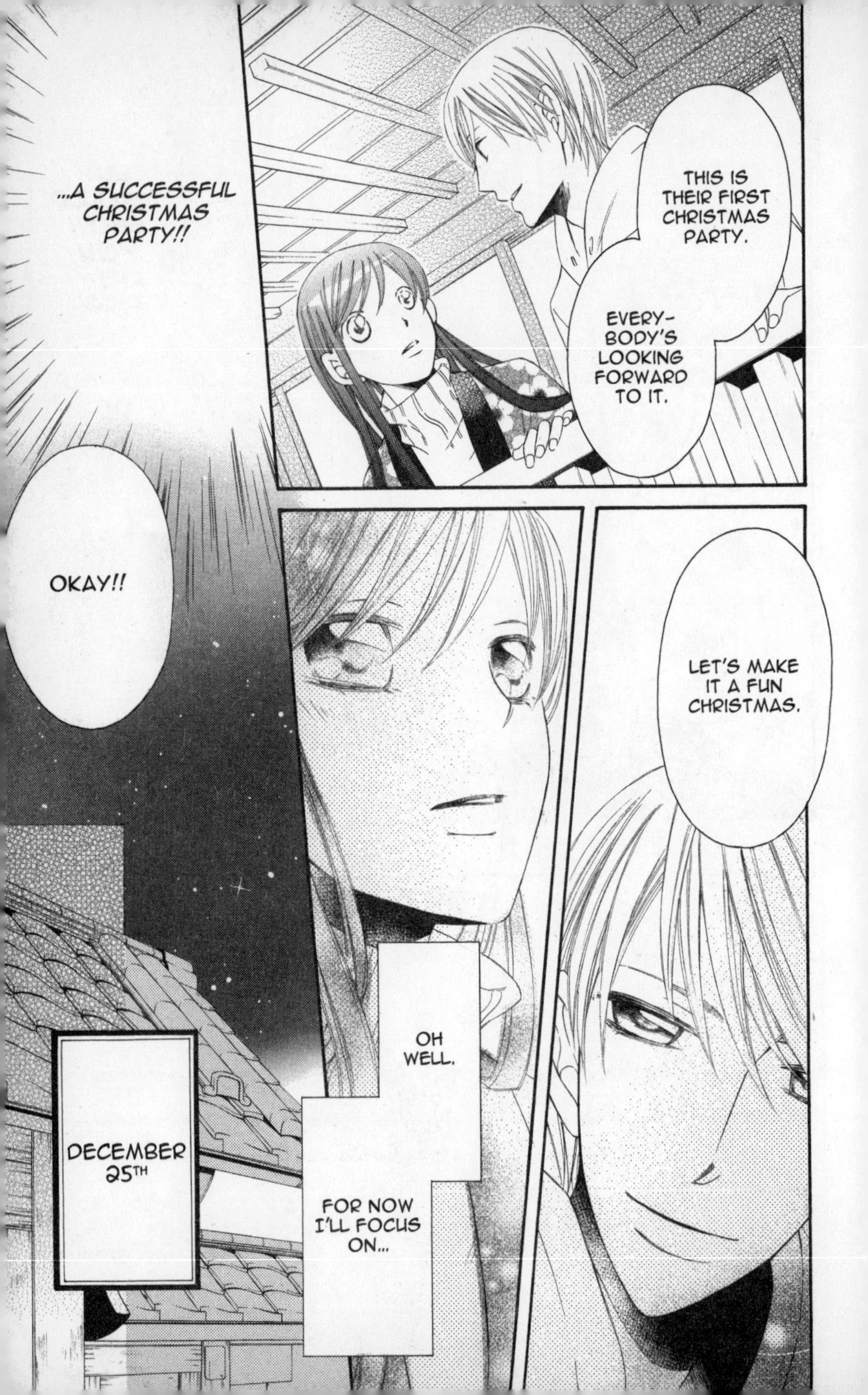
THIS IS THEIR FIRST CHRISTMAS PARTY.
EVERY-BODY'S LOOKING FORWARD TO IT.
LET'S MAKE IT A FUN CHRISTMAS.
OH WELL.
FOR NOW I'LL FOCUS ON...
...A SUCCESSFUL CHRISTMAS PARTY!!
OKAY!!
DECEMBER 25TH

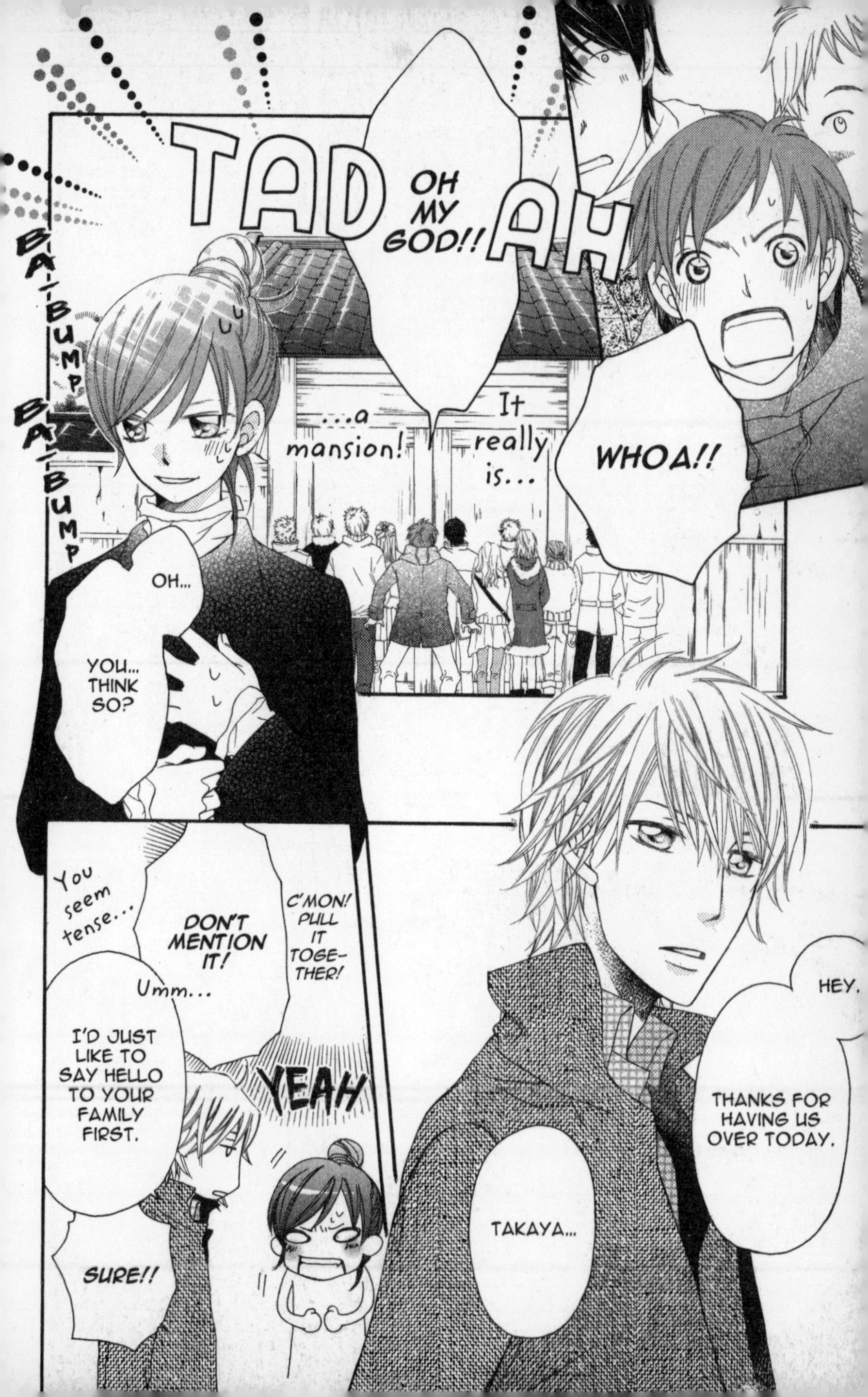
TADAH
OH MY GOD!!
WHOA!!
It really is...
...a mansion!
BA-BUMP
BA-BUMP
OH...
YOU... THINK SO?
HEY.
THANKS FOR HAVING US OVER TODAY.
TAKAYA...
C'MON! PULL IT TOGE-THER!
DON'T MENTION IT!
You seem tense...
Umm...
I'D JUST LIKE TO SAY HELLO TO YOUR FAMILY FIRST.
YEAH
SURE!!

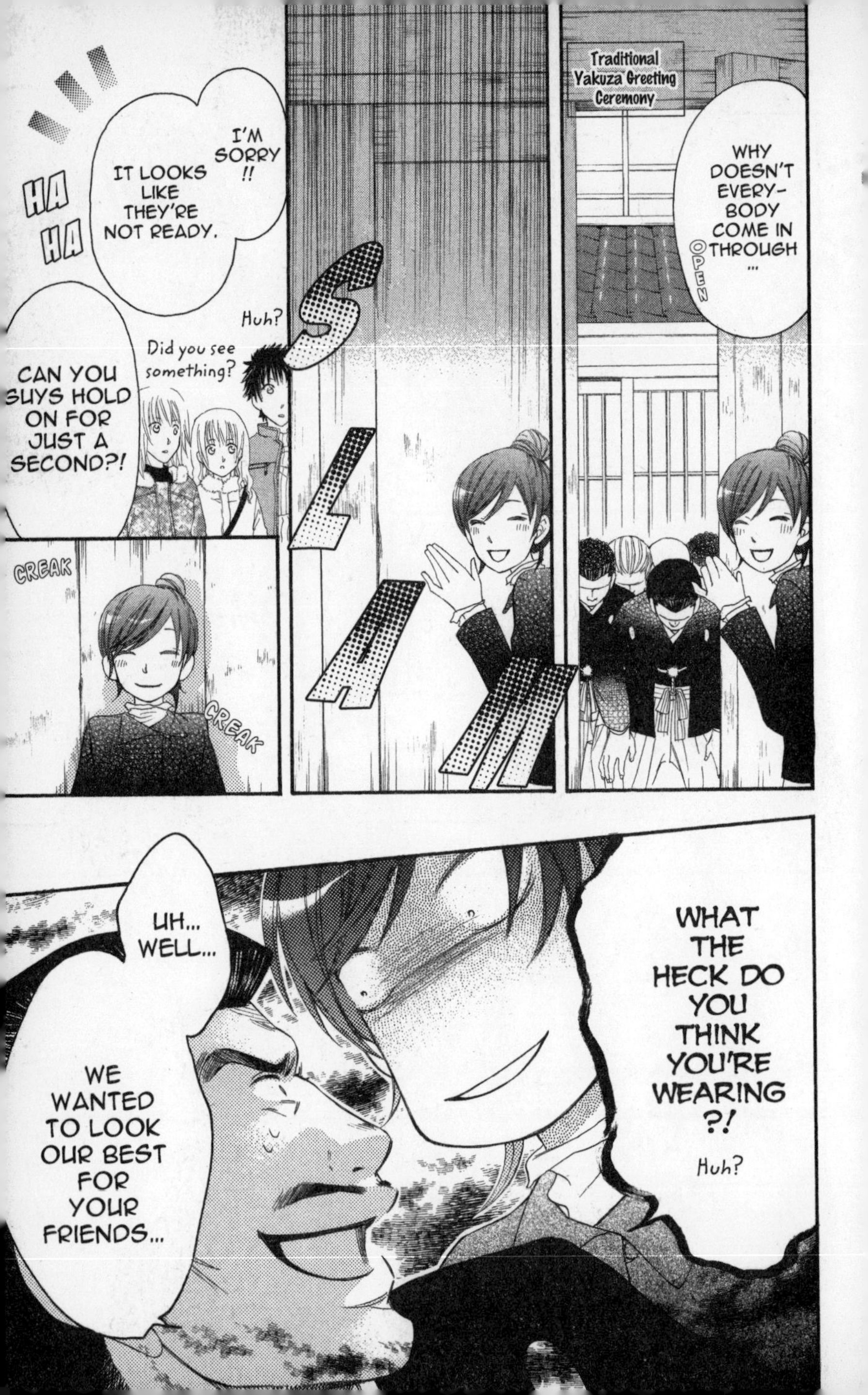

Traditional Yakuza Greeting Ceremony
WHY DOESN'T EVERY-BODY COME IN THROUGH ...
OPEN
SLAM
I'M SORRY !!
IT LOOKS LIKE THEY'RE NOT READY.
HA HA
Huh?
Did you see something?
CAN YOU GUYS HOLD ON FOR JUST A SECOND?!
CREAK
CREAK
WHAT THE HECK DO YOU THINK YOU'RE WEARING ?!
Huh?
UH... WELL...
WE WANTED TO LOOK OUR BEST FOR YOUR FRIENDS...

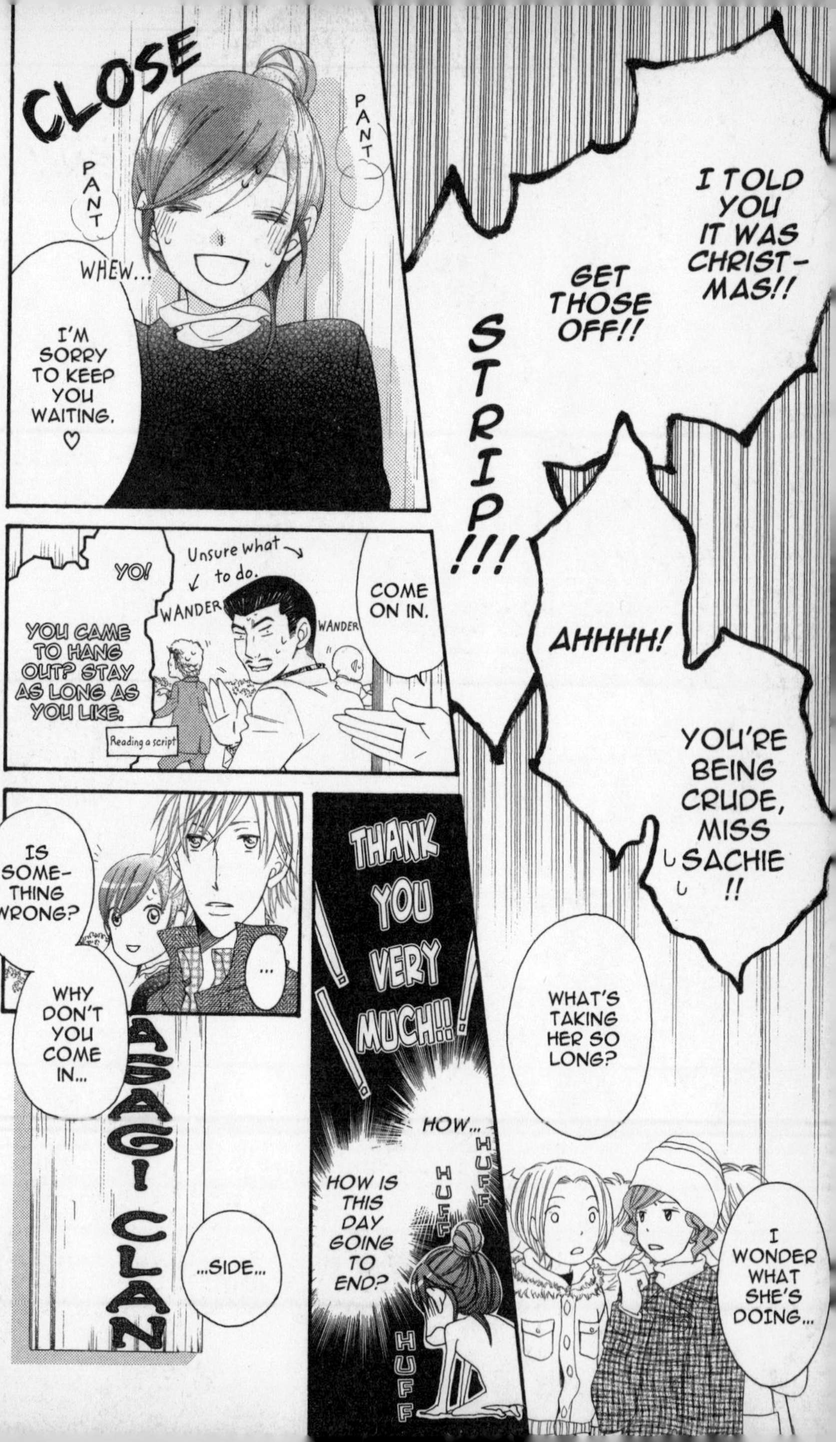
I TOLD YOU IT WAS CHRISTMAS!!
GET THOSE OFF!!
STRIP!!!
AHHHH!
YOU'RE BEING CRUDE, MISS SACHIE!!
WHAT'S TAKING HER SO LONG?
I WONDER WHAT SHE'S DOING...
CLOSE
PANT
PANT
WHEW...
I'M SORRY TO KEEP YOU WAITING. ♡
YO!
Unsure what to do.
WANDER
WANDER
COME ON IN.
YOU CAME TO HANG OUT? STAY AS LONG AS YOU LIKE.
Reading a script
THANK YOU VERY MUCH!!
HOW...
HUFF
HUFF
HOW IS THIS DAY GOING TO END?
HUFF
HUFF
IS SOME-THING WRONG?
...
WHY DON'T YOU COME IN...
AGI CLAN
...SIDE...

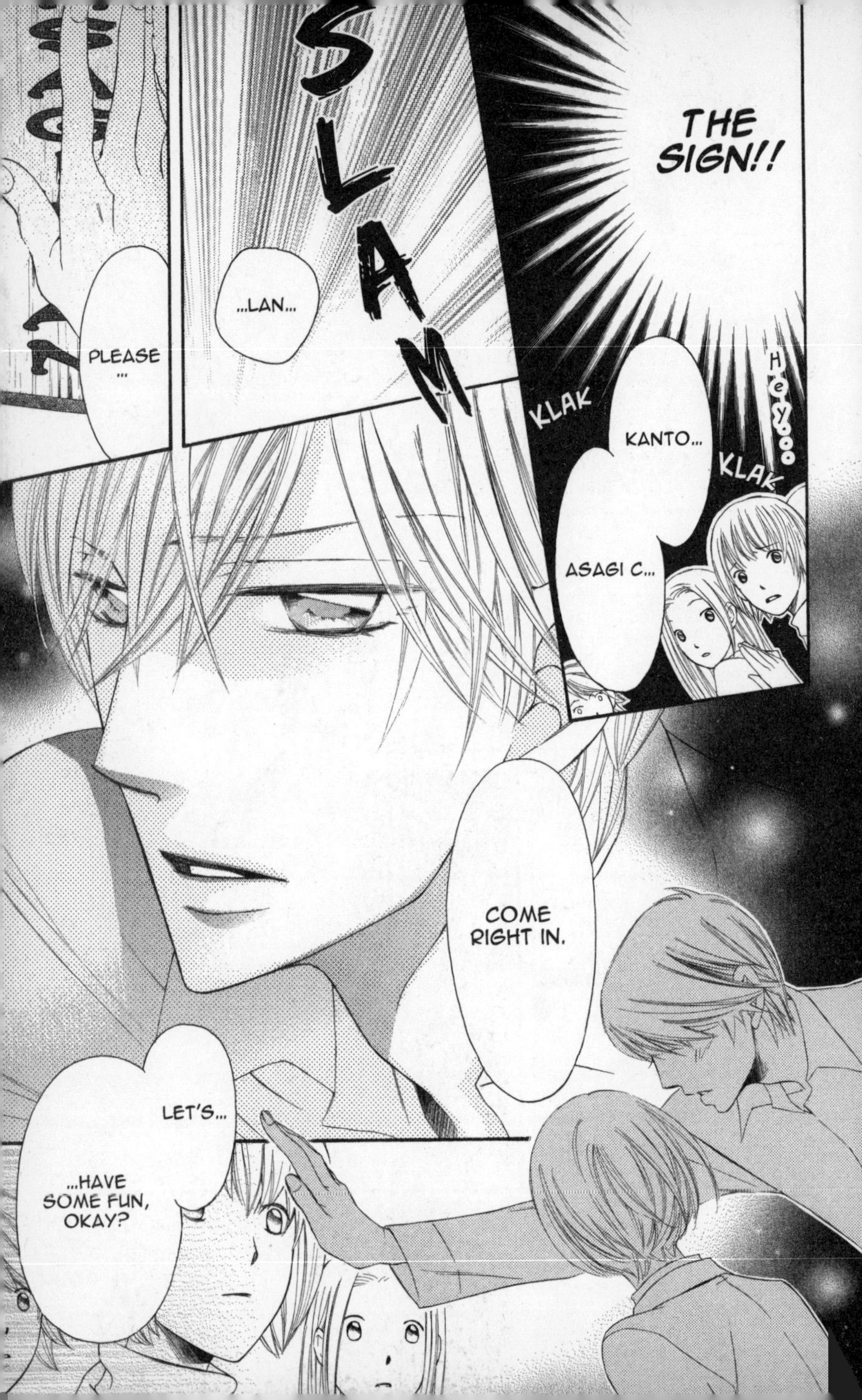
THE SIGN!!
Hey...
KLAK KLAK
KANTO...
ASAGI C...
SLAM
...LAN...
PLEASE ...
COME RIGHT IN.
LET'S...
...HAVE SOME FUN, OKAY?

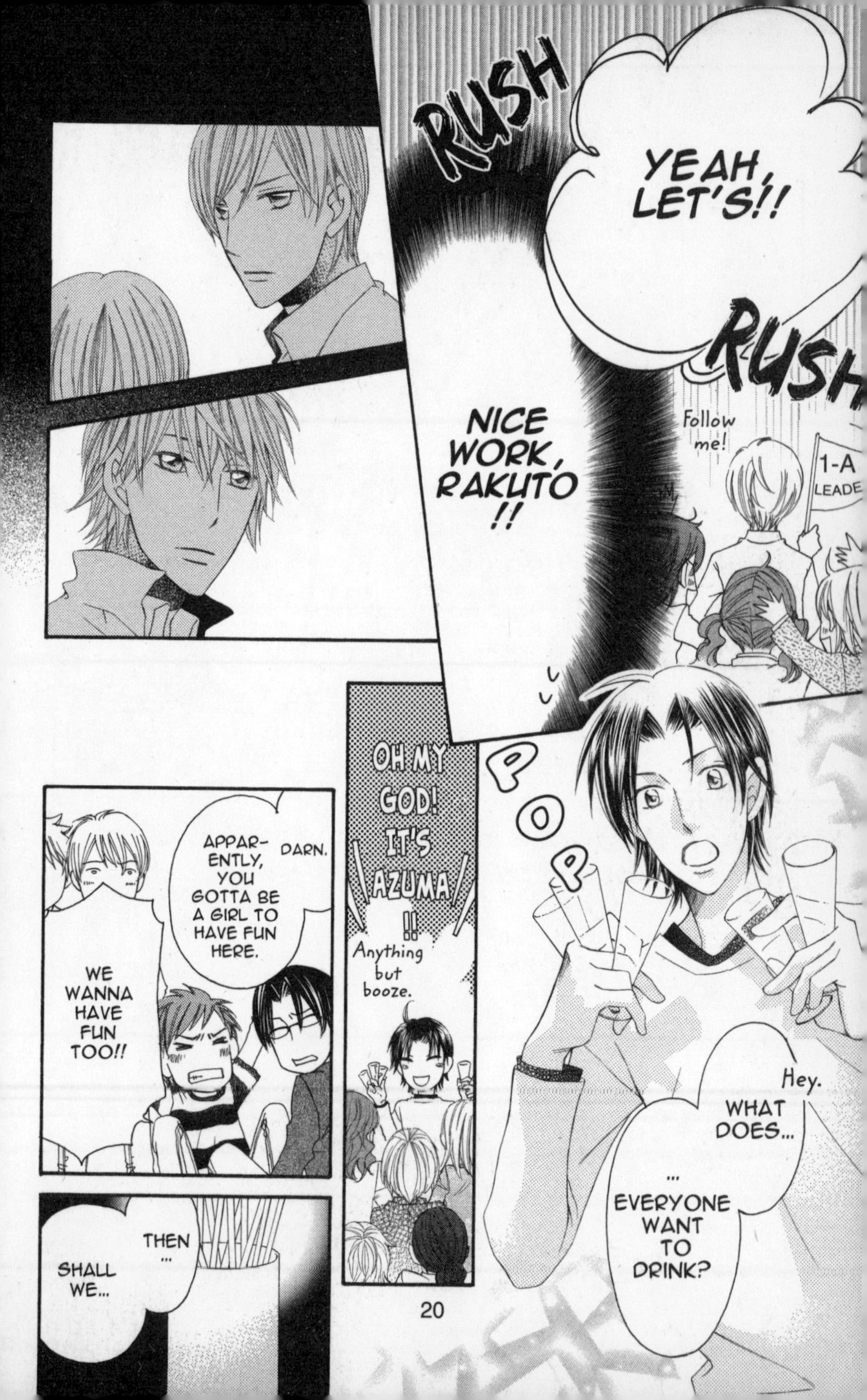
RUSH
YEAH, LET'S!!
RUSH
Follow me!
1-A LEADE
NICE WORK, RAKUTO!!
POP
Hey.
WHAT DOES...
... EVERYONE WANT TO DRINK?
OH MY GOD! IT'S AZUMA!!
Anything but booze.
DARN.
APPARENTLY, YOU GOTTA BE A GIRL TO HAVE FUN HERE.
WE WANNA HAVE FUN TOO!!
THEN ...
SHALL WE...

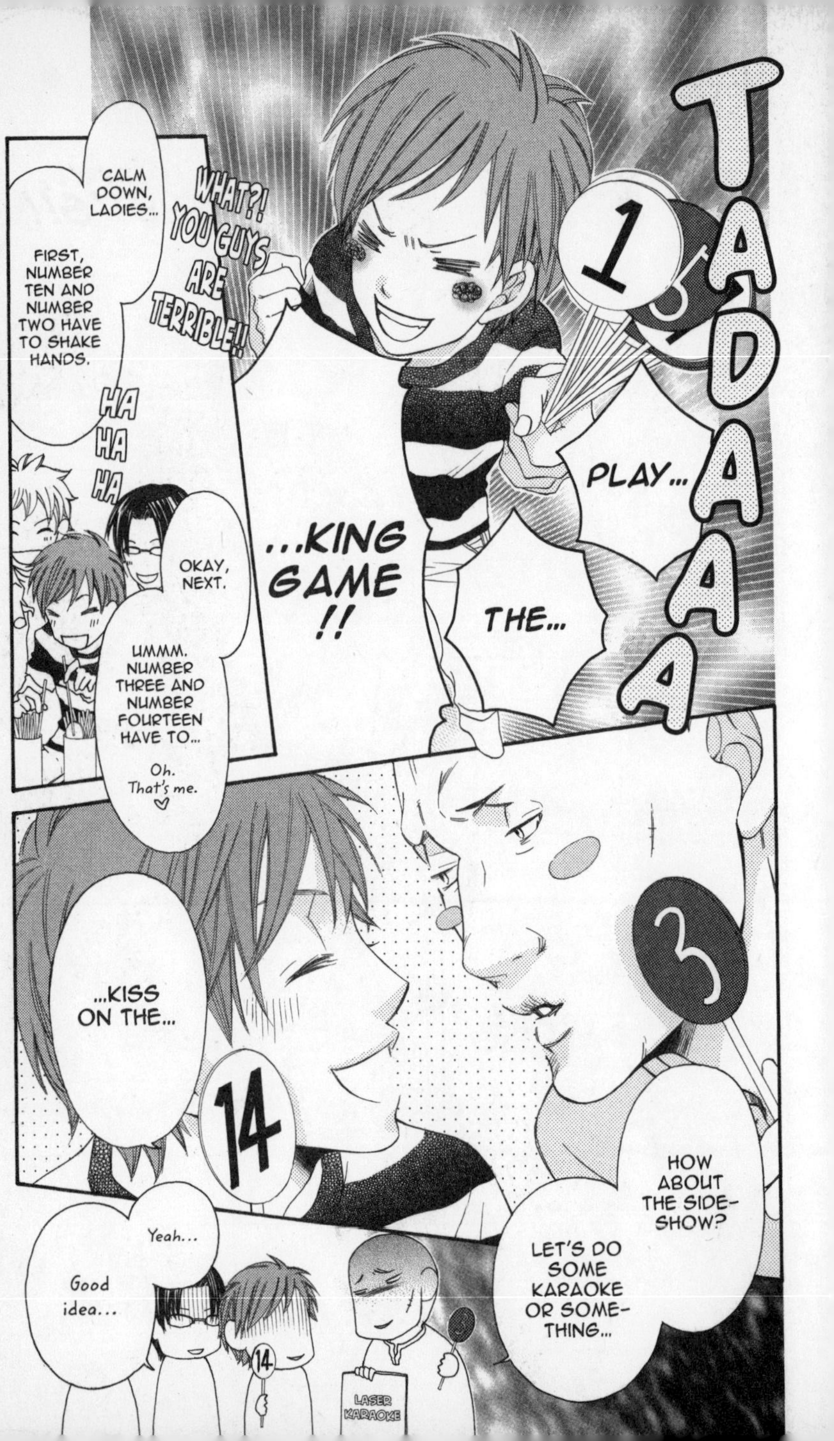
TADAAAA
PLAY...
THE...
...KING GAME !!
WHAT?! YOU GUYS ARE TERRIBLE!!
CALM DOWN, LADIES...
FIRST, NUMBER TEN AND NUMBER TWO HAVE TO SHAKE HANDS.
HA HA HA
OKAY, NEXT.
UMMM. NUMBER THREE AND NUMBER FOURTEEN HAVE TO...
Oh. That's me. ♡
...KISS ON THE...
HOW ABOUT THE SIDE-SHOW?
LET'S DO SOME KARAOKE OR SOME-THING...
Yeah...
Good idea...
LASER KARAOKE

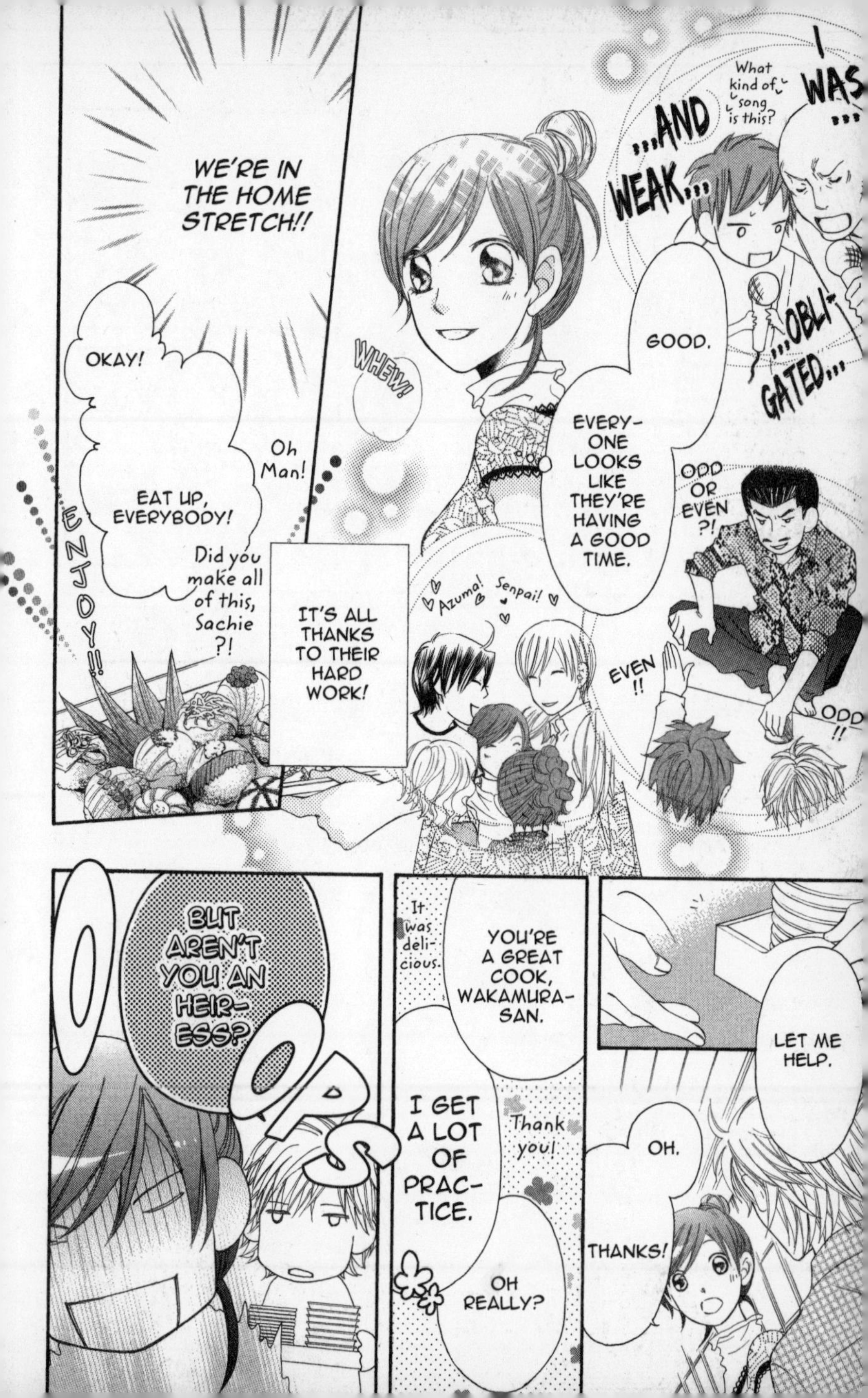
I WAS...
What kind of song is this?
...AND WEAK...
...OBLIGATED...
GOOD.
EVERYONE LOOKS LIKE THEY'RE HAVING A GOOD TIME.
ODD OR EVEN?!
EVEN!!
ODD!!
Azuma! Senpai!
WHEW!
WE'RE IN THE HOME STRETCH!!
OKAY!
Oh Man!
EAT UP, EVERYBODY!
Did you make all of this, Sachie?!
ENJOY!!
IT'S ALL THANKS TO THEIR HARD WORK!
LET ME HELP.
OH.
THANKS!
YOU'RE A GREAT COOK, WAKAMURA-SAN.
It was delicious.
I GET A LOT OF PRACTICE.
Thank you!
OH REALLY?
BUT AREN'T YOU AN HEIRESS?
OOPS

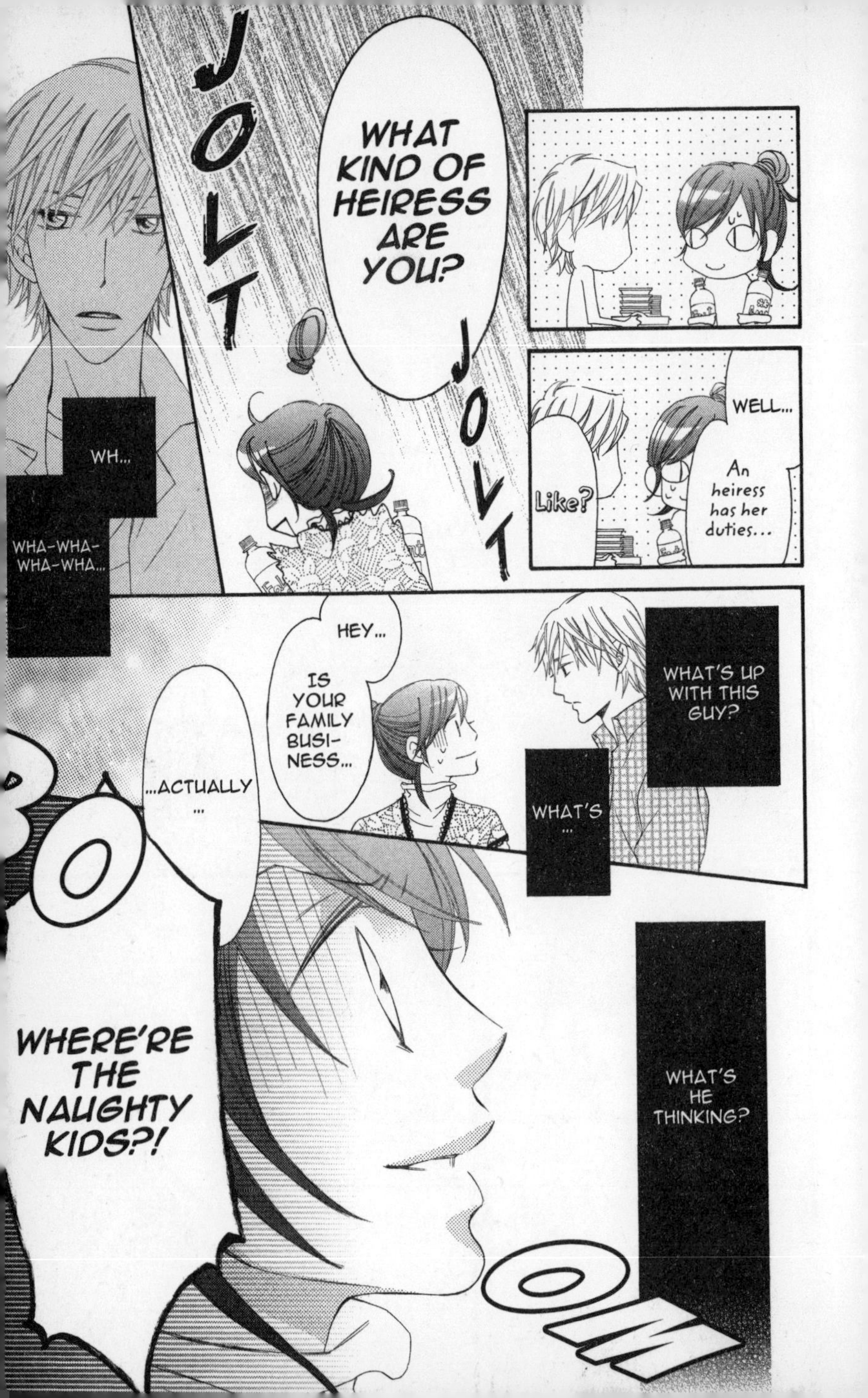
WELL...
An heiress has her duties...
Like?
WHAT KIND OF HEIRESS ARE YOU?
JOLT
JOLT
WH...
WHA-WHA-WHA-WHA...
WHAT'S UP WITH THIS GUY?
WHAT'S ...
HEY...
IS YOUR FAMILY BUSI-NESS...
...ACTUALLY ...
WHAT'S HE THINKING?
WHERE'RE THE NAUGHTY KIDS?!

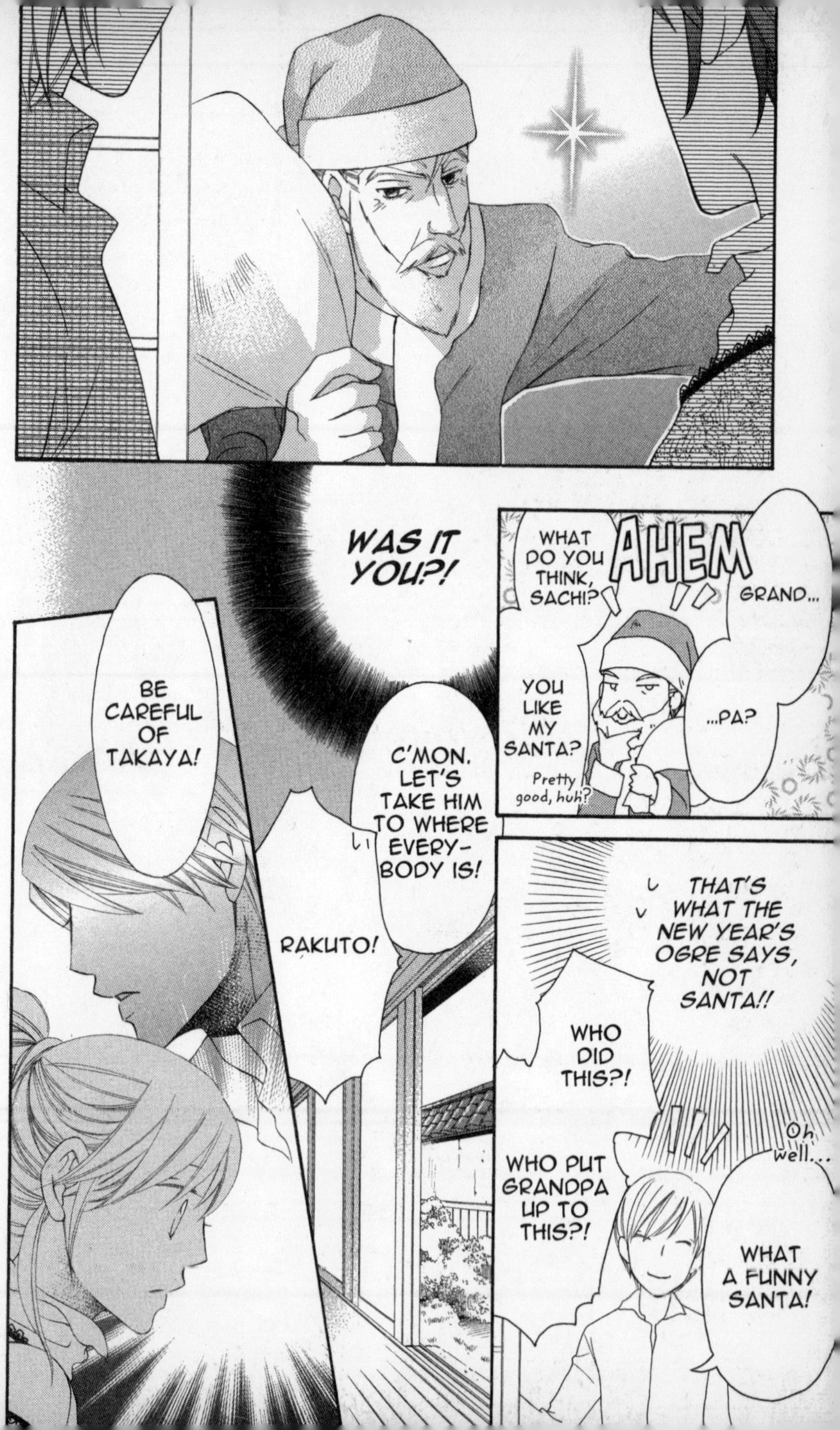
GRAND...
...PA?
AHEM
WHAT DO YOU THINK, SACHI?
YOU LIKE MY SANTA?
Pretty good, huh?
THAT'S WHAT THE NEW YEAR'S OGRE SAYS, NOT SANTA!!
WHO DID THIS?!
WHO PUT GRANDPA UP TO THIS?!
Oh well...
WHAT A FUNNY SANTA!
WAS IT YOU?!
C'MON. LET'S TAKE HIM TO WHERE EVERY-BODY IS!
RAKUTO!
BE CAREFUL OF TAKAYA!

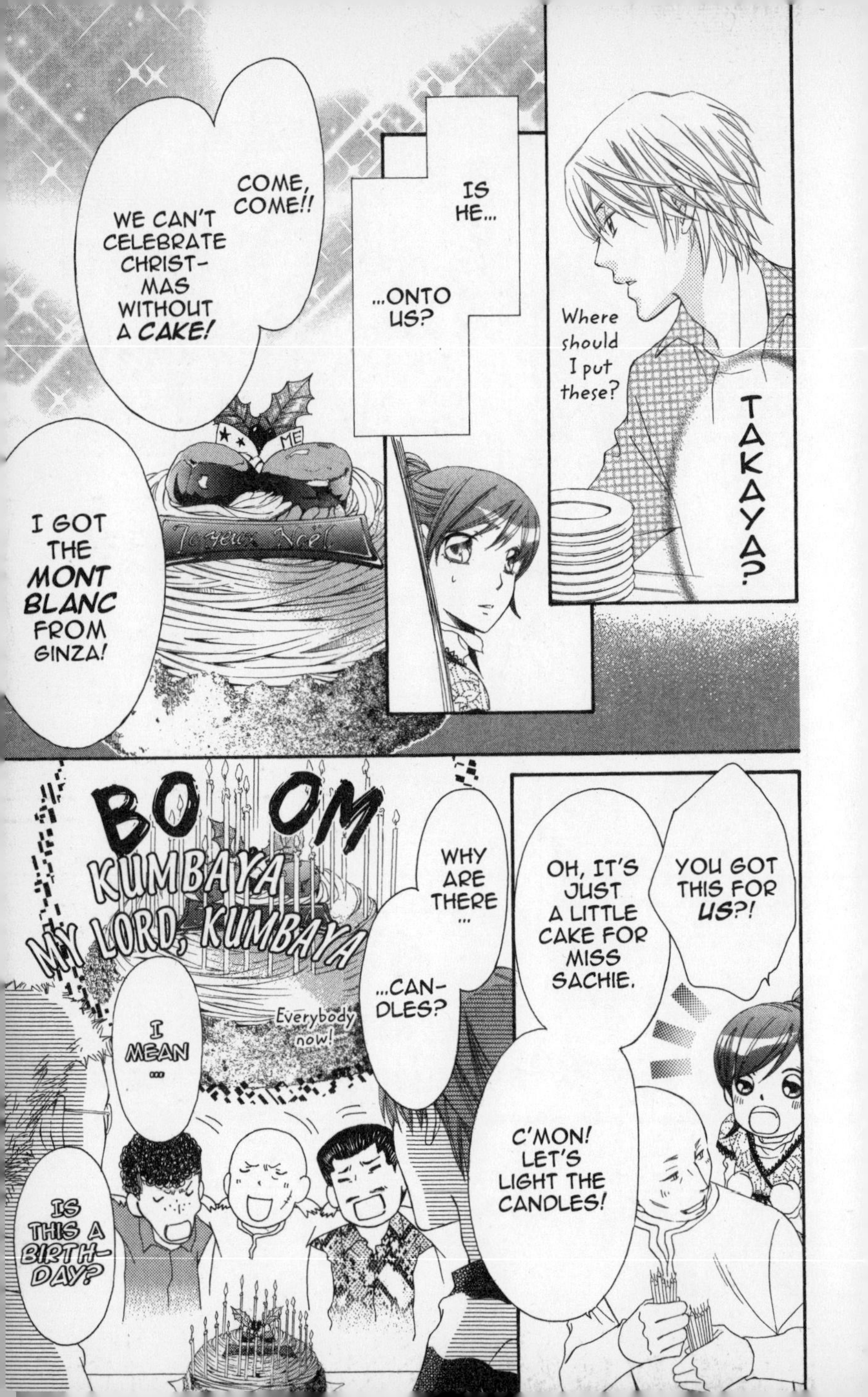
TAKAYA?
Where should I put these?
IS HE...
...ONTO US?
COME, COME!!
WE CAN'T CELEBRATE CHRIST-MAS WITHOUT A CAKE!
I GOT THE MONT BLANC FROM GINZA!
Joyeux Noël
YOU GOT THIS FOR US?!
OH, IT'S JUST A LITTLE CAKE FOR MISS SACHIE.
C'MON! LET'S LIGHT THE CANDLES!
WHY ARE THERE ...
...CAN-DLES?
BO OM
KUMBAYA MY LORD, KUMBAYA
Everybody now!
I MEAN ...
IS THIS A BIRTH-DAY?

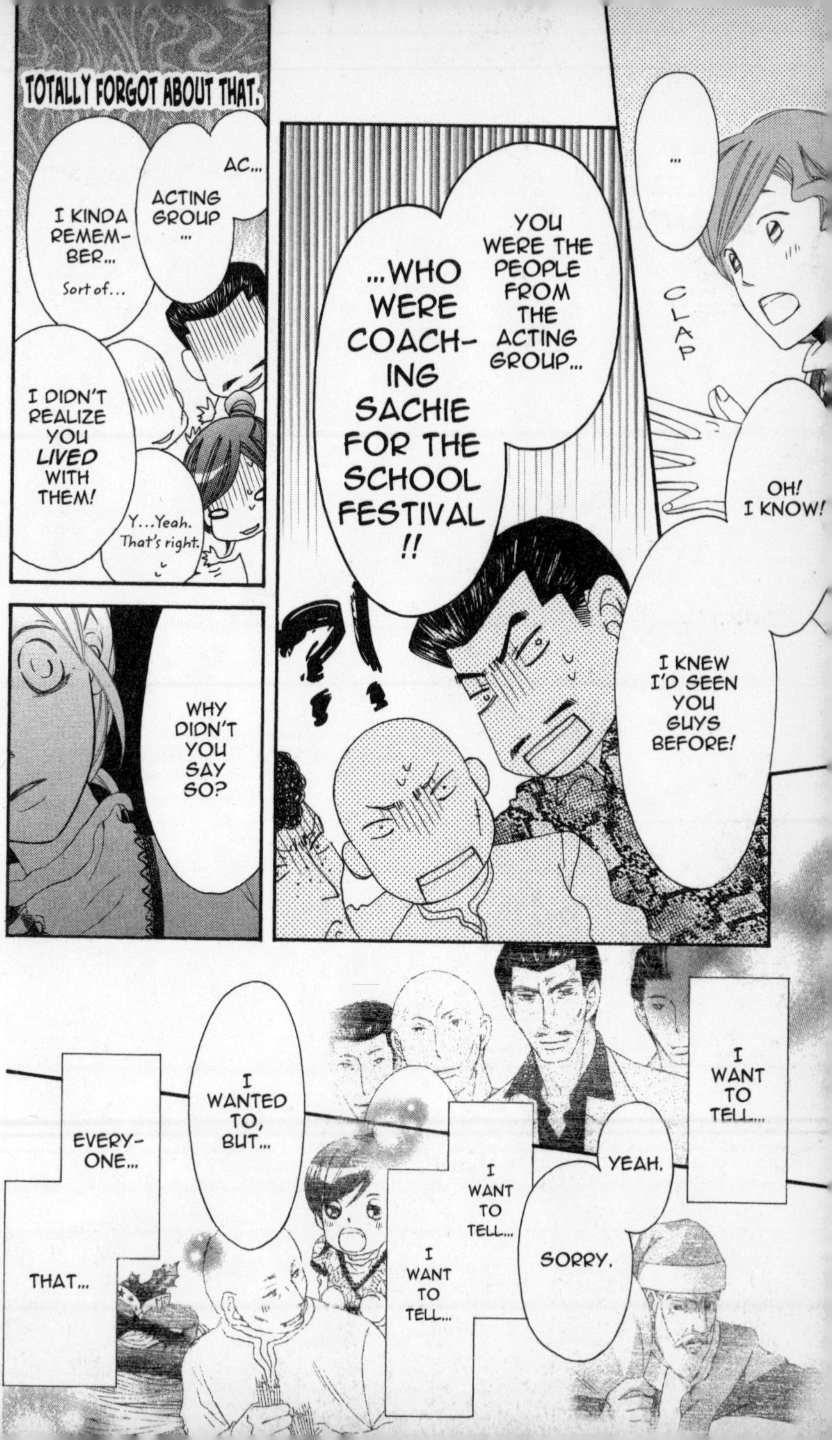
...
CLAP
OH! I KNOW!
I KNEW I'D SEEN YOU GUYS BEFORE!
YOU WERE THE PEOPLE FROM THE ACTING GROUP...
...WHO WERE COACHING SACHIE FOR THE SCHOOL FESTIVAL !!
AC...
ACTING GROUP ...
I KINDA REMEMBER...
Sort of...
I DIDN'T REALIZE YOU LIVED WITH THEM!
Y...Yeah. That's right.
TOTALLY FORGOT ABOUT THAT.
WHY DIDN'T YOU SAY SO?
I WANT TO TELL...
YEAH.
SORRY.
I WANT TO TELL...
I WANT TO TELL...
I WANTED TO, BUT...
EVERYONE...
THAT...

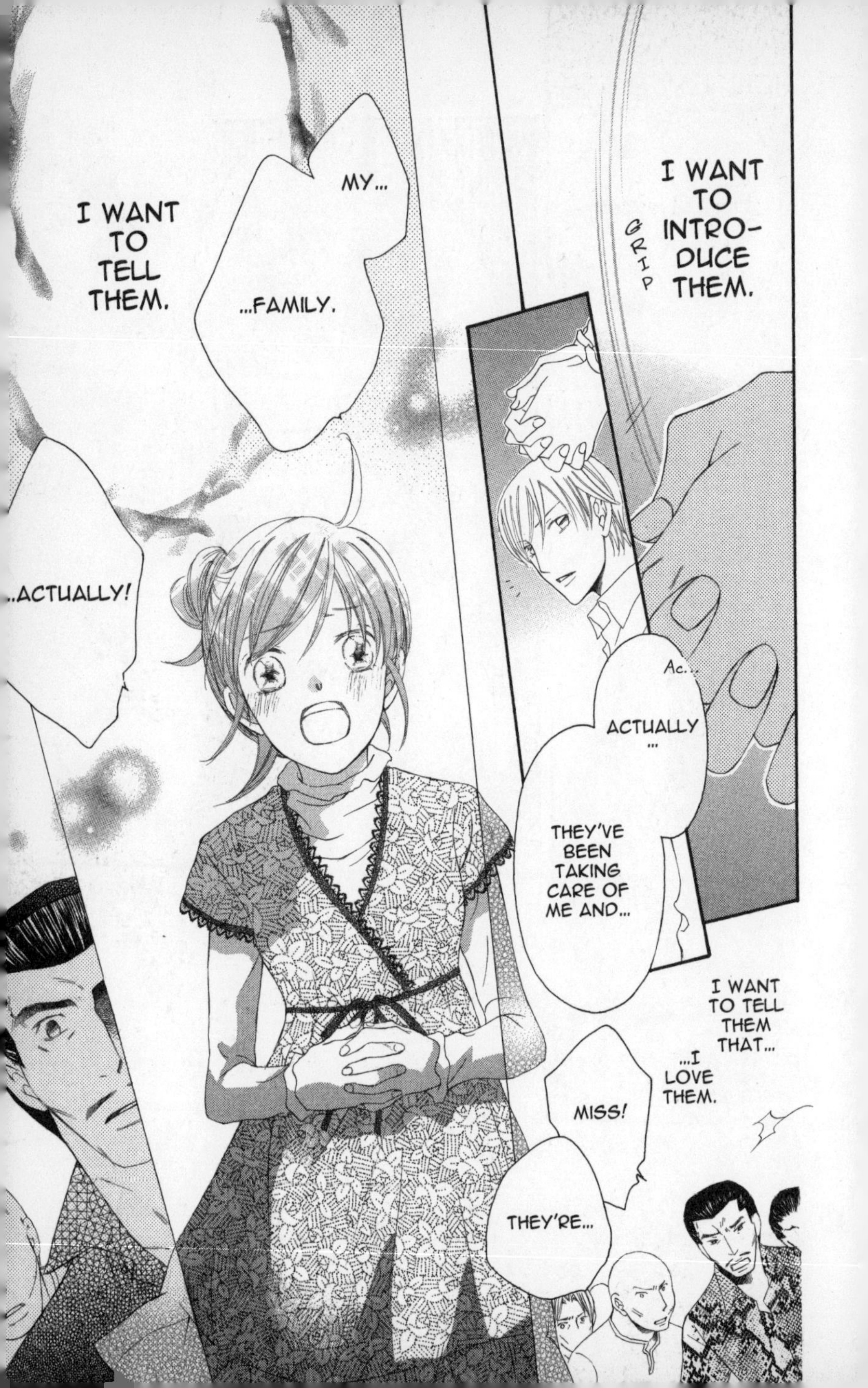
I WANT TO INTRODUCE THEM.
GRIP
I WANT TO TELL THEM.
MY...
...FAMILY.
Ac...
ACTUALLY...
THEY'VE BEEN TAKING CARE OF ME AND...
..ACTUALLY!
I WANT TO TELL THEM THAT...
...I LOVE THEM.
MISS!
THEY'RE...

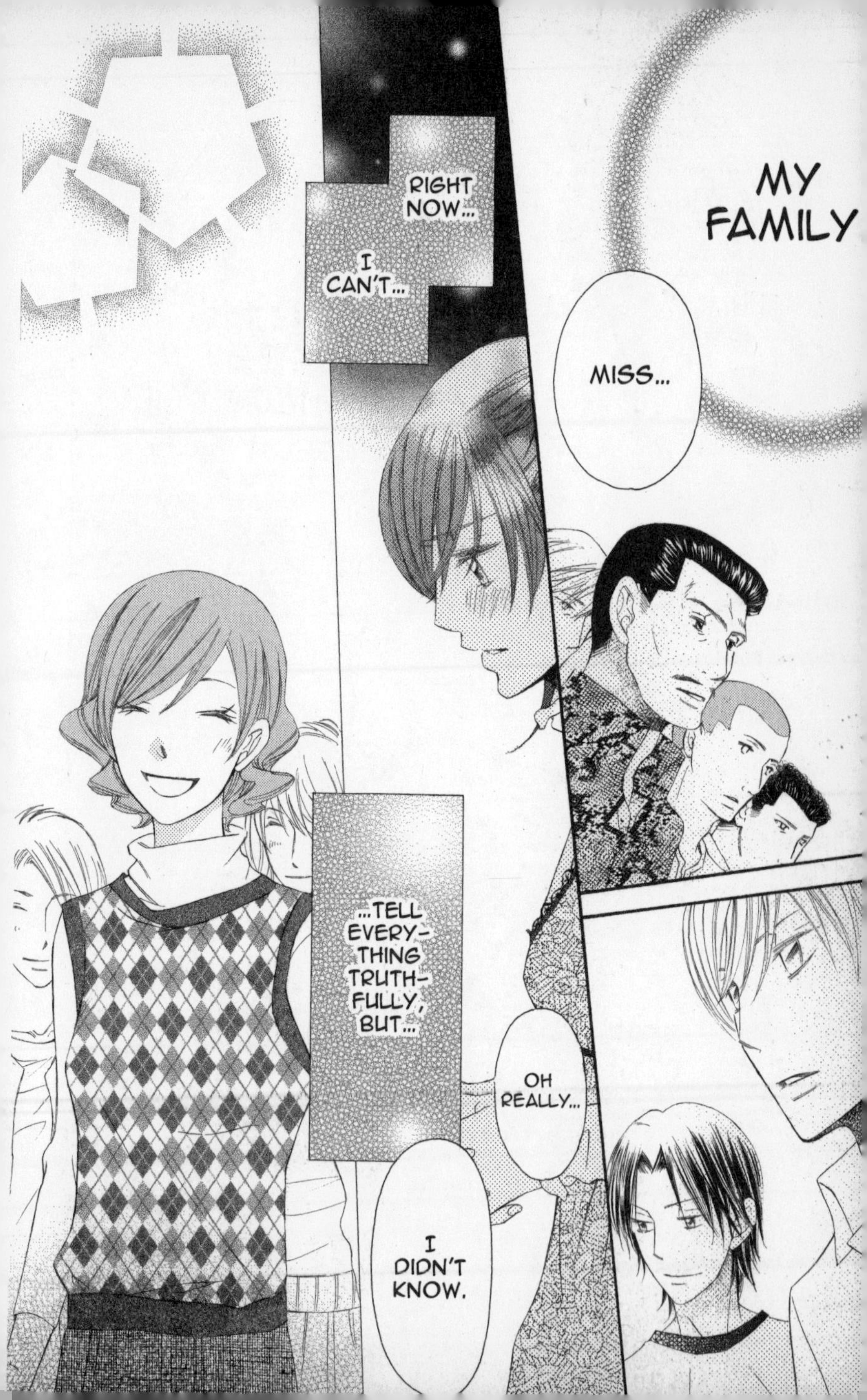
MY FAMILY
MISS...
OH REALLY...
I DIDN'T KNOW.
RIGHT NOW...
I CAN'T...
...TELL EVERYTHING TRUTHFULLY, BUT...

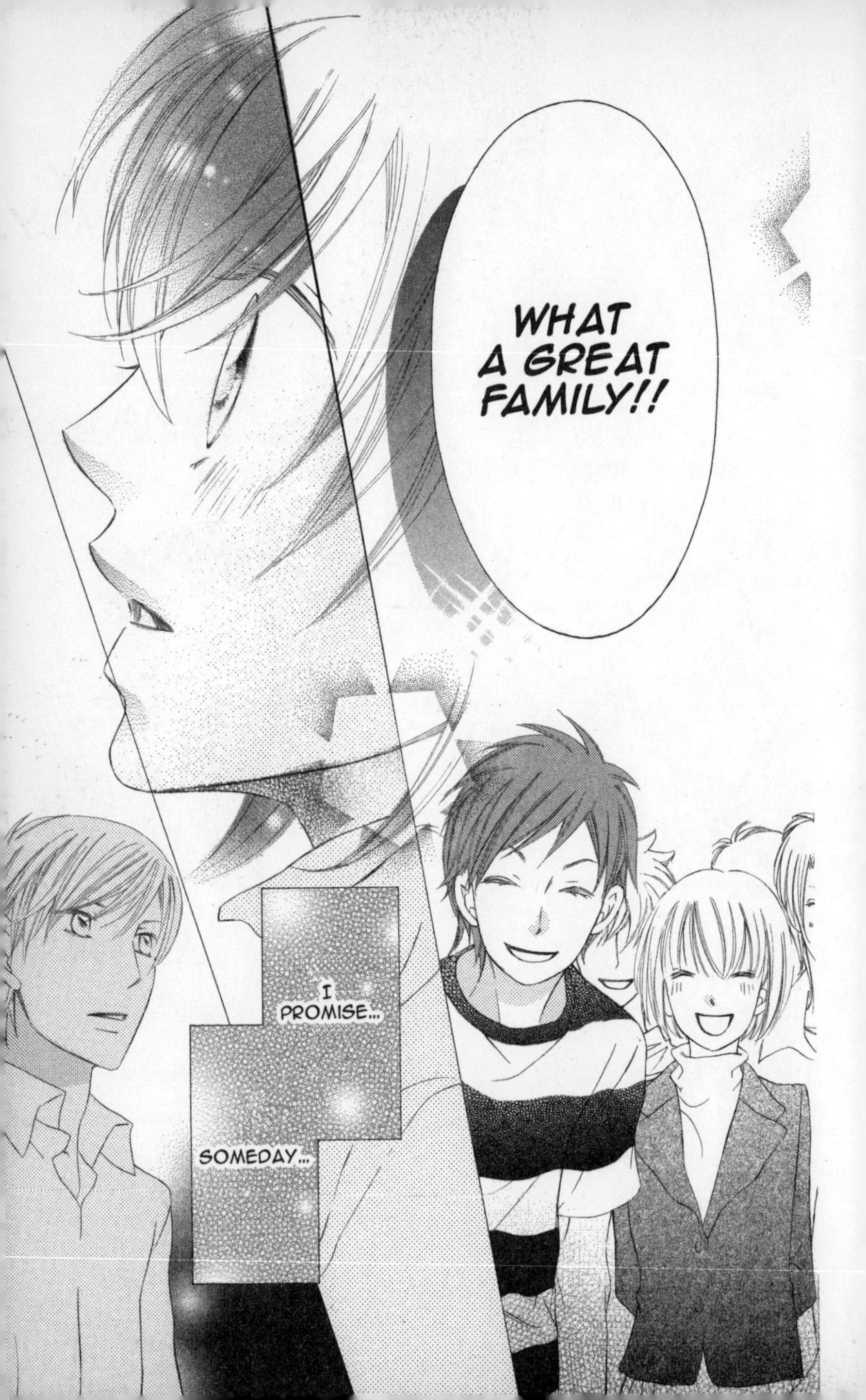
WHAT A GREAT FAMILY!!
I PROMISE...
SOMEDAY...

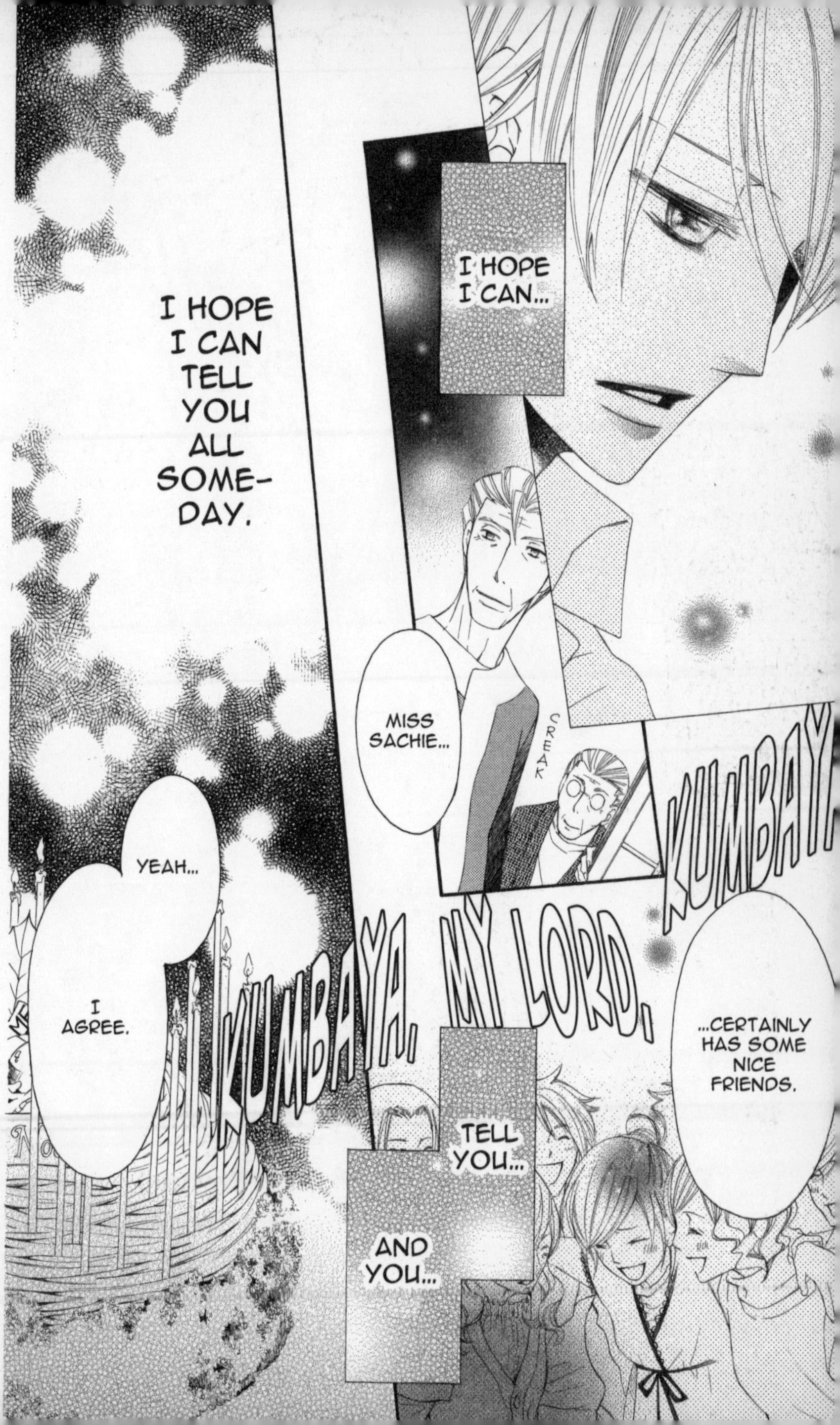
I HOPE I CAN...
MISS SACHIE...
CREAK
KUMBAYA
...CERTAINLY HAS SOME NICE FRIENDS.
KUMBAYA, MY LORD,
TELL YOU...
AND YOU...
I HOPE I CAN TELL YOU ALL SOME-DAY.
YEAH...
I AGREE.

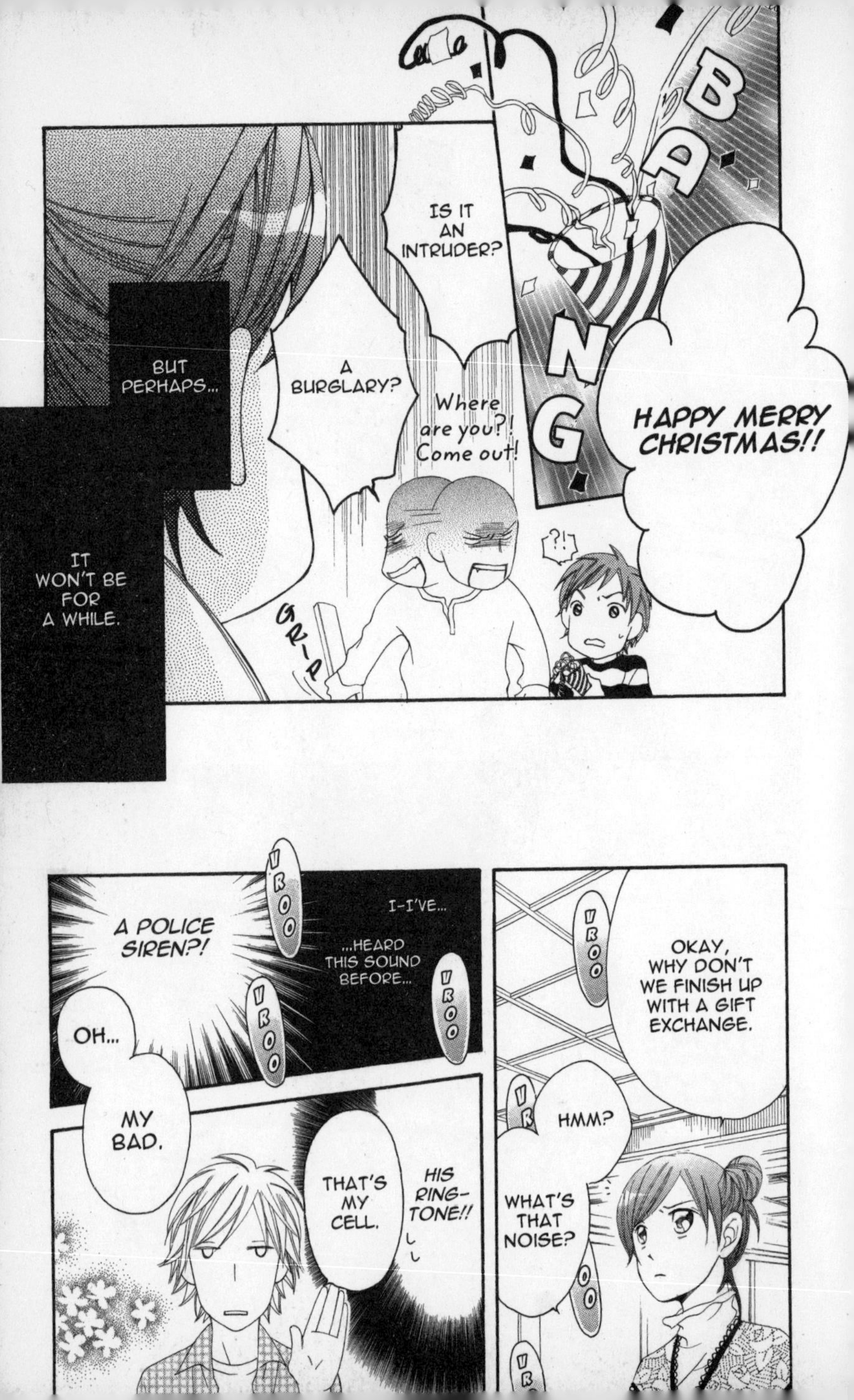
BANG
HAPPY MERRY CHRISTMAS!!
?!
IS IT AN INTRUDER?
Where are you?! Come out!
A BURGLARY?
GRIP
BUT PERHAPS...
IT WON'T BE FOR A WHILE.
OKAY, WHY DON'T WE FINISH UP WITH A GIFT EXCHANGE.
VROO
HMM?
WHAT'S THAT NOISE?
VROO
I-I'VE...
...HEARD THIS SOUND BEFORE...
A POLICE SIREN?!
OH...
MY BAD.
HIS RINGTONE!!
THAT'S MY CELL.

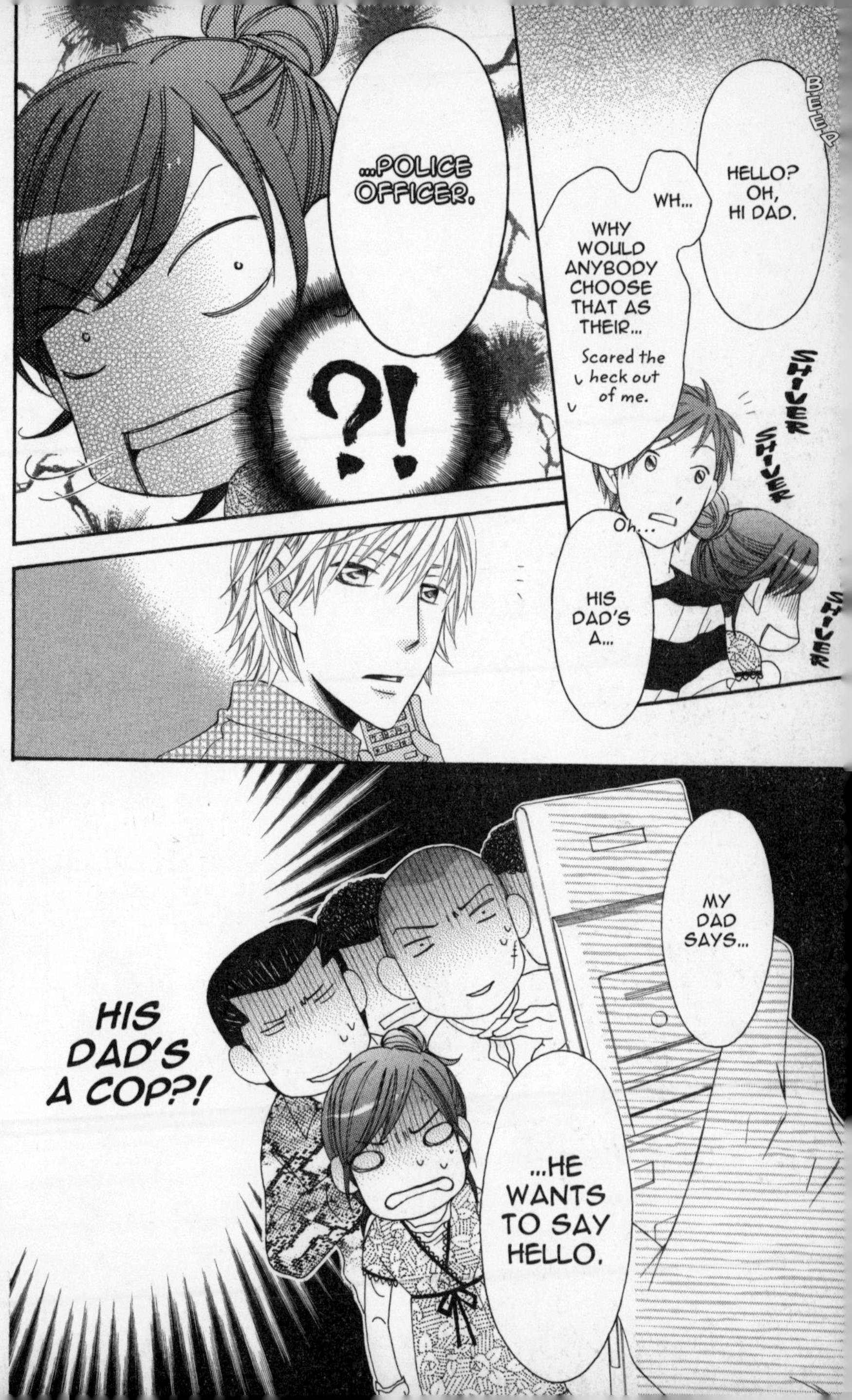
BEEP
HELLO? OH, HI DAD.
WH...
WHY WOULD ANYBODY CHOOSE THAT AS THEIR...
Scared the heck out of me.
SHIVER SHIVER SHIVER
...POLICE OFFICER.
?!
Oh...
HIS DAD'S A...
MY DAD SAYS...
...HE WANTS TO SAY HELLO.
HIS DAD'S A COP?!

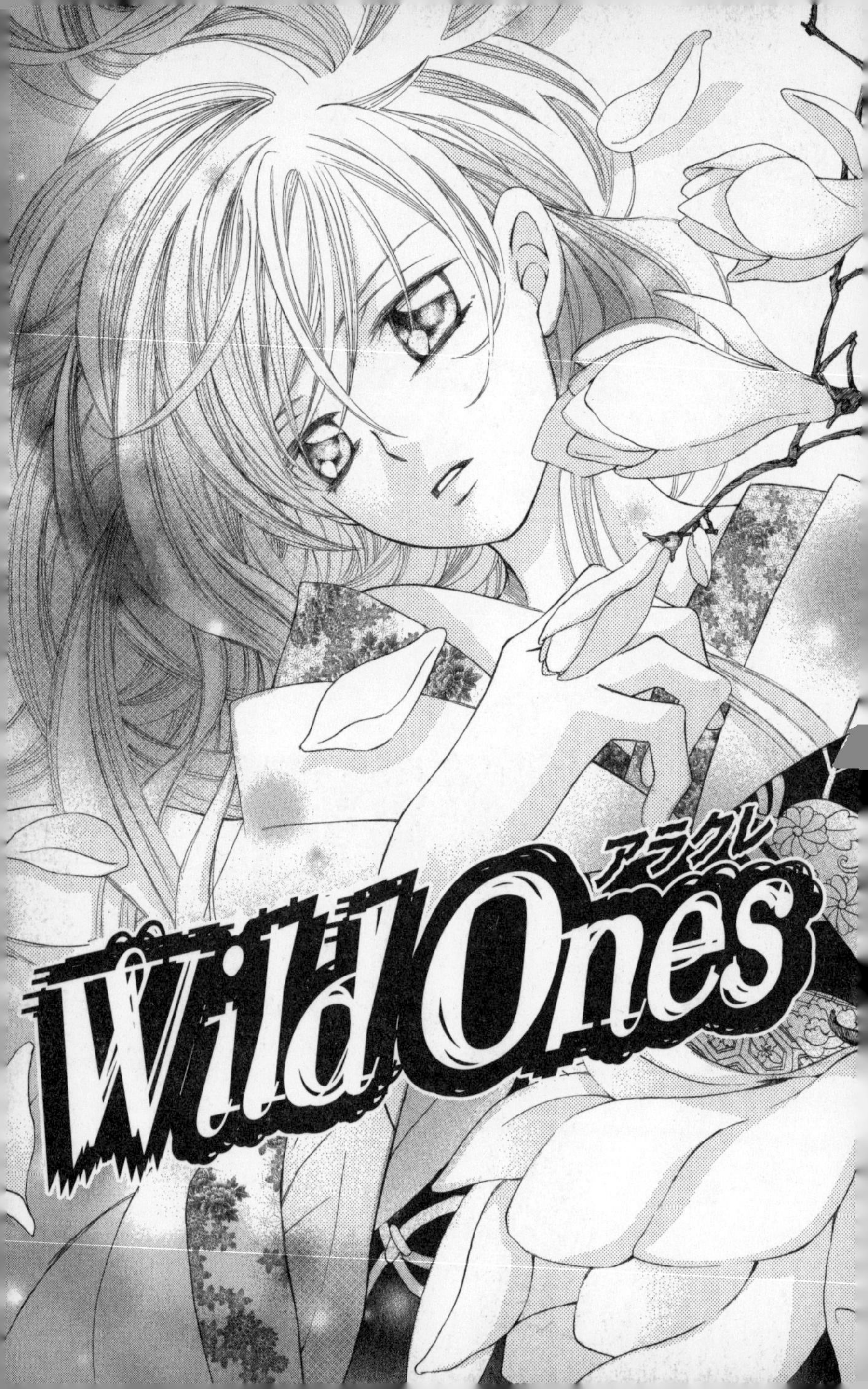
アラクレ
Wild Ones

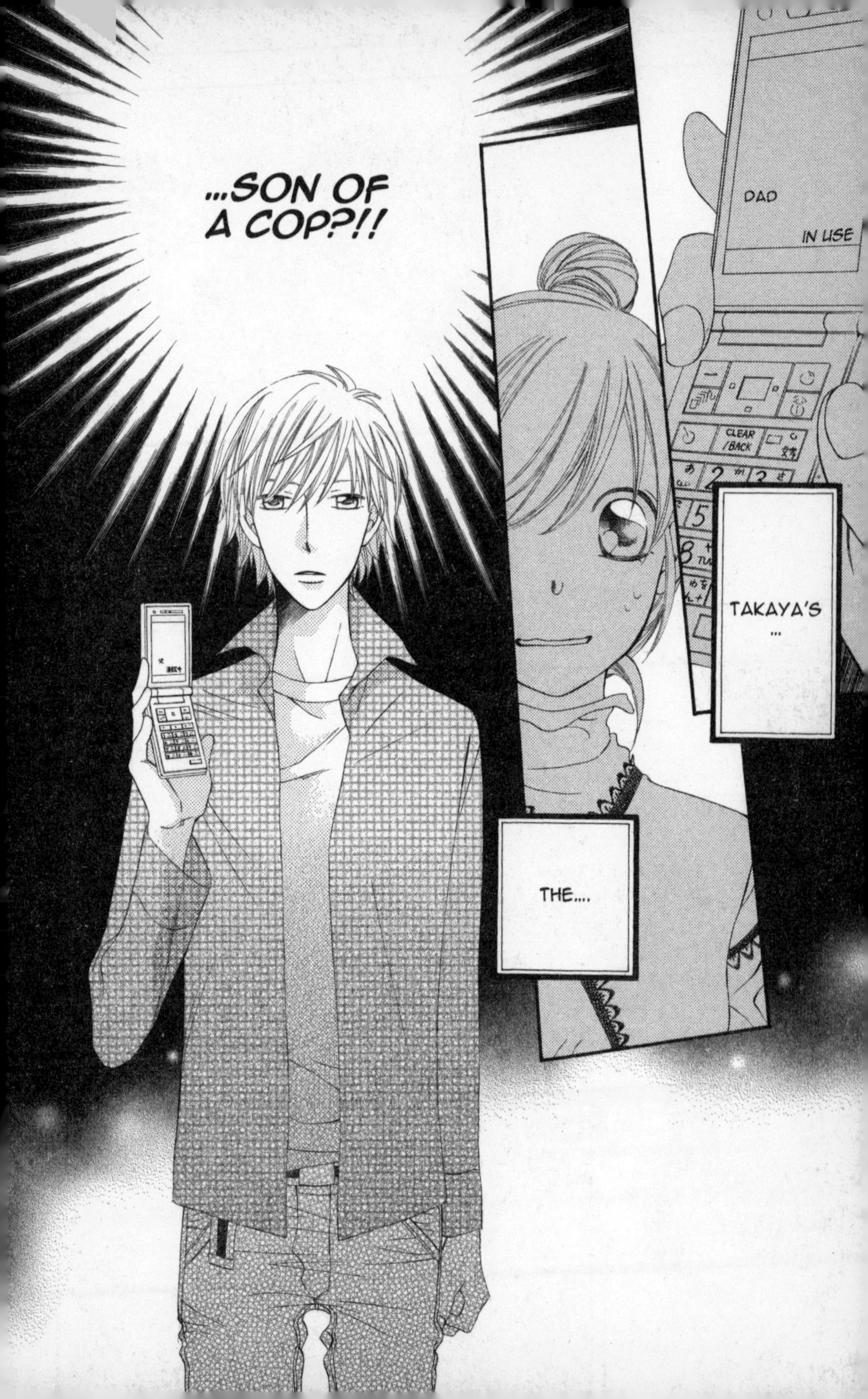
DAD
IN USE
CLEAR /BACK
TAKAYA'S ...
THE....
...SON OF A COP?!!

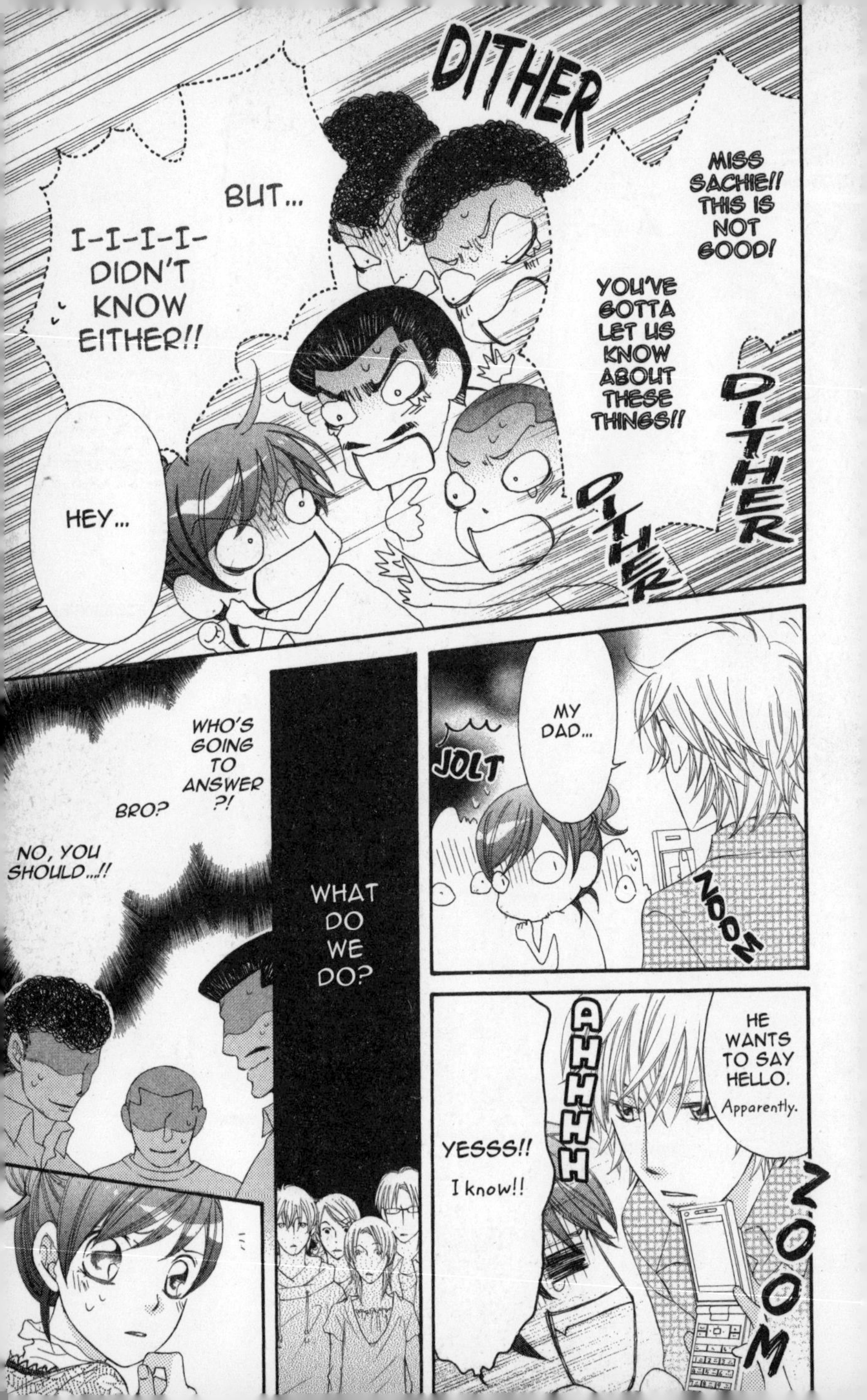
DITHER
MISS SACHIE!! THIS IS NOT GOOD!
YOU'VE GOTTA LET US KNOW ABOUT THESE THINGS!!
DITHER
DITHER
BUT...
I-I-I-I-DIDN'T KNOW EITHER!!
HEY...
MY DAD...
JOLT
ZOOM
HE WANTS TO SAY HELLO.
Apparently.
AHHHHH
ZOOM
YESSS!!
I know!!
WHAT DO WE DO?
WHO'S GOING TO ANSWER?!
BRO?
NO, YOU SHOULD...!!

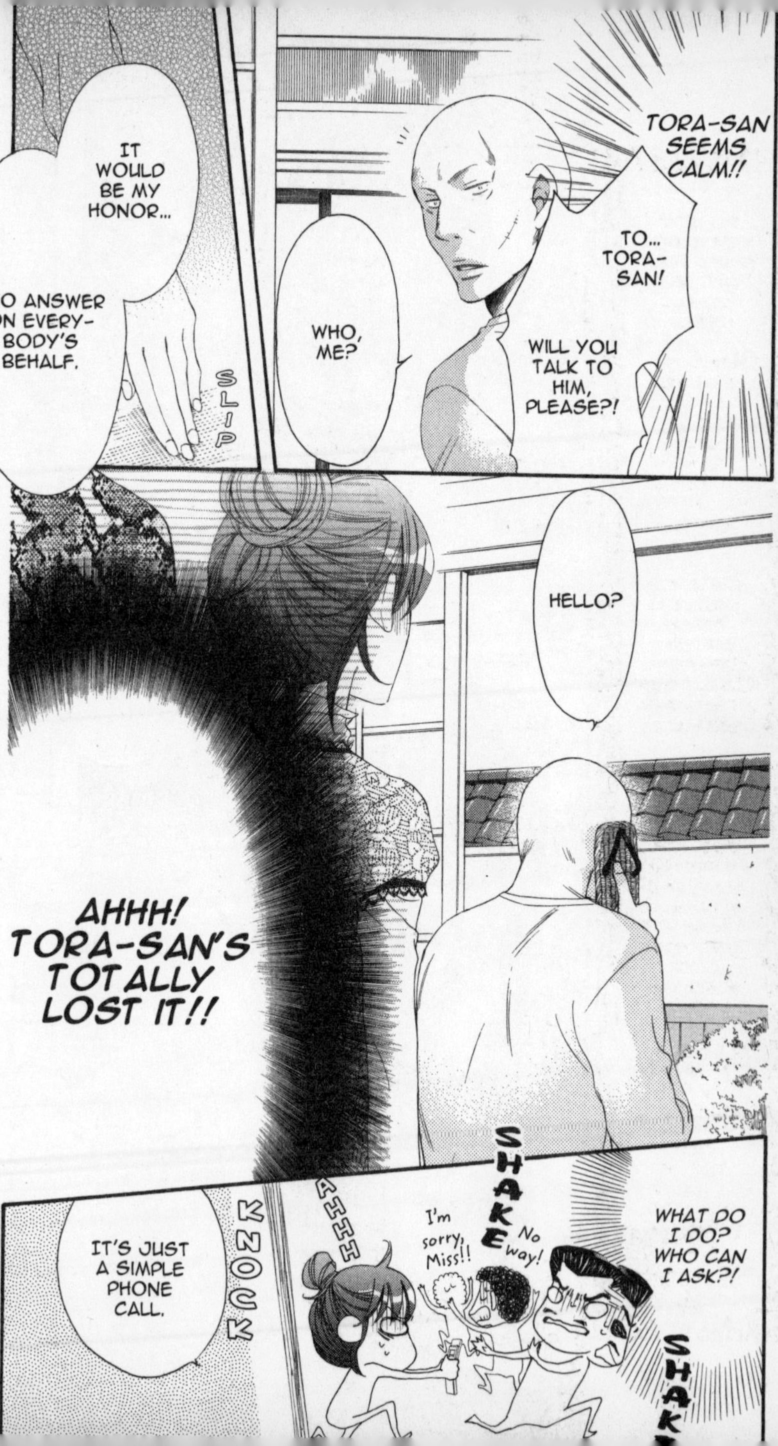
TORA-SAN SEEMS CALM!!
TO... TORA-SAN!
WILL YOU TALK TO HIM, PLEASE?!
WHO, ME?
IT WOULD BE MY HONOR...
...TO ANSWER ON EVERY-BODY'S BEHALF.
SLIP
HELLO?
AHHH! TORA-SAN'S TOTALLY LOST IT!!
SHAKE
WHAT DO I DO? WHO CAN I ASK?!
No way!
I'm sorry, Miss!!
AHHH
KNOCK
IT'S JUST A SIMPLE PHONE CALL.
SHAKE

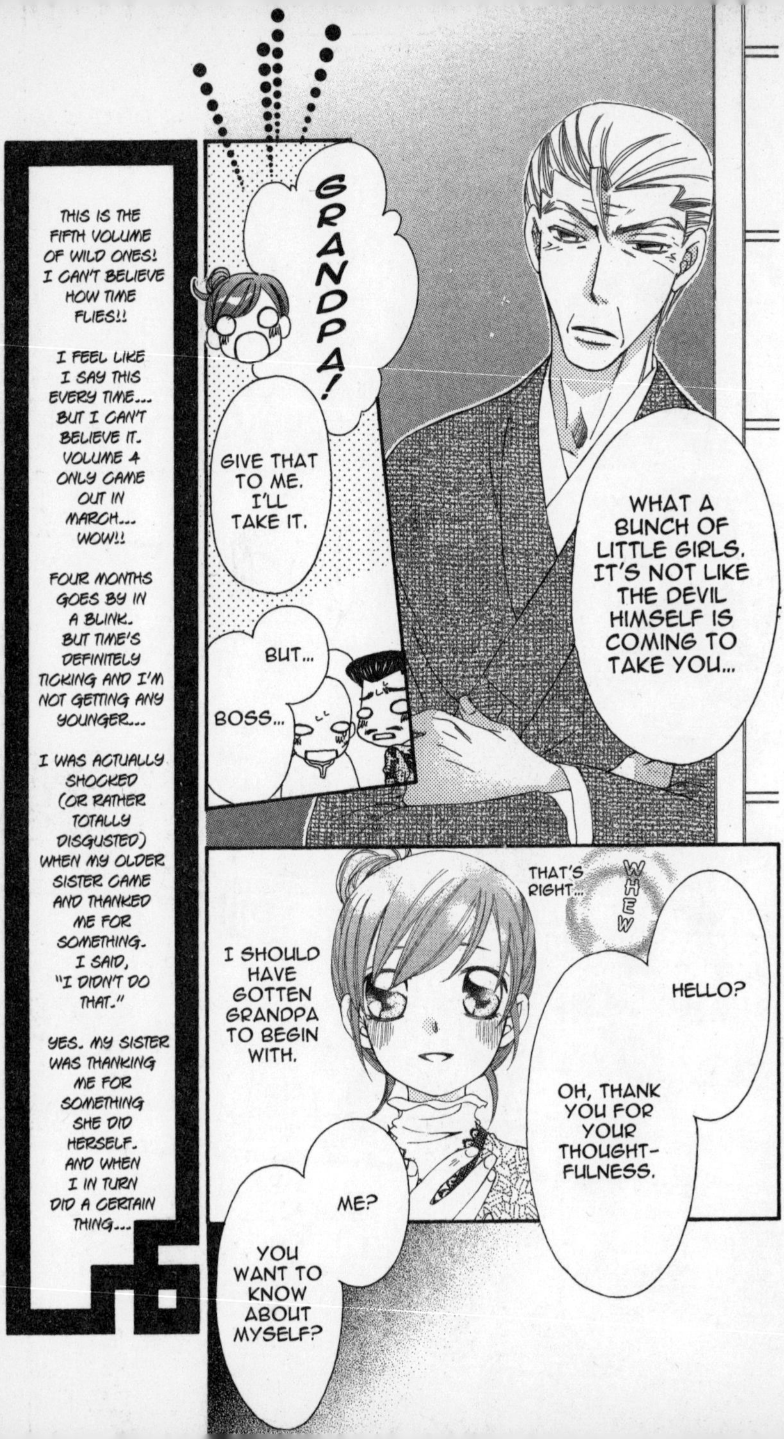
WHAT A BUNCH OF LITTLE GIRLS. IT'S NOT LIKE THE DEVIL HIMSELF IS COMING TO TAKE YOU...
GRANDPA!
GIVE THAT TO ME. I'LL TAKE IT.
BUT...
BOSS...
WHEW
THAT'S RIGHT...
I SHOULD HAVE GOTTEN GRANDPA TO BEGIN WITH.
HELLO?
OH, THANK YOU FOR YOUR THOUGHT-FULNESS.
ME?
YOU WANT TO KNOW ABOUT MYSELF?

THIS IS THE FIFTH VOLUME OF WILD ONES! I CAN'T BELIEVE HOW TIME FLIES!!

I FEEL LIKE I SAY THIS EVERY TIME... BUT I CAN'T BELIEVE IT. VOLUME 4 ONLY CAME OUT IN MARCH... WOW!!

FOUR MONTHS GOES BY IN A BLINK. BUT TIME'S DEFINITELY TICKING AND I'M NOT GETTING ANY YOUNGER...

I WAS ACTUALLY SHOCKED (OR RATHER TOTALLY DISGUSTED) WHEN MY OLDER SISTER CAME AND THANKED ME FOR SOMETHING. I SAID, "I DIDN'T DO THAT."

YES. MY SISTER WAS THANKING ME FOR SOMETHING SHE DID HERSELF. AND WHEN I IN TURN DID A CERTAIN THING...

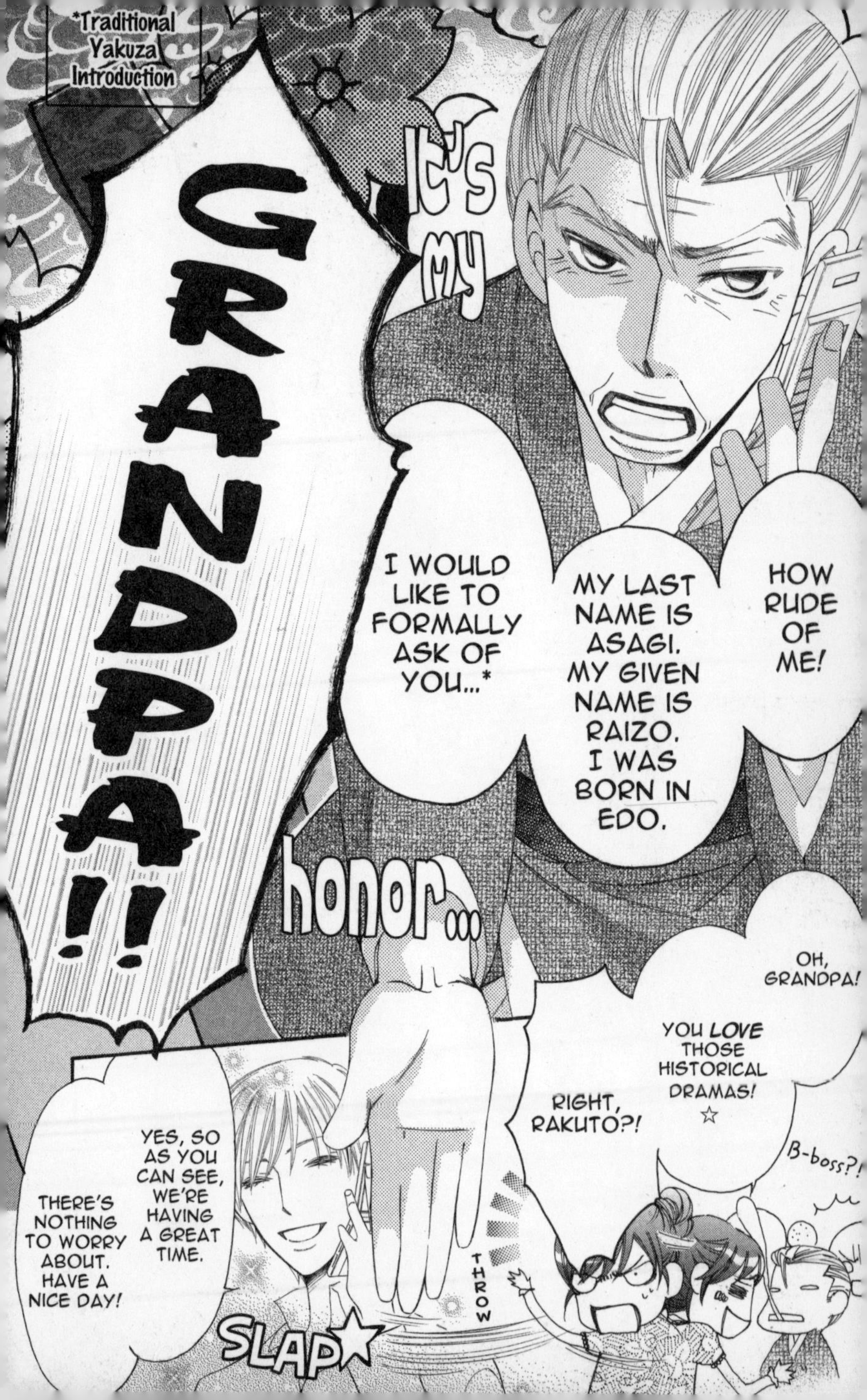
HOW RUDE OF ME!
MY LAST NAME IS ASAGI. MY GIVEN NAME IS RAIZO. I WAS BORN IN EDO.
I WOULD LIKE TO FORMALLY ASK OF YOU...*
It's my honor...
GRANDPA!!
OH, GRANDPA!
YOU LOVE THOSE HISTORICAL DRAMAS! ☆
RIGHT, RAKUTO?!
B-boss?!
THROW
YES, SO AS YOU CAN SEE, WE'RE HAVING A GREAT TIME.
THERE'S NOTHING TO WORRY ABOUT. HAVE A NICE DAY!
SLAP☆
*Traditional Yakuza Introduction

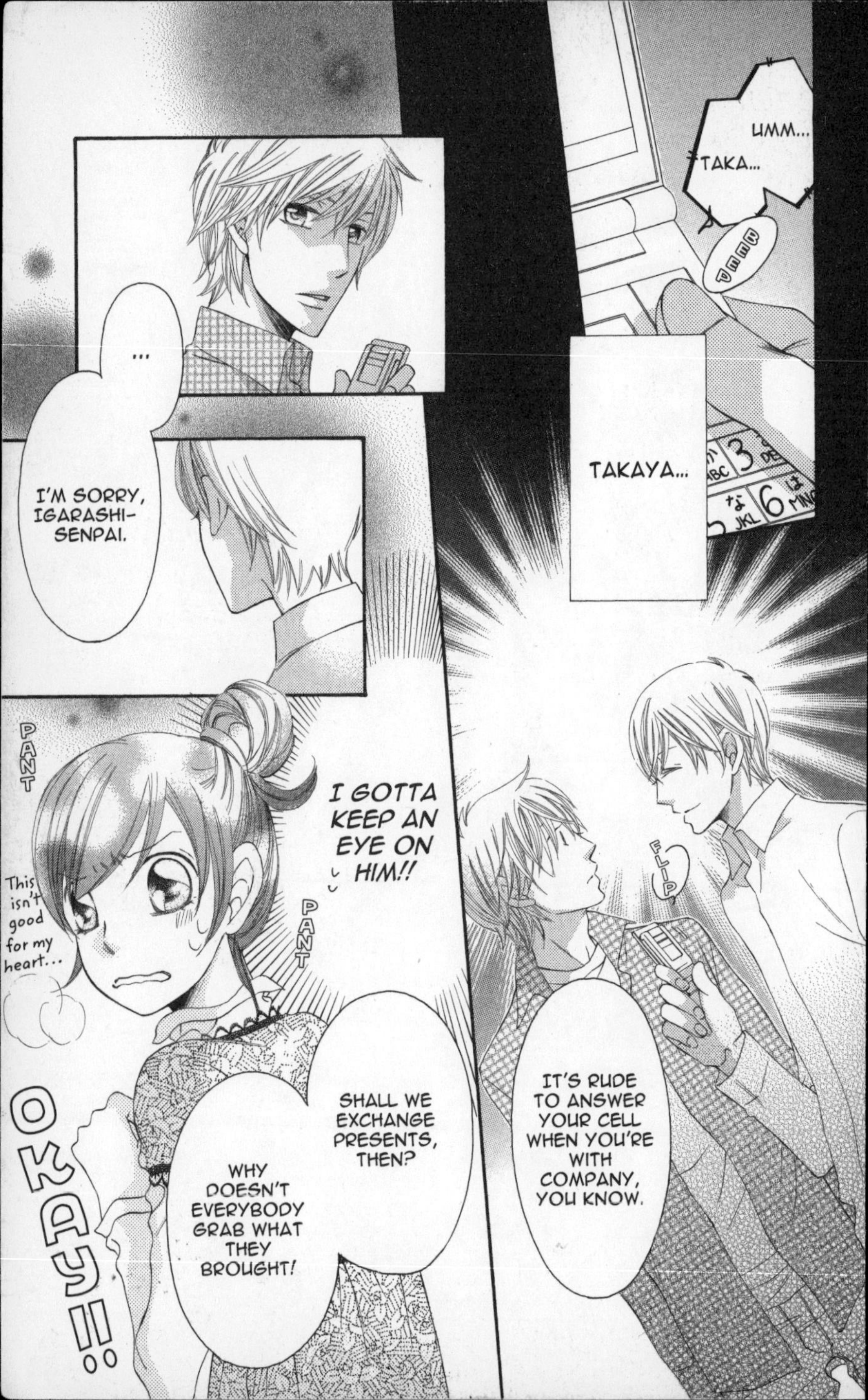
UMM... TAKA...
BEEP
TAKAYA...
...
I'M SORRY, IGARASHI-SENPAI.
FLIP
IT'S RUDE TO ANSWER YOUR CELL WHEN YOU'RE WITH COMPANY, YOU KNOW.
I GOTTA KEEP AN EYE ON HIM!!
PANT
PANT
This isn't good for my heart...
SHALL WE EXCHANGE PRESENTS, THEN?
WHY DOESN'T EVERYBODY GRAB WHAT THEY BROUGHT!
OKAY!!

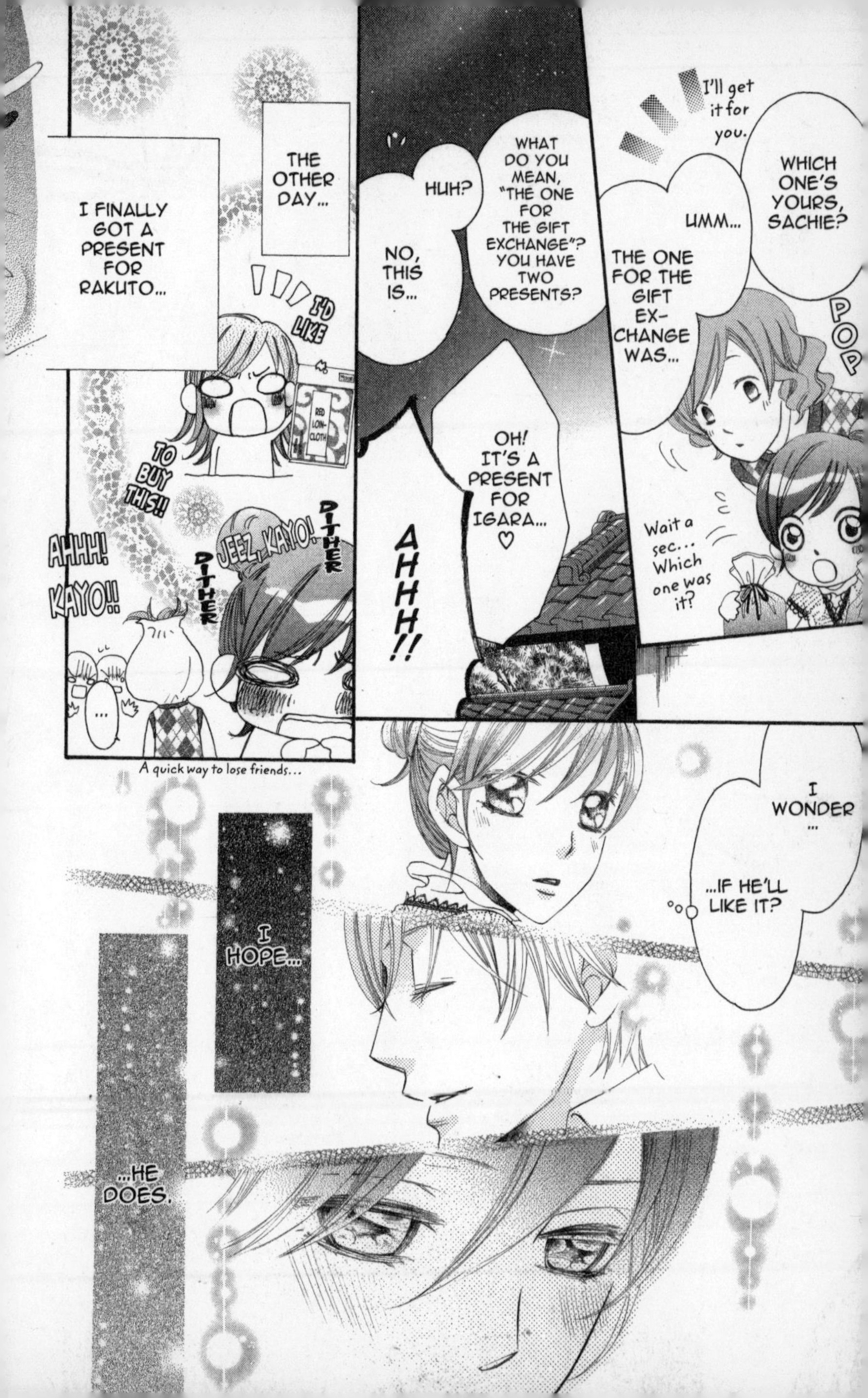
WHICH ONE'S YOURS, SACHIE?
I'll get it for you.
UMM...
THE ONE FOR THE GIFT EX-CHANGE WAS...
POP
Wait a sec... Which one was it?
WHAT DO YOU MEAN, "THE ONE FOR THE GIFT EXCHANGE"? YOU HAVE TWO PRESENTS?
HUH?
NO, THIS IS...
OH! IT'S A PRESENT FOR IGARA... ♡
AHHHH!!
THE OTHER DAY...
I FINALLY GOT A PRESENT FOR RAKUTO...
I'D LIKE
RED LOIN-CLOTH
TO BUY THIS!!
DITHER
JEEZ, KAYO!
DITHER
AHHH! KAYO!!
...
A quick way to lose friends...
I WONDER ...
...IF HE'LL LIKE IT?
I HOPE...
...HE DOES.

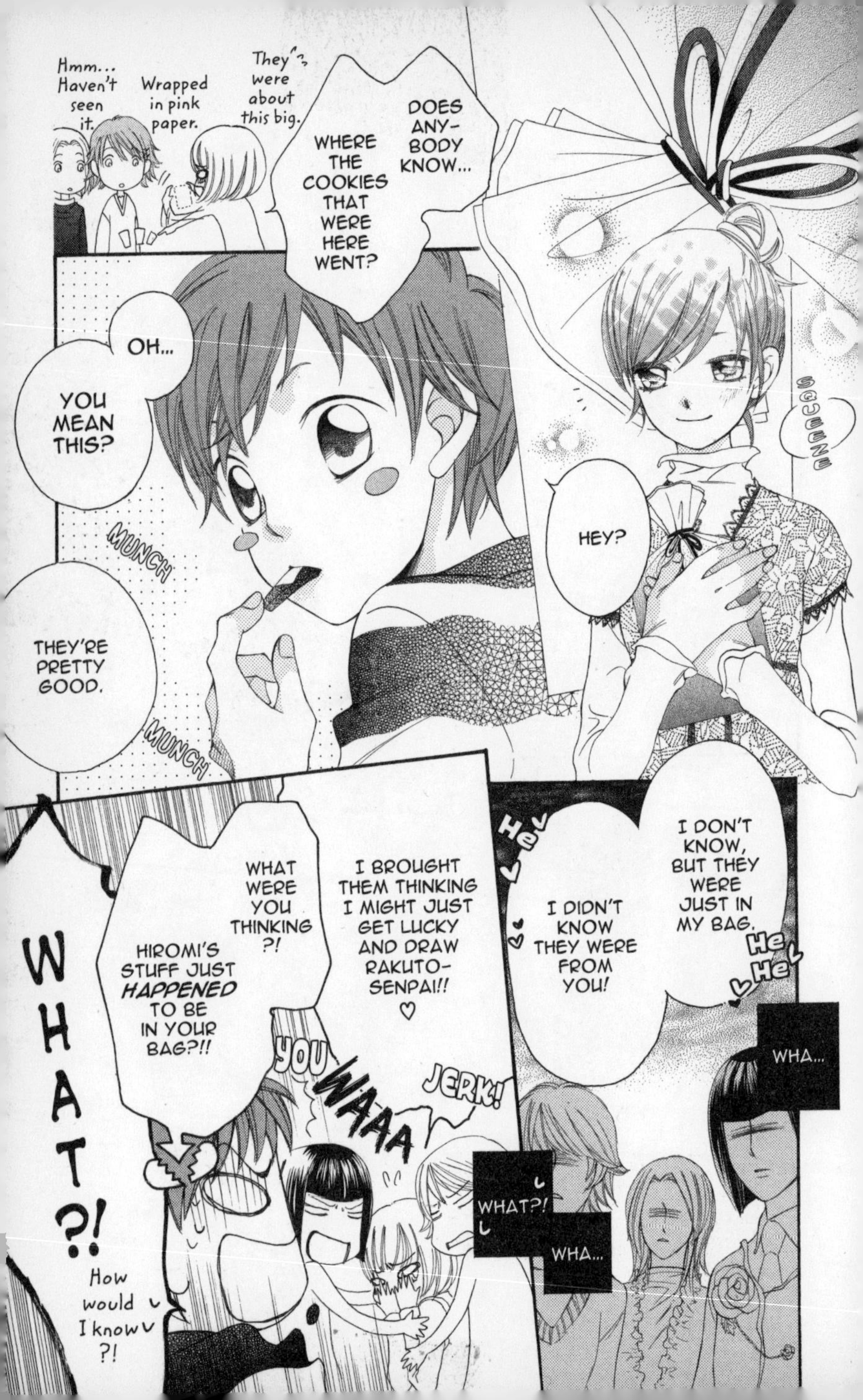
DOES ANYBODY KNOW... WHERE THE COOKIES THAT WERE HERE WENT?
They're were about this big.
Wrapped in pink paper.
Hmm... Haven't seen it.
OH...
YOU MEAN THIS?
MUNCH
THEY'RE PRETTY GOOD.
MUNCH
HEY?
SQUEEZE
I DON'T KNOW, BUT THEY WERE JUST IN MY BAG.
He He
I DIDN'T KNOW THEY WERE FROM YOU!
He He
WHA...
WHAT?!
WHA...
WHAT WERE YOU THINKING ?!
I BROUGHT THEM THINKING I MIGHT JUST GET LUCKY AND DRAW RAKUTO-SENPAI!! ♡
HIROMI'S STUFF JUST HAPPENED TO BE IN YOUR BAG?!!
YOU JERK!
WAAAA
WHAT?!
How would I know ?!

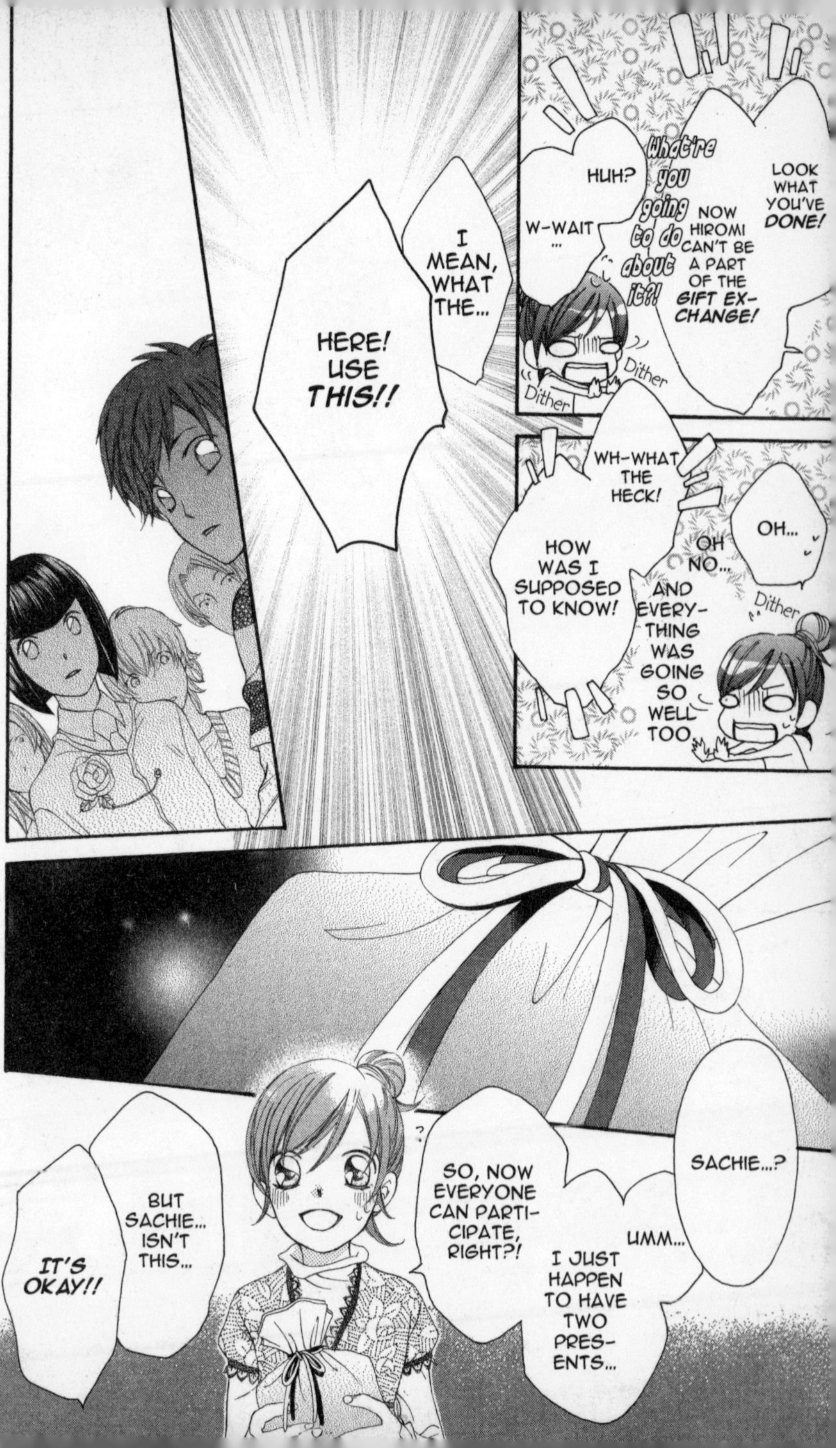
LOOK WHAT YOU'VE DONE! NOW HIROMI CAN'T BE A PART OF THE GIFT EX-CHANGE!
What're you going to do about it?!
HUH?
W-WAIT ...
Dither
Dither
OH...
OH NO... AND EVERY-THING WAS GOING SO WELL TOO
Dither
WH-WHAT THE HECK!
HOW WAS I SUPPOSED TO KNOW!
I MEAN, WHAT THE...
HERE! USE THIS!!
SACHIE...?
UMM... I JUST HAPPEN TO HAVE TWO PRES-ENTS...
SO, NOW EVERYONE CAN PARTI-CIPATE, RIGHT?!
BUT SACHIE... ISN'T THIS...
IT'S OKAY!!

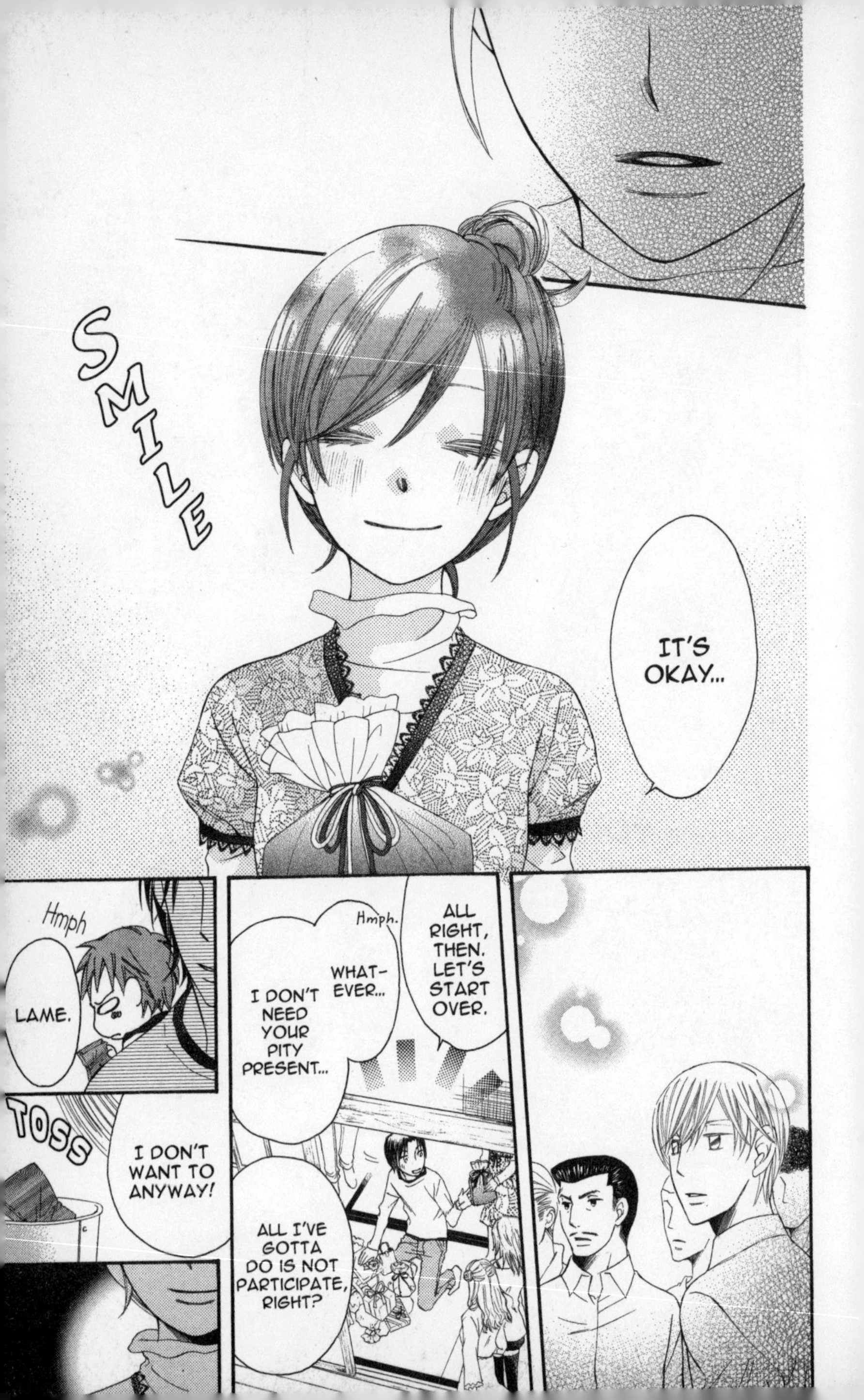
IT'S OKAY...
SMILE
ALL RIGHT, THEN. LET'S START OVER.
Hmph.
WHATEVER...
I DON'T NEED YOUR PITY PRESENT...
ALL I'VE GOTTA DO IS NOT PARTICIPATE, RIGHT?
Hmph
LAME.
TOSS
I DON'T WANT TO ANYWAY!

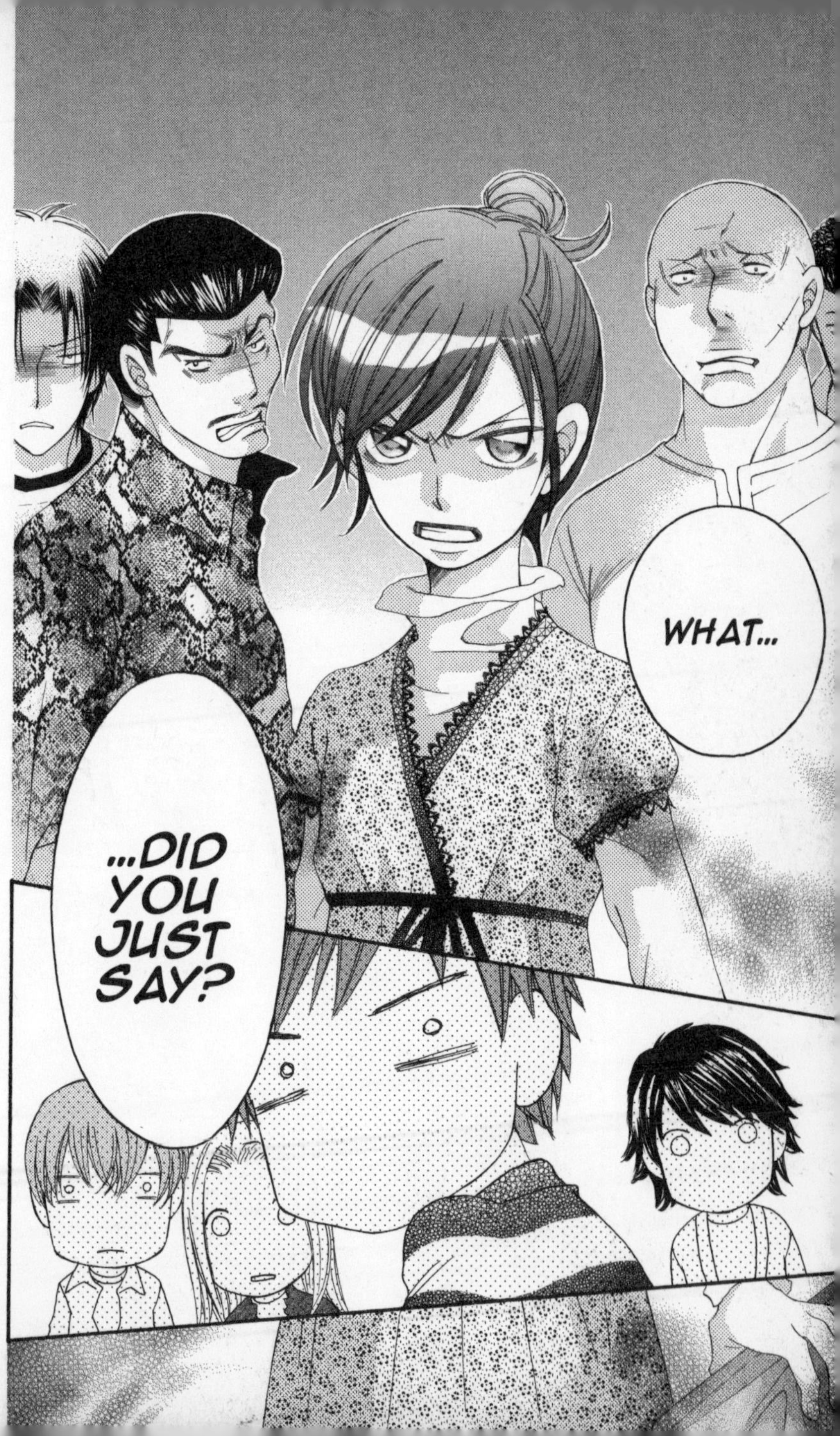
WHAT...
...DID YOU JUST SAY?

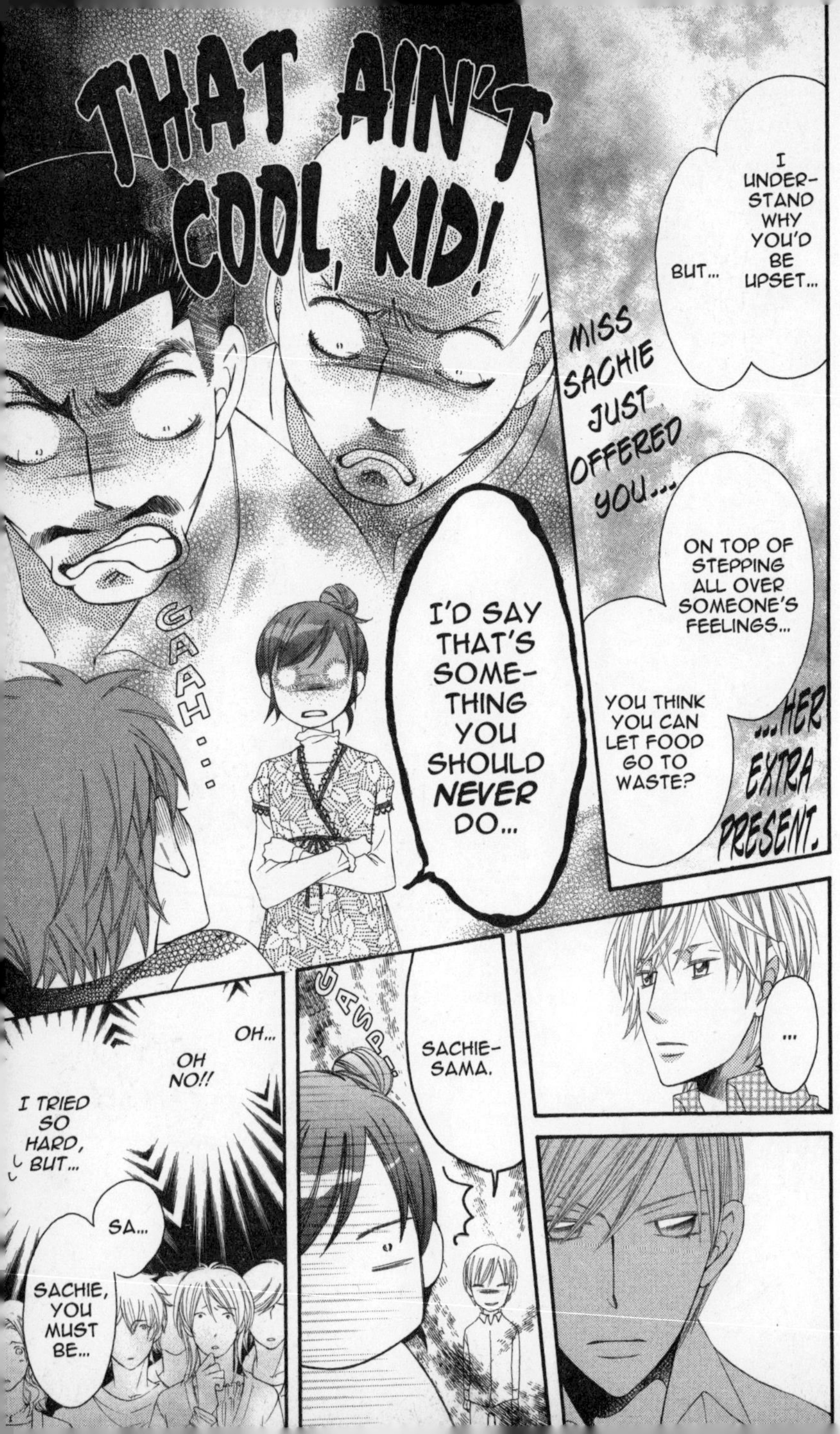
I UNDERSTAND WHY YOU'D BE UPSET...
BUT...
MISS SACHIE JUST OFFERED YOU...
...HER EXTRA PRESENT.
ON TOP OF STEPPING ALL OVER SOMEONE'S FEELINGS...
YOU THINK YOU CAN LET FOOD GO TO WASTE?
I'D SAY THAT'S SOMETHING YOU SHOULD NEVER DO...
THAT AIN'T COOL, KID!
GAAH...
...
SACHIE-SAMA.
GASA...
OH...
OH NO!!
I TRIED SO HARD, BUT...
SA...
SACHIE, YOU MUST BE...

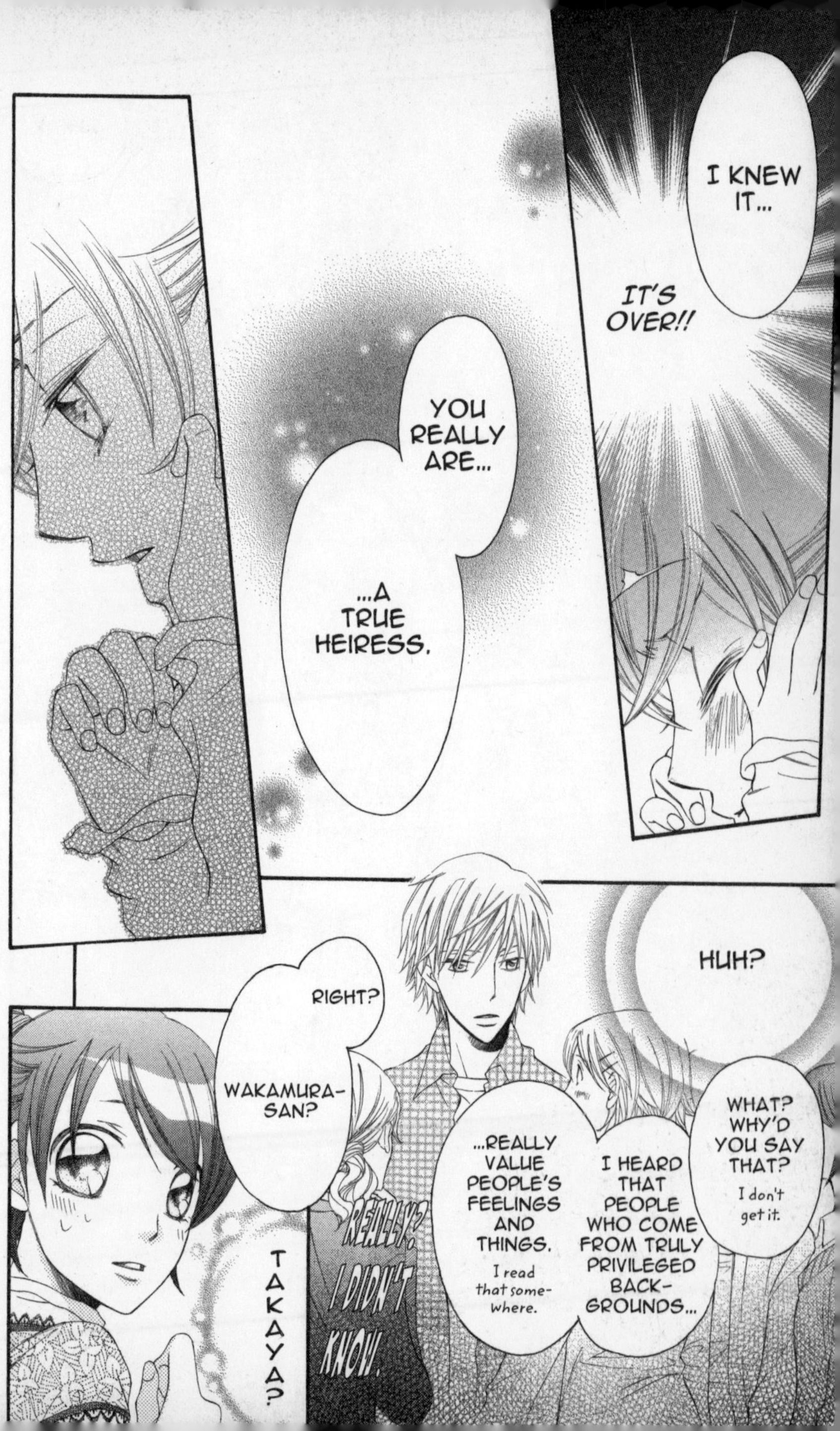
I KNEW IT...
IT'S OVER!!
YOU REALLY ARE...
...A TRUE HEIRESS.
HUH?
WHAT? WHY'D YOU SAY THAT?
I don't get it.
I HEARD THAT PEOPLE WHO COME FROM TRULY PRIVILEGED BACK-GROUNDS...
...REALLY VALUE PEOPLE'S FEELINGS AND THINGS.
I read that some-where.
REALLY? I DIDN'T KNOW.
RIGHT?
WAKAMURA-SAN?
TAKAYA?

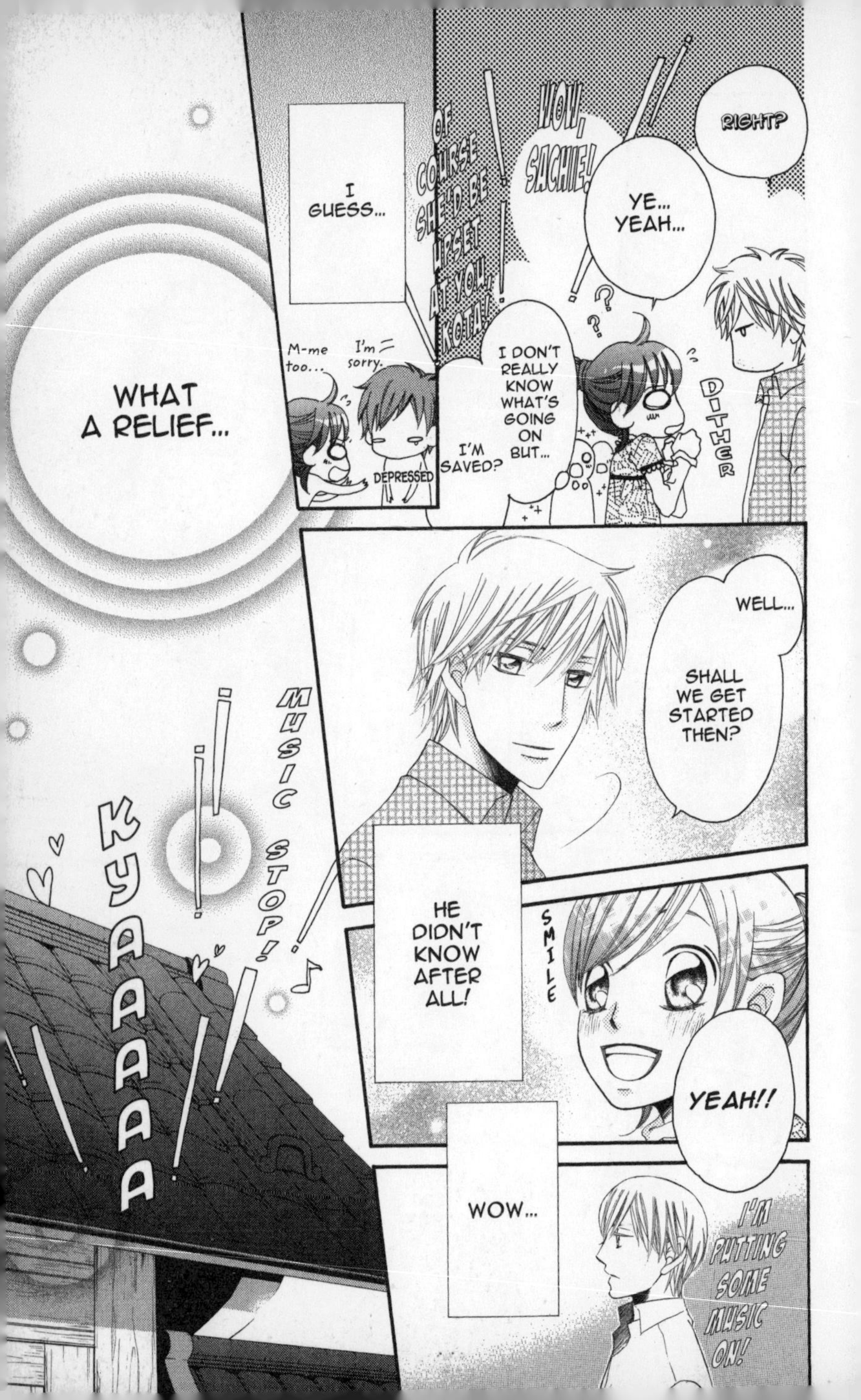
RIGHT?
YE... YEAH...
WOW, SACHIE!
OF COURSE SHE'D BE UPSET AT YOU, KOTA!
I GUESS...
DITHER
I DON'T REALLY KNOW WHAT'S GOING ON BUT...
I'M SAVED?
I'm sorry.
M-me too...
DEPRESSED
WHAT A RELIEF...
WELL...
SHALL WE GET STARTED THEN?
SMILE
YEAH!!
HE DIDN'T KNOW AFTER ALL!
I'M PUTTING SOME MUSIC ON!
WOW...
MUSIC STOP!
KYAAAAAA!!

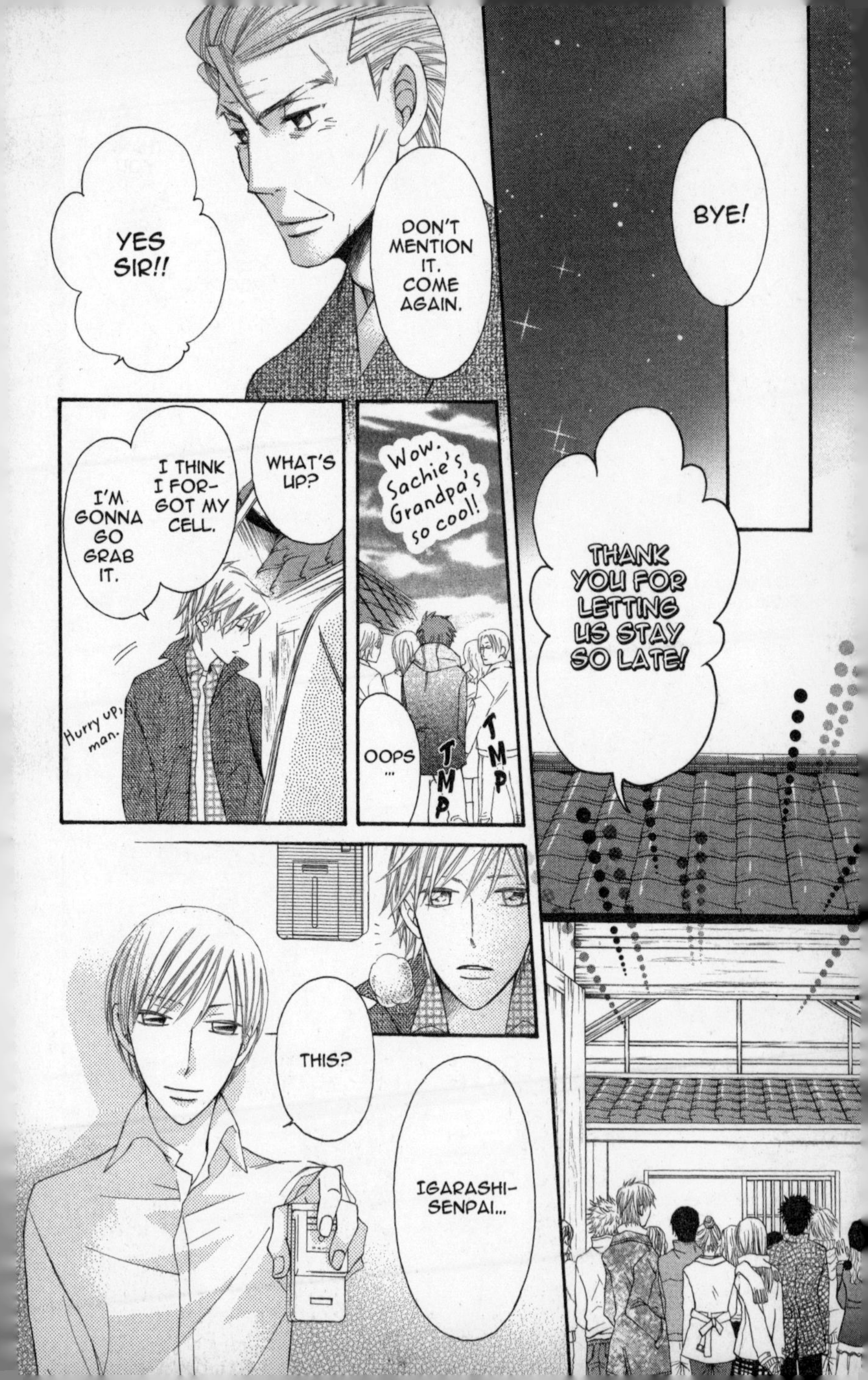
BYE!
THANK YOU FOR LETTING US STAY SO LATE!
DON'T MENTION IT. COME AGAIN.
YES SIR!!
Wow. Sachie's Grandpa's so cool!
OOPS...
TMP TMP
WHAT'S UP?
I THINK I FORGOT MY CELL.
I'M GONNA GO GRAB IT.
Hurry up, man.
IGARASHI-SENPAI...
THIS?

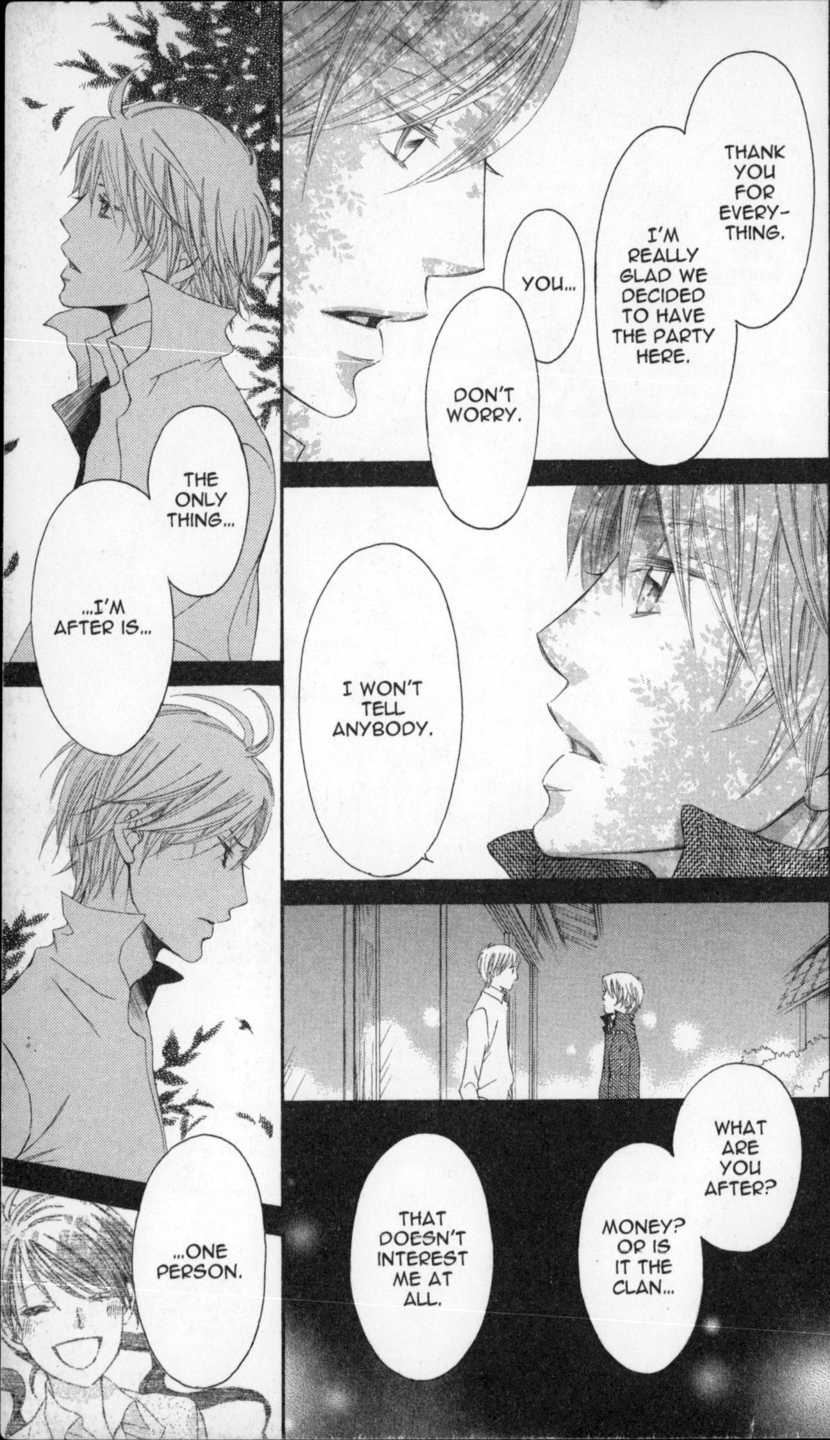
THANK YOU FOR EVERY-THING.
I'M REALLY GLAD WE DECIDED TO HAVE THE PARTY HERE.
YOU...
DON'T WORRY.
I WON'T TELL ANYBODY.
WHAT ARE YOU AFTER?
MONEY? OR IS IT THE CLAN...
THAT DOESN'T INTEREST ME AT ALL.
THE ONLY THING...
...I'M AFTER IS...
...ONE PERSON.

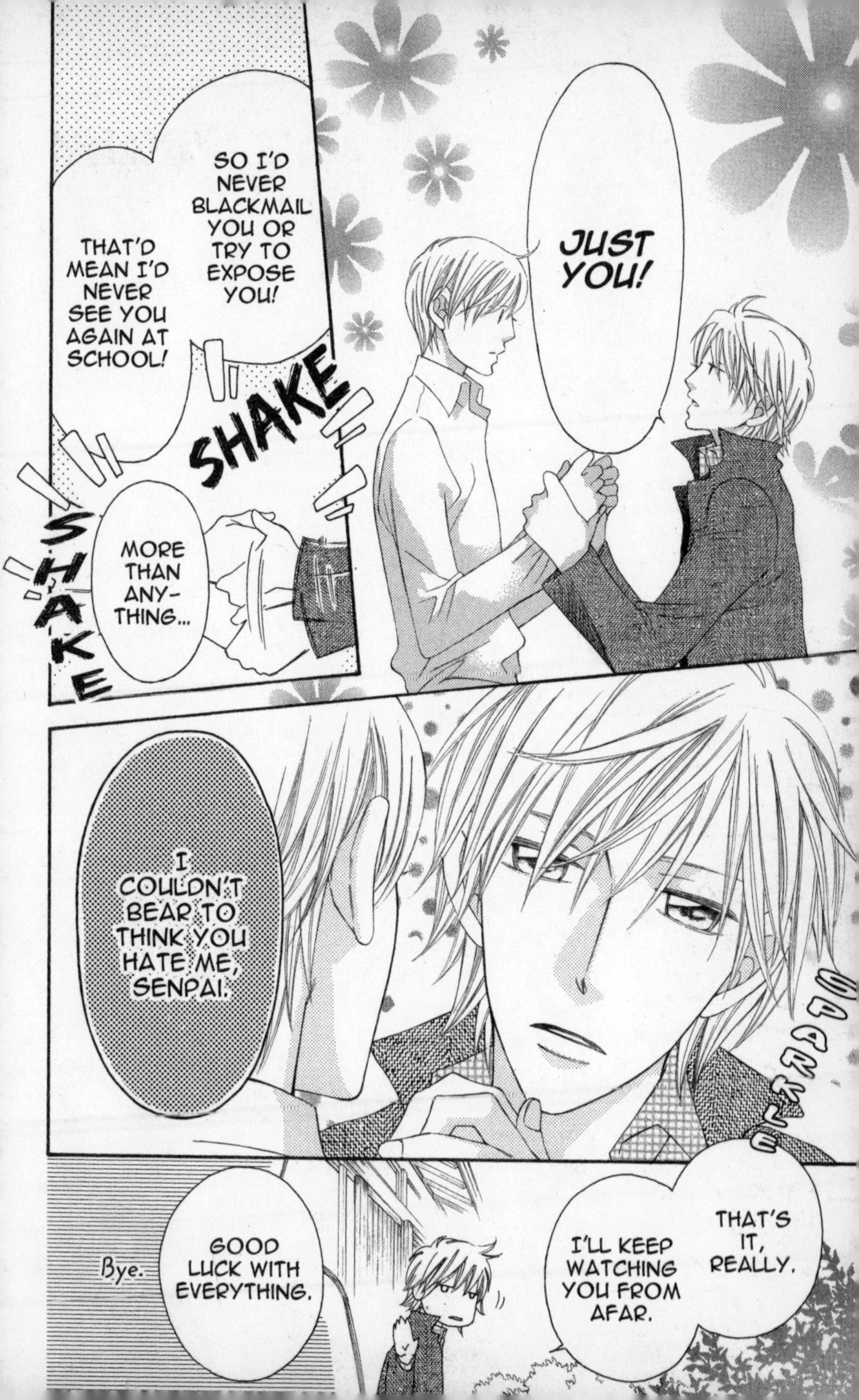
JUST YOU!
SO I'D NEVER BLACKMAIL YOU OR TRY TO EXPOSE YOU!
THAT'D MEAN I'D NEVER SEE YOU AGAIN AT SCHOOL!
SHAKE
SHAKE
MORE THAN ANY-THING...
I COULDN'T BEAR TO THINK YOU HATE ME, SENPAI.
SPARKLE
THAT'S IT, REALLY.
I'LL KEEP WATCHING YOU FROM AFAR.
GOOD LUCK WITH EVERYTHING.
Bye.

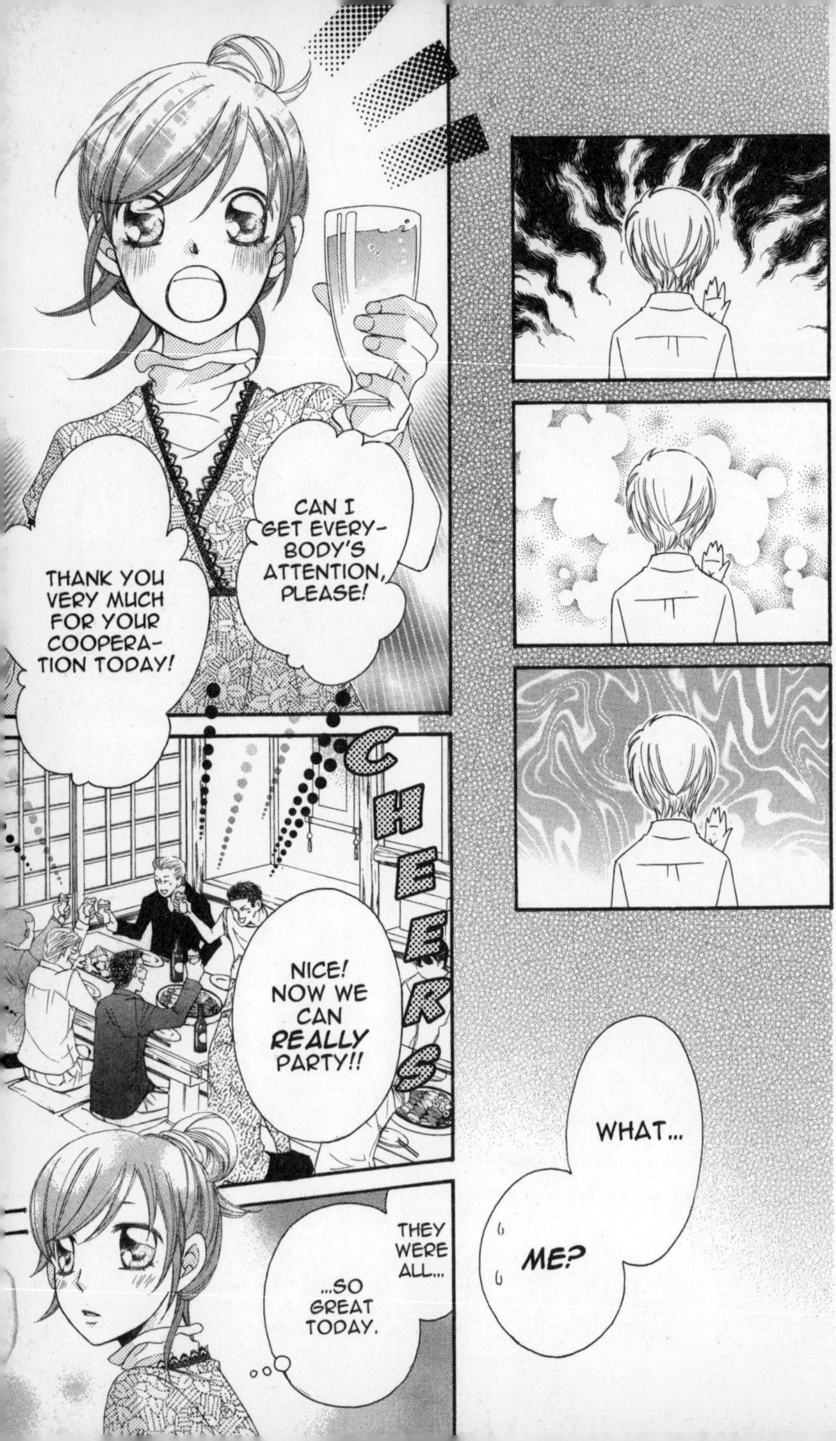
WHAT...
ME?
CAN I GET EVERY-BODY'S ATTENTION, PLEASE!
THANK YOU VERY MUCH FOR YOUR COOPERA-TION TODAY!
CHEERS
NICE! NOW WE CAN REALLY PARTY!!
THEY WERE ALL...
...SO GREAT TODAY.

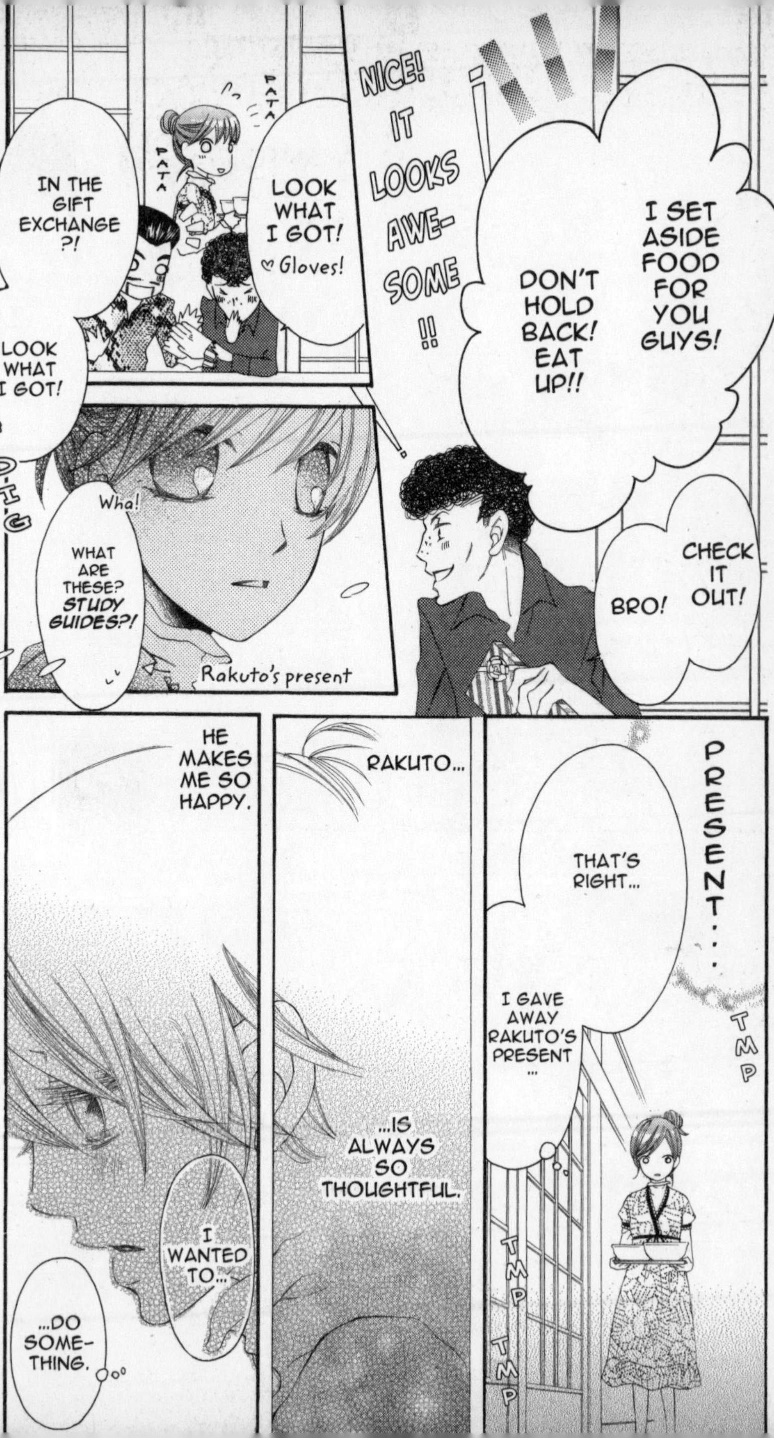
I SET ASIDE FOOD FOR YOU GUYS!
DON'T HOLD BACK! EAT UP!!
NICE! IT LOOKS AWE-SOME!!
LOOK WHAT I GOT!
♡ Gloves!
PATA PATA
IN THE GIFT EXCHANGE?!
LOOK WHAT I GOT!
DIG DIG
CHECK IT OUT!
BRO!
Wha!
WHAT ARE THESE? STUDY GUIDES?!
Rakuto's present
PRESENT...
THAT'S RIGHT...
I GAVE AWAY RAKUTO'S PRESENT...
TMP
TMP TMP
RAKUTO...
...IS ALWAYS SO THOUGHTFUL.
HE MAKES ME SO HAPPY.
I WANTED TO...
...DO SOMETHING.

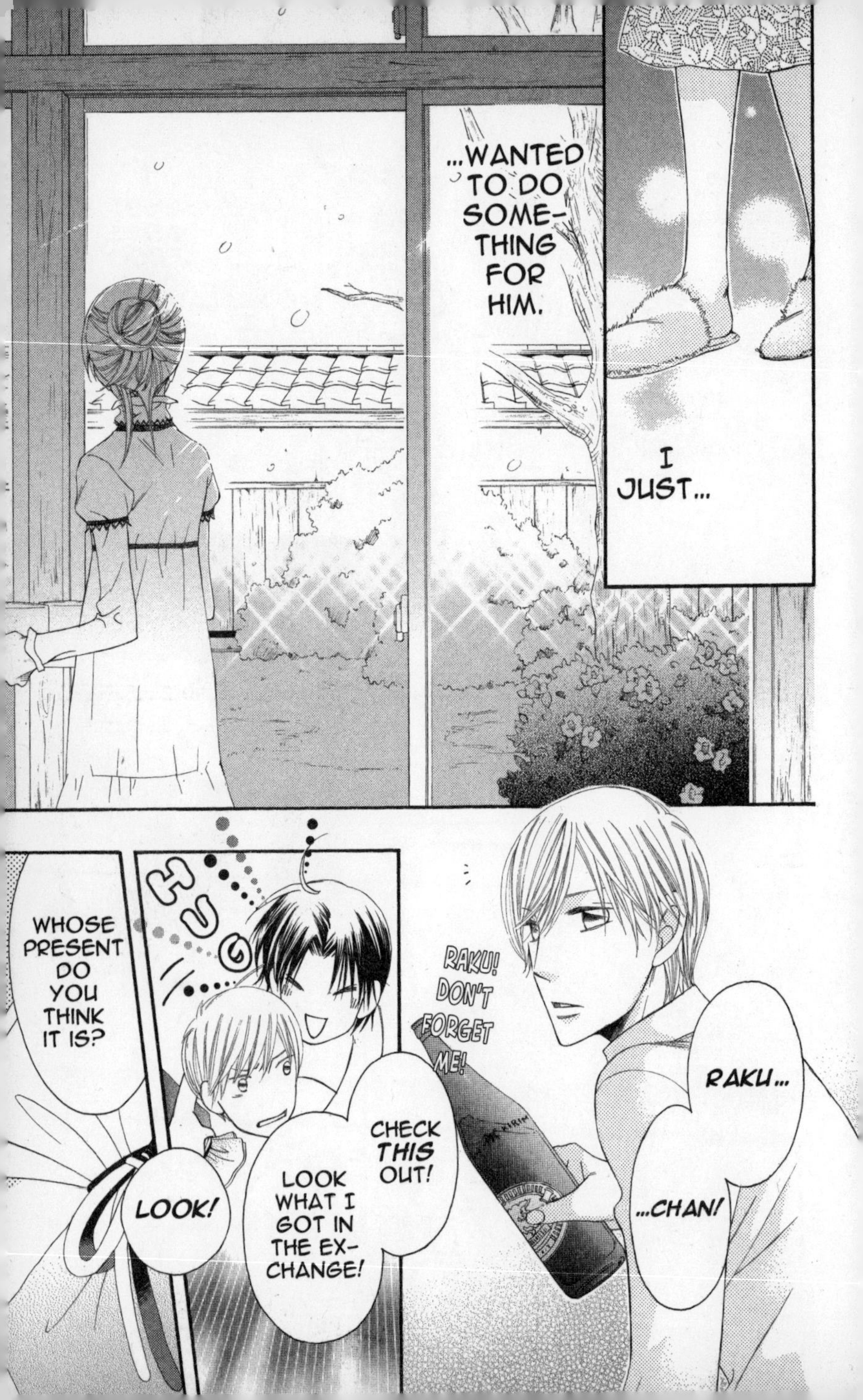
I JUST...
...WANTED TO DO SOME-THING FOR HIM.
RAKU...
...CHAN!
RAKU! DON'T FORGET ME!
CHECK THIS OUT!
LOOK WHAT I GOT IN THE EX-CHANGE!
HUG
LOOK!
WHOSE PRESENT DO YOU THINK IT IS?

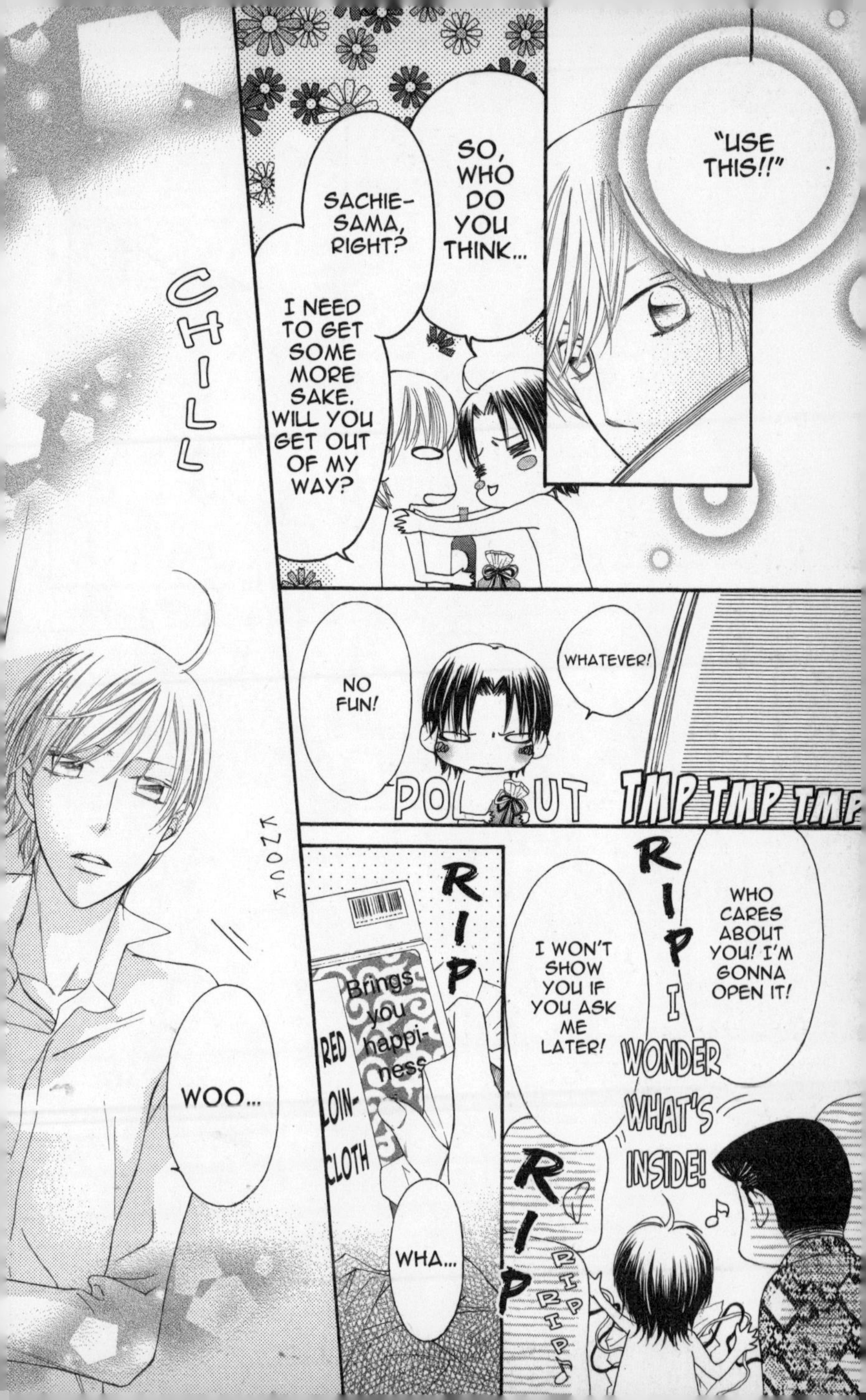
"USE THIS!!"
SO, WHO DO YOU THINK...
SACHIE-SAMA, RIGHT?
I NEED TO GET SOME MORE SAKE. WILL YOU GET OUT OF MY WAY?
WHATEVER!
TMP TMP TMP
NO FUN!
POUT
WHO CARES ABOUT YOU! I'M GONNA OPEN IT!
RIP
I WONDER WHAT'S INSIDE!
I WON'T SHOW YOU IF YOU ASK ME LATER!
RIP
RIP
RIPPIPIP
RIP
Brings you happi-ness
RED LOIN-CLOTH
WHA...
CHILL
KNOCK
WOO...

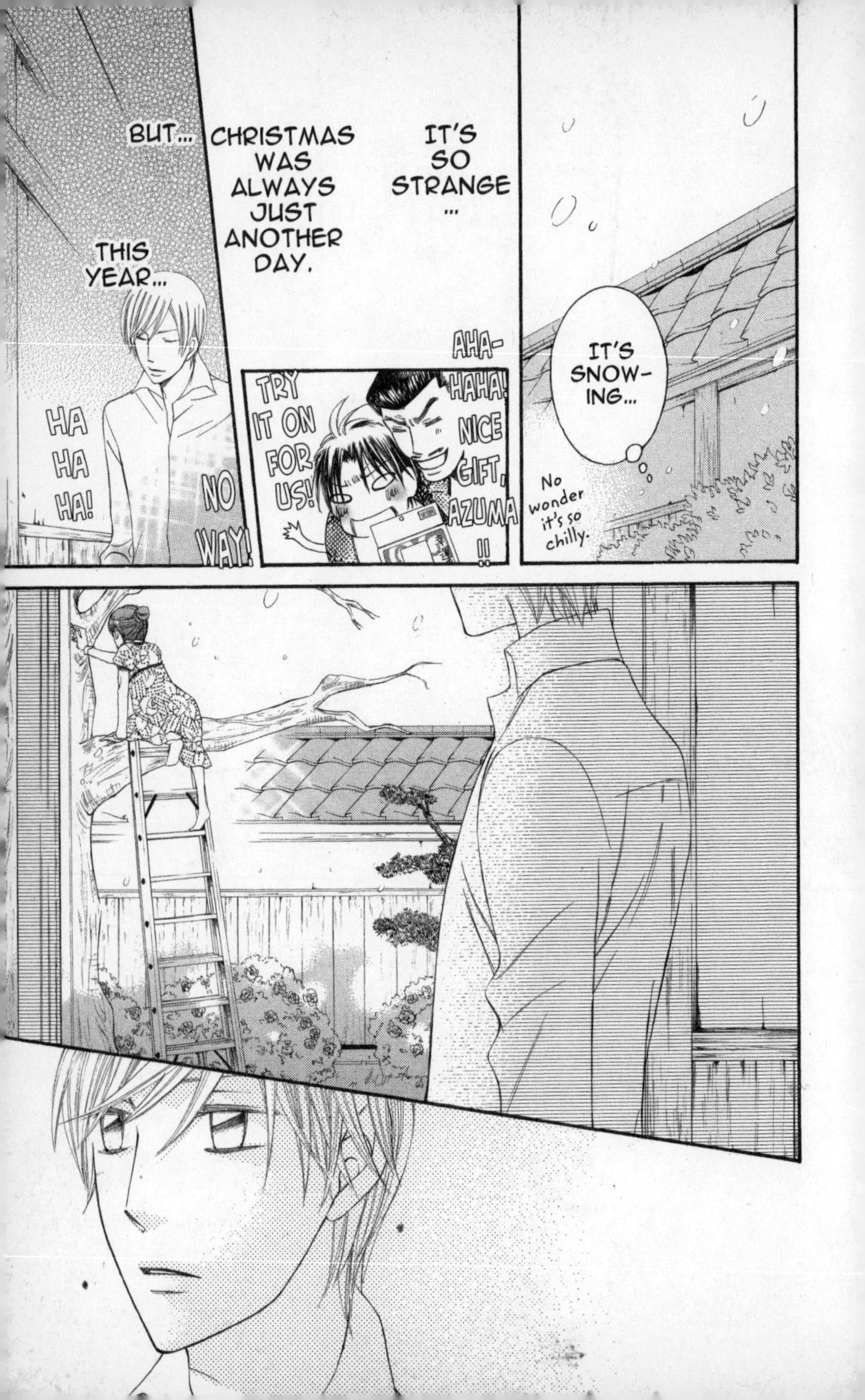
IT'S SNOW-ING...
No wonder it's so chilly.
IT'S SO STRANGE ...
AHA-HAHA! NICE GIFT, AZUMA !!
TRY IT ON FOR US!
CHRISTMAS WAS ALWAYS JUST ANOTHER DAY.
BUT...
THIS YEAR...
NO WAY!
HA HA HA!

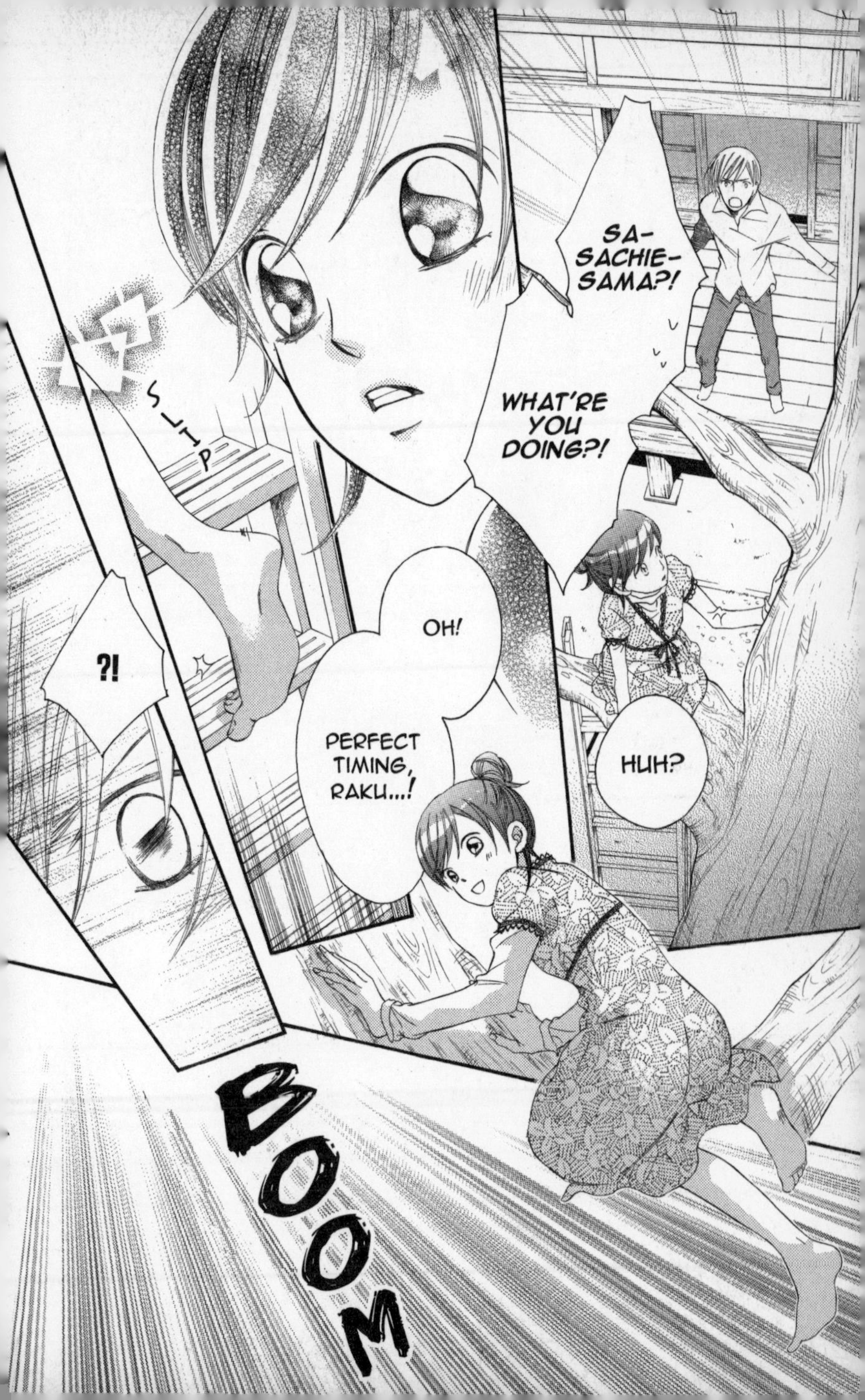
SA-SACHIE-SAMA?!
WHAT'RE YOU DOING?!
HUH?
OH!
PERFECT TIMING, RAKU...!
SLIP
?!
BOOM

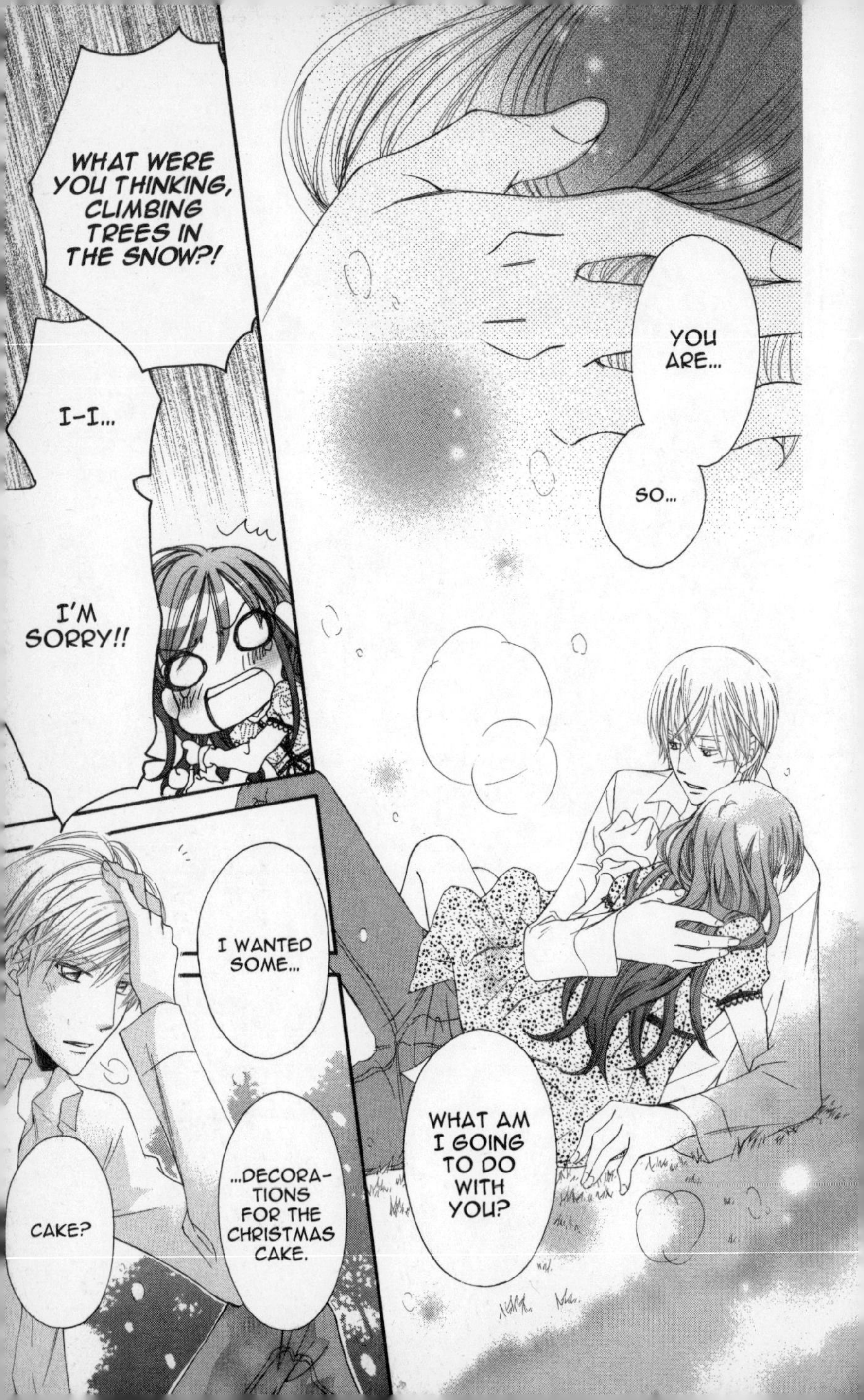
YOU ARE...
SO...
WHAT AM I GOING TO DO WITH YOU?
WHAT WERE YOU THINKING, CLIMBING TREES IN THE SNOW?!
I-I...
I'M SORRY!!
I WANTED SOME...
...DECORA-TIONS FOR THE CHRISTMAS CAKE.
CAKE?

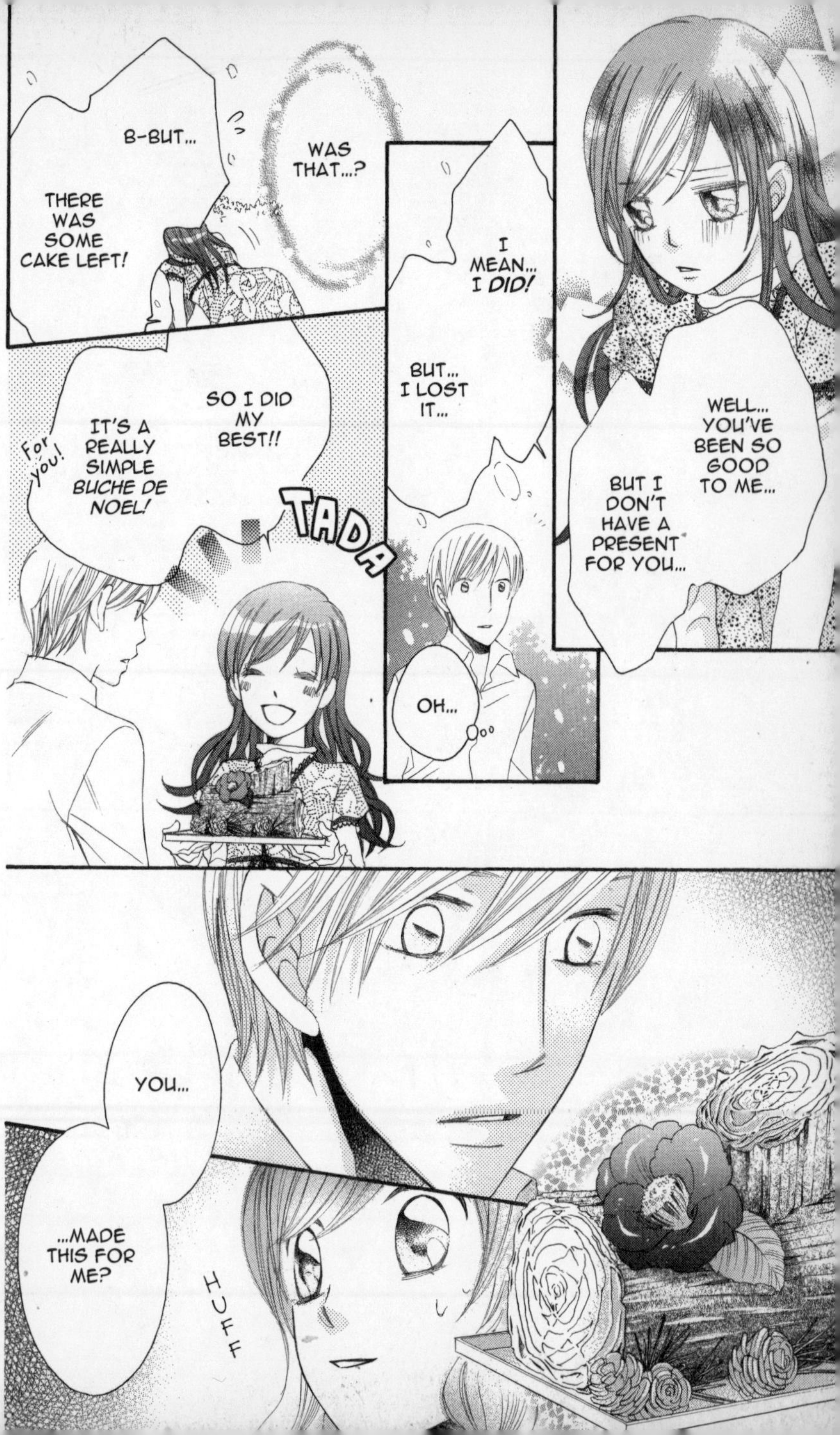
WELL... YOU'VE BEEN SO GOOD TO ME...
BUT I DON'T HAVE A PRESENT FOR YOU...
I MEAN... I DID!
BUT... I LOST IT...
OH...
B-BUT...
THERE WAS SOME CAKE LEFT!
WAS THAT...?
SO I DID MY BEST!!
IT'S A REALLY SIMPLE BUCHE DE NOEL!
For you!
TADA
YOU...
...MADE THIS FOR ME?
HUFF

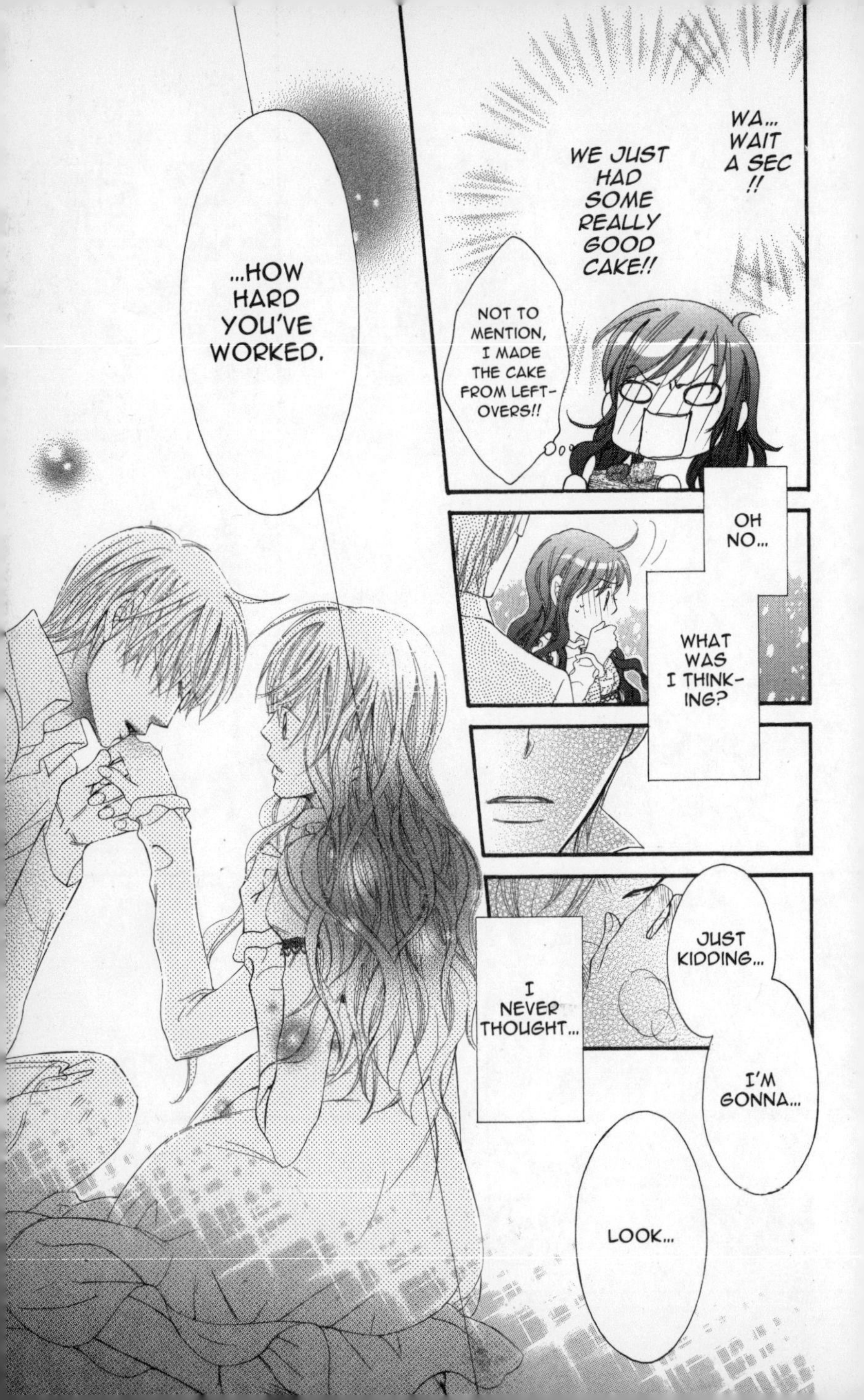
WA... WAIT A SEC !!
WE JUST HAD SOME REALLY GOOD CAKE!!
NOT TO MENTION, I MADE THE CAKE FROM LEFT-OVERS!!
OH NO...
WHAT WAS I THINK-ING?
JUST KIDDING...
I NEVER THOUGHT...
I'M GONNA...
LOOK...
...HOW HARD YOU'VE WORKED.

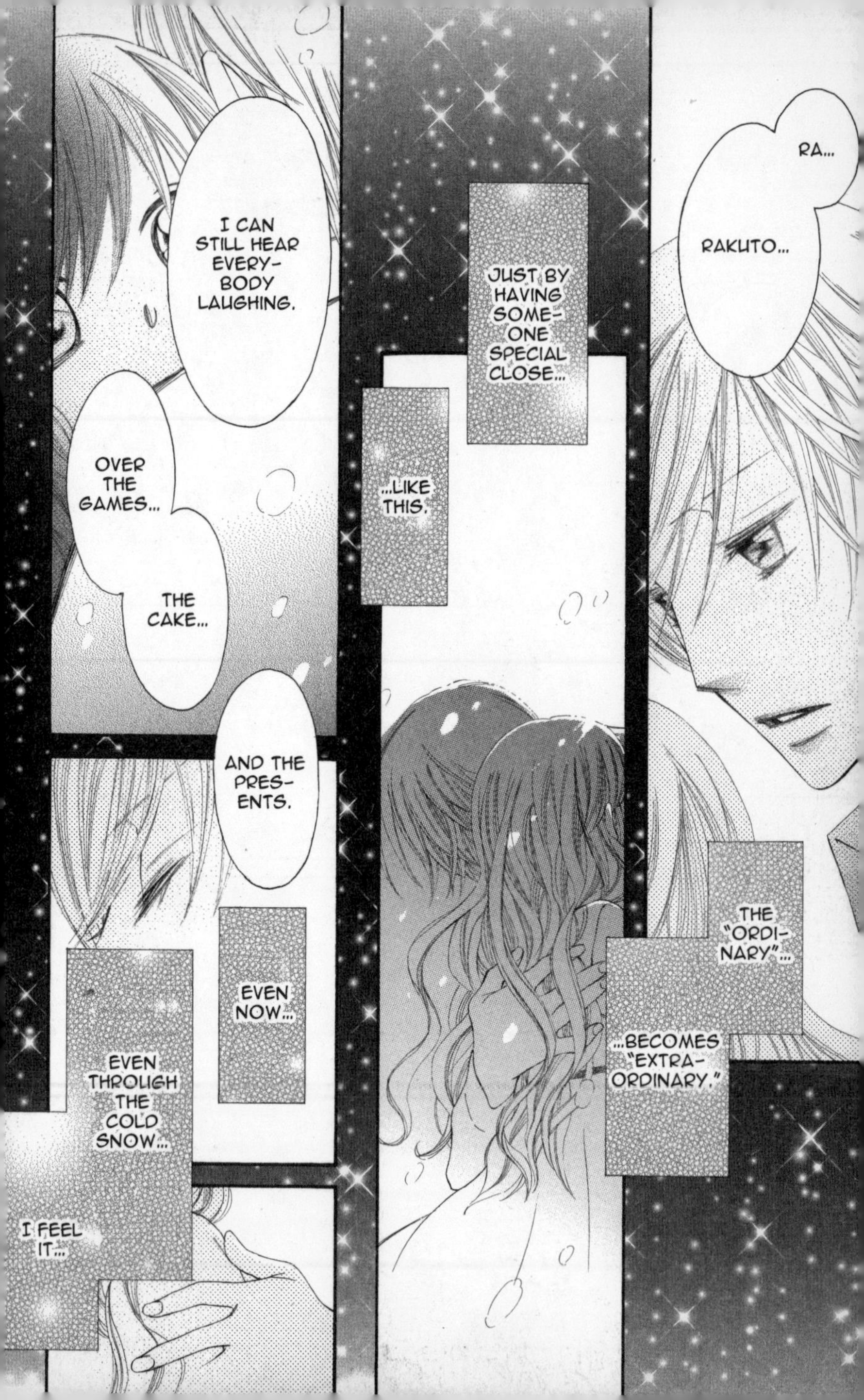
RA...
RAKUTO...
THE "ORDI-NARY"...
...BECOMES "EXTRA-ORDINARY."
JUST BY HAVING SOME-ONE SPECIAL CLOSE...
...LIKE THIS.
I CAN STILL HEAR EVERY-BODY LAUGHING.
OVER THE GAMES...
THE CAKE...
AND THE PRES-ENTS.
EVEN NOW...
EVEN THROUGH THE COLD SNOW...
I FEEL IT...

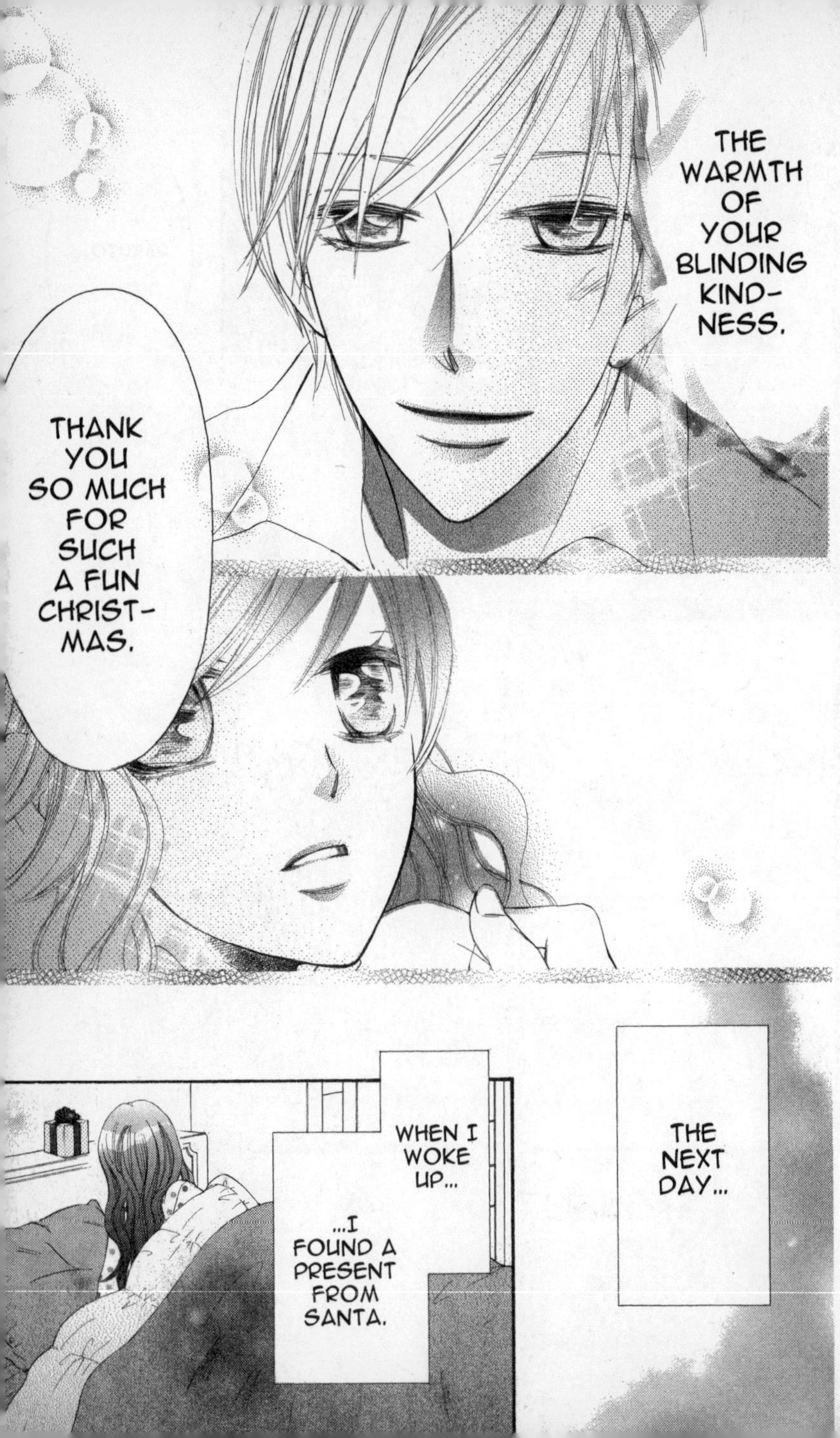
THE WARMTH OF YOUR BLINDING KIND-NESS.
THANK YOU SO MUCH FOR SUCH A FUN CHRIST-MAS.
THE NEXT DAY...
WHEN I WOKE UP...
...I FOUND A PRESENT FROM SANTA.

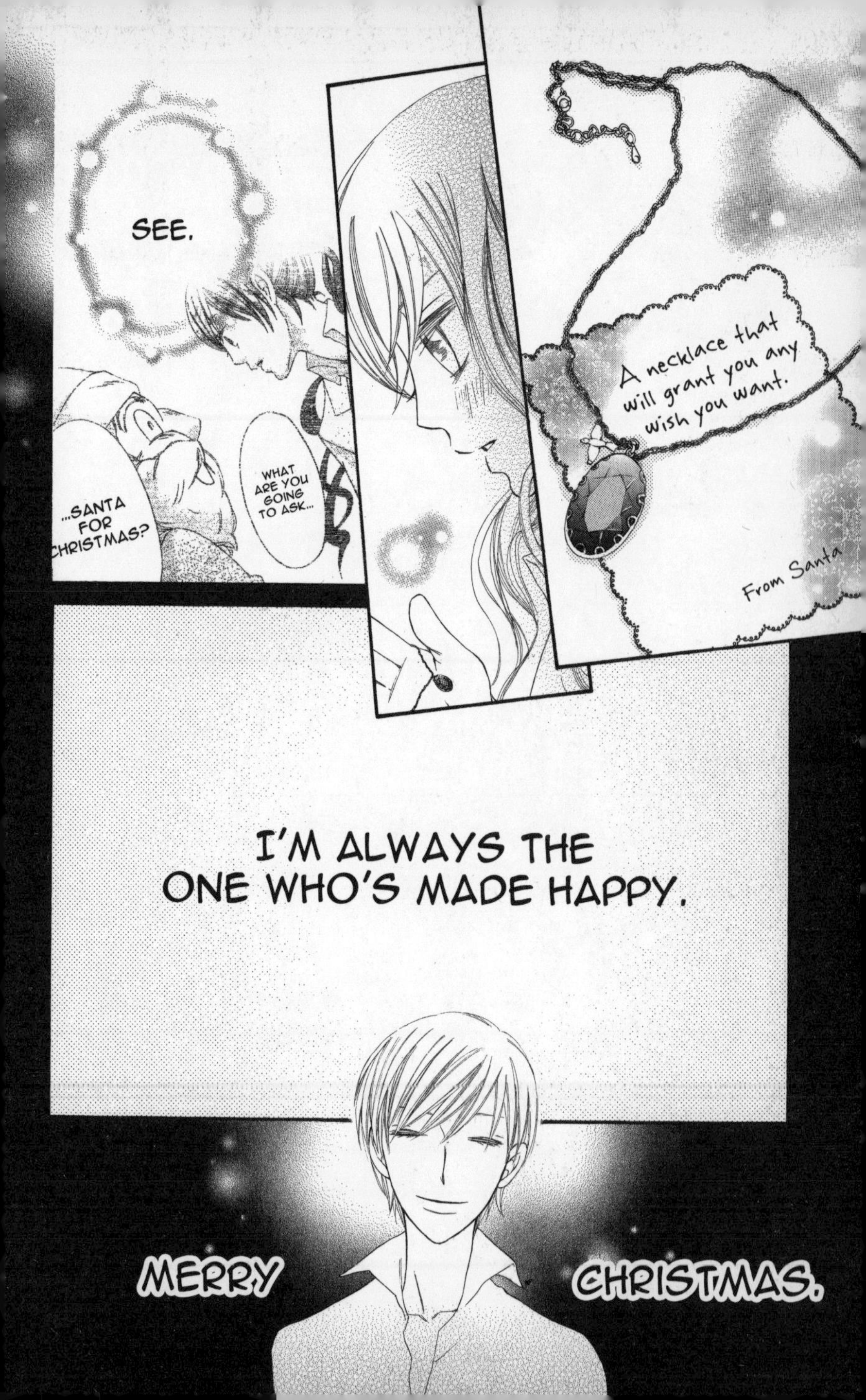
A necklace that will grant you any wish you want.
From Santa
SEE.
WHAT ARE YOU GOING TO ASK...
...SANTA FOR CHRISTMAS?
I'M ALWAYS THE ONE WHO'S MADE HAPPY.
MERRY
CHRISTMAS.

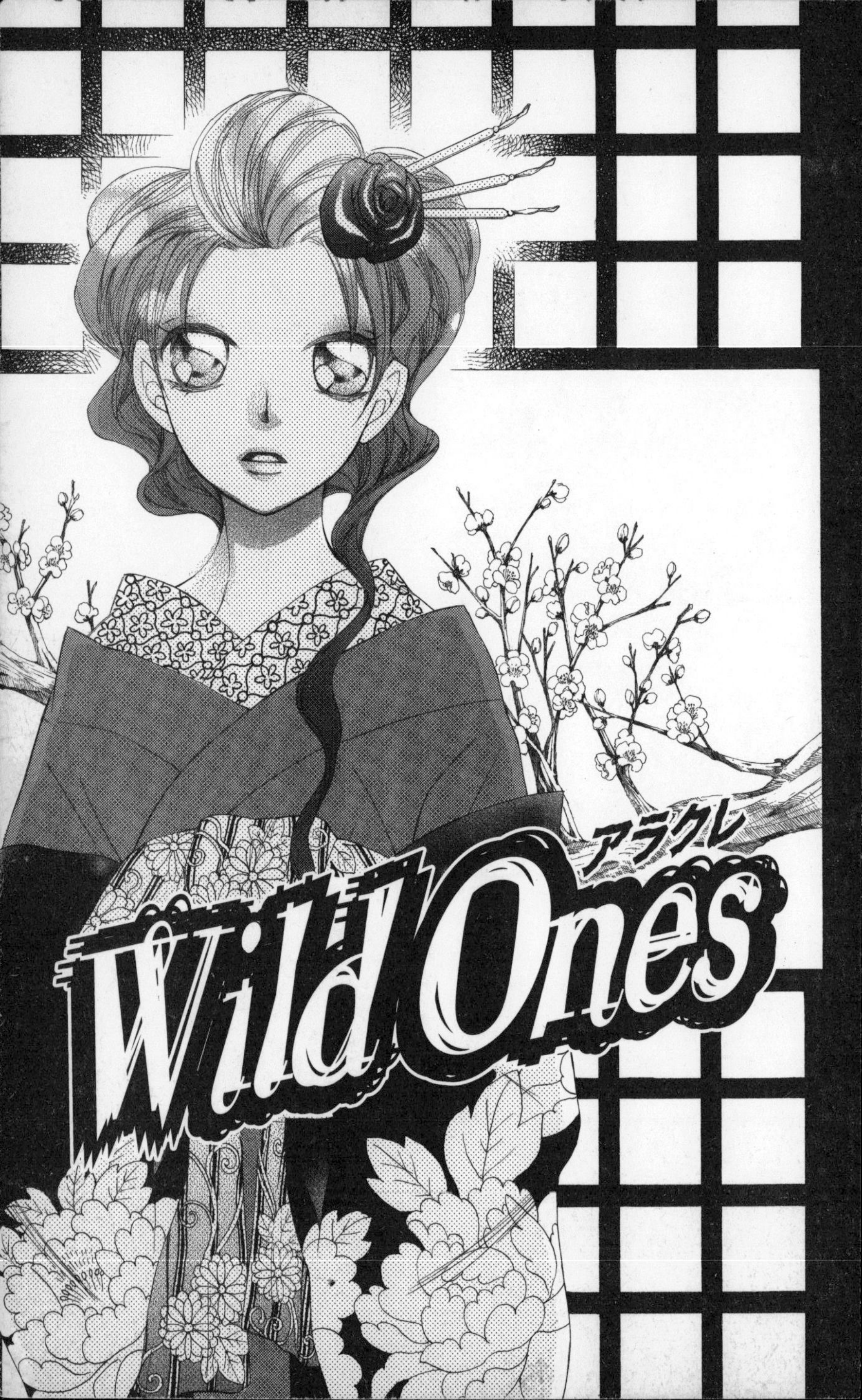
アラクレ
Wild Ones

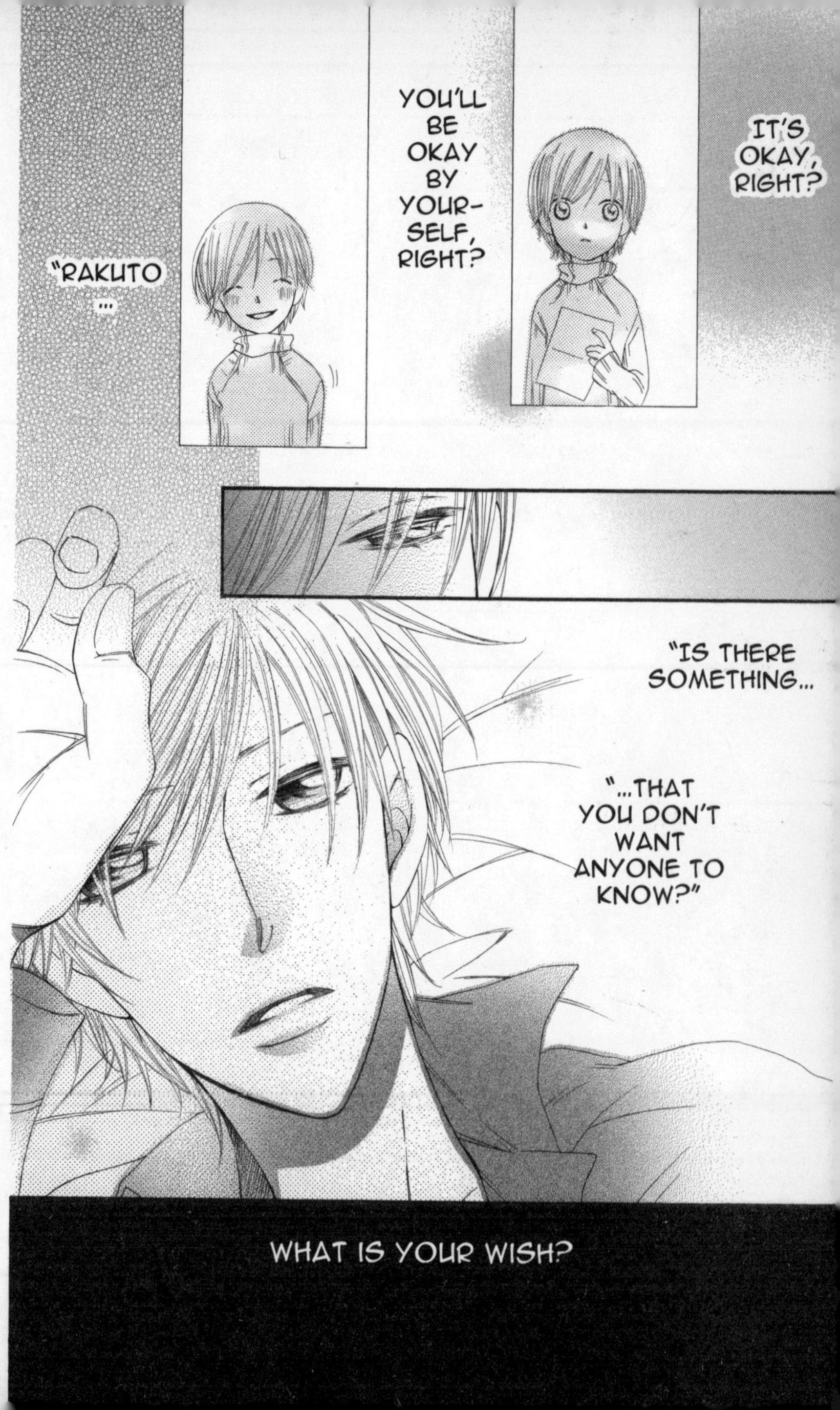

IT'S OKAY, RIGHT?
YOU'LL BE OKAY BY YOURSELF, RIGHT?
"RAKUTO ...
"IS THERE SOMETHING...
"...THAT YOU DON'T WANT ANYONE TO KNOW?"
WHAT IS YOUR WISH?

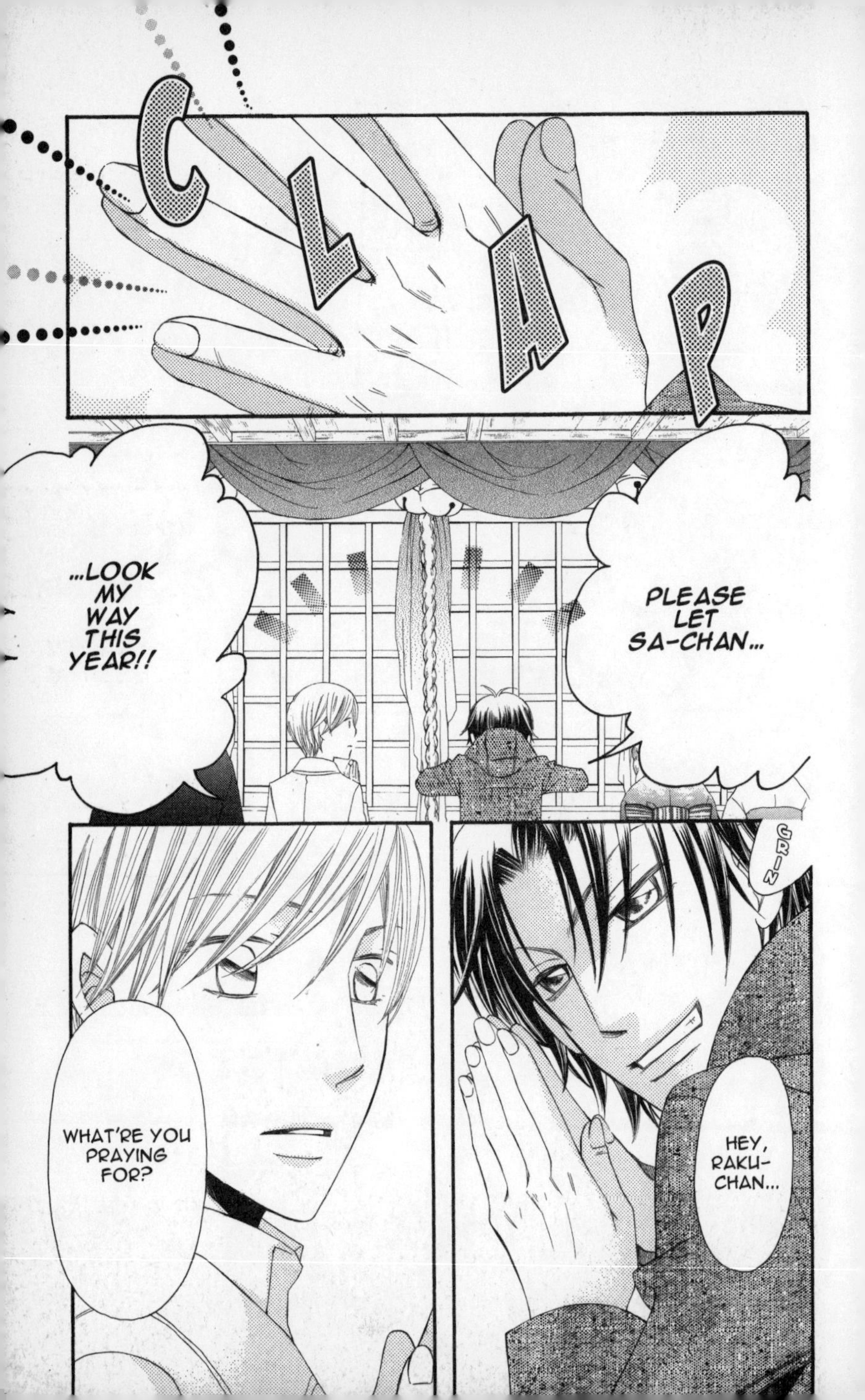
CLAP
PLEASE LET SA-CHAN...
...LOOK MY WAY THIS YEAR!!
GRIN
HEY, RAKU-CHAN...
WHAT'RE YOU PRAYING FOR?

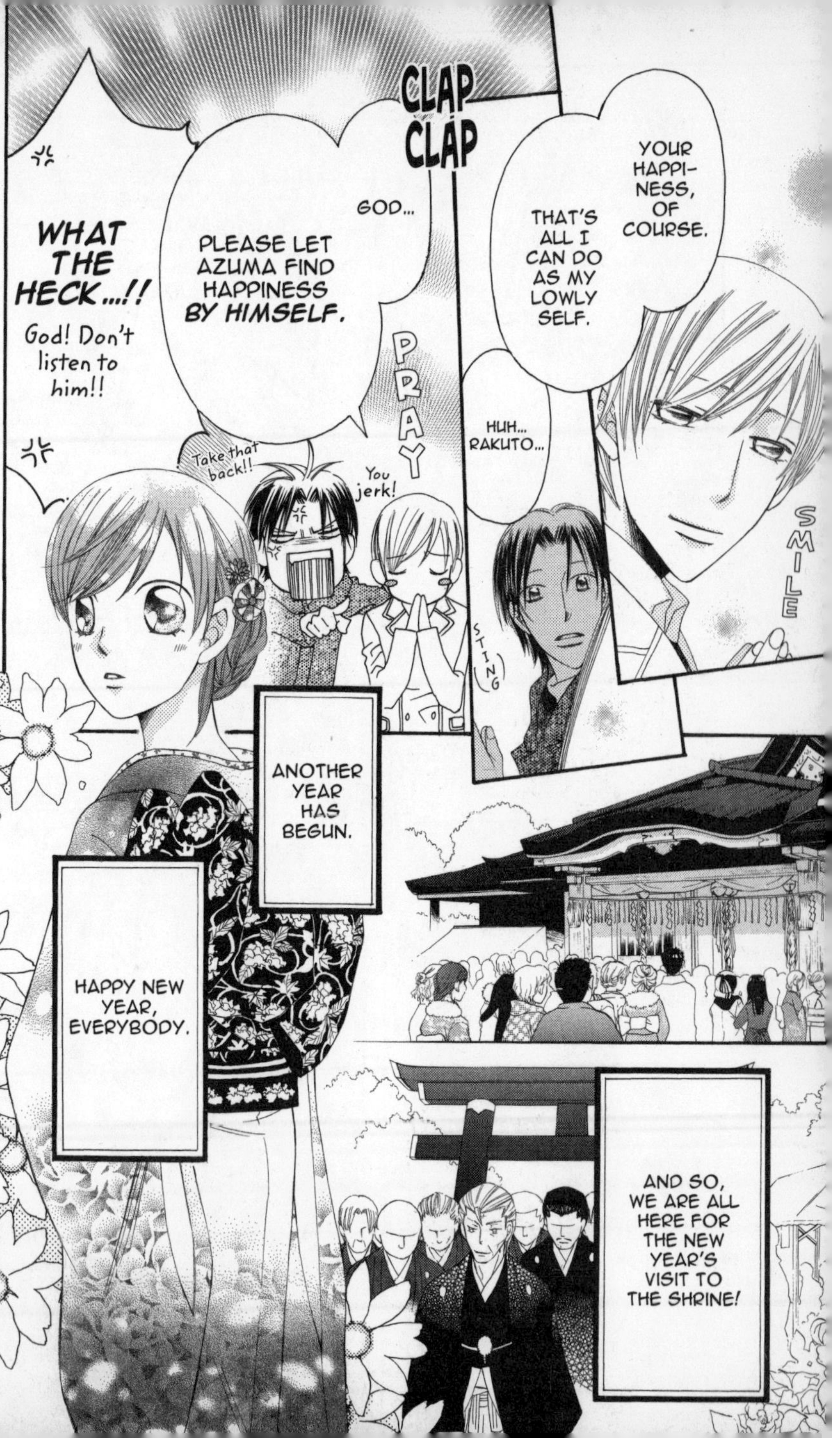
CLAP CLAP
YOUR HAPPI- NESS, OF COURSE.
THAT'S ALL I CAN DO AS MY LOWLY SELF.
SMILE
HUH... RAKUTO...
STING
GOD...
PLEASE LET AZUMA FIND HAPPINESS BY HIMSELF.
PRAY
You jerk!
Take that back!!
WHAT THE HECK...!!
God! Don't listen to him!!
ANOTHER YEAR HAS BEGUN.
HAPPY NEW YEAR, EVERYBODY.
AND SO, WE ARE ALL HERE FOR THE NEW YEAR'S VISIT TO THE SHRINE!

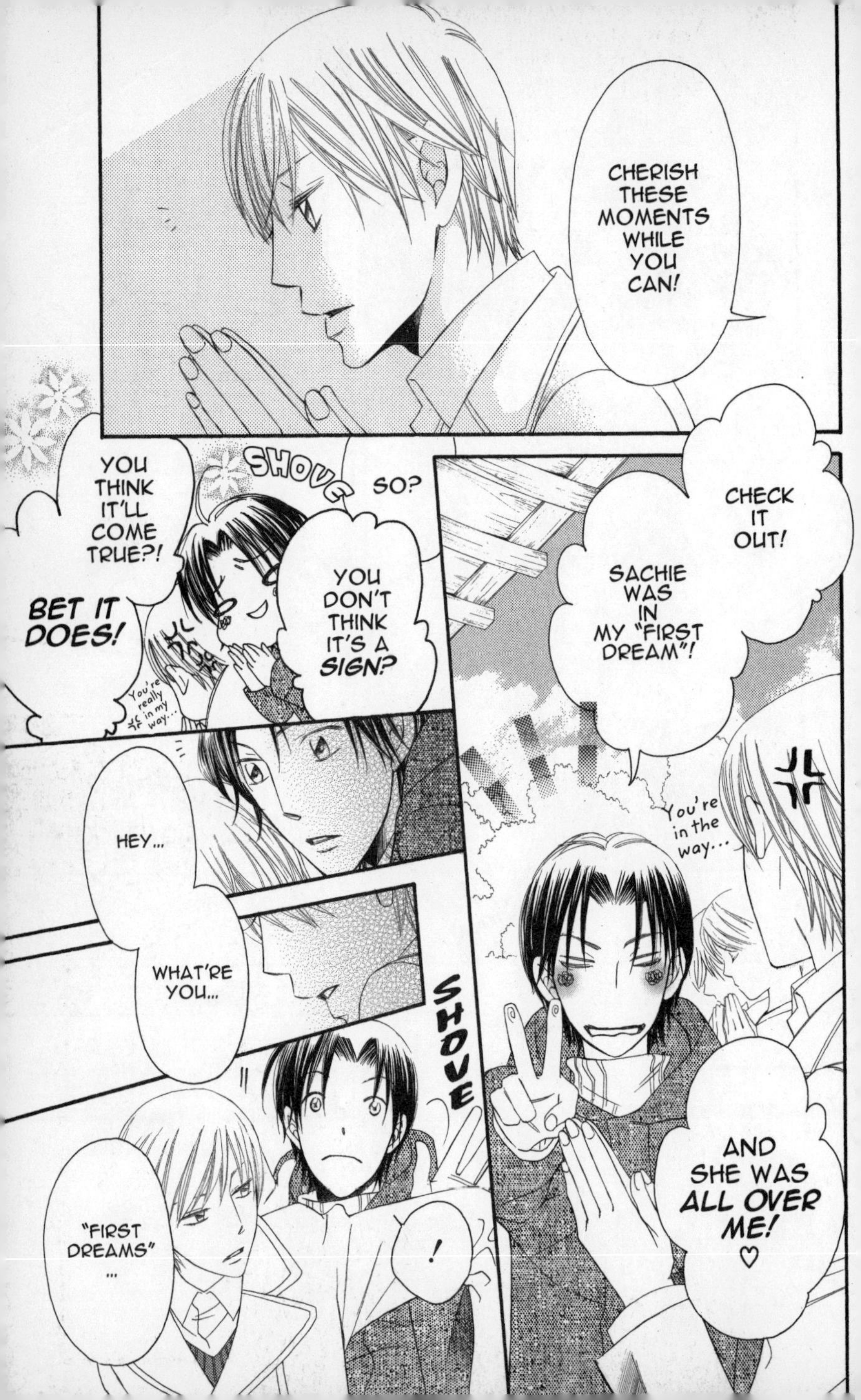
CHERISH THESE MOMENTS WHILE YOU CAN!
CHECK IT OUT!
SACHIE WAS IN MY "FIRST DREAM"!
You're in the way...
AND SHE WAS ALL OVER ME! ♡
SHOVE
SO?
YOU DON'T THINK IT'S A SIGN?
YOU THINK IT'LL COME TRUE?!
BET IT DOES!
You're really in my way...
HEY...
WHAT'RE YOU...
SHOVE
!
"FIRST DREAMS"...

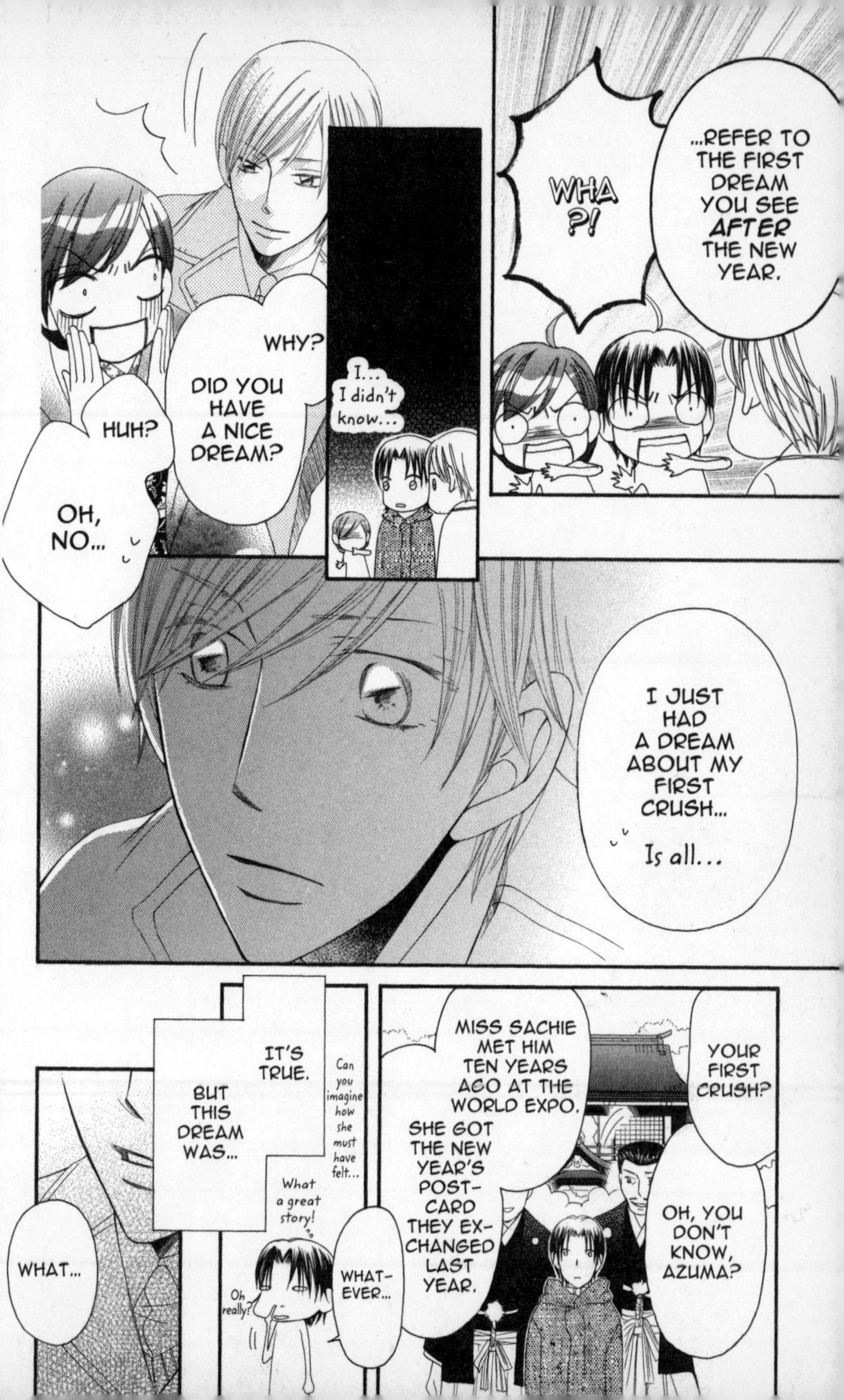
...REFER TO THE FIRST DREAM YOU SEE AFTER THE NEW YEAR.
WHA ?!
WHY?
DID YOU HAVE A NICE DREAM?
HUH?
OH, NO...
I... I didn't know...
I JUST HAD A DREAM ABOUT MY FIRST CRUSH...
Is all...
YOUR FIRST CRUSH?
OH, YOU DON'T KNOW, AZUMA?
MISS SACHIE MET HIM TEN YEARS AGO AT THE WORLD EXPO.
SHE GOT THE NEW YEAR'S POST-CARD THEY EX-CHANGED LAST YEAR.
WHAT-EVER...
Oh really?
What a great story!
Can you imagine how she must have felt...
IT'S TRUE.
BUT THIS DREAM WAS...
WHAT...

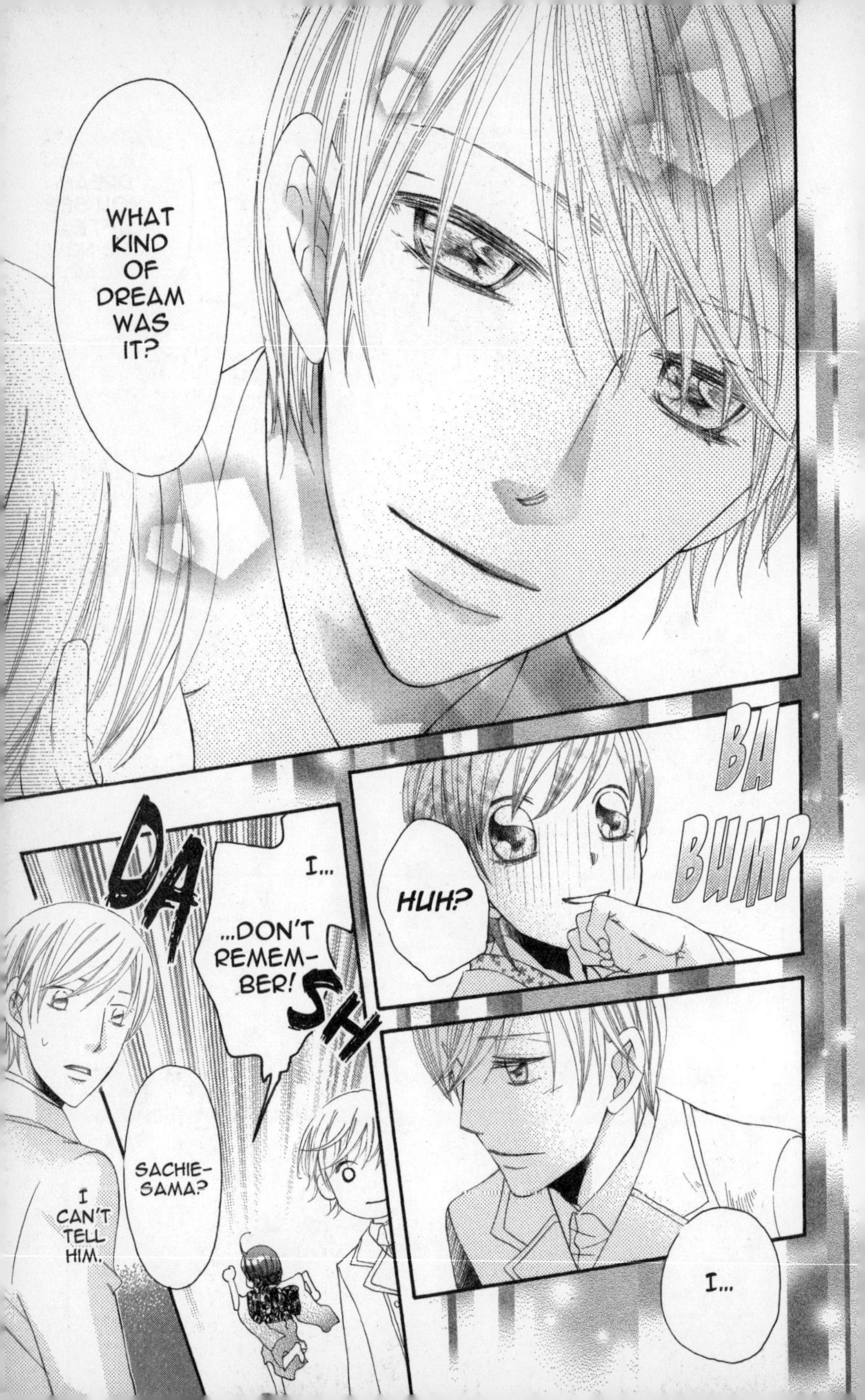
WHAT KIND OF DREAM WAS IT?
BA BUMP
HUH?
I...
I...
...DON'T REMEM-BER!
DASH
SACHIE-SAMA?
I CAN'T TELL HIM.

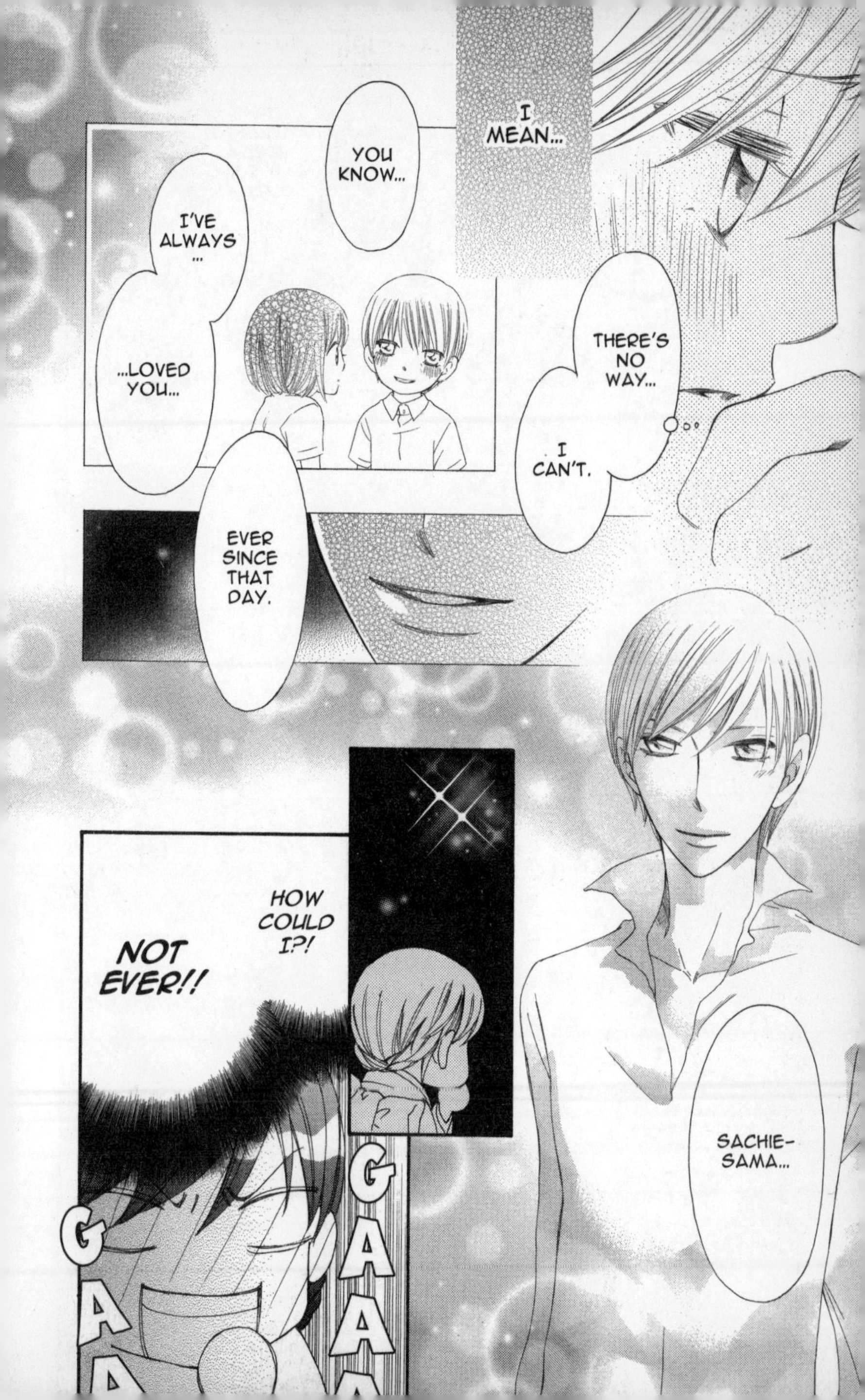
I MEAN...
THERE'S NO WAY...
I CAN'T.
YOU KNOW...
I'VE ALWAYS ...
...LOVED YOU...
EVER SINCE THAT DAY.
SACHIE-SAMA...
HOW COULD I?!
NOT EVER!!
GAA
GAA

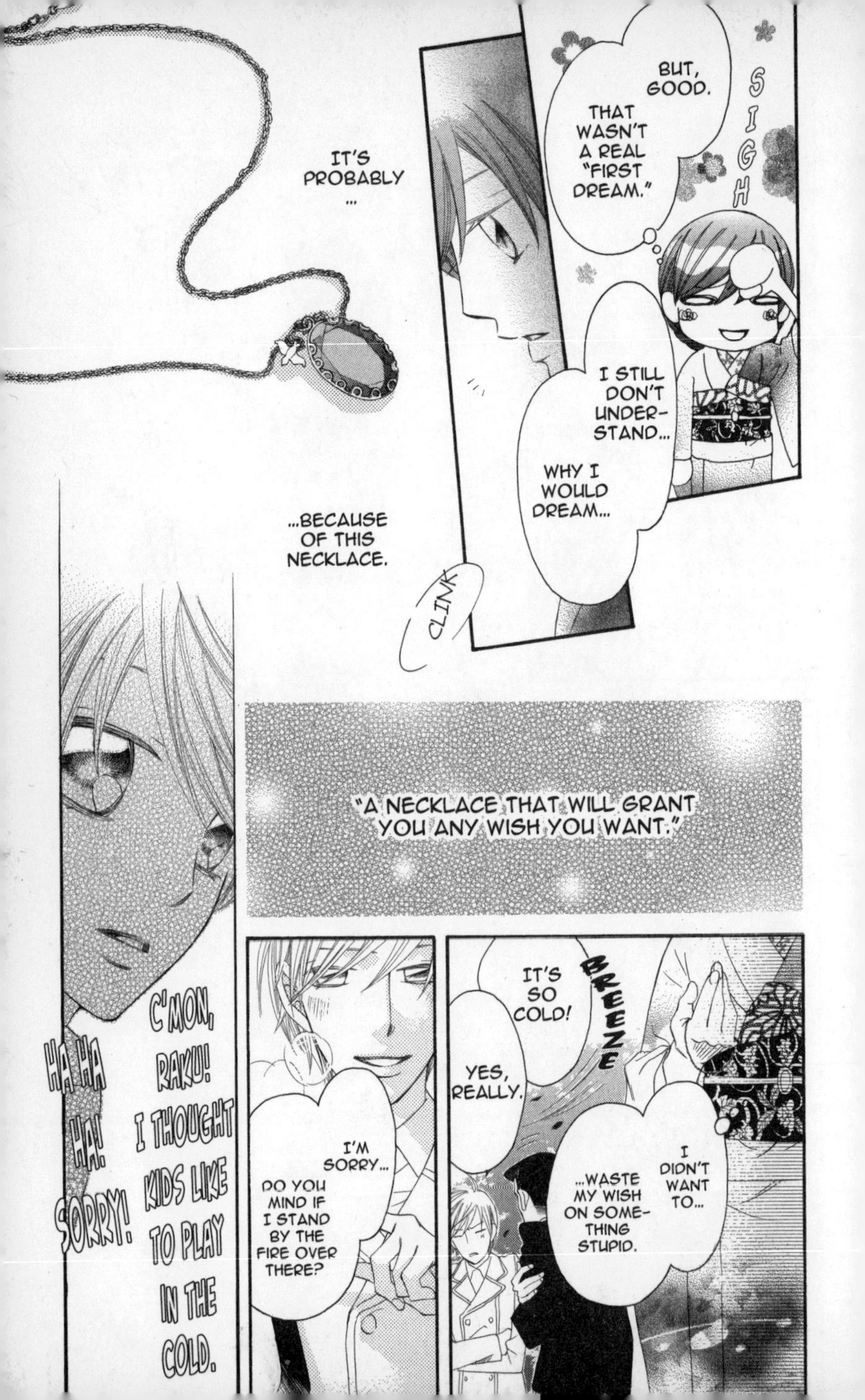
SIGH
BUT, GOOD.
THAT WASN'T A REAL "FIRST DREAM."
I STILL DON'T UNDER-STAND...
WHY I WOULD DREAM...
CLINK
IT'S PROBABLY ...
...BECAUSE OF THIS NECKLACE.
"A NECKLACE THAT WILL GRANT YOU ANY WISH YOU WANT."
I DIDN'T WANT TO...
...WASTE MY WISH ON SOME-THING STUPID.
BREEZE
IT'S SO COLD!
YES, REALLY.
I'M SORRY...
DO YOU MIND IF I STAND BY THE FIRE OVER THERE?
C'MON, RAKU! I THOUGHT KIDS LIKE TO PLAY IN THE COLD.
HA HA HA! SORRY!

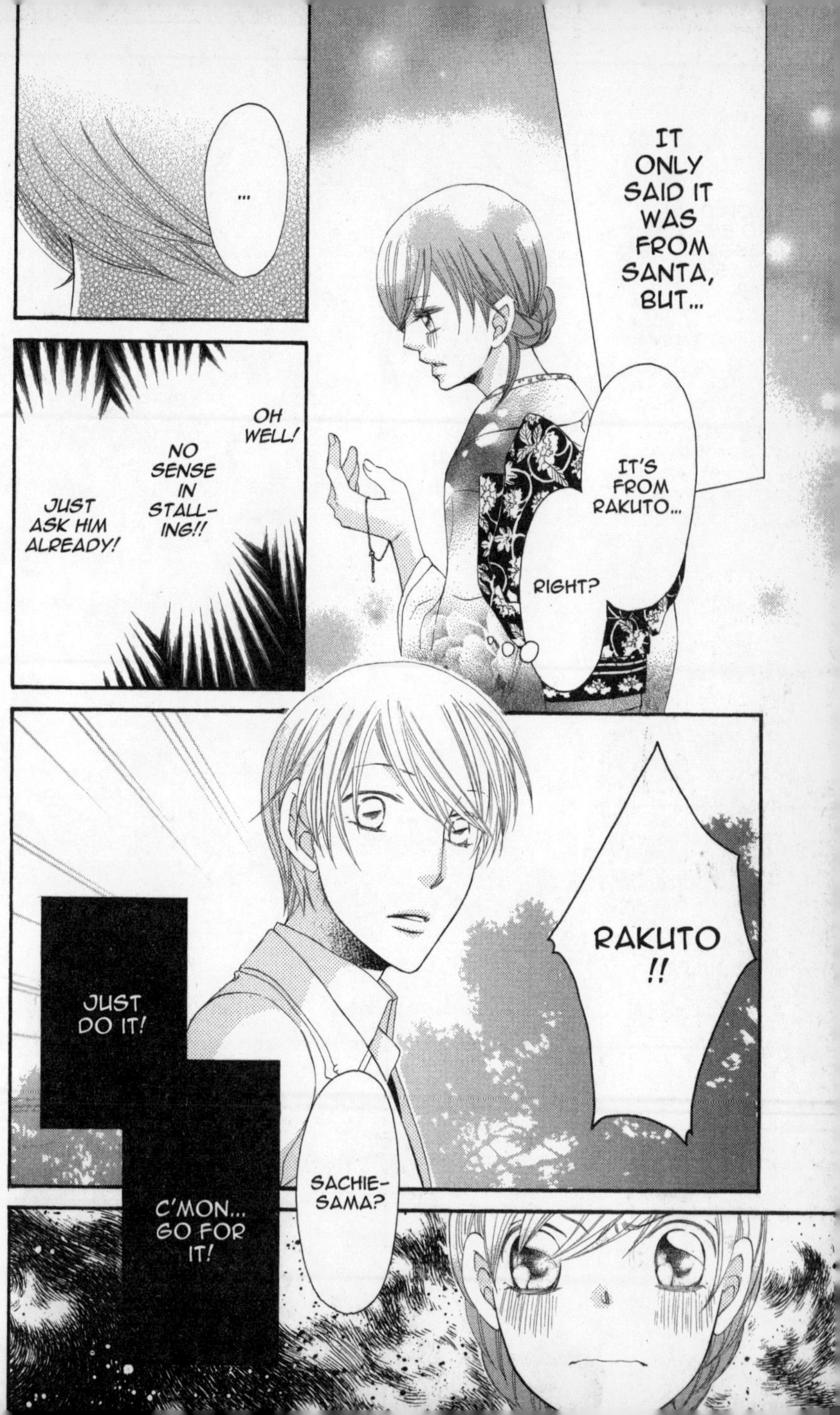
IT ONLY SAID IT WAS FROM SANTA, BUT...
IT'S FROM RAKUTO...
RIGHT?
...
OH WELL!
NO SENSE IN STALL-ING!!
JUST ASK HIM ALREADY!
RAKUTO!!
SACHIE-SAMA?
JUST DO IT!
C'MON... GO FOR IT!

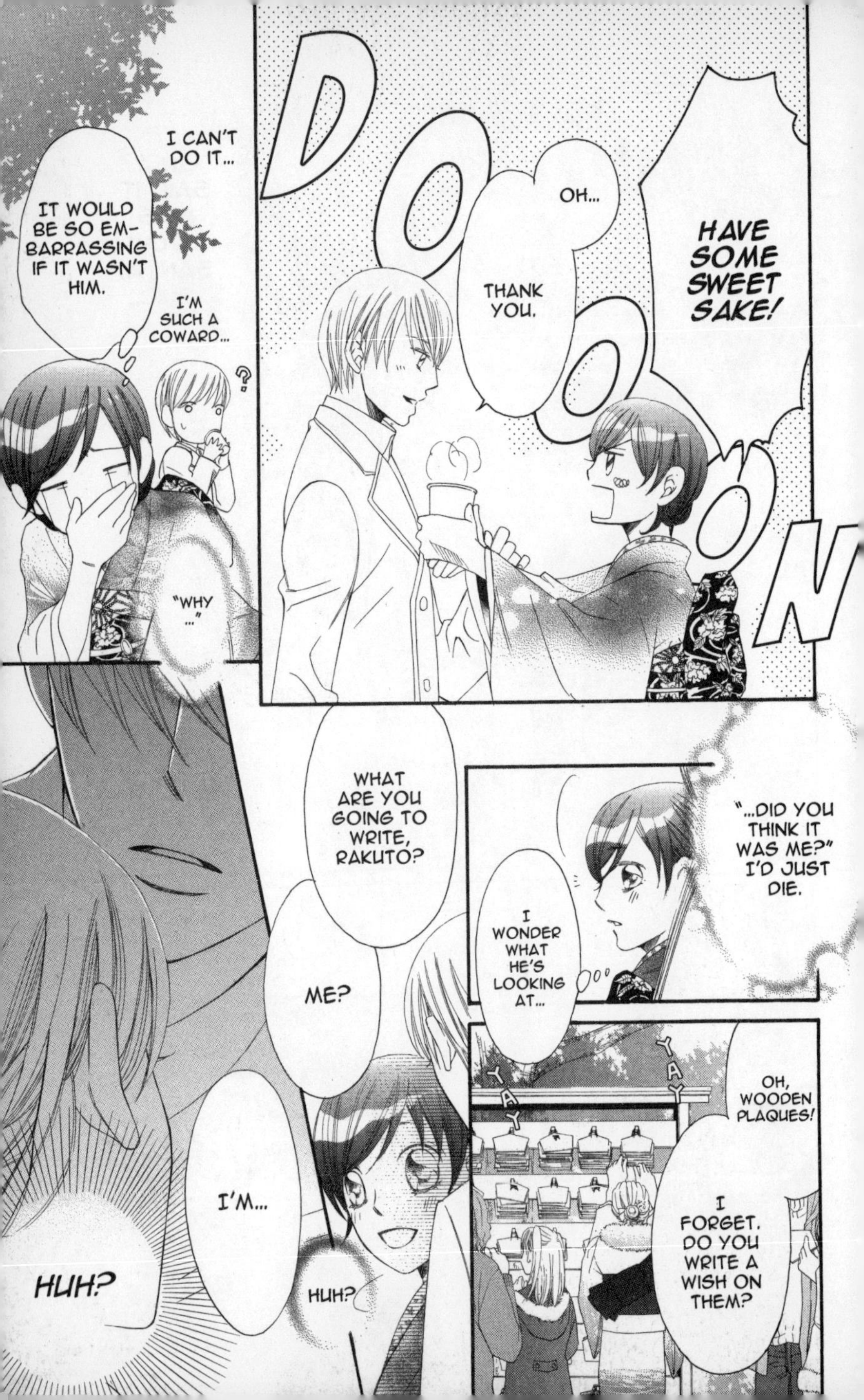
HAVE SOME SWEET SAKE!
DOOOON
OH...
THANK YOU.
I CAN'T DO IT...
IT WOULD BE SO EM-BARRASSING IF IT WASN'T HIM.
I'M SUCH A COWARD...
?
"WHY..."
"...DID YOU THINK IT WAS ME?" I'D JUST DIE.
I WONDER WHAT HE'S LOOKING AT...
OH, WOODEN PLAQUES!
YAY
YAY
I FORGET. DO YOU WRITE A WISH ON THEM?
WHAT ARE YOU GOING TO WRITE, RAKUTO?
ME?
I'M...
HUH?
HUH?

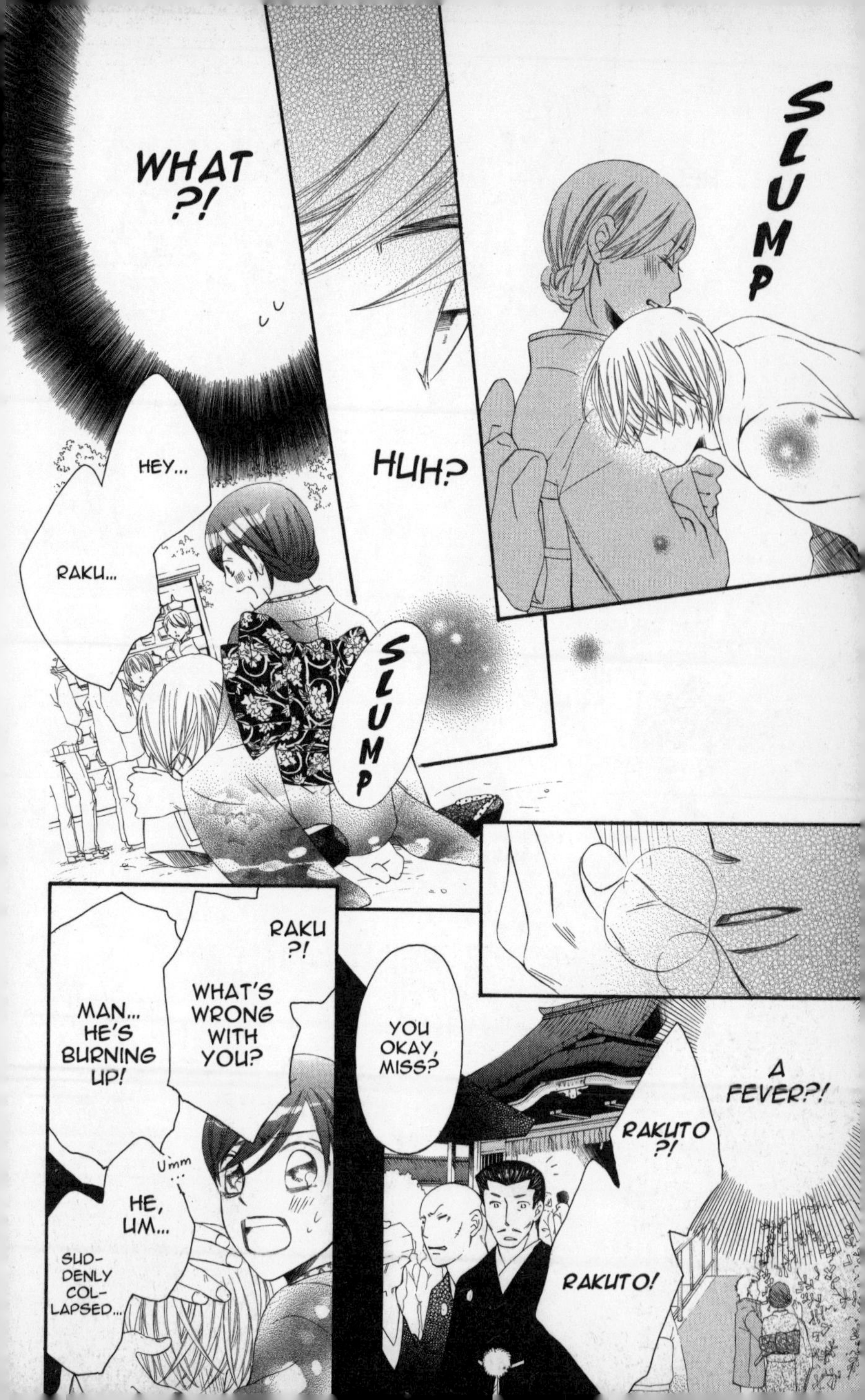
SLUMP
HUH?
WHAT?!
HEY...
RAKU...
SLUMP
A FEVER?!
RAKUTO?!
RAKUTO!
YOU OKAY, MISS?
RAKU?!
WHAT'S WRONG WITH YOU?
MAN... HE'S BURNING UP!
Umm...
HE, UM...
SUD-DENLY COL-LAPSED...

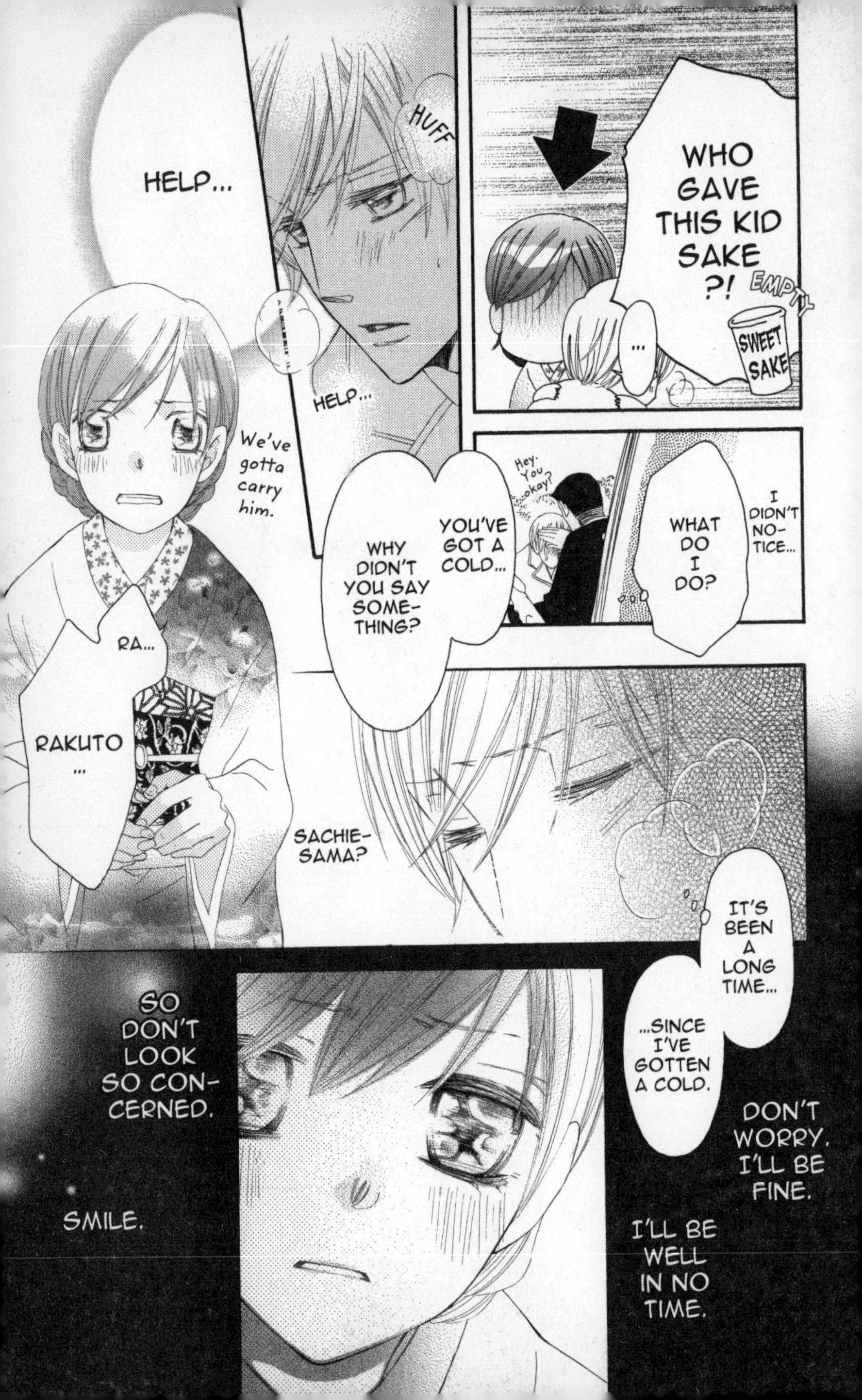
WHO GAVE THIS KID SAKE ?!
EMPTY
SWEET SAKE
...
HUFF
HELP...
HELP...
I DIDN'T NO-TICE...
WHAT DO I DO?
Hey. You okay?
YOU'VE GOT A COLD...
WHY DIDN'T YOU SAY SOME-THING?
We've gotta carry him.
SACHIE-SAMA?
RA...
RAKUTO ...
IT'S BEEN A LONG TIME...
...SINCE I'VE GOTTEN A COLD.
DON'T WORRY. I'LL BE FINE.
I'LL BE WELL IN NO TIME.
SO DON'T LOOK SO CON-CERNED.
SMILE.

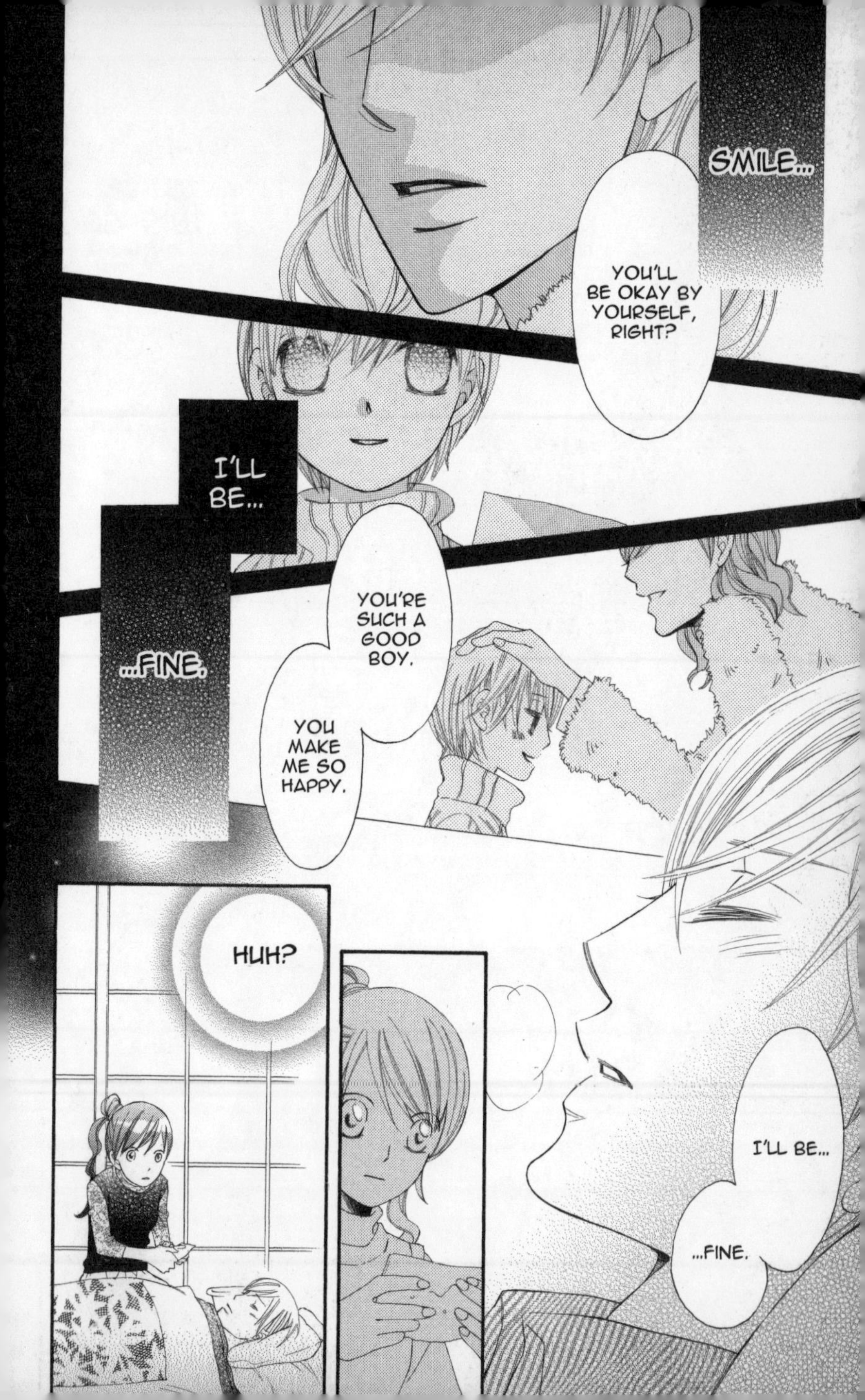
SMILE...
YOU'LL BE OKAY BY YOURSELF, RIGHT?
I'LL BE...
YOU'RE SUCH A GOOD BOY.
YOU MAKE ME SO HAPPY.
...FINE.
I'LL BE...
...FINE.
HUH?

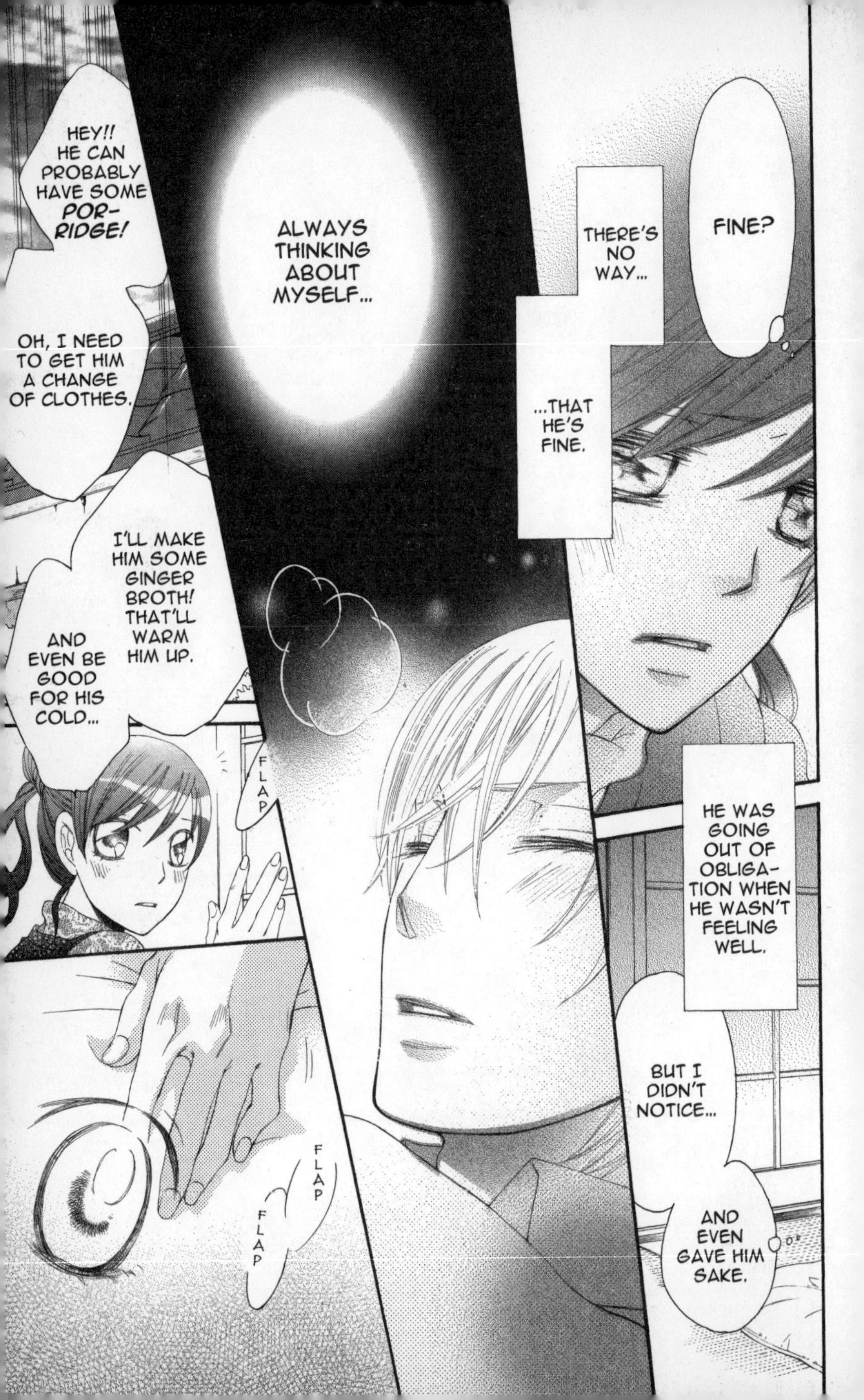
FINE?
THERE'S NO WAY...
...THAT HE'S FINE.
HE WAS GOING OUT OF OBLIGA-TION WHEN HE WASN'T FEELING WELL.
BUT I DIDN'T NOTICE...
AND EVEN GAVE HIM SAKE.
ALWAYS THINKING ABOUT MYSELF...
HEY!! HE CAN PROBABLY HAVE SOME POR-RIDGE!
OH, I NEED TO GET HIM A CHANGE OF CLOTHES.
I'LL MAKE HIM SOME GINGER BROTH! THAT'LL WARM HIM UP.
AND EVEN BE GOOD FOR HIS COLD...
FLAP
FLAP
FLAP

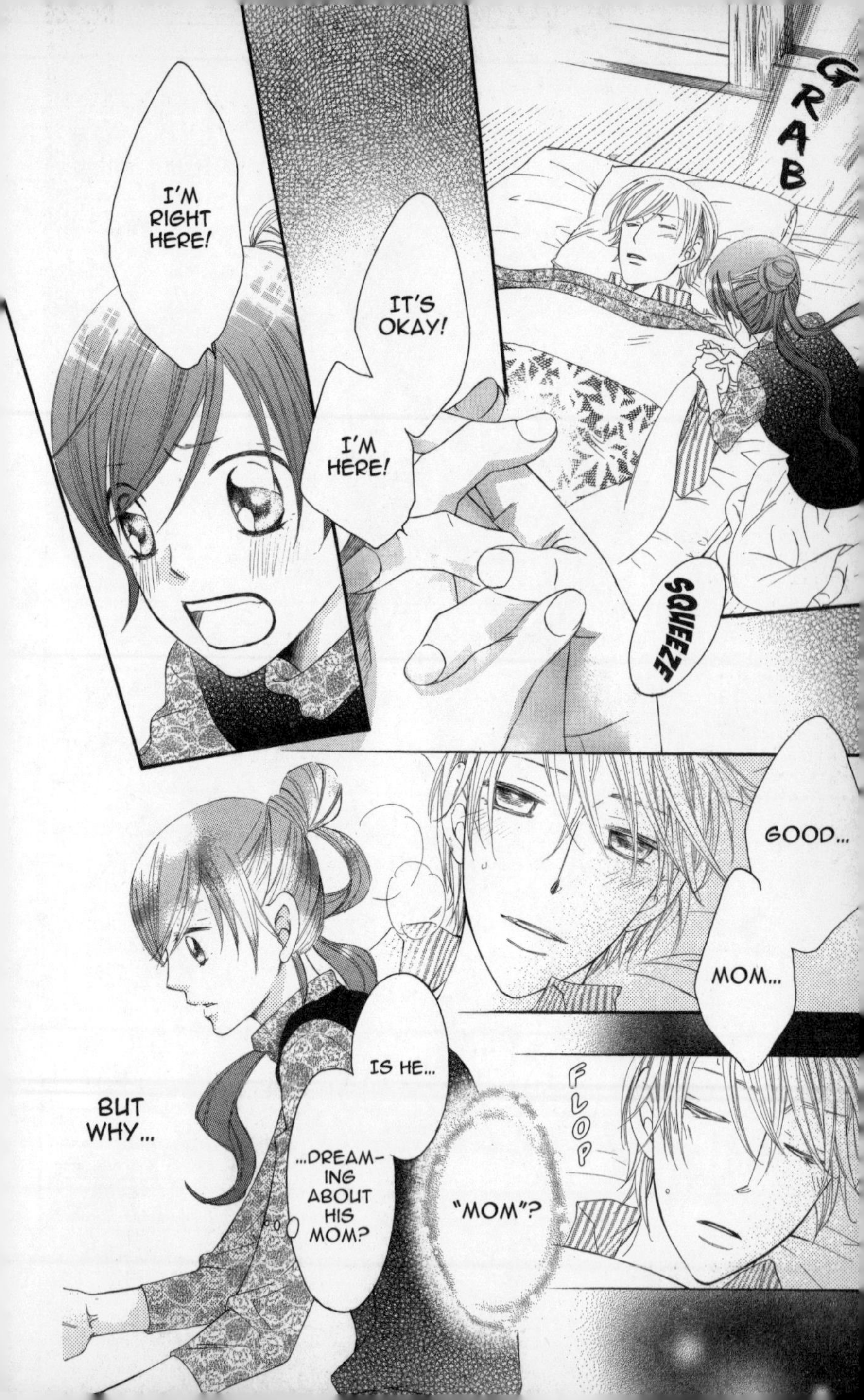
GRAB
SQUEEZE
IT'S OKAY!
I'M HERE!
I'M RIGHT HERE!
GOOD...
MOM...
FLOP
"MOM"?
IS HE...
...DREAMING ABOUT HIS MOM?
BUT WHY...

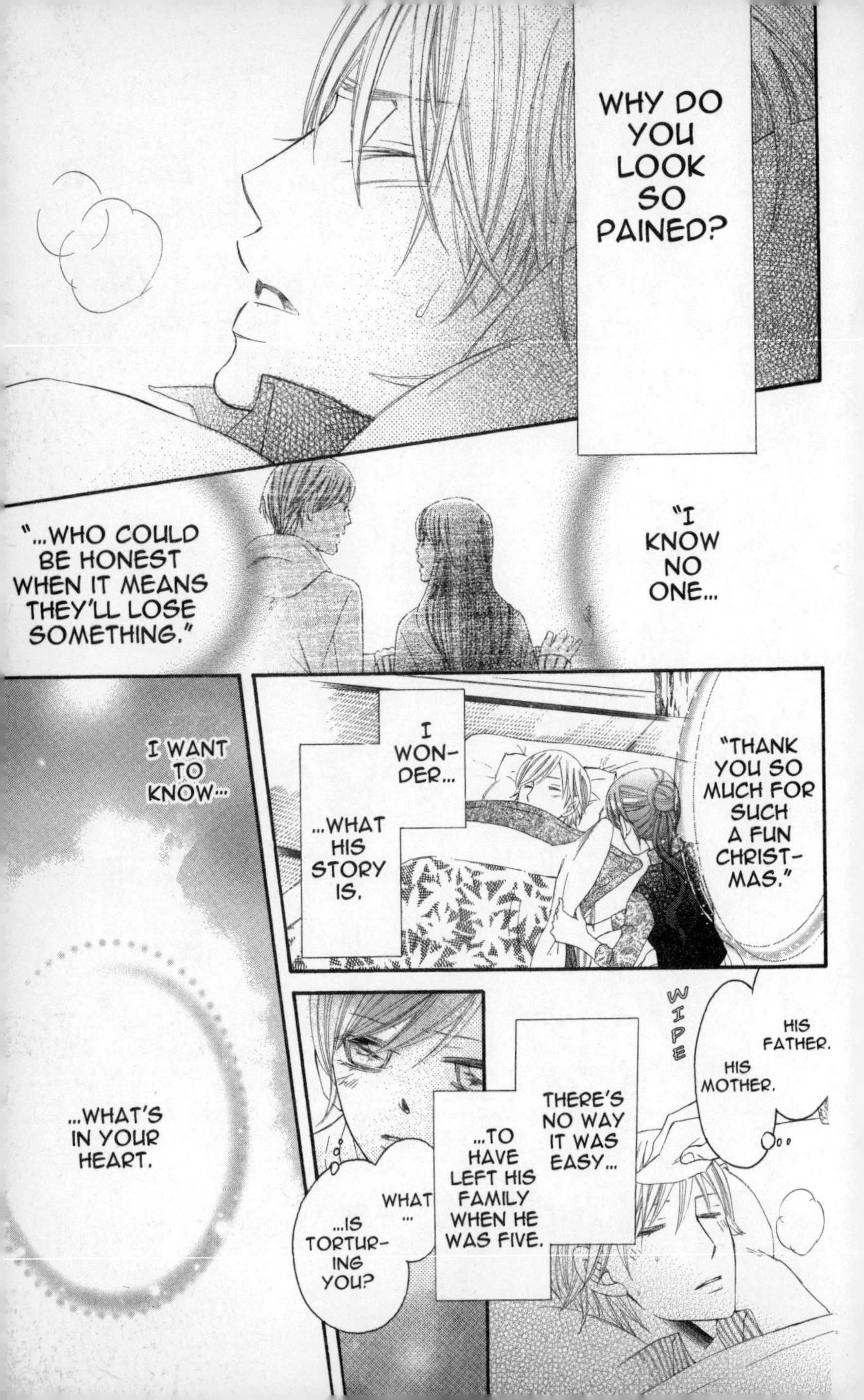
WHY DO YOU LOOK SO PAINED?
"I KNOW NO ONE...
"...WHO COULD BE HONEST WHEN IT MEANS THEY'LL LOSE SOMETHING."
"THANK YOU SO MUCH FOR SUCH A FUN CHRISTMAS."
I WONDER...
...WHAT HIS STORY IS.
I WANT TO KNOW...
HIS FATHER.
HIS MOTHER.
WIPE
THERE'S NO WAY IT WAS EASY...
...TO HAVE LEFT HIS FAMILY WHEN HE WAS FIVE.
WHAT...
...IS TORTURING YOU?
...WHAT'S IN YOUR HEART.

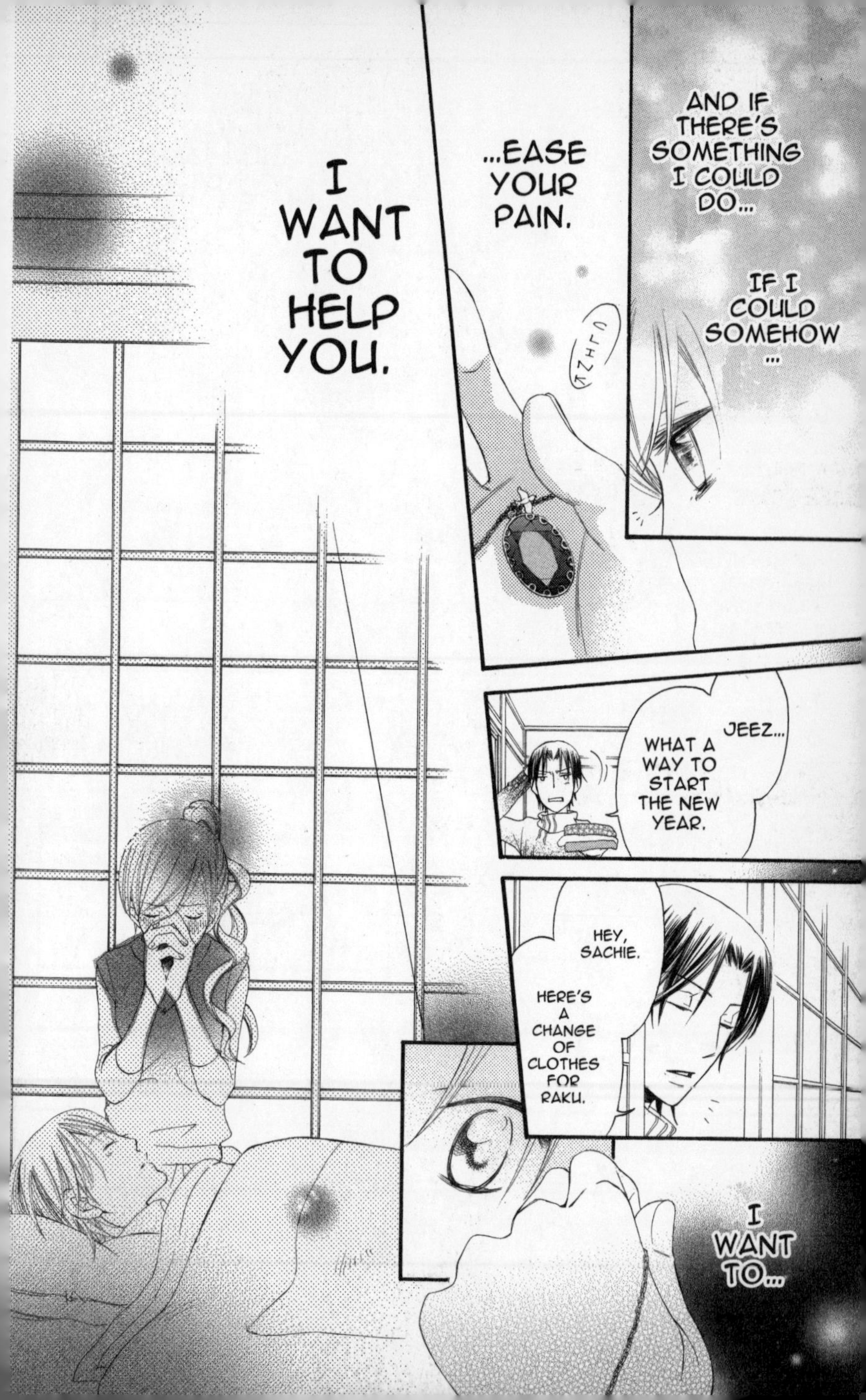
AND IF THERE'S SOMETHING I COULD DO...
IF I COULD SOMEHOW ...
...EASE YOUR PAIN.
JEEZ...
WHAT A WAY TO START THE NEW YEAR.
HEY, SACHIE.
HERE'S A CHANGE OF CLOTHES FOR RAKU.
I WANT TO...
I WANT TO HELP YOU.

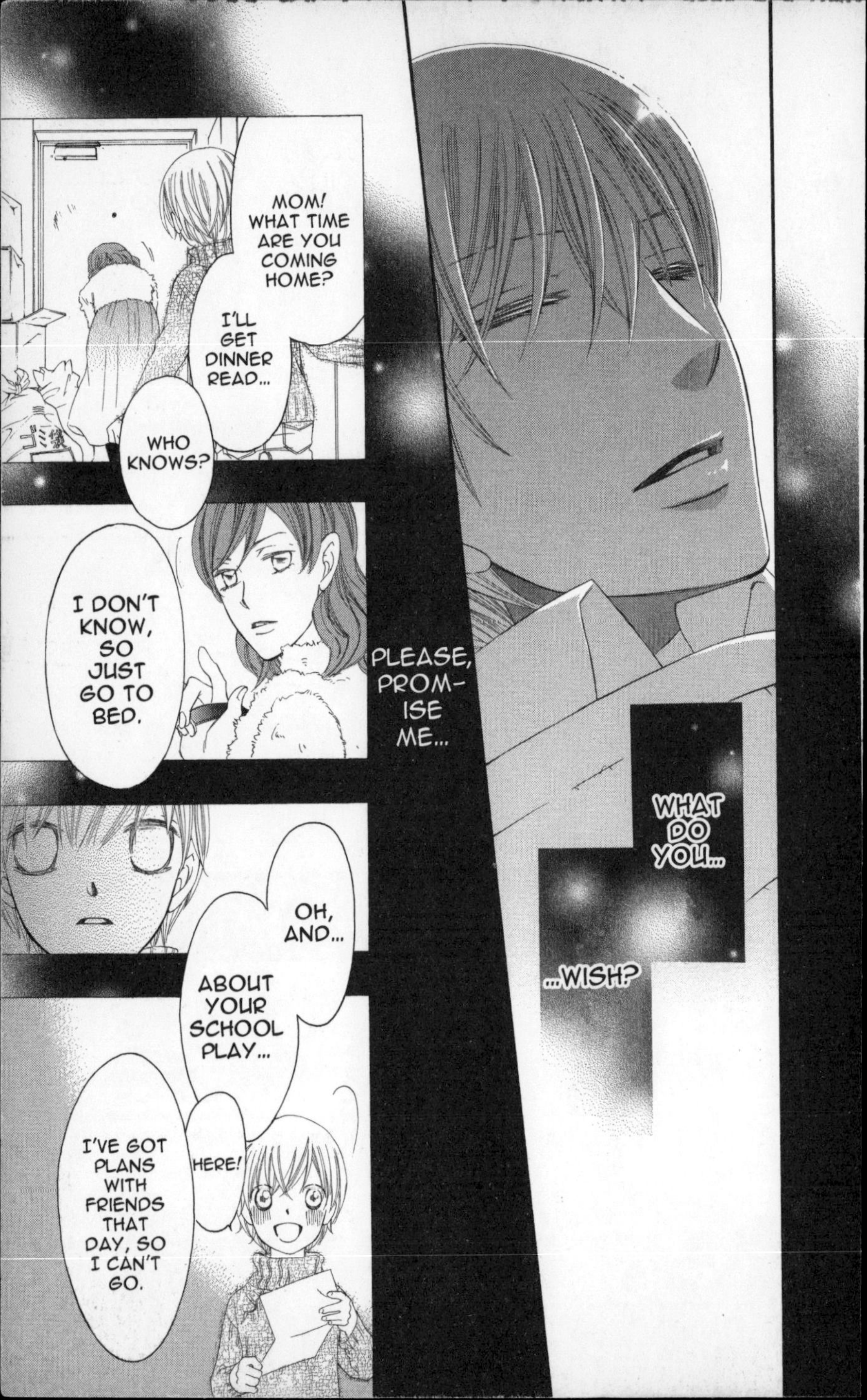
PLEASE, PROM-ISE ME...
WHAT DO YOU...
...WISH?
MOM! WHAT TIME ARE YOU COMING HOME?
I'LL GET DINNER READ...
WHO KNOWS?
I DON'T KNOW, SO JUST GO TO BED.
OH, AND...
ABOUT YOUR SCHOOL PLAY...
HERE!
I'VE GOT PLANS WITH FRIENDS THAT DAY, SO I CAN'T GO.

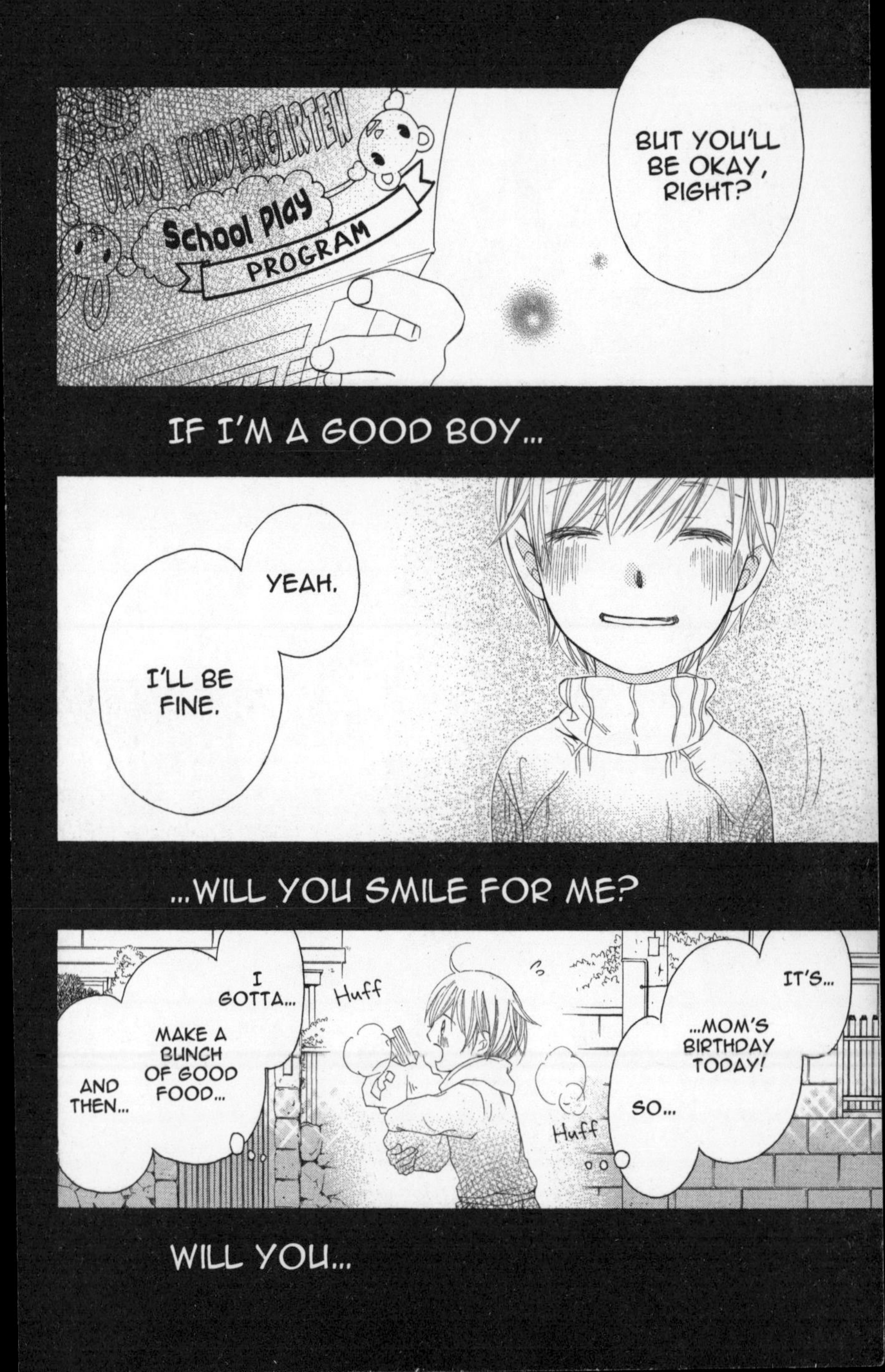
BUT YOU'LL BE OKAY, RIGHT?
OEDO KINDERGARTEN
School Play
PROGRAM
IF I'M A GOOD BOY...
YEAH.
I'LL BE FINE.
...WILL YOU SMILE FOR ME?
IT'S...
...MOM'S BIRTHDAY TODAY!
SO...
Huff
I GOTTA...
Huff
MAKE A BUNCH OF GOOD FOOD...
AND THEN...
WILL YOU...

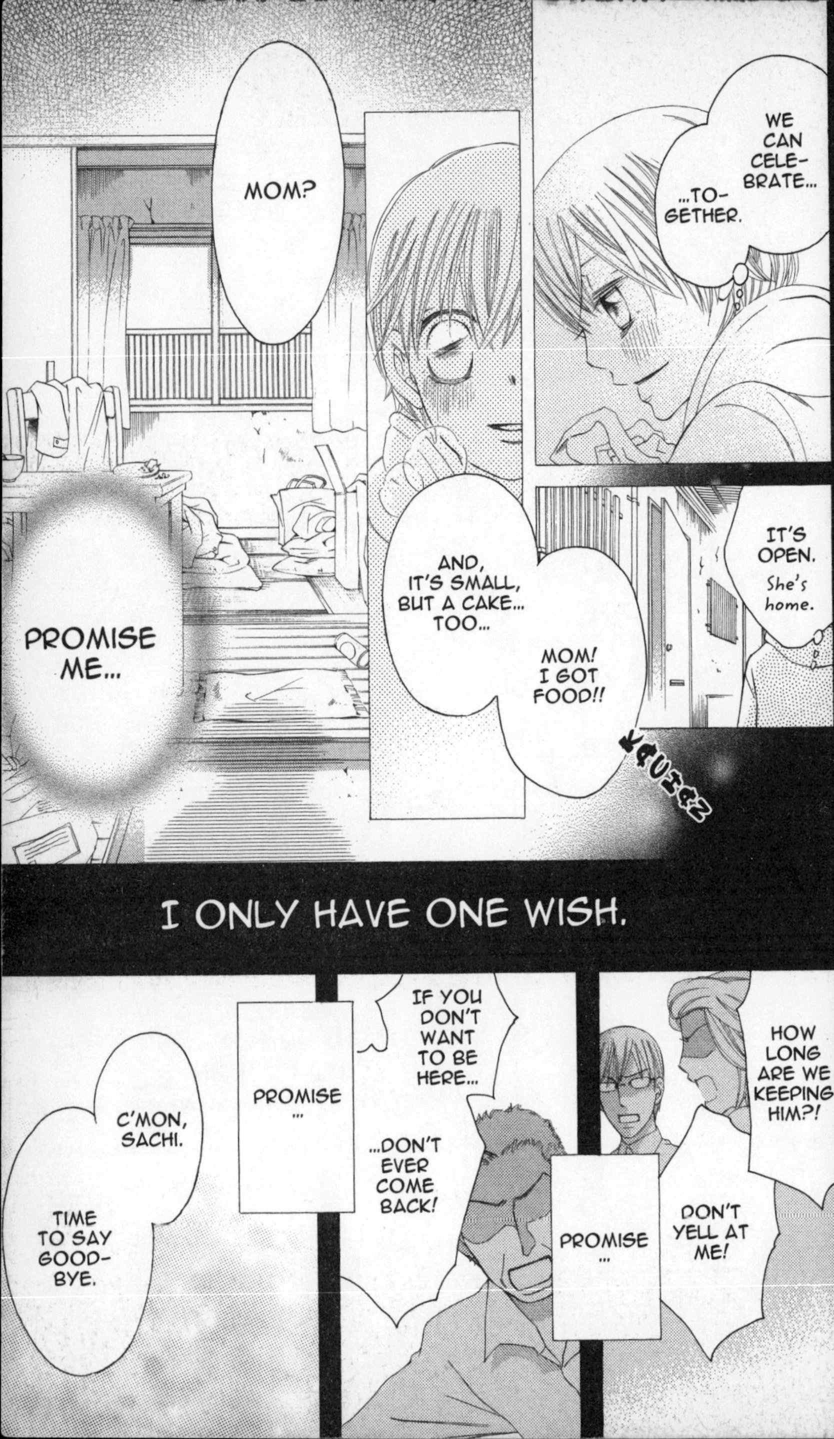
WE CAN CELEBRATE...
...TO-GETHER.
IT'S OPEN.
She's home.
MOM! I GOT FOOD!!
AND, IT'S SMALL, BUT A CAKE... TOO...
MOM?
PROMISE ME...
I ONLY HAVE ONE WISH.
HOW LONG ARE WE KEEPING HIM?!
DON'T YELL AT ME!
PROMISE ...
IF YOU DON'T WANT TO BE HERE...
...DON'T EVER COME BACK!
PROMISE ...
C'MON, SACHI.
TIME TO SAY GOOD-BYE.

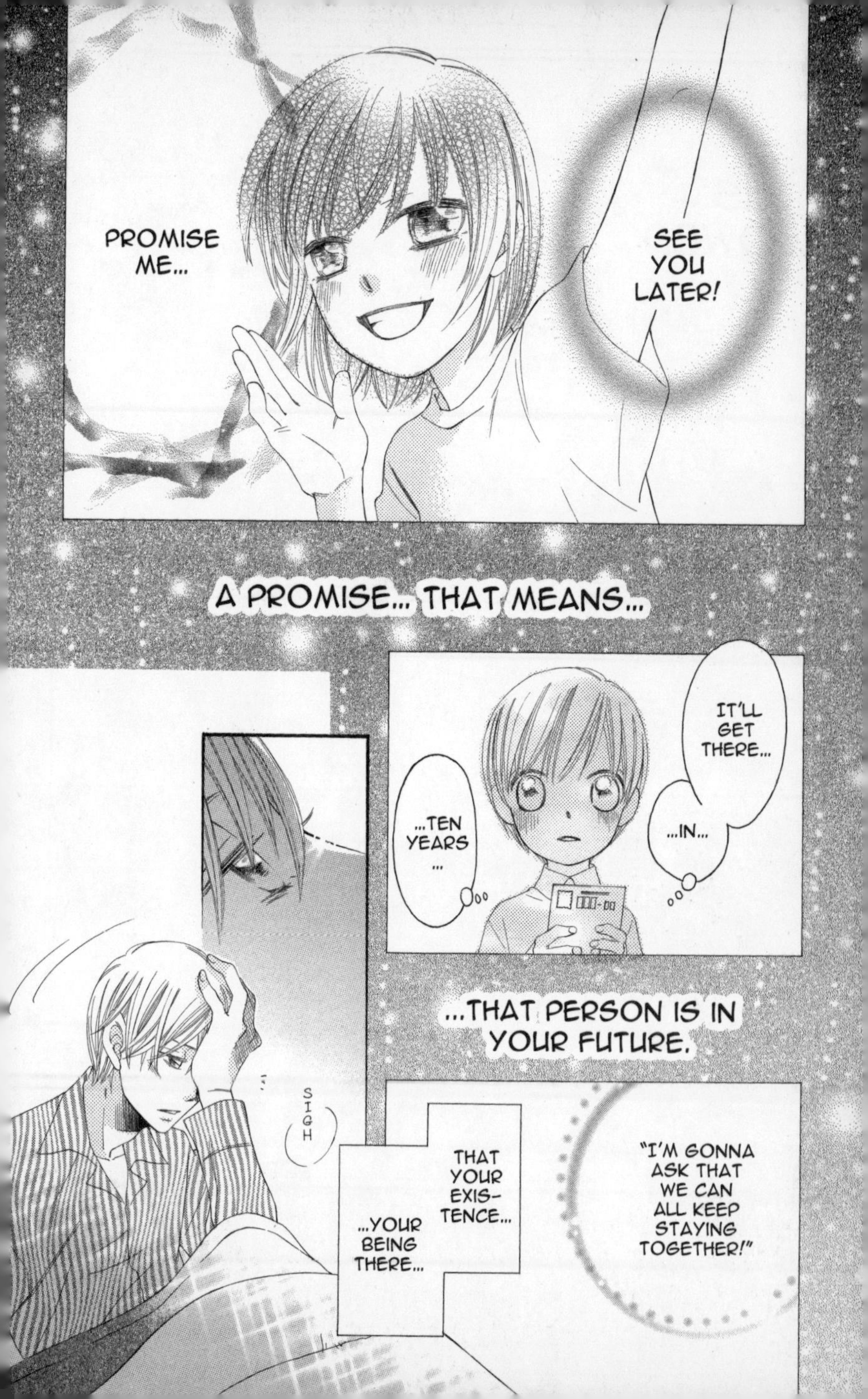
SEE YOU LATER!
PROMISE ME...
A PROMISE... THAT MEANS...
IT'LL GET THERE...
...IN...
...TEN YEARS...
...THAT PERSON IS IN YOUR FUTURE.
"I'M GONNA ASK THAT WE CAN ALL KEEP STAYING TOGETHER!"
THAT YOUR EXIS-TENCE...
...YOUR BEING THERE...
SIGH

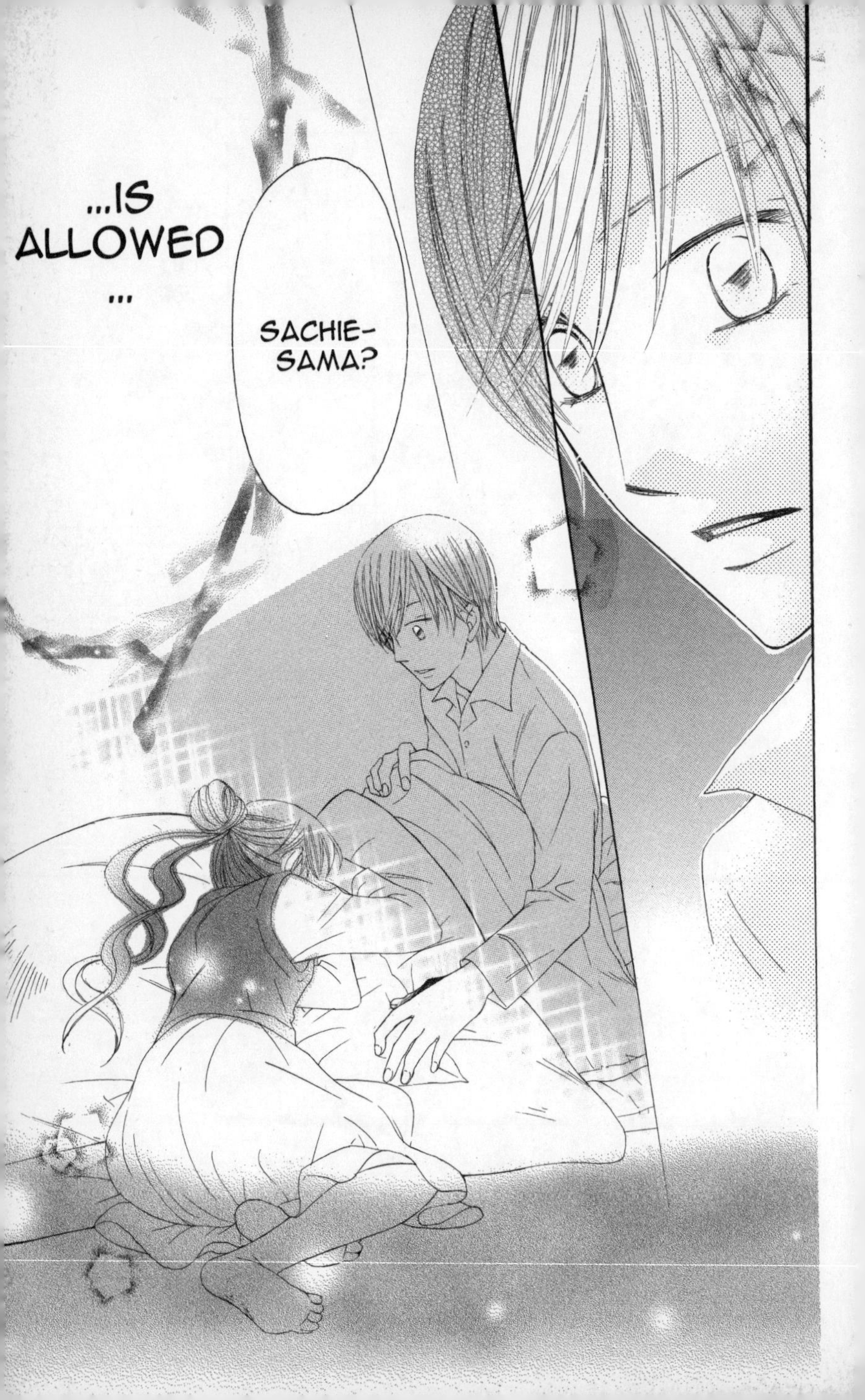
SACHIE-SAMA?
...IS ALLOWED ...

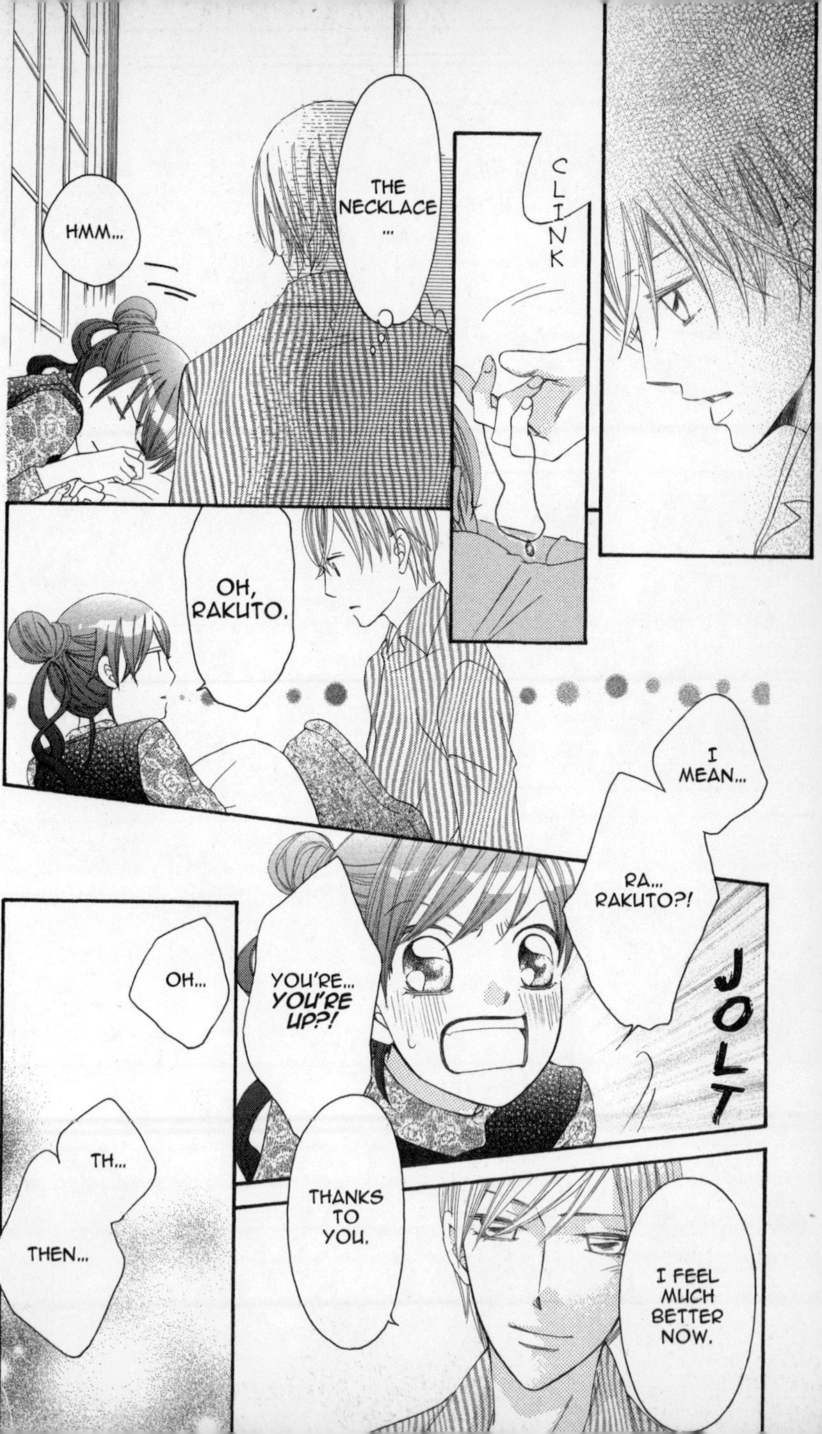
CLINK
THE NECKLACE...
HMM...
OH, RAKUTO.
I MEAN...
RA... RAKUTO?!
JOLT
YOU'RE... YOU'RE UP?!
OH...
I FEEL MUCH BETTER NOW.
THANKS TO YOU.
TH...
THEN...

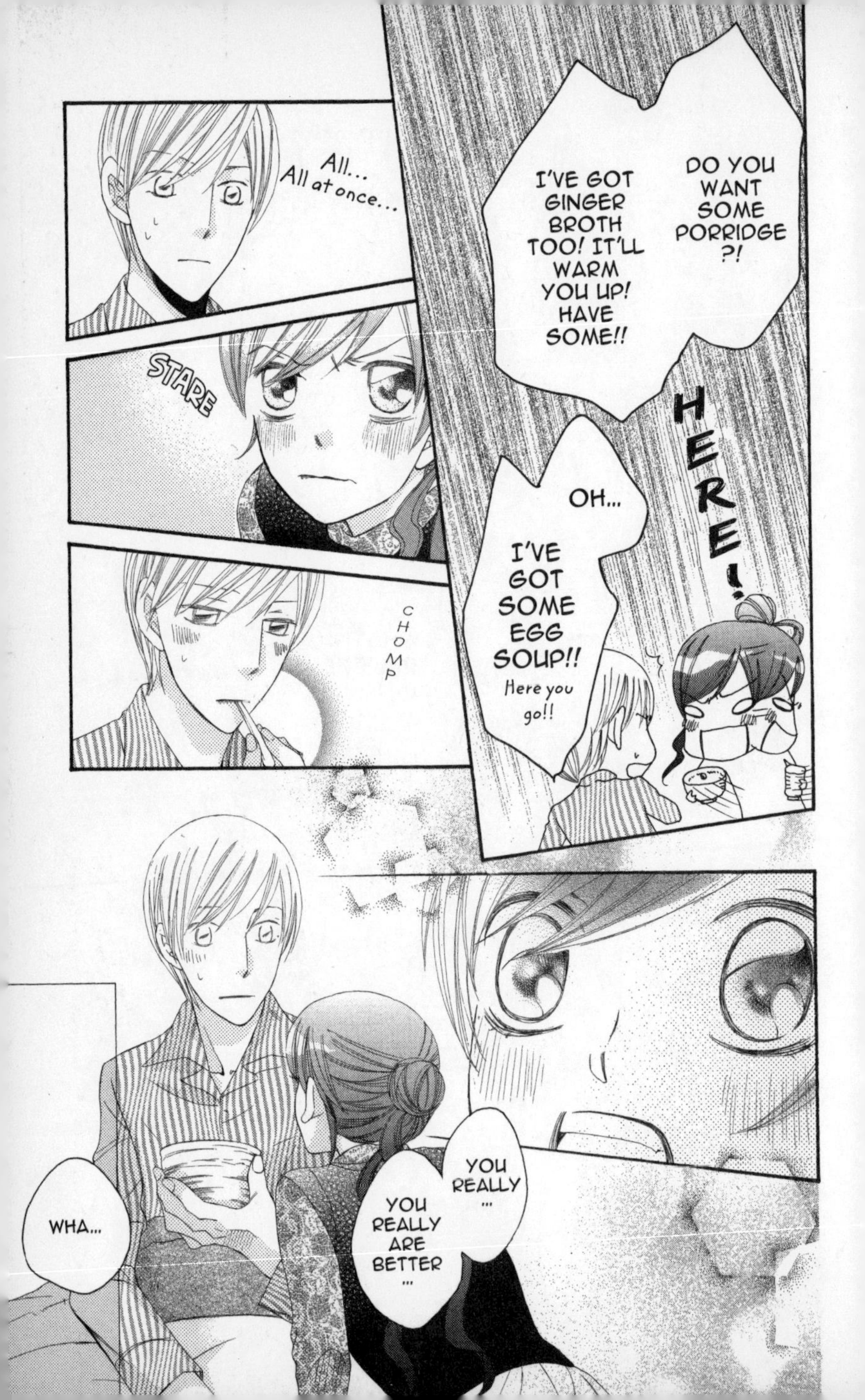

DO YOU WANT SOME PORRIDGE ?!
I'VE GOT GINGER BROTH TOO! IT'LL WARM YOU UP! HAVE SOME!!
HERE!
OH...
I'VE GOT SOME EGG SOUP!!
Here you go!!
All... All at once...
STARE
CHOMP
YOU REALLY ...
YOU REALLY ARE BETTER ...
WHA...

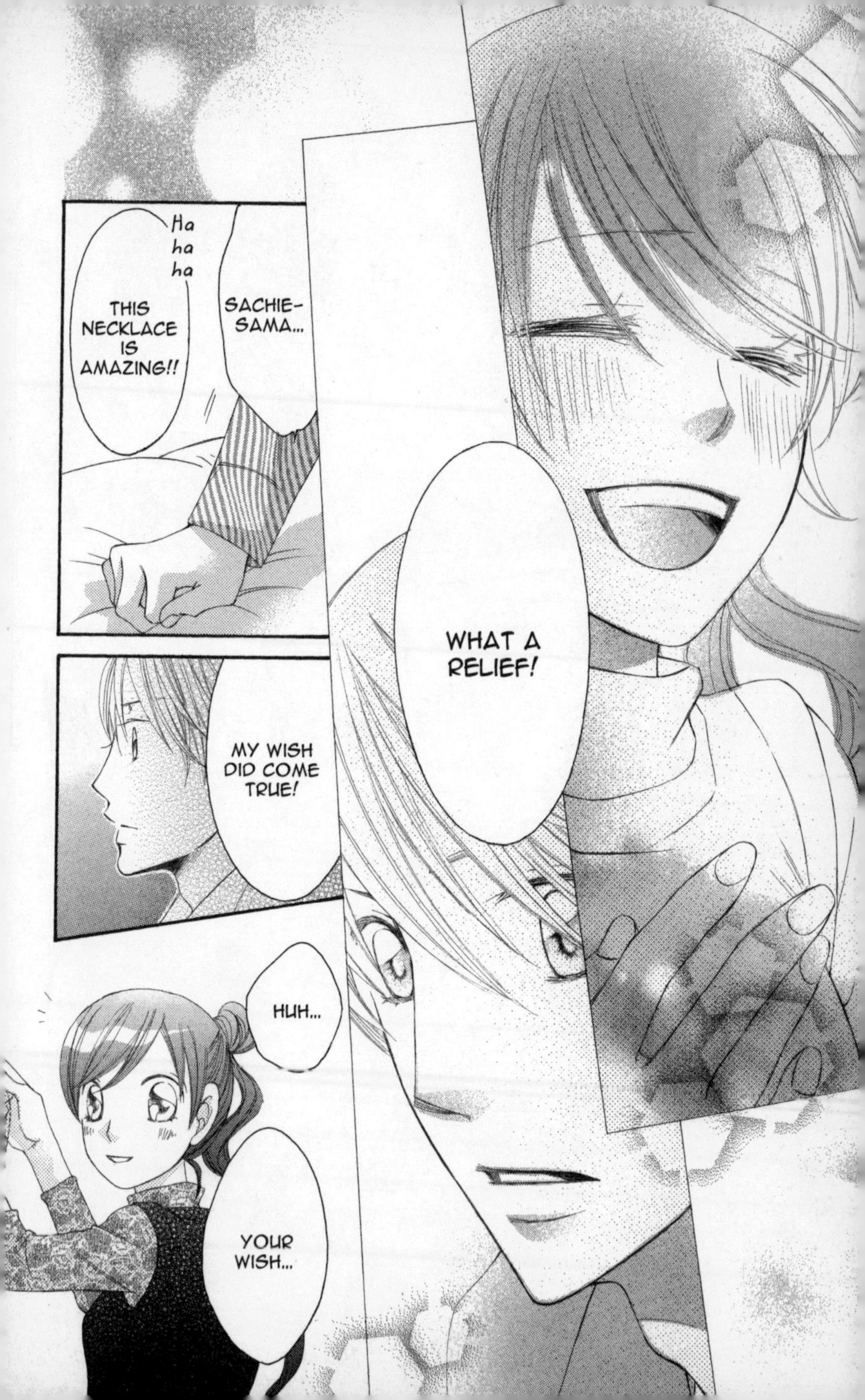
WHAT A RELIEF!
SACHIE-SAMA...
Ha ha ha
THIS NECKLACE IS AMAZING!!
MY WISH DID COME TRUE!
HUH...
YOUR WISH...

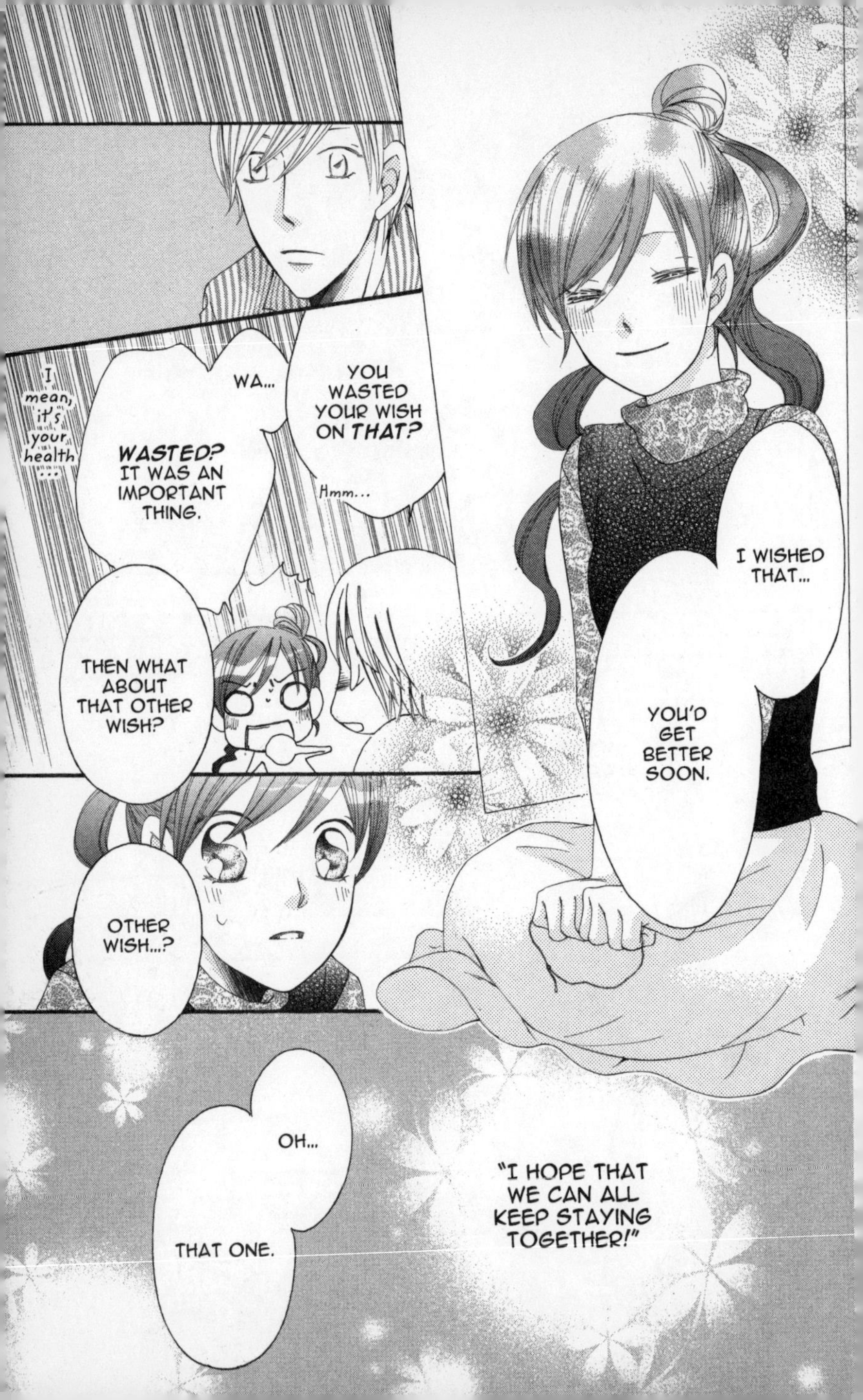
I WISHED THAT...
YOU'D GET BETTER SOON.
YOU WASTED YOUR WISH ON *THAT?*
Hmm...
WA...
WASTED? IT WAS AN IMPORTANT THING.
I mean, it's your health...
THEN WHAT ABOUT THAT OTHER WISH?
OTHER WISH...?
"I HOPE THAT WE CAN ALL KEEP STAYING TOGETHER!"
OH...
THAT ONE.

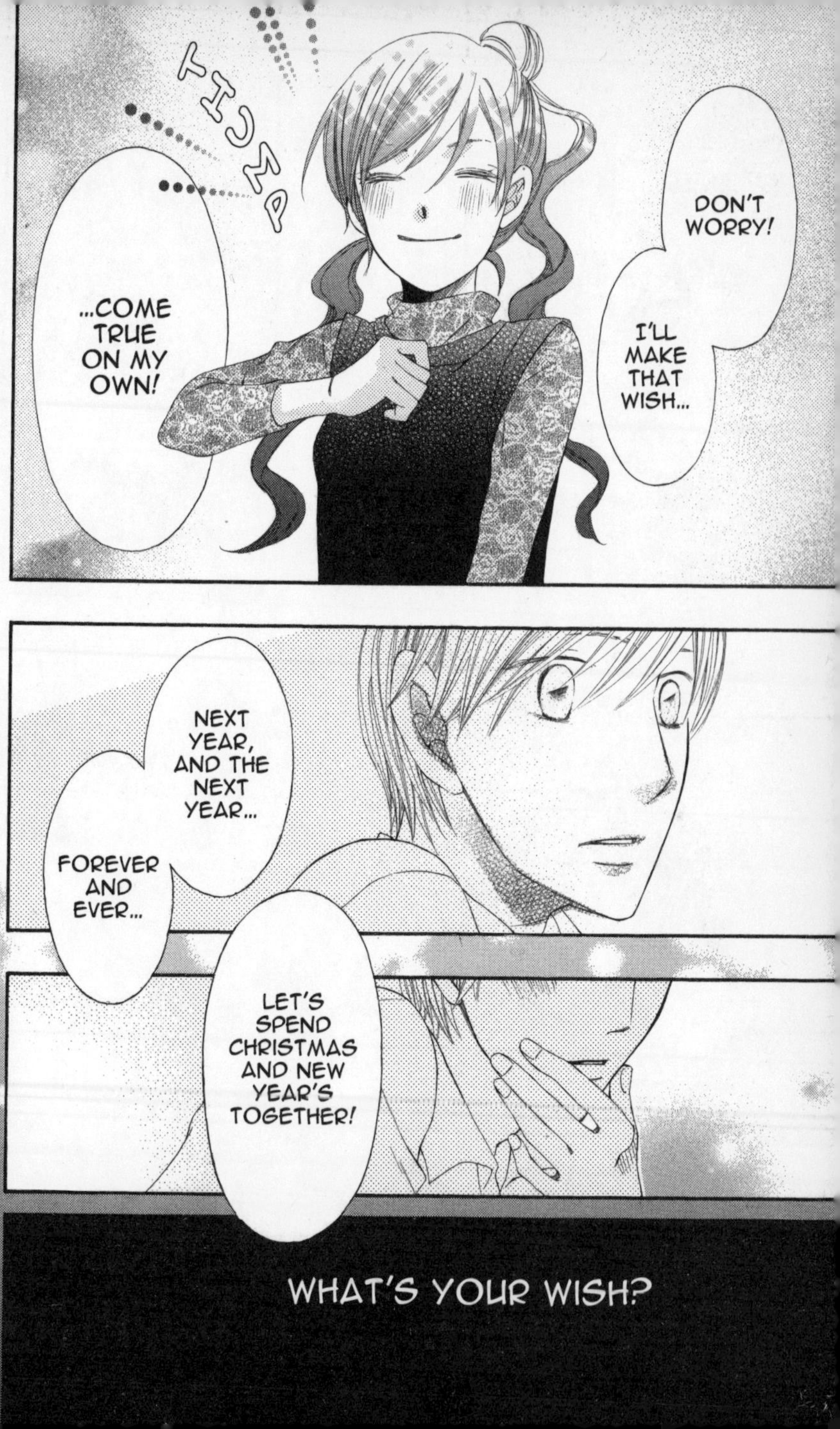
DON'T WORRY!
I'LL MAKE THAT WISH...
THUMP
...COME TRUE ON MY OWN!
NEXT YEAR, AND THE NEXT YEAR...
FOREVER AND EVER...
LET'S SPEND CHRISTMAS AND NEW YEAR'S TOGETHER!
WHAT'S YOUR WISH?

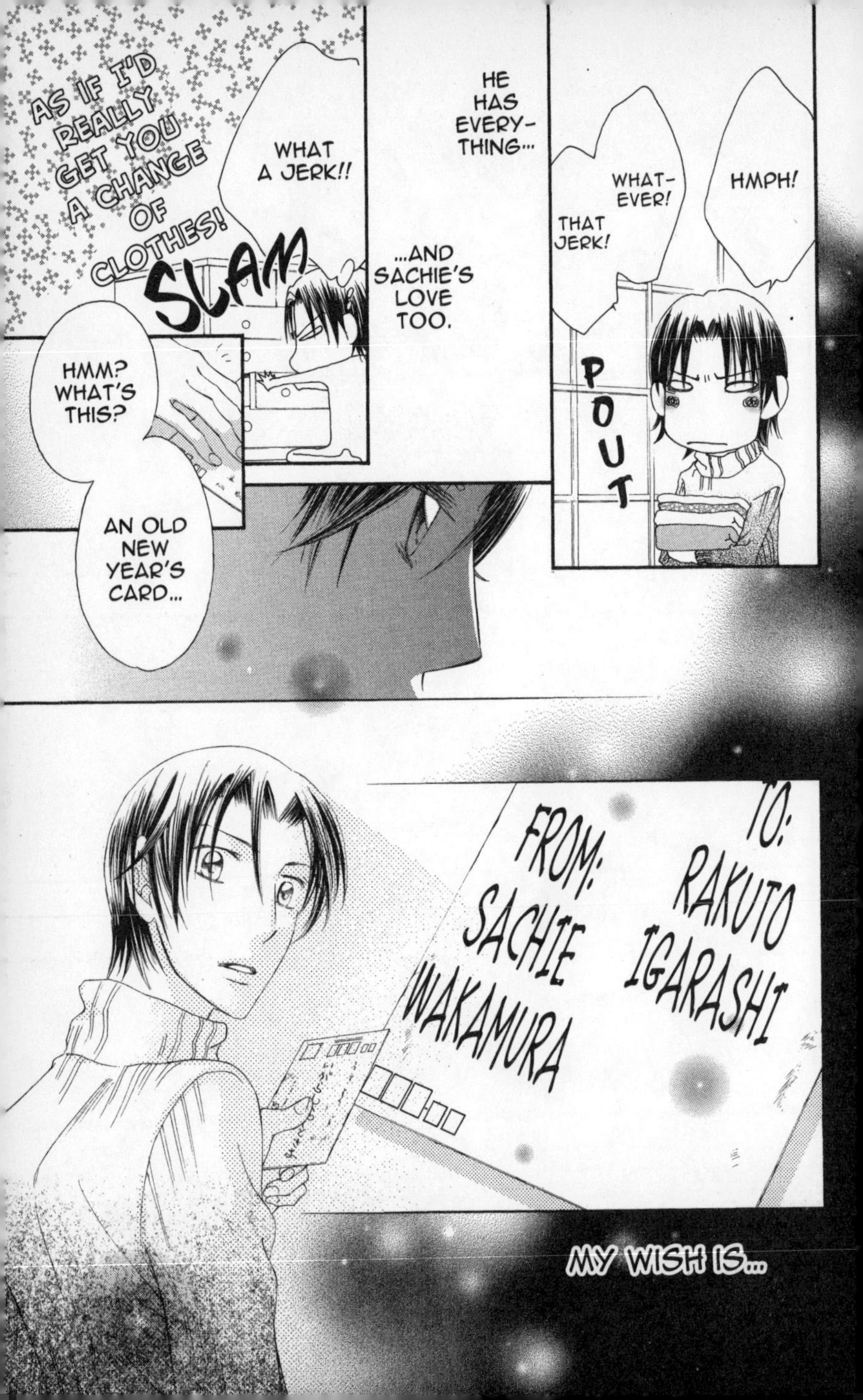
HMPH!
WHAT-EVER!
THAT JERK!
POUT
HE HAS EVERY-THING...
...AND SACHIE'S LOVE TOO.
WHAT A JERK!!
AS IF I'D REALLY GET YOU A CHANGE OF CLOTHES!
SLAM
HMM? WHAT'S THIS?
AN OLD NEW YEAR'S CARD...
TO: RAKUTO IGARASHI
FROM: SACHIE WAKAMURA
MY WISH IS...

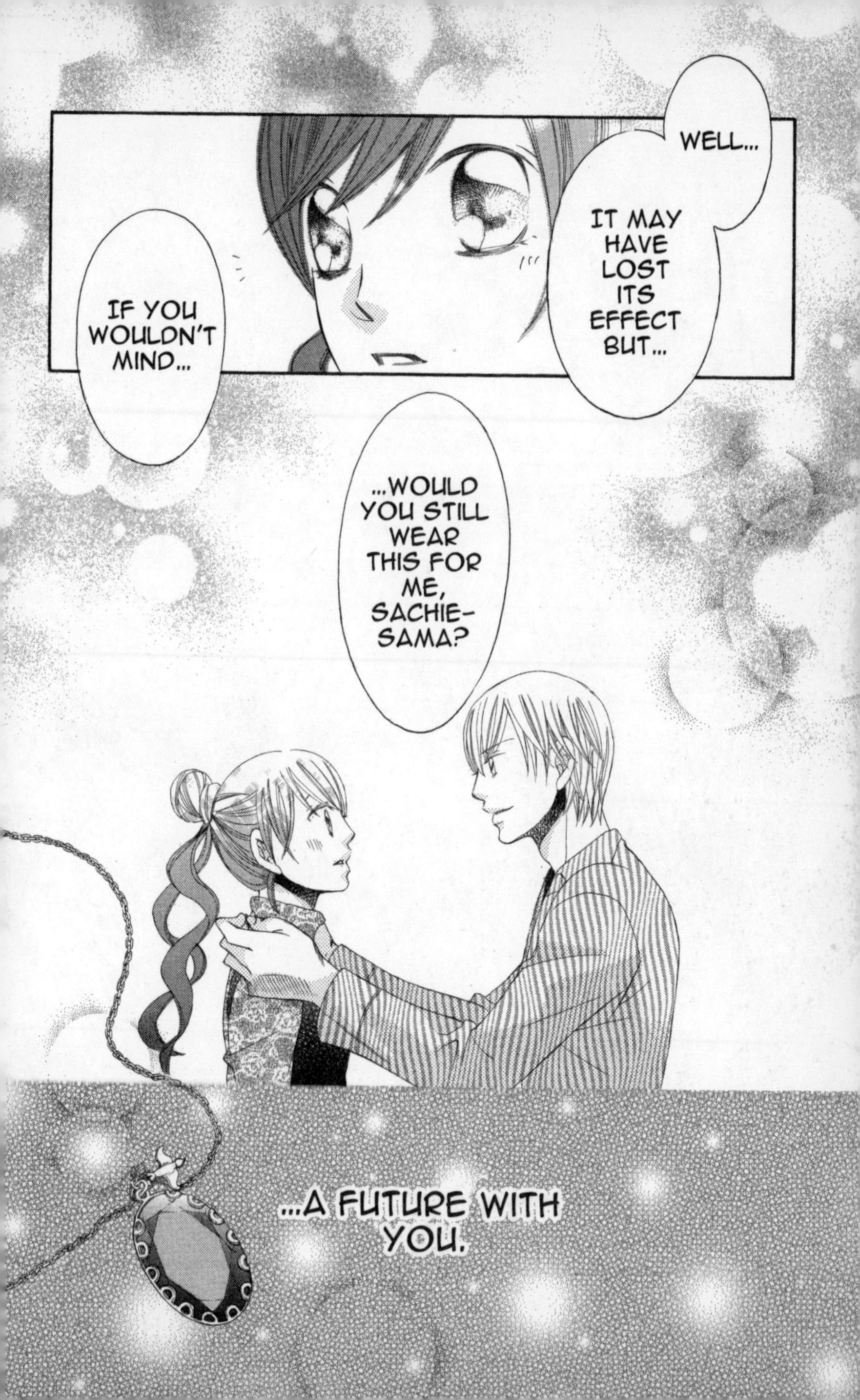
WELL...
IT MAY HAVE LOST ITS EFFECT BUT...
IF YOU WOULDN'T MIND...
...WOULD YOU STILL WEAR THIS FOR ME, SACHIE-SAMA?
...A FUTURE WITH YOU.

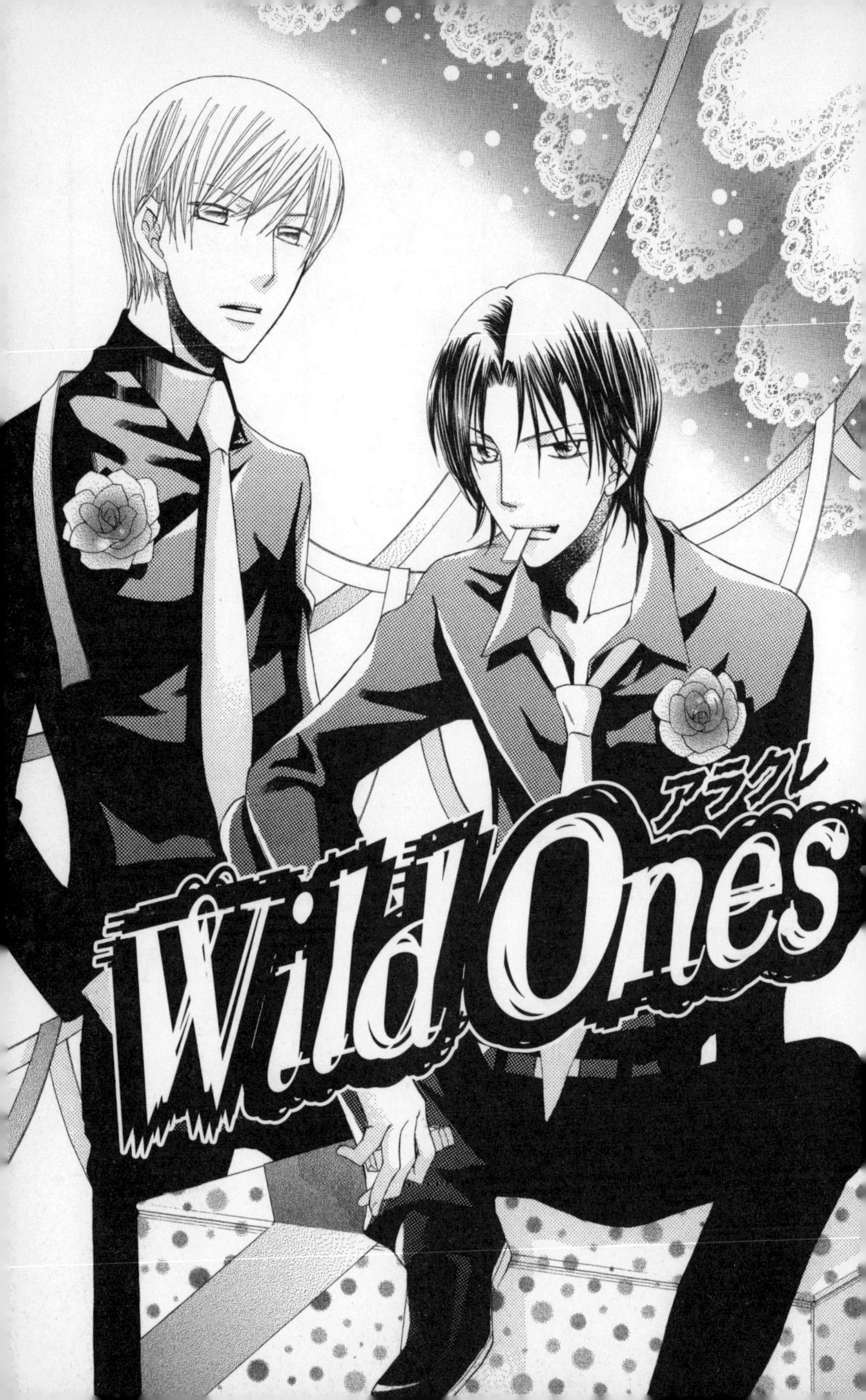
アラクレ
Wild Ones

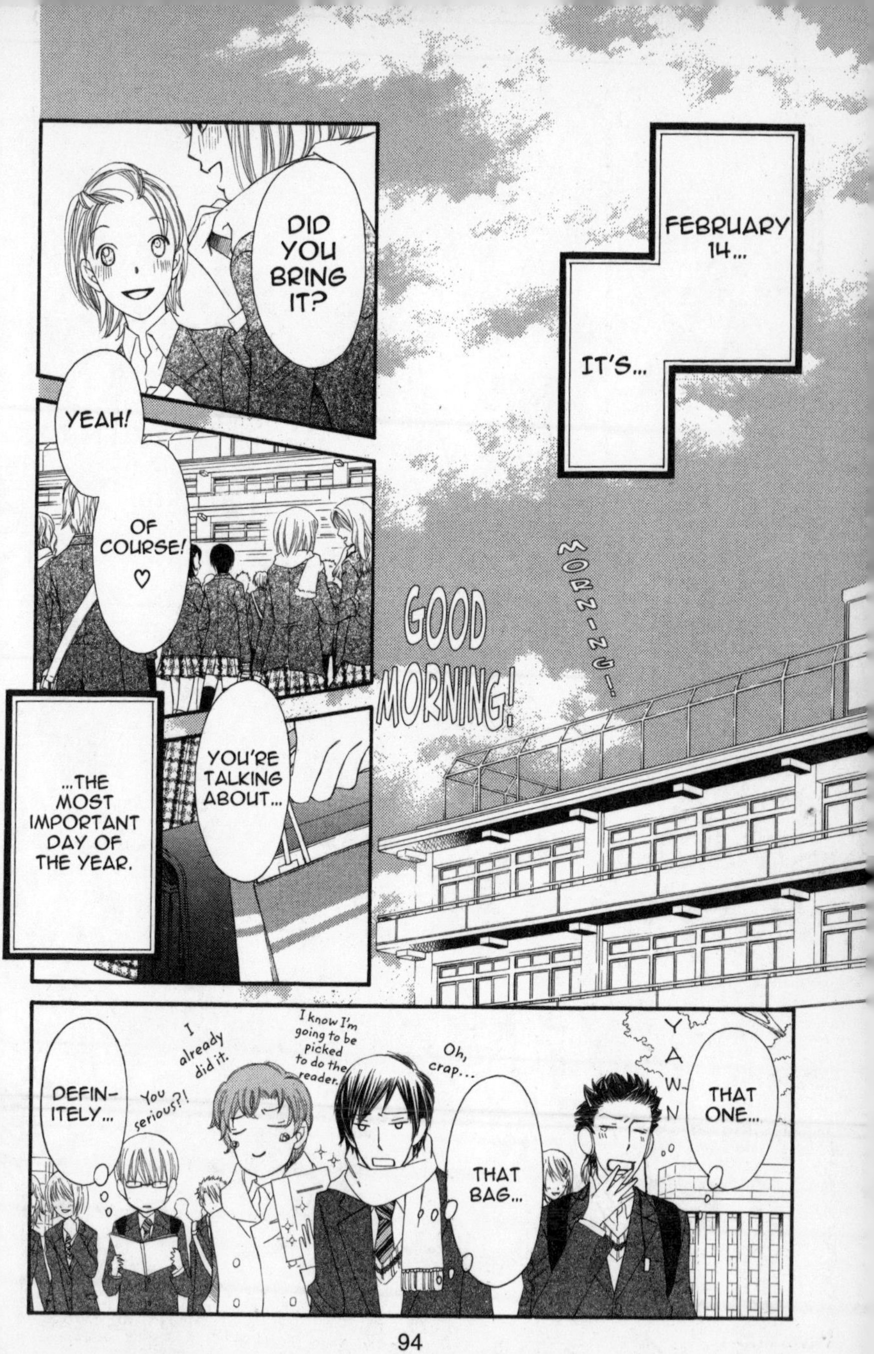
FEBRUARY 14...
IT'S...
GOOD MORNING!
MORNING!
DID YOU BRING IT?
YEAH!
OF COURSE! ♡
YOU'RE TALKING ABOUT...
...THE MOST IMPORTANT DAY OF THE YEAR.
THAT ONE...
YAWN
THAT BAG...
Oh, crap...
I know I'm going to be picked to do the reader.
I already did it.
You serious?!
DEFINITELY...

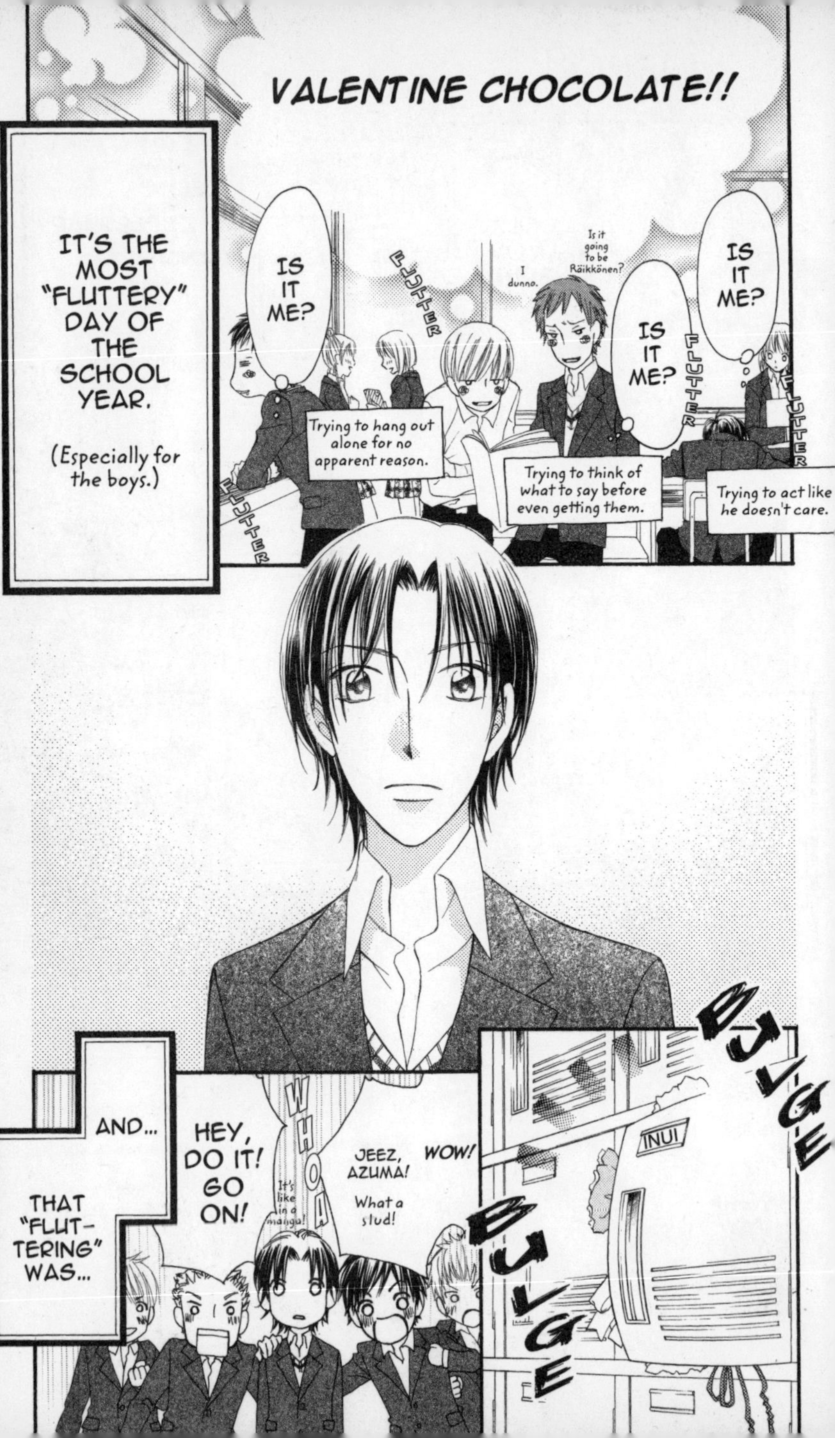
VALENTINE CHOCOLATE!!
IS IT ME?
Is it going to be Räikkönen?
I dunno.
IS IT ME?
FLUTTER
FLUTTER
Trying to act like he doesn't care.
Trying to think of what to say before even getting them.
IS IT ME?
FLUTTER
Trying to hang out alone for no apparent reason.
FLUTTER
IT'S THE MOST "FLUTTERY" DAY OF THE SCHOOL YEAR.
(Especially for the boys.)
BULGE
BULGE
INUI
WOW!
JEEZ, AZUMA!
What a stud!
WHOA
It's like in a manga!
HEY, DO IT! GO ON!
AND...
THAT "FLUT-TERING" WAS...

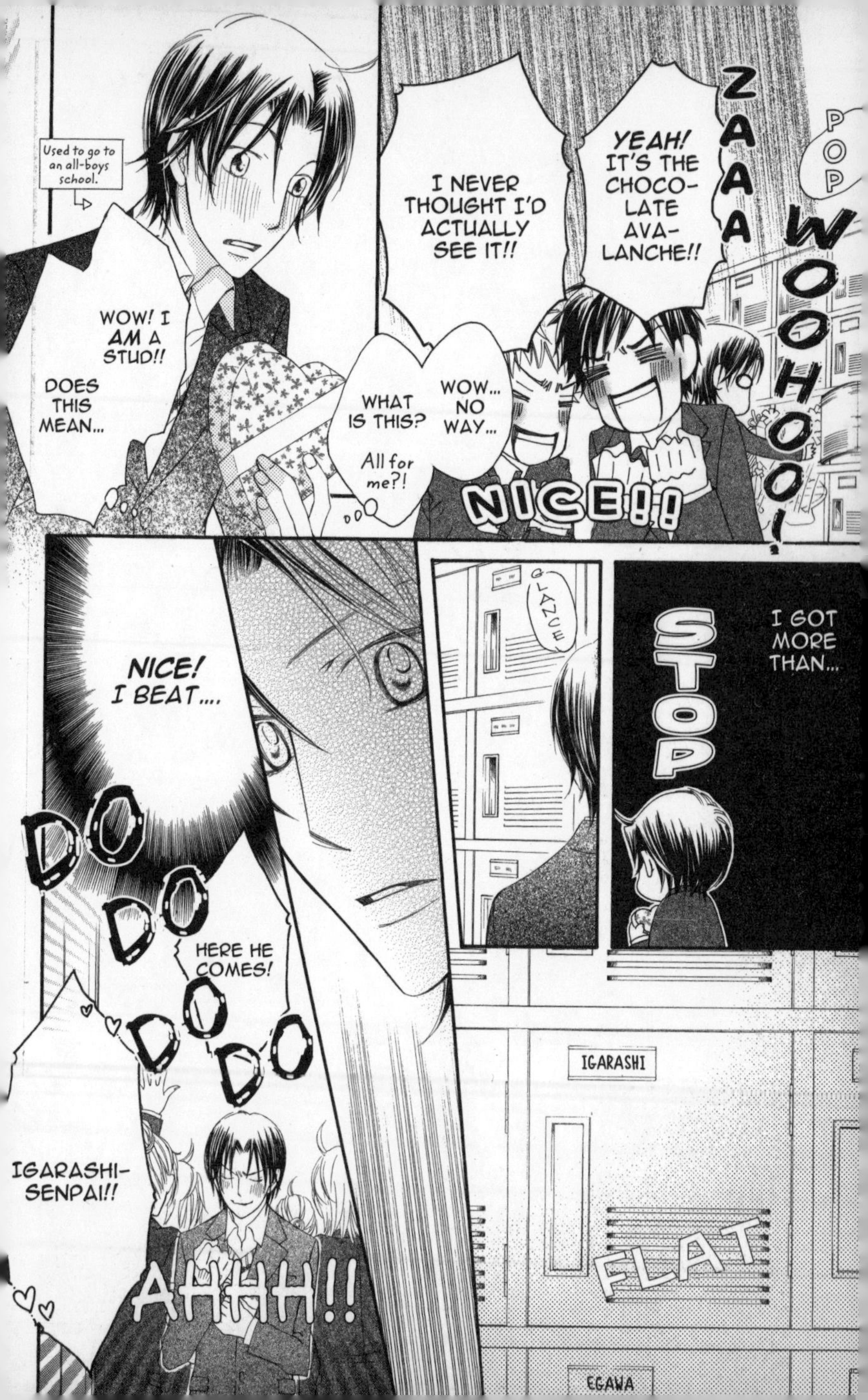
POP
ZAAAA
WOOHOO!
YEAH! IT'S THE CHOCO-LATE AVA-LANCHE!!
I NEVER THOUGHT I'D ACTUALLY SEE IT!!
NICE!!
WOW... NO WAY...
WHAT IS THIS?
All for me?!
Used to go to an all-boys school.
WOW! I AM A STUD!!
DOES THIS MEAN...
I GOT MORE THAN...
STOP
GLANCE
NICE! I BEAT....
DODODODODO
HERE HE COMES!
IGARASHI-SENPAI!!
AHHH!!
IGARASHI
FLAT
EGAWA

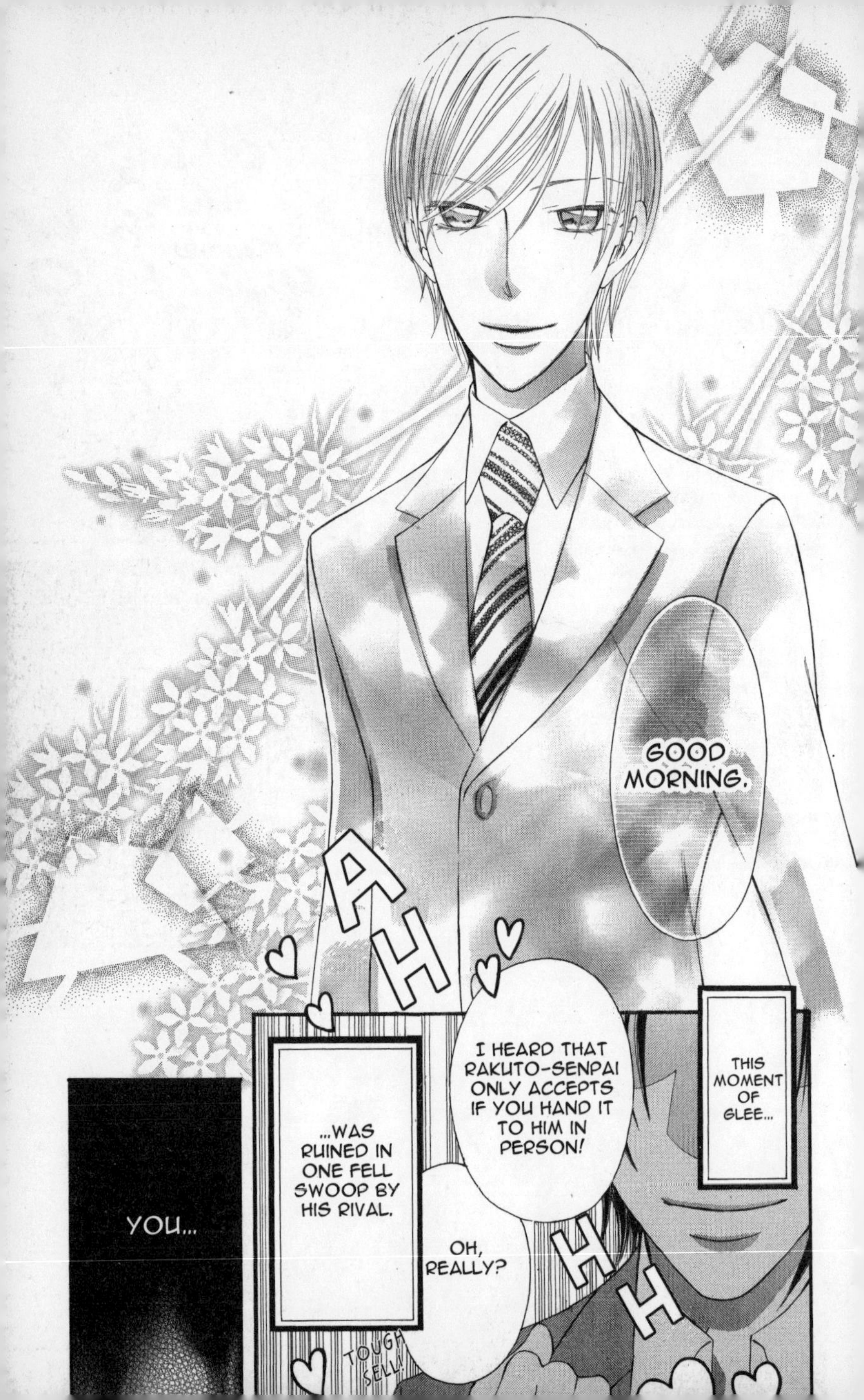
GOOD MORNING.
THIS MOMENT OF GLEE...
AHHHH
I HEARD THAT RAKUTO-SENPAI ONLY ACCEPTS IF YOU HAND IT TO HIM IN PERSON!
OH, REALLY?
TOUGH SELL!
...WAS RUINED IN ONE FELL SWOOP BY HIS RIVAL.
YOU...

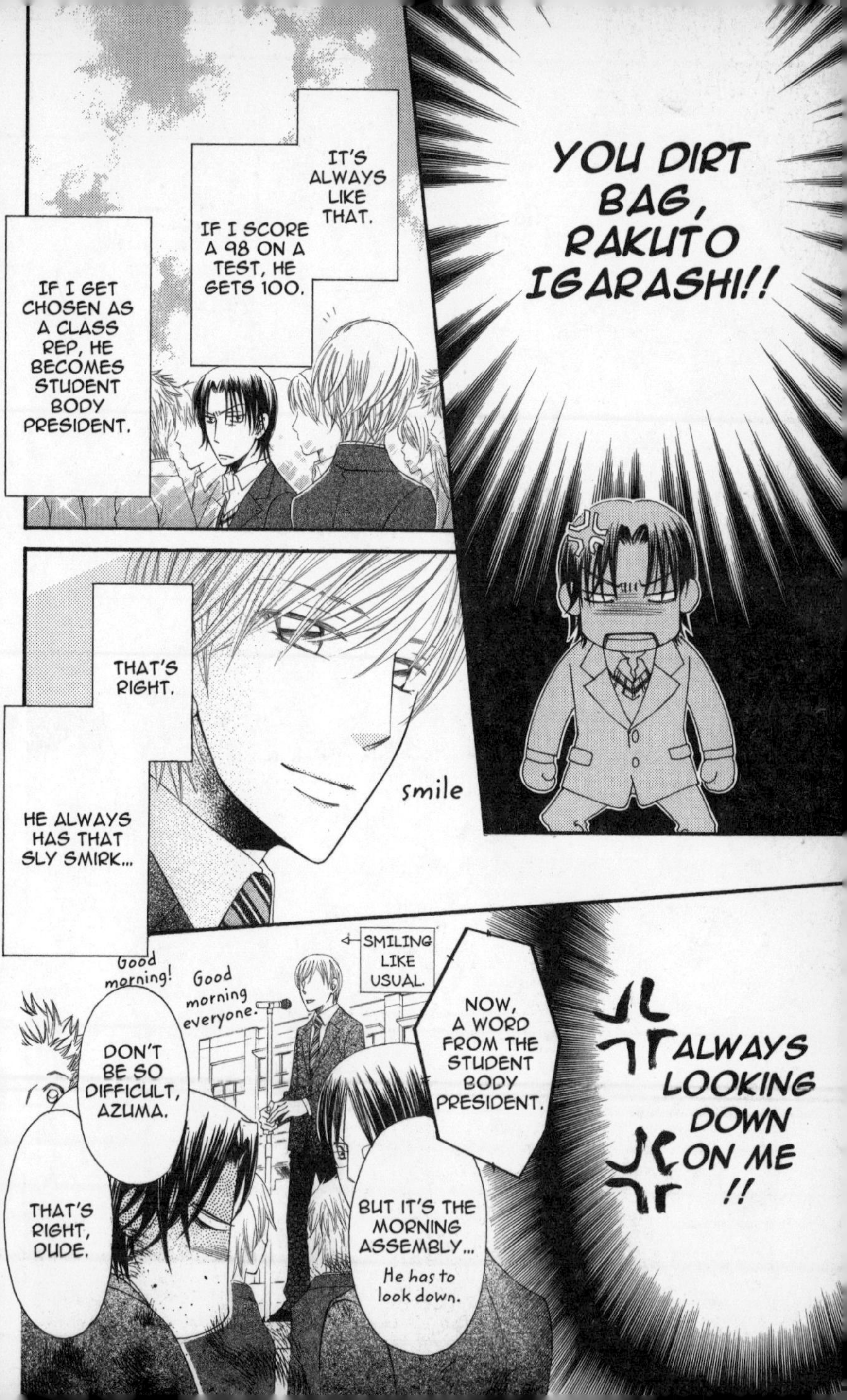
YOU DIRT BAG, RAKUTO IGARASHI!!
IF I GET CHOSEN AS A CLASS REP, HE BECOMES STUDENT BODY PRESIDENT.
IT'S ALWAYS LIKE THAT.
IF I SCORE A 98 ON A TEST, HE GETS 100.
THAT'S RIGHT.
HE ALWAYS HAS THAT SLY SMIRK...
smile
ALWAYS LOOKING DOWN ON ME !!
NOW, A WORD FROM THE STUDENT BODY PRESIDENT.
SMILING LIKE USUAL.
Good morning everyone.
Good morning!
BUT IT'S THE MORNING ASSEMBLY...
He has to look down.
DON'T BE SO DIFFICULT, AZUMA.
THAT'S RIGHT, DUDE.

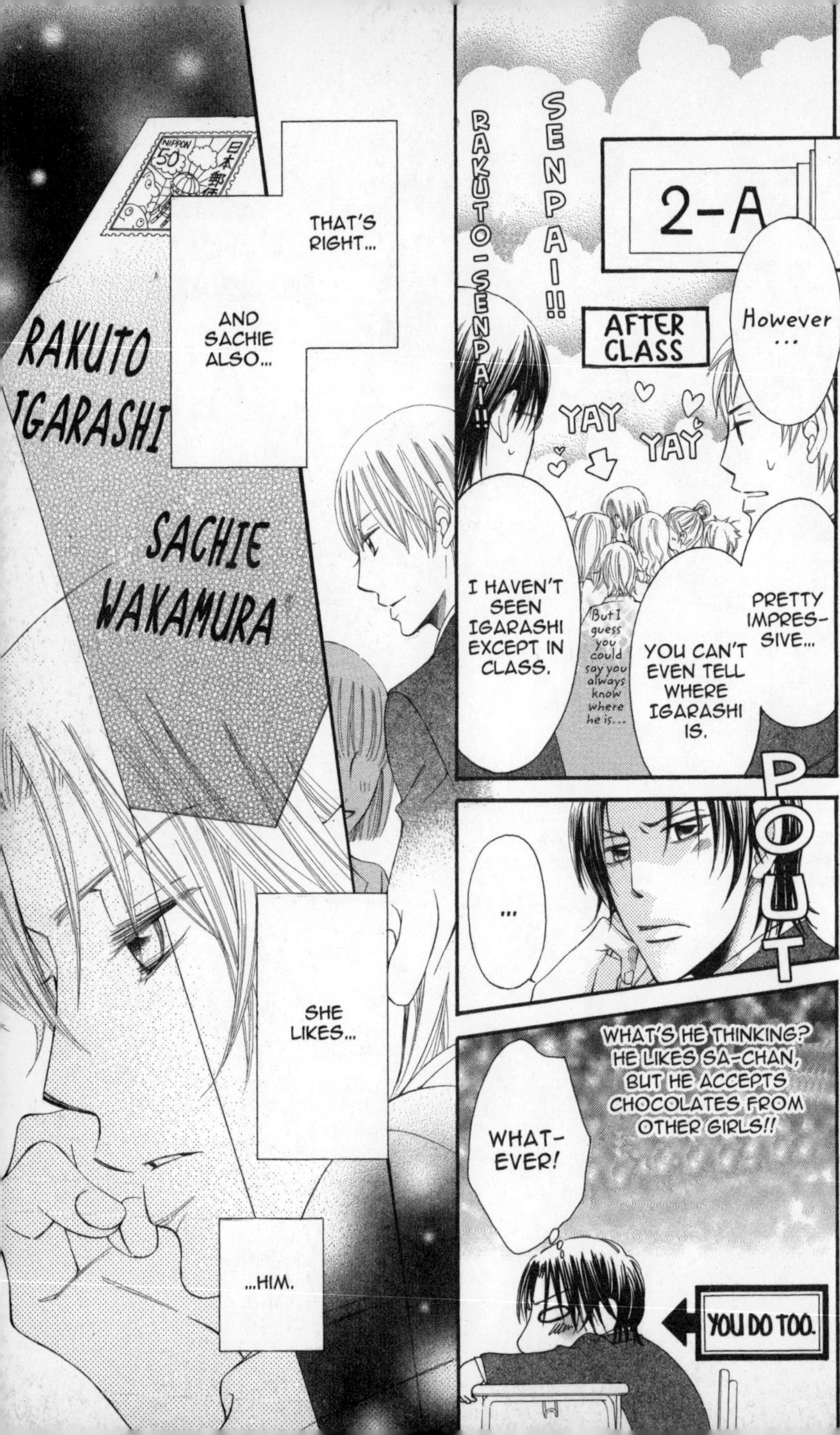
2-A
SENPAI!!
RAKUTO-SENPAI!!
AFTER CLASS
However...
YAY
YAY
PRETTY IMPRES-SIVE...
YOU CAN'T EVEN TELL WHERE IGARASHI IS.
But I guess you could say you always know where he is...
I HAVEN'T SEEN IGARASHI EXCEPT IN CLASS.
POUT
...
WHAT'S HE THINKING? HE LIKES SA-CHAN, BUT HE ACCEPTS CHOCOLATES FROM OTHER GIRLS!!
WHAT-EVER!
YOU DO TOO.
NIPPON 50
THAT'S RIGHT...
AND SACHIE ALSO...
RAKUTO IGARASHI
SACHIE WAKAMURA
SHE LIKES...
...HIM.

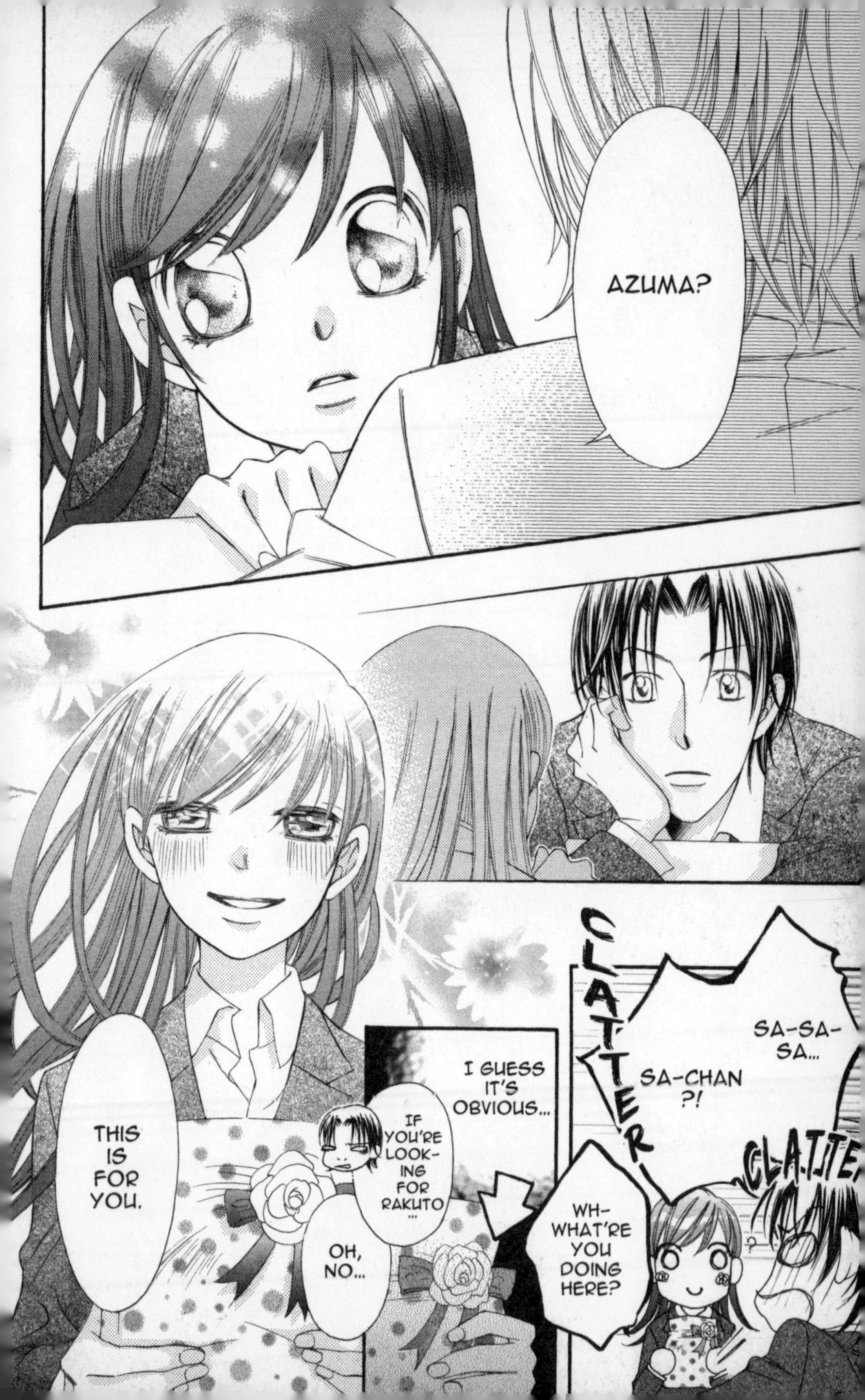
AZUMA?
SA-SA-SA...
SA-CHAN?!
CLATTER
CLATTER
WH-WHAT'RE YOU DOING HERE?
I GUESS IT'S OBVIOUS...
IF YOU'RE LOOKING FOR RAKUTO...
OH, NO...
THIS IS FOR YOU.

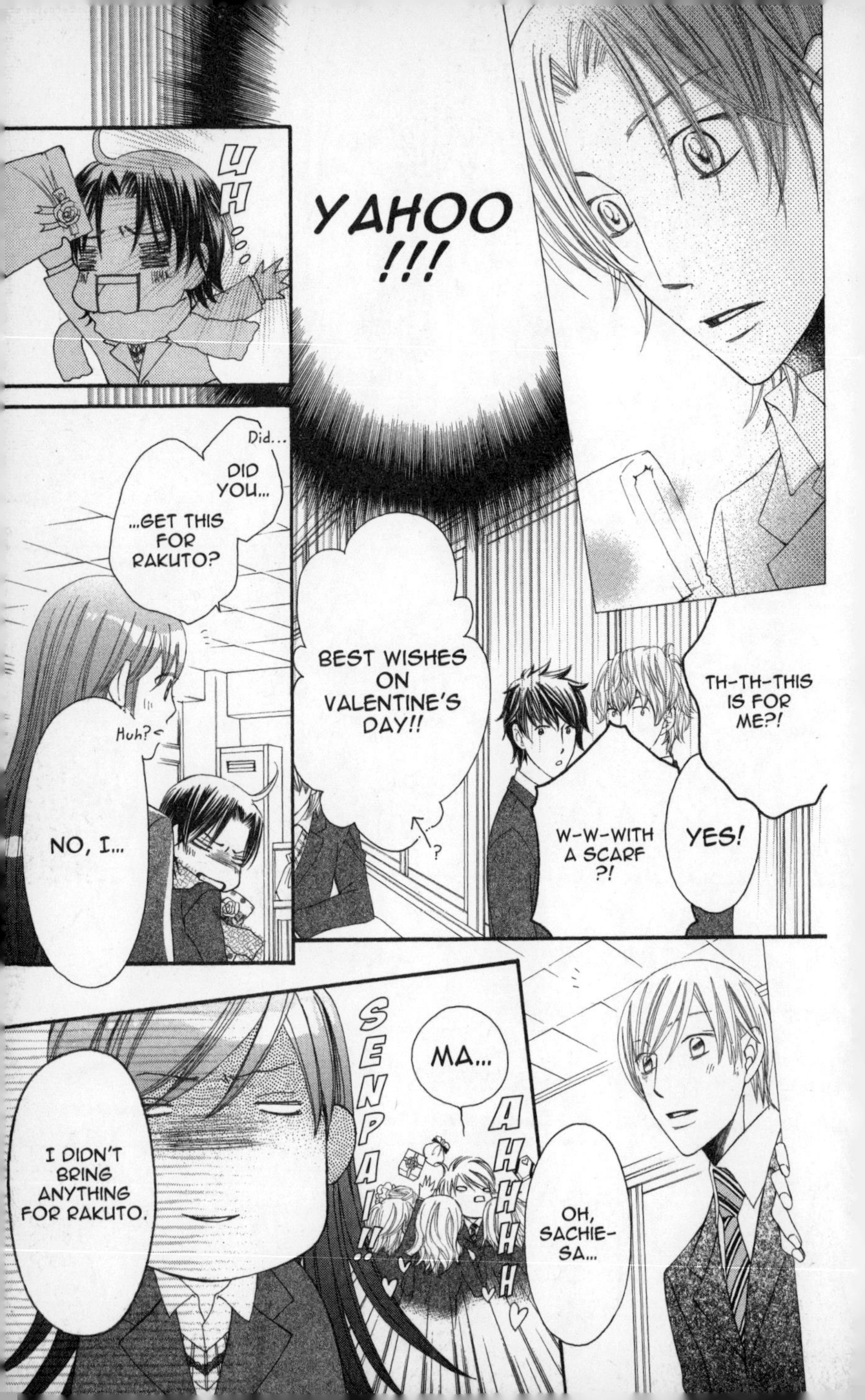
YAHOO !!!
UH ooo
TH-TH-THIS IS FOR ME?!
YES!
W-W-WITH A SCARF ?!
BEST WISHES ON VALENTINE'S DAY!!
?
Did...
DID YOU...
...GET THIS FOR RAKUTO?
Huh?
NO, I...
OH, SACHIE-SA...
AHHHHH
MA...
SENPAI!!
I DIDN'T BRING ANYTHING FOR RAKUTO.

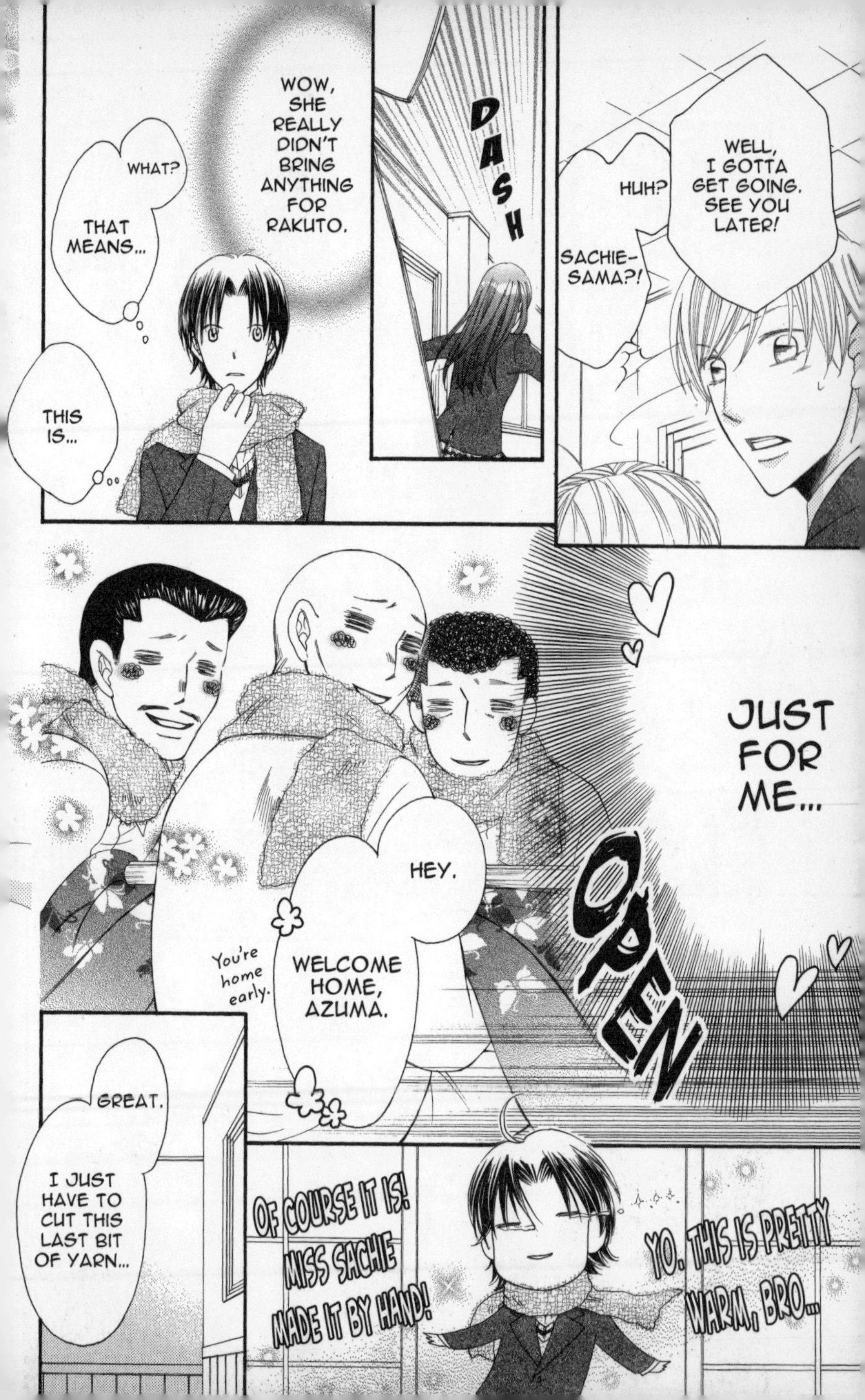
WELL, I GOTTA GET GOING. SEE YOU LATER!
HUH?
SACHIE-SAMA?!
DASH
WOW, SHE REALLY DIDN'T BRING ANYTHING FOR RAKUTO.
WHAT?
THAT MEANS...
THIS IS...
JUST FOR ME...
OPEN
HEY.
WELCOME HOME, AZUMA.
You're home early.
YO. THIS IS PRETTY WARM, BRO...
OF COURSE IT IS! MISS SACHIE MADE IT BY HAND!
GREAT.
I JUST HAVE TO CUT THIS LAST BIT OF YARN...

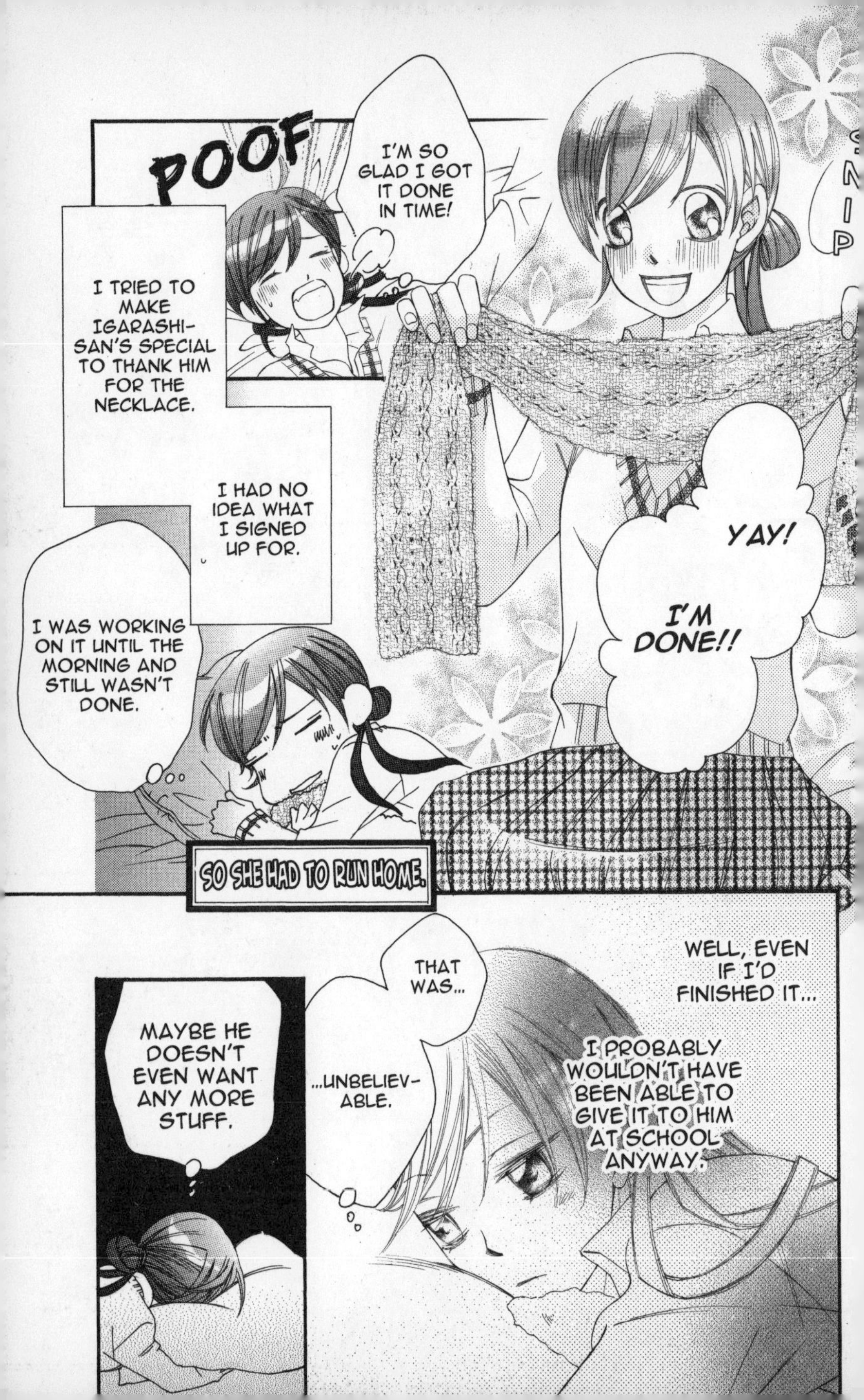
SNIP
YAY!
I'M DONE!!
POOF
I'M SO GLAD I GOT IT DONE IN TIME!
I TRIED TO MAKE IGARASHI-SAN'S SPECIAL TO THANK HIM FOR THE NECKLACE.
I HAD NO IDEA WHAT I SIGNED UP FOR.
I WAS WORKING ON IT UNTIL THE MORNING AND STILL WASN'T DONE.
SO SHE HAD TO RUN HOME.
WELL, EVEN IF I'D FINISHED IT...
I PROBABLY WOULDN'T HAVE BEEN ABLE TO GIVE IT TO HIM AT SCHOOL ANYWAY.
THAT WAS...
...UNBELIEV-ABLE.
MAYBE HE DOESN'T EVEN WANT ANY MORE STUFF.

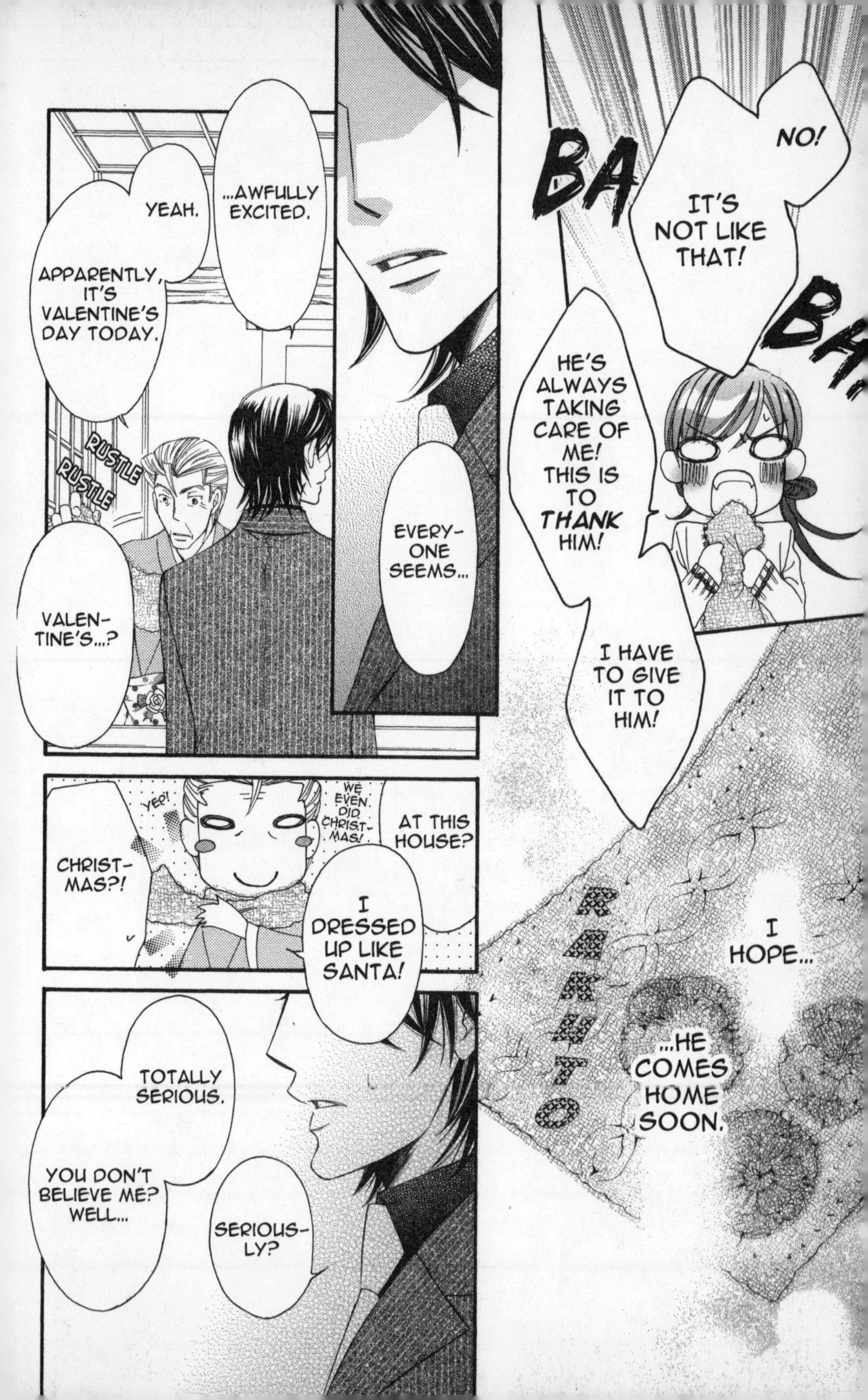
NO!
IT'S NOT LIKE THAT!
BA
BA
HE'S ALWAYS TAKING CARE OF ME! THIS IS TO *THANK* HIM!
I HAVE TO GIVE IT TO HIM!
RAKUTO
I HOPE...
...HE COMES HOME SOON.
...AWFULLY EXCITED.
EVERY-ONE SEEMS...
YEAH.
APPARENTLY, IT'S VALENTINE'S DAY TODAY.
RUSTLE RUSTLE
VALEN-TINE'S...?
AT THIS HOUSE?
WE EVEN DID CHRIST-MAS!
YEP!
I DRESSED UP LIKE SANTA!
CHRIST-MAS?!
TOTALLY SERIOUS.
SERIOUS-LY?
YOU DON'T BELIEVE ME? WELL...

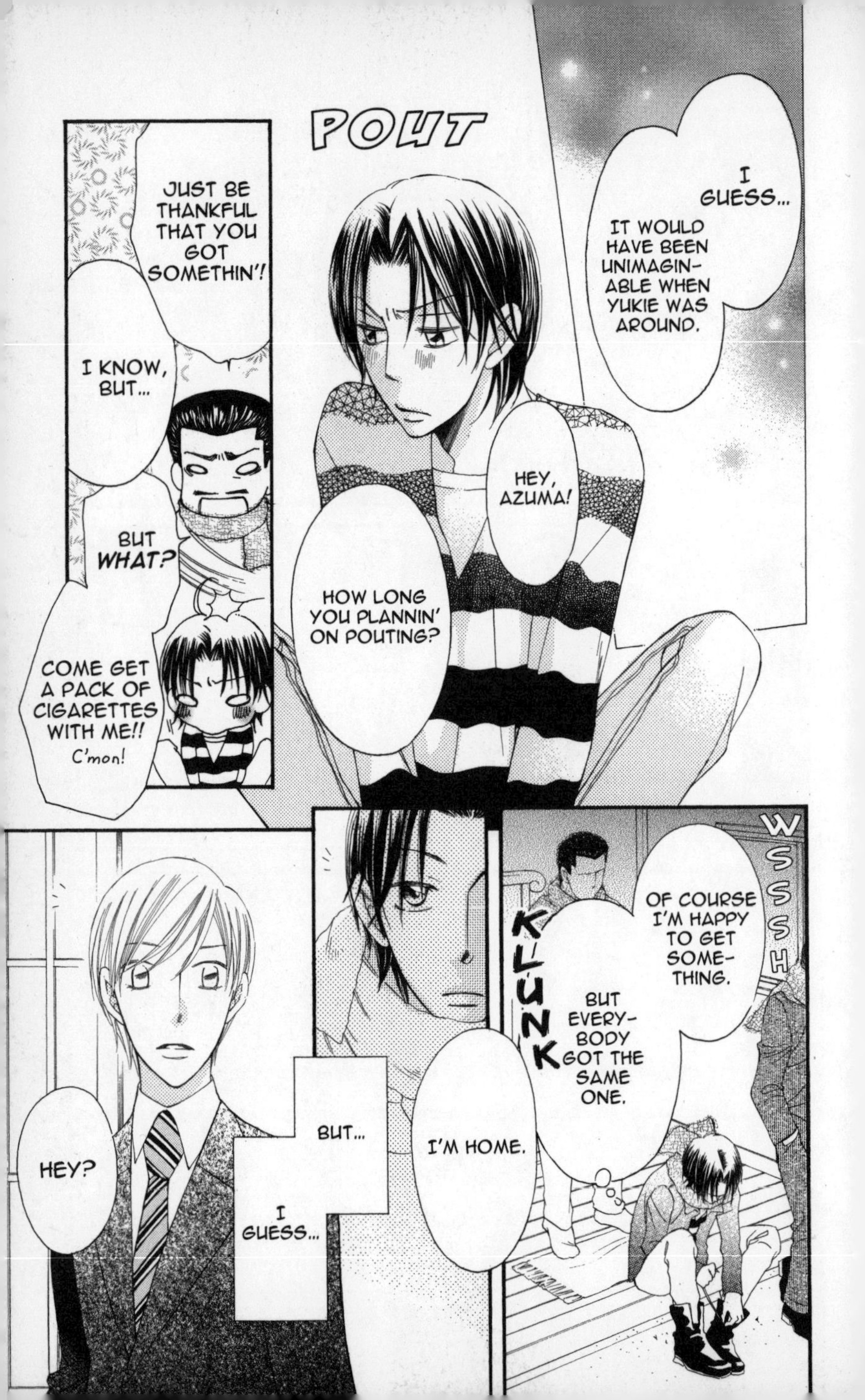
I GUESS...
IT WOULD HAVE BEEN UNIMAGIN-ABLE WHEN YUKIE WAS AROUND.
POUT
HEY, AZUMA!
HOW LONG YOU PLANNIN' ON POUTING?
JUST BE THANKFUL THAT YOU GOT SOMETHIN'!
I KNOW, BUT...
BUT WHAT?
COME GET A PACK OF CIGARETTES WITH ME!!
C'mon!
WSSSH
OF COURSE I'M HAPPY TO GET SOME-THING.
BUT EVERY-BODY GOT THE SAME ONE.
KLUNK
I'M HOME.
BUT...
I GUESS...
HEY?

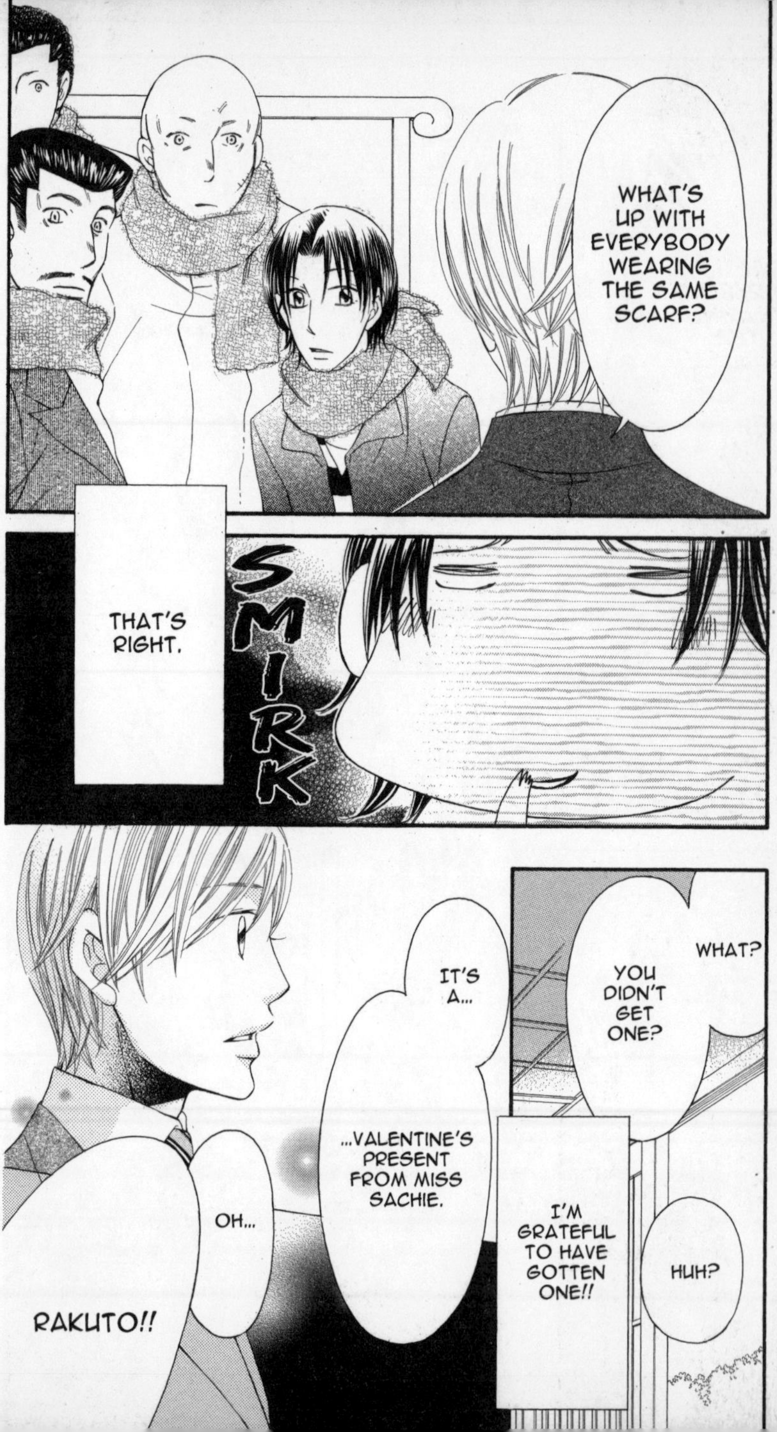
WHAT'S UP WITH EVERYBODY WEARING THE SAME SCARF?
THAT'S RIGHT.
SMIRK
WHAT?
YOU DIDN'T GET ONE?
IT'S A...
...VALENTINE'S PRESENT FROM MISS SACHIE.
I'M GRATEFUL TO HAVE GOTTEN ONE!!
HUH?
OH...
RAKUTO!!

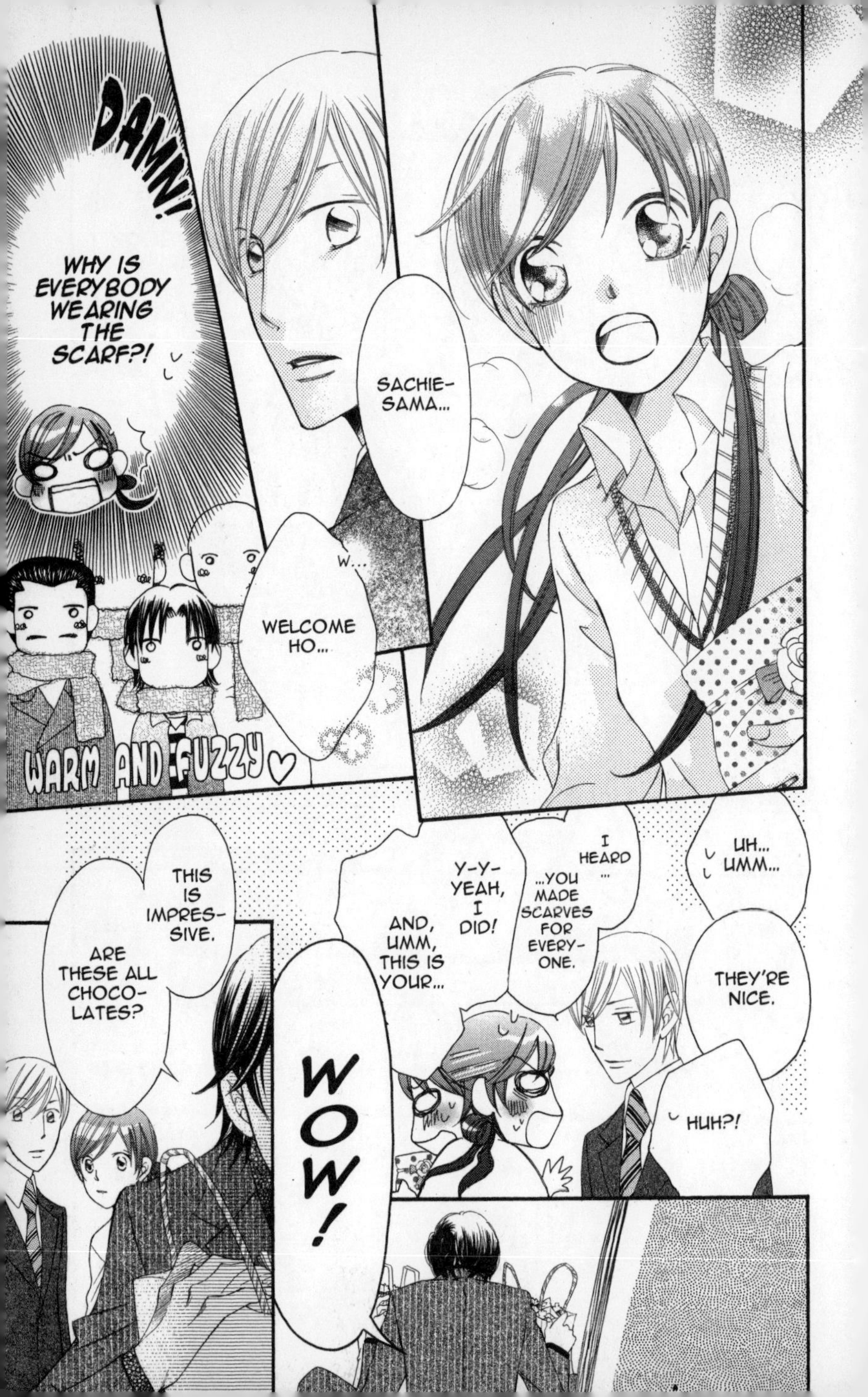
SACHIE-SAMA...
W...
WELCOME HO...
DAMN!
WHY IS EVERYBODY WEARING THE SCARF?!
WARM AND FUZZY♥
UH... UMM...
THEY'RE NICE.
HUH?!
I HEARD ...
...YOU MADE SCARVES FOR EVERYONE.
Y-Y-YEAH, I DID!
AND, UMM, THIS IS YOUR...
WOW!
THIS IS IMPRESSIVE.
ARE THESE ALL CHOCOLATES?

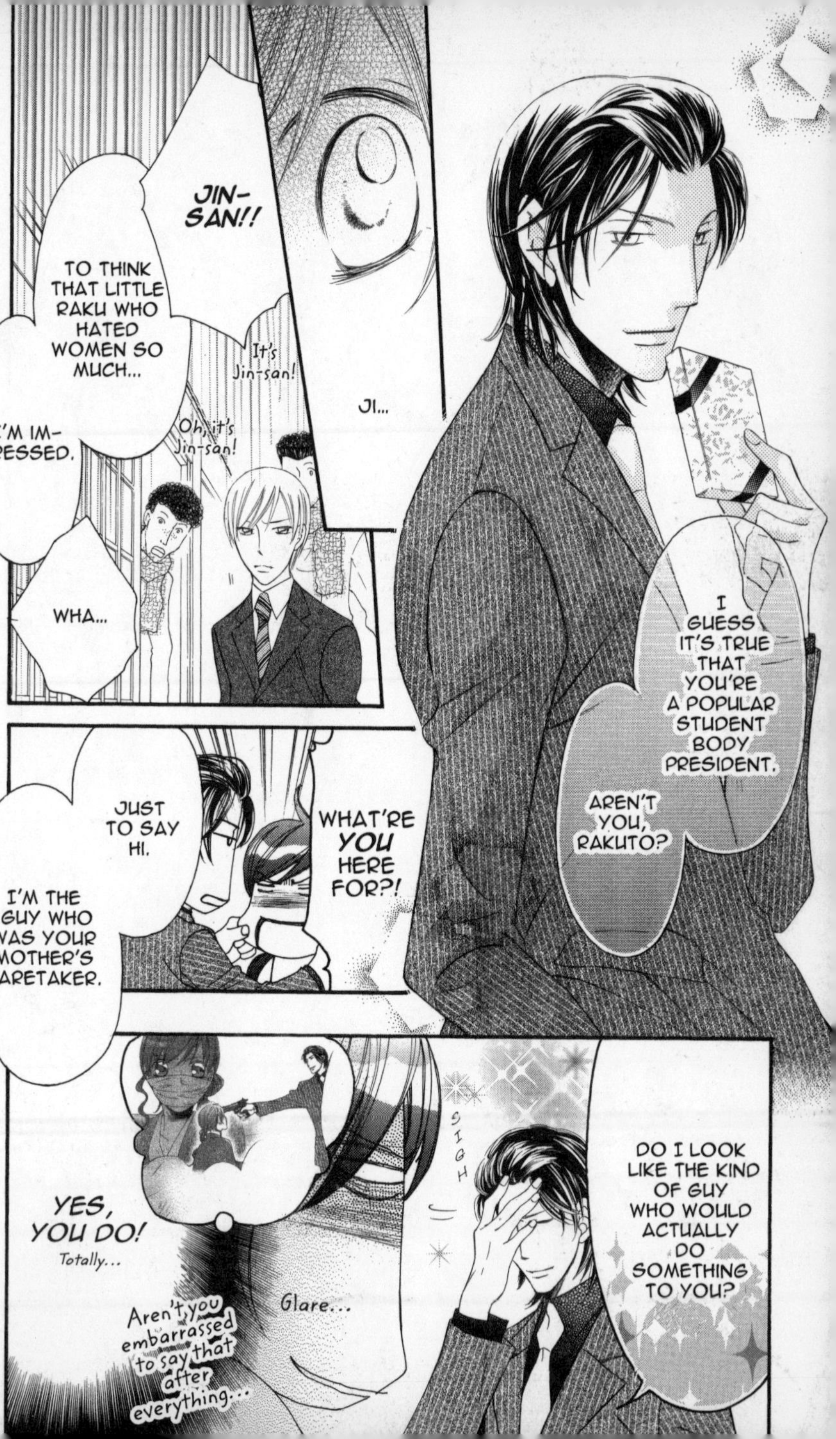
I GUESS IT'S TRUE THAT YOU'RE A POPULAR STUDENT BODY PRESIDENT.
AREN'T YOU, RAKUTO?
JI...
JIN-SAN!!
It's Jin-san!
TO THINK THAT LITTLE RAKU WHO HATED WOMEN SO MUCH...
I'M IM-PRESSED.
Oh, it's Jin-san!
WHA...
WHAT'RE *YOU* HERE FOR?!
JUST TO SAY HI.
I'M THE GUY WHO WAS YOUR MOTHER'S CARETAKER.
DO I LOOK LIKE THE KIND OF GUY WHO WOULD ACTUALLY DO SOMETHING TO YOU?
SIGH
YES, YOU DO!
Totally...
Glare...
Aren't you embarrassed to say that after everything...

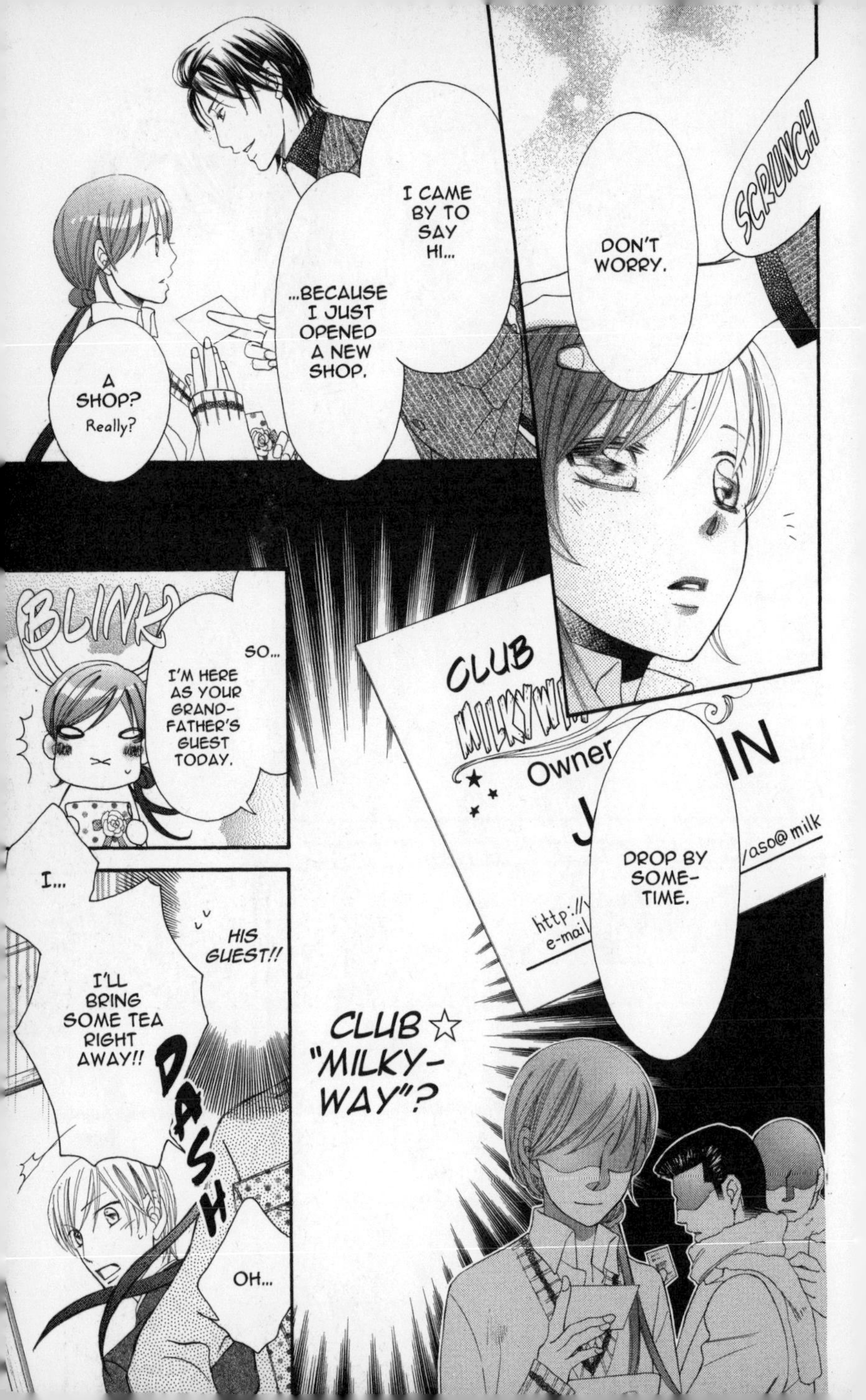
SCRUNCH
DON'T WORRY.
I CAME BY TO SAY HI...
...BECAUSE I JUST OPENED A NEW SHOP.
A SHOP? Really?
DROP BY SOME-TIME.
CLUB MILKYWA
Owner
IN
J
/aso@milk
http://
e-mail
CLUB☆ "MILKY-WAY"?
BLINK
SO... I'M HERE AS YOUR GRAND-FATHER'S GUEST TODAY.
I...
HIS GUEST!!
I'LL BRING SOME TEA RIGHT AWAY!!
DASH
OH...

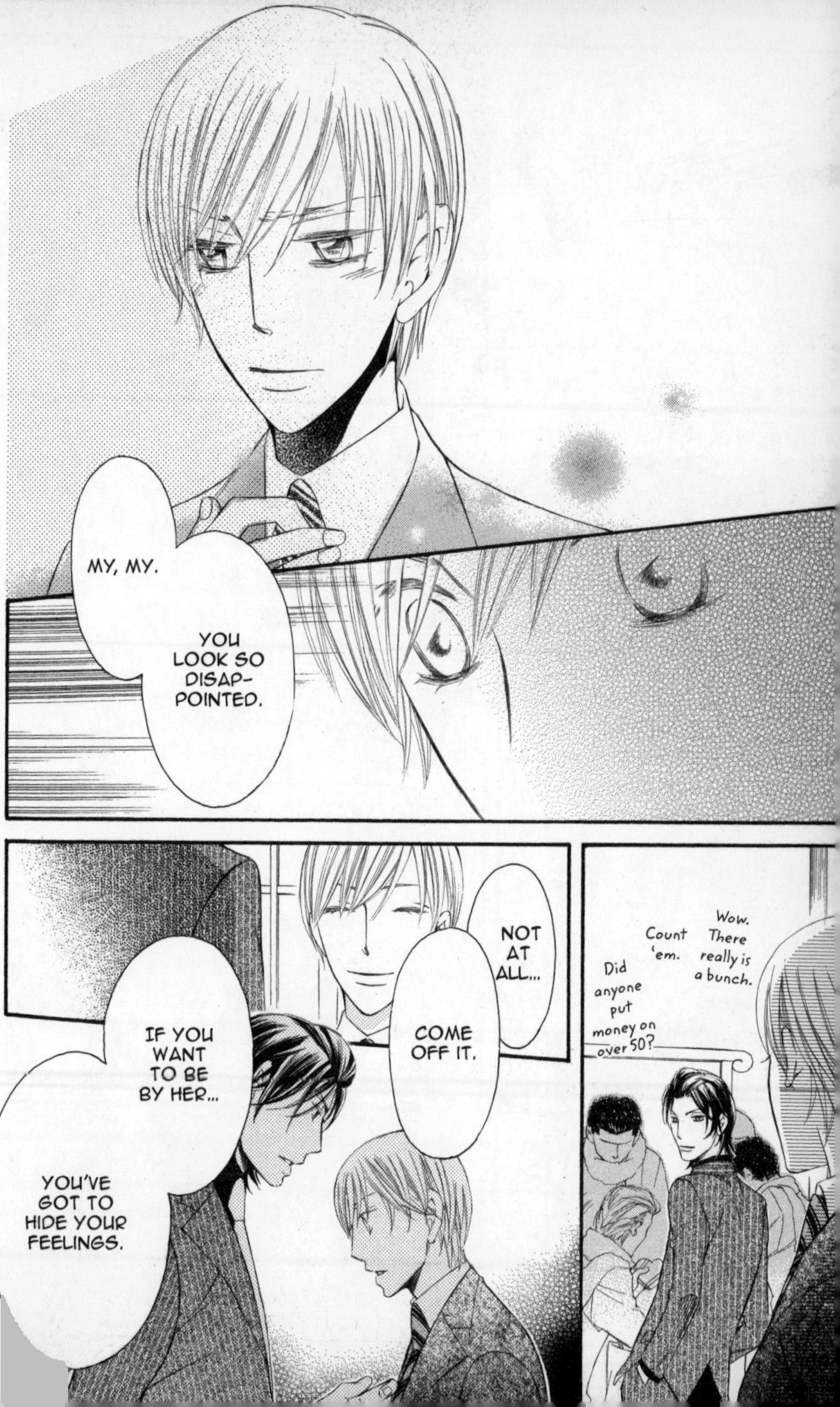
MY, MY.
YOU LOOK SO DISAP-POINTED.
Wow. There really is a bunch.
Count 'em.
Did anyone put money on over 50?
NOT AT ALL...
COME OFF IT.
IF YOU WANT TO BE BY HER...
YOU'VE GOT TO HIDE YOUR FEELINGS.

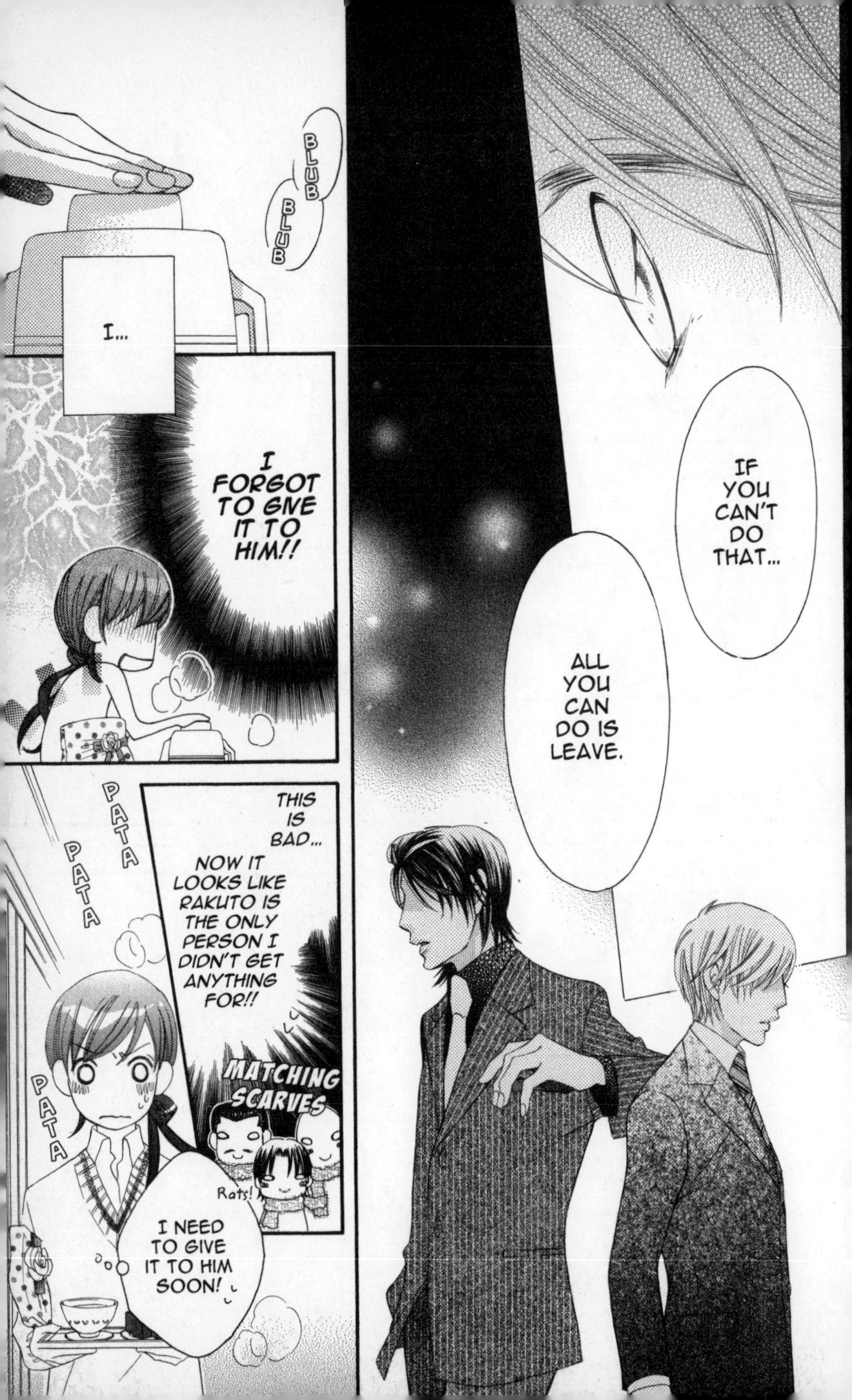
IF YOU CAN'T DO THAT...
ALL YOU CAN DO IS LEAVE.
BLUB BLUB
I...
I FORGOT TO GIVE IT TO HIM!!
THIS IS BAD...
NOW IT LOOKS LIKE RAKUTO IS THE ONLY PERSON I DIDN'T GET ANYTHING FOR!!
PATA PATA PATA
MATCHING SCARVES
Rats!
PATA
I NEED TO GIVE IT TO HIM SOON!

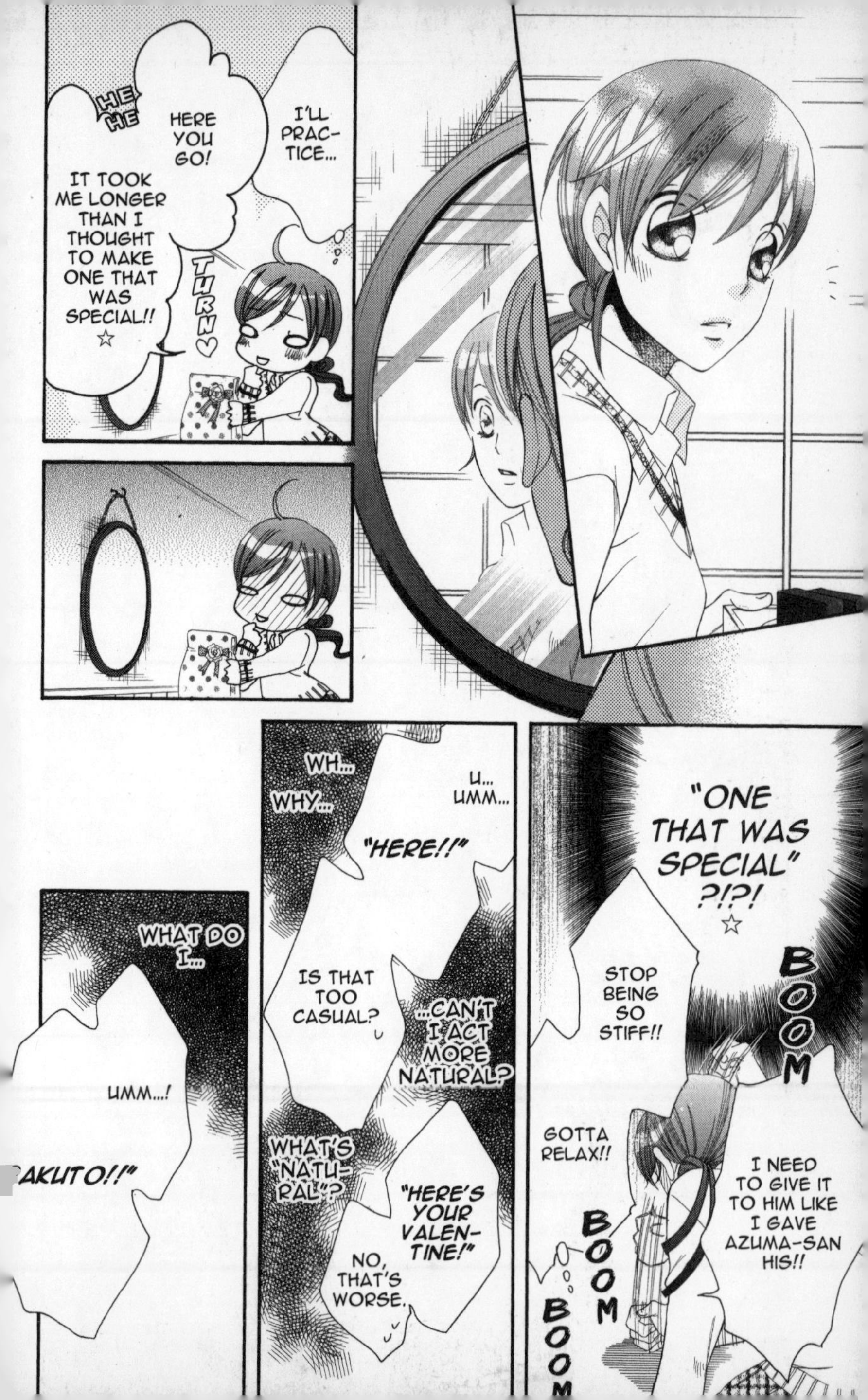
HE HE
HERE YOU GO!
IT TOOK ME LONGER THAN I THOUGHT TO MAKE ONE THAT WAS SPECIAL!! ☆
TURN♡
I'LL PRAC-TICE...
"ONE THAT WAS SPECIAL" ?!?! ☆
STOP BEING SO STIFF!!
BOOM
GOTTA RELAX!!
I NEED TO GIVE IT TO HIM LIKE I GAVE AZUMA-SAN HIS!!
BOOM
BOOM
U... UMM...
WH... WHY...
"HERE!!"
IS THAT TOO CASUAL?
...CAN'T I ACT MORE NATURAL?
"HERE'S YOUR VALEN-TINE!"
NO, THAT'S WORSE.
WHAT'S "NATU-RAL"?
WHAT DO I...
UMM...!
AKUTO!!"

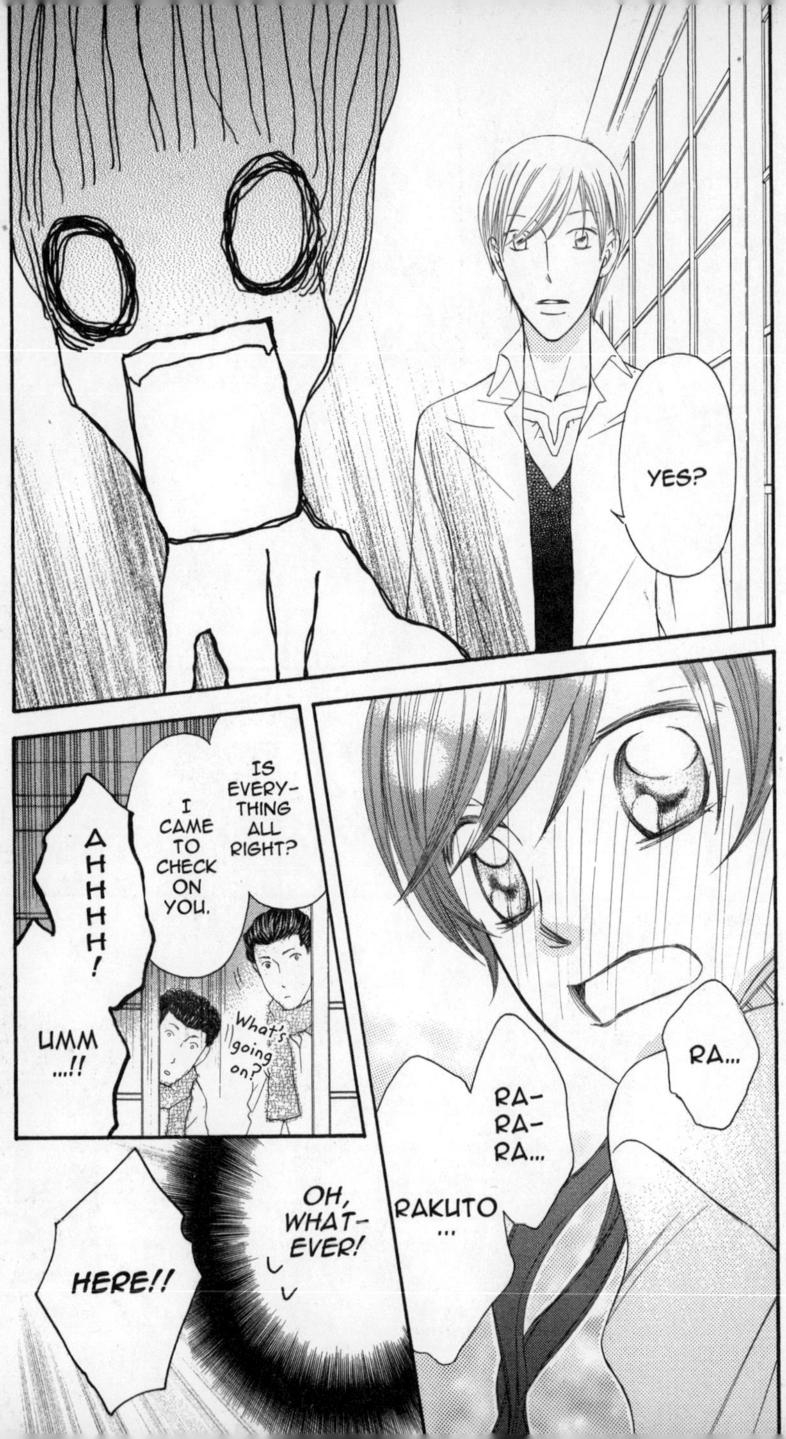
YES?
RA...
RA-RA-RA...
RAKUTO...
IS EVERYTHING ALL RIGHT?
I CAME TO CHECK ON YOU.
AHHHH!
UMM ...!!
What's going on?
OH, WHAT-EVER!
HERE!!

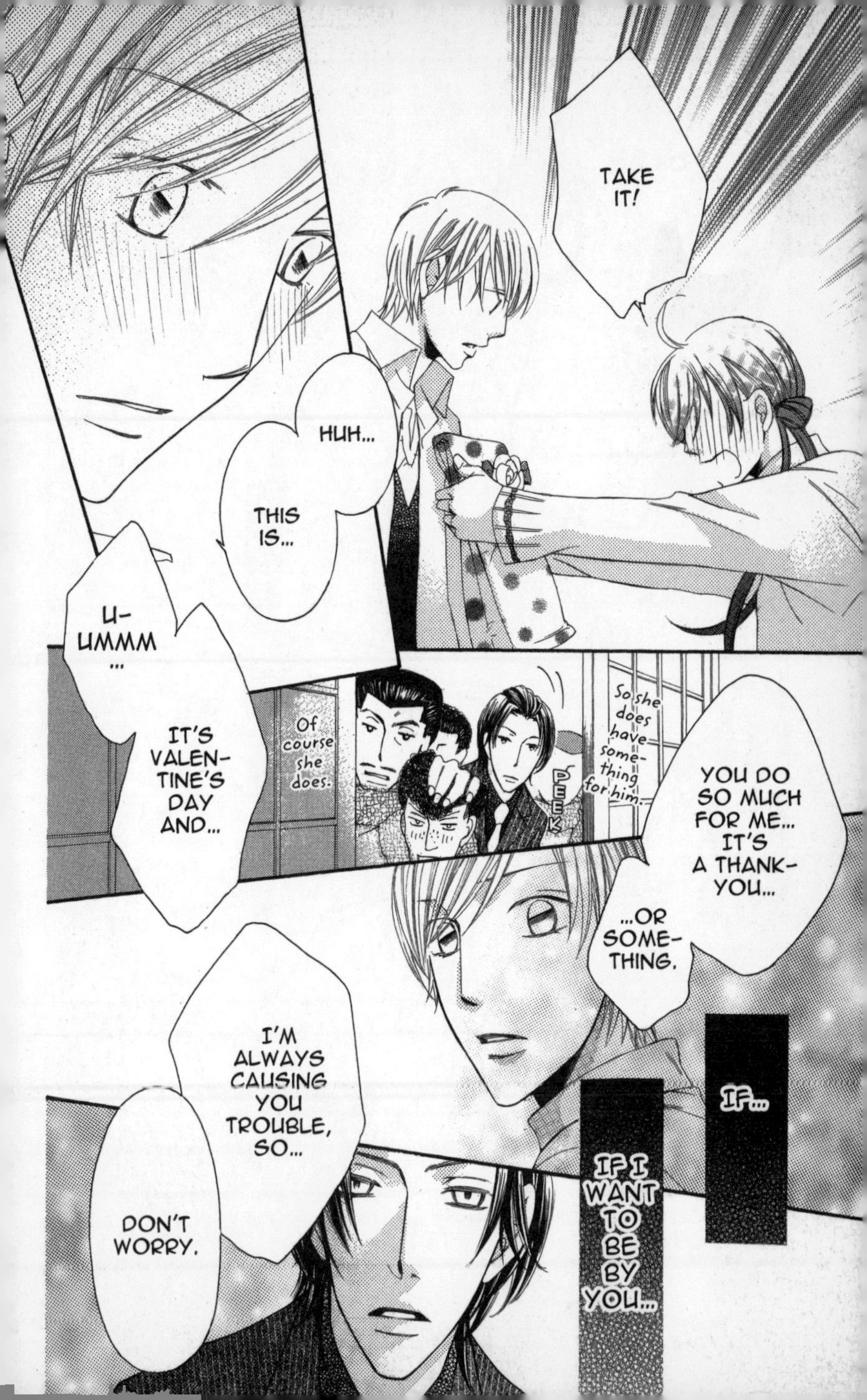
TAKE IT!
HUH...
THIS IS...
U-UMMM...
IT'S VALENTINE'S DAY AND...
So she does have something for him.
PEEK
Of course she does.
YOU DO SO MUCH FOR ME... IT'S A THANK-YOU...
...OR SOMETHING.
I'M ALWAYS CAUSING YOU TROUBLE, SO...
IF...
IF I WANT TO BE BY YOU...
DON'T WORRY.

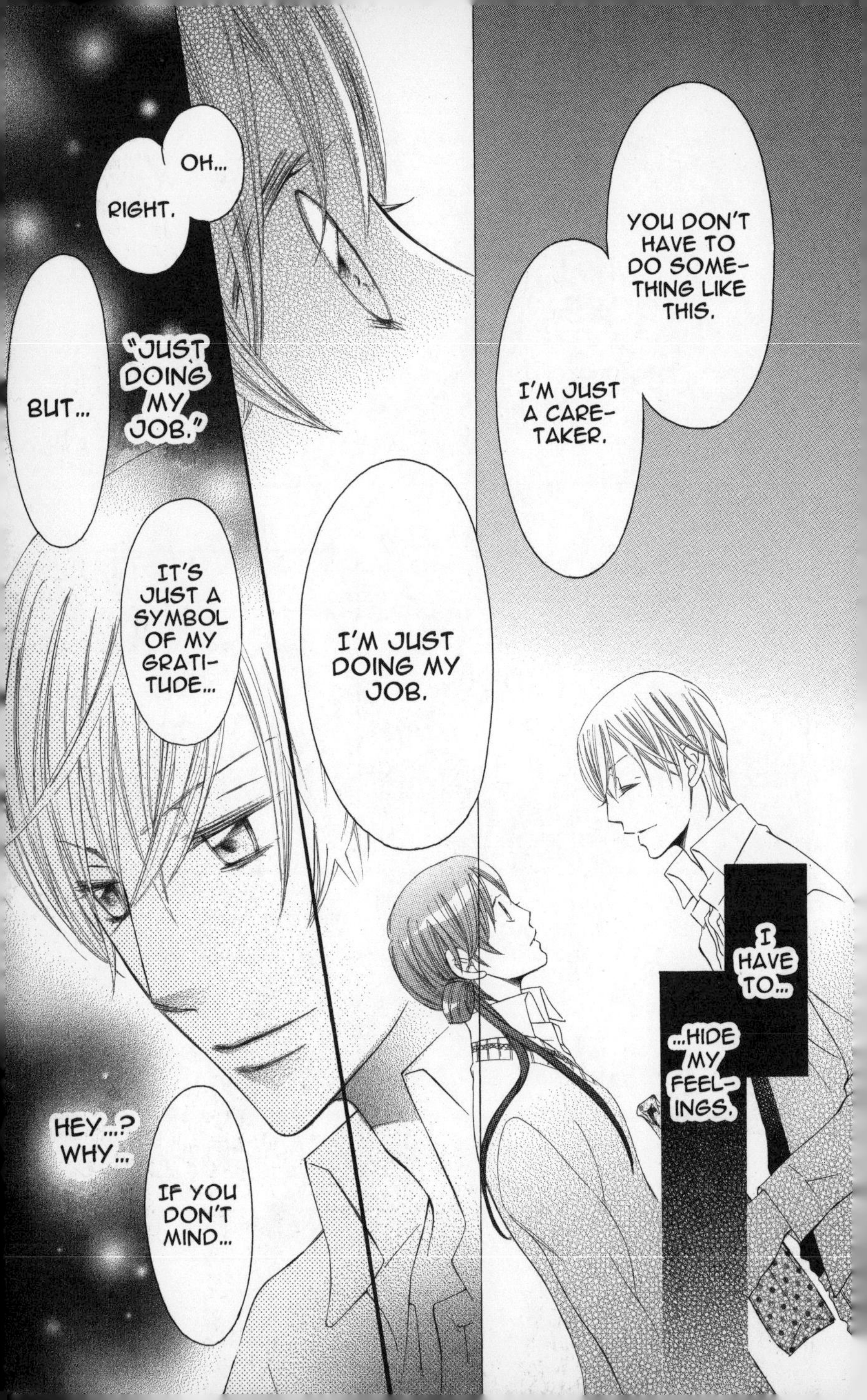
YOU DON'T HAVE TO DO SOME-THING LIKE THIS.
I'M JUST A CARE-TAKER.
I HAVE TO...
...HIDE MY FEEL-INGS.
I'M JUST DOING MY JOB.
OH... RIGHT.
"JUST DOING MY JOB."
BUT...
IT'S JUST A SYMBOL OF MY GRATI-TUDE...
IF YOU DON'T MIND...
HEY...? WHY...

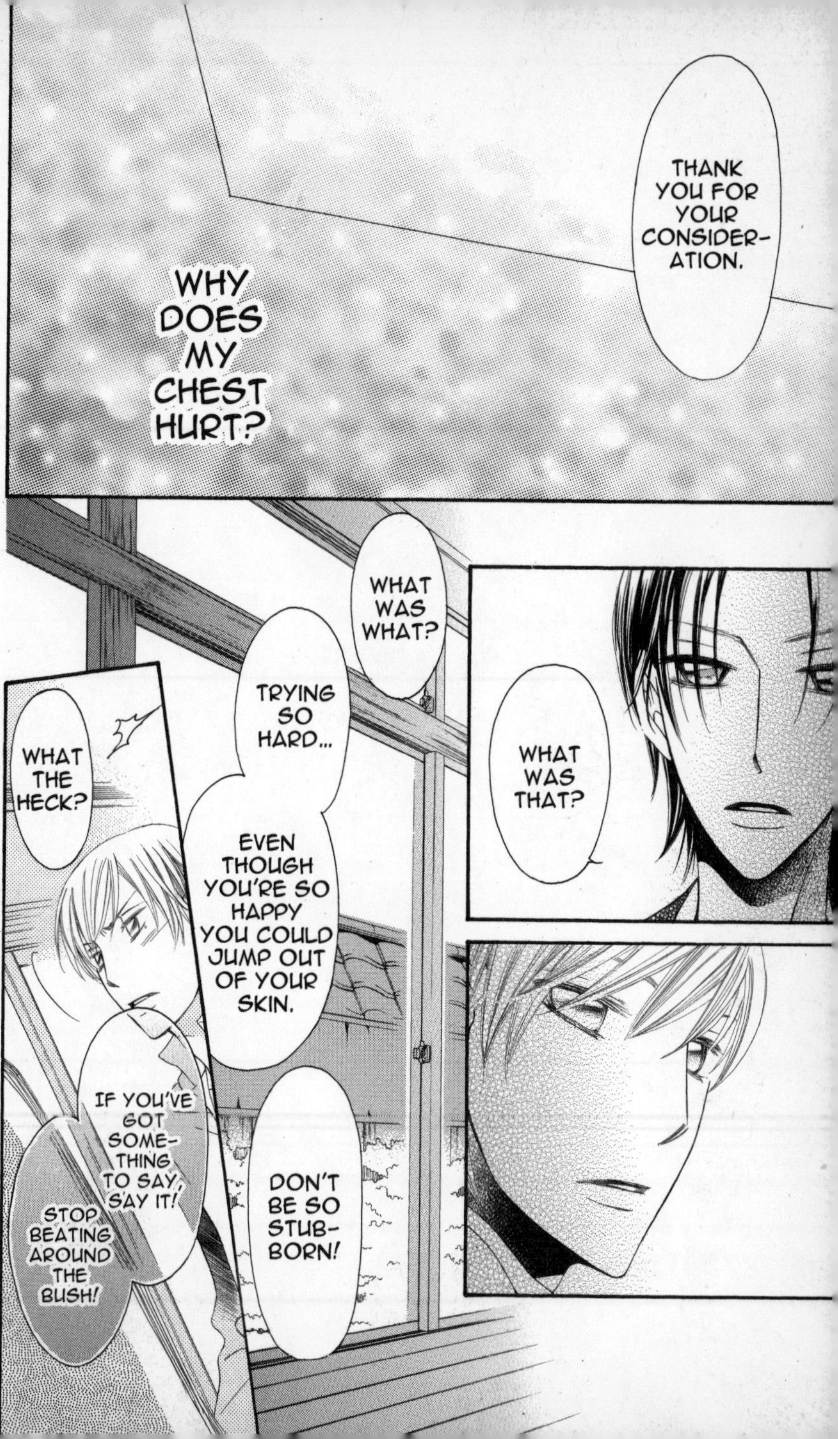
THANK YOU FOR YOUR CONSIDER-ATION.
WHY DOES MY CHEST HURT?
WHAT WAS THAT?
WHAT WAS WHAT?
TRYING SO HARD...
EVEN THOUGH YOU'RE SO HAPPY YOU COULD JUMP OUT OF YOUR SKIN.
DON'T BE SO STUB-BORN!
WHAT THE HECK?
IF YOU'VE GOT SOME-THING TO SAY, SAY IT!
STOP BEATING AROUND THE BUSH!

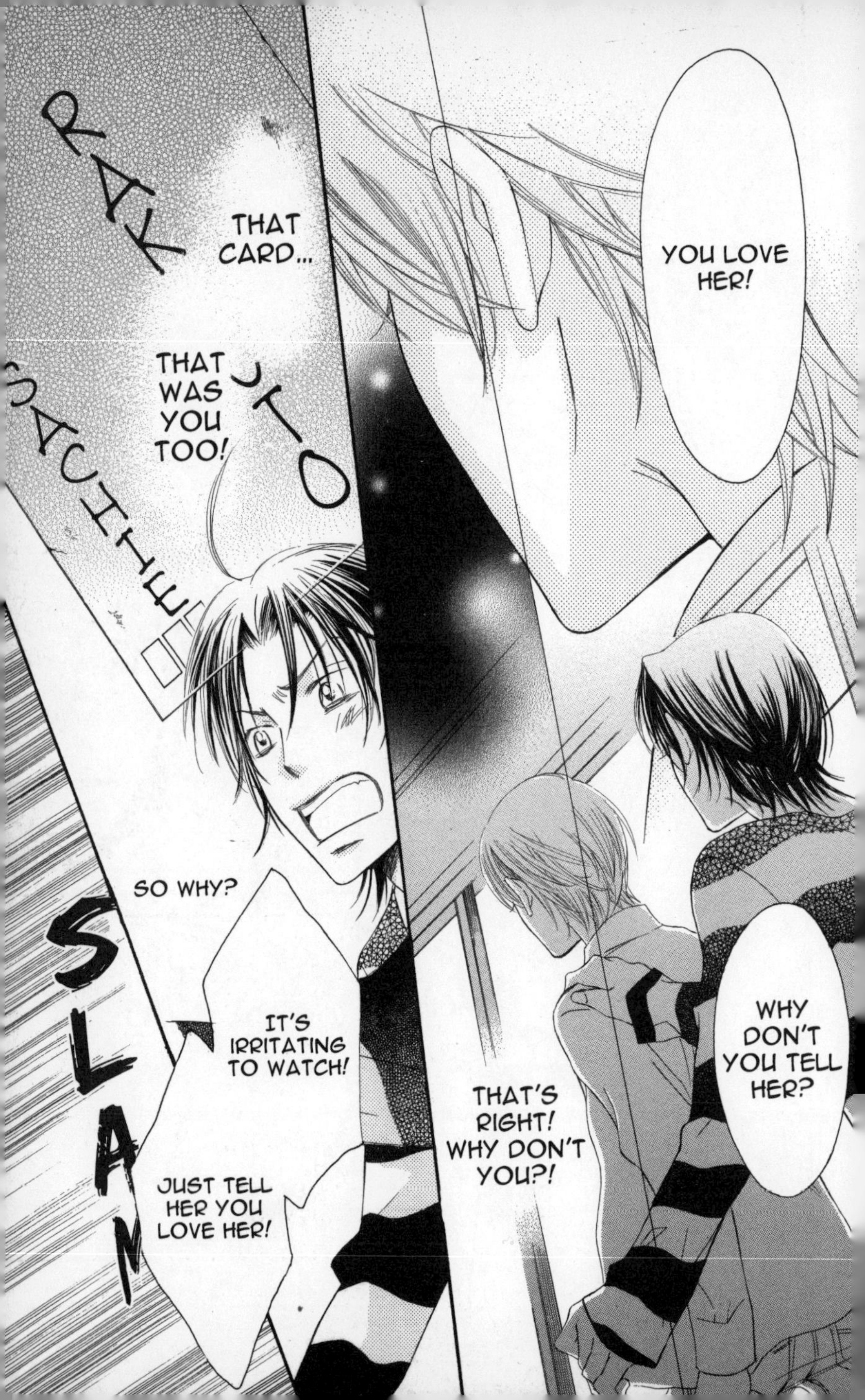
YOU LOVE HER!
WHY DON'T YOU TELL HER?
THAT'S RIGHT! WHY DON'T YOU?!
THAT CARD...
THAT WAS YOU TOO!
SO WHY?
IT'S IRRITATING TO WATCH!
JUST TELL HER YOU LOVE HER!
SLAM

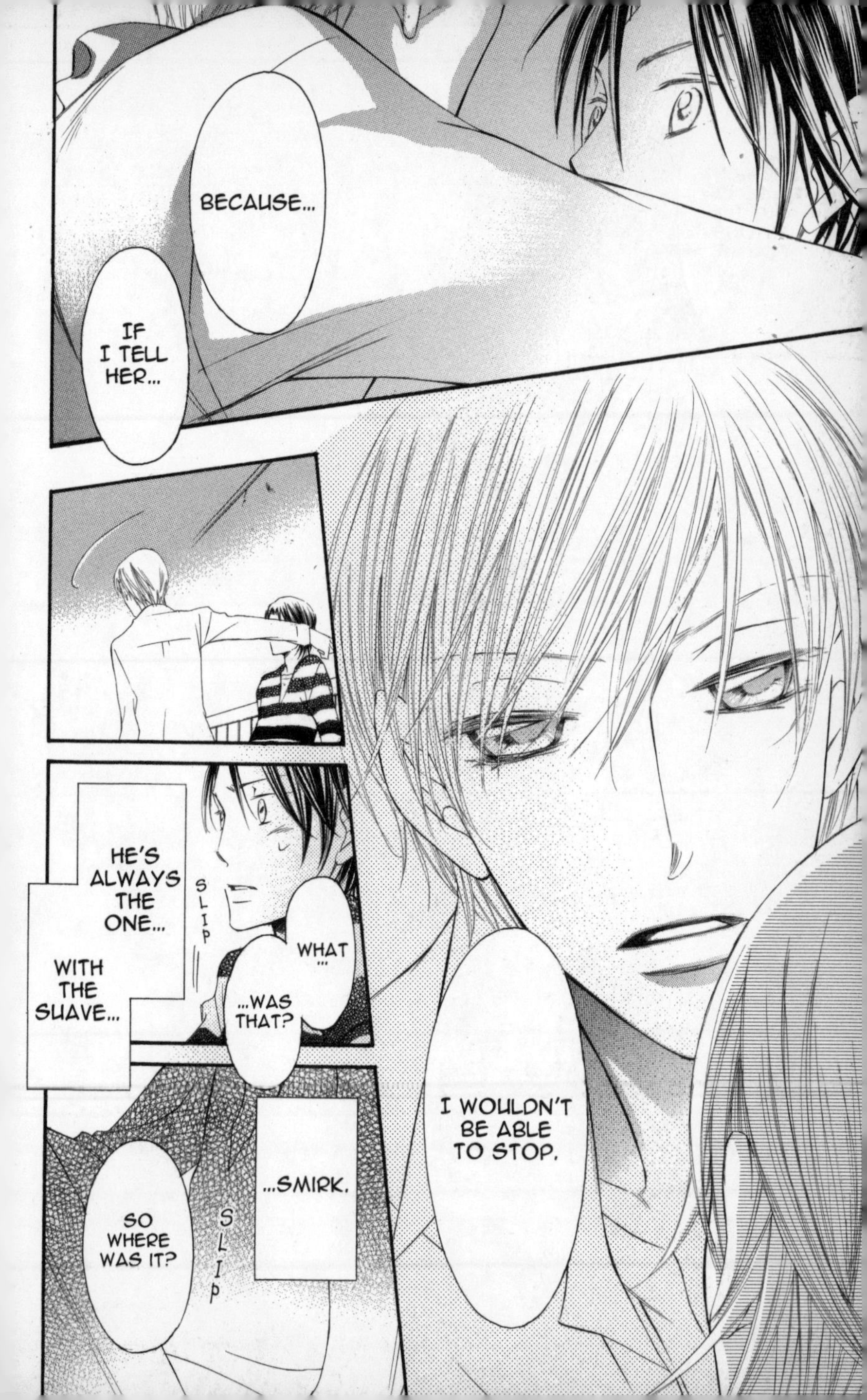
BECAUSE...
IF I TELL HER...
I WOULDN'T BE ABLE TO STOP.
HE'S ALWAYS THE ONE...
WITH THE SUAVE...
SLIP
WHAT...
...WAS THAT?
...SMIRK.
SLIP
SO WHERE WAS IT?

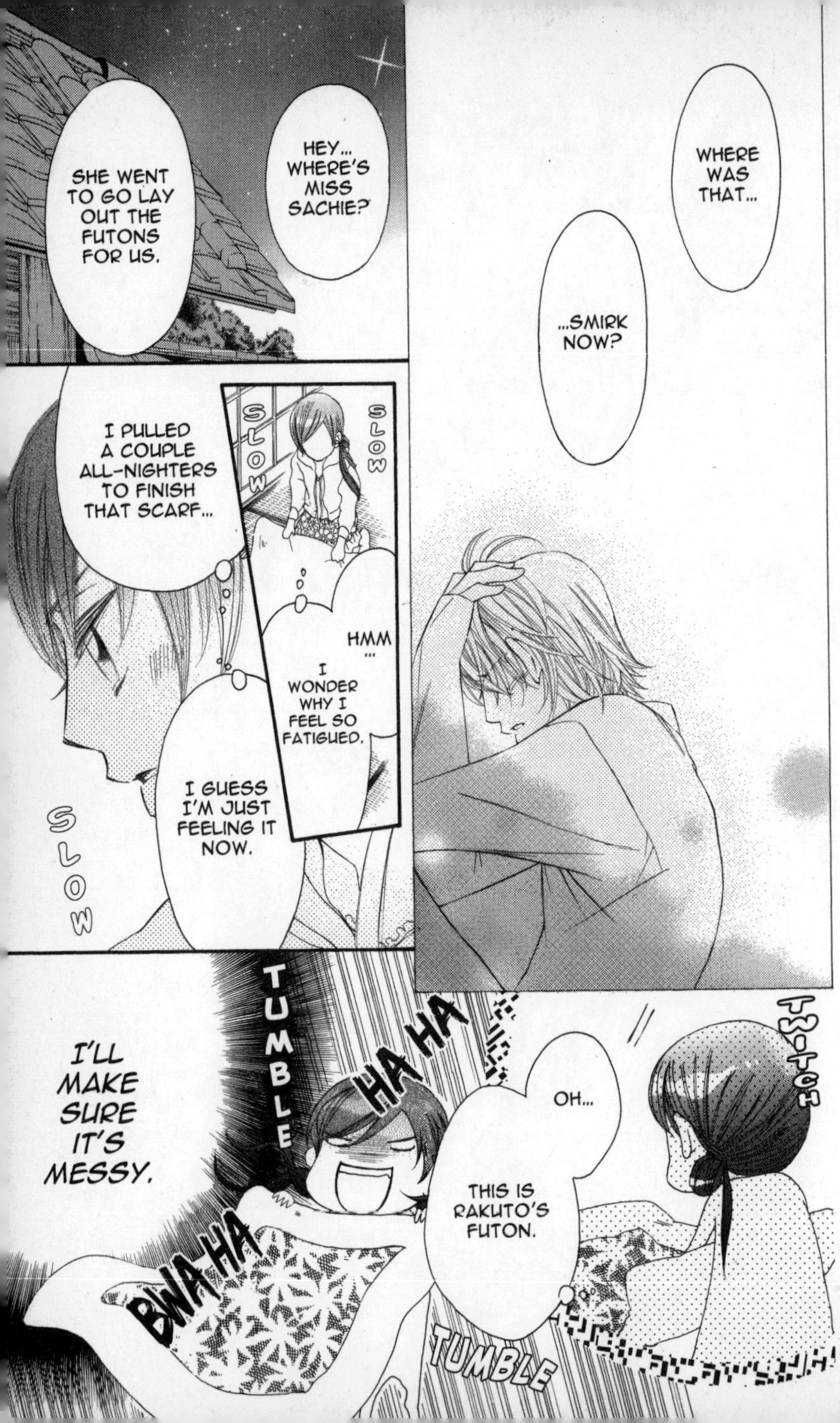
WHERE WAS THAT...
...SMIRK NOW?
HEY... WHERE'S MISS SACHIE?
SHE WENT TO GO LAY OUT THE FUTONS FOR US.
SLOW
SLOW
HMM...
I WONDER WHY I FEEL SO FATIGUED.
I PULLED A COUPLE ALL-NIGHTERS TO FINISH THAT SCARF...
I GUESS I'M JUST FEELING IT NOW.
SLOW
TWITCH
OH...
THIS IS RAKUTO'S FUTON.
HA HA
TUMBLE
I'LL MAKE SURE IT'S MESSY.
BWA HA
TUMBLE

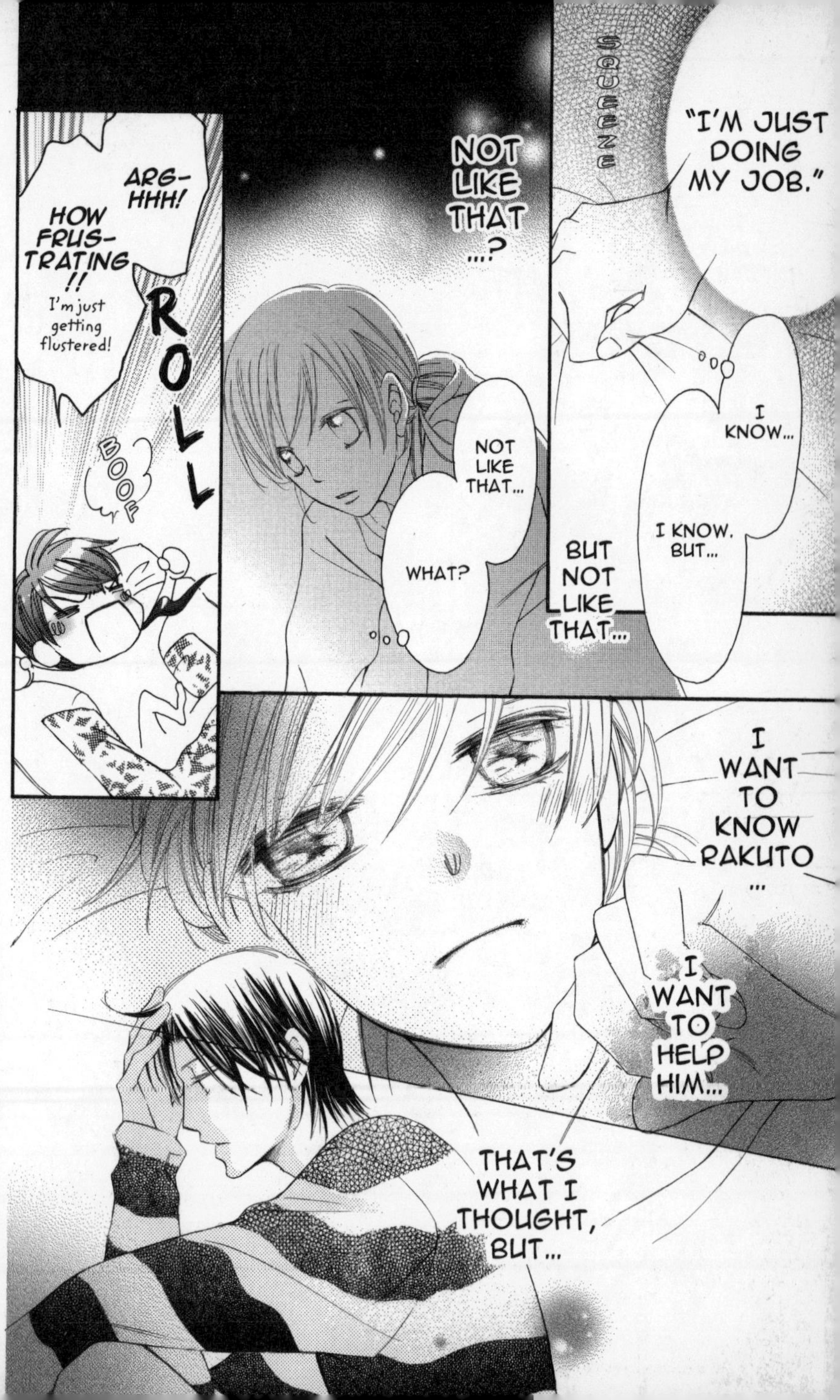
"I'M JUST DOING MY JOB."
SQUEEZE
I KNOW...
I KNOW. BUT...
BUT NOT LIKE THAT...
NOT LIKE THAT...
WHAT?
NOT LIKE THAT ...?
ARG-HHH! HOW FRUS-TRATING !!
I'm just getting flustered!
ROLL
BOOF
I WANT TO KNOW RAKUTO ...
I WANT TO HELP HIM...
THAT'S WHAT I THOUGHT, BUT...

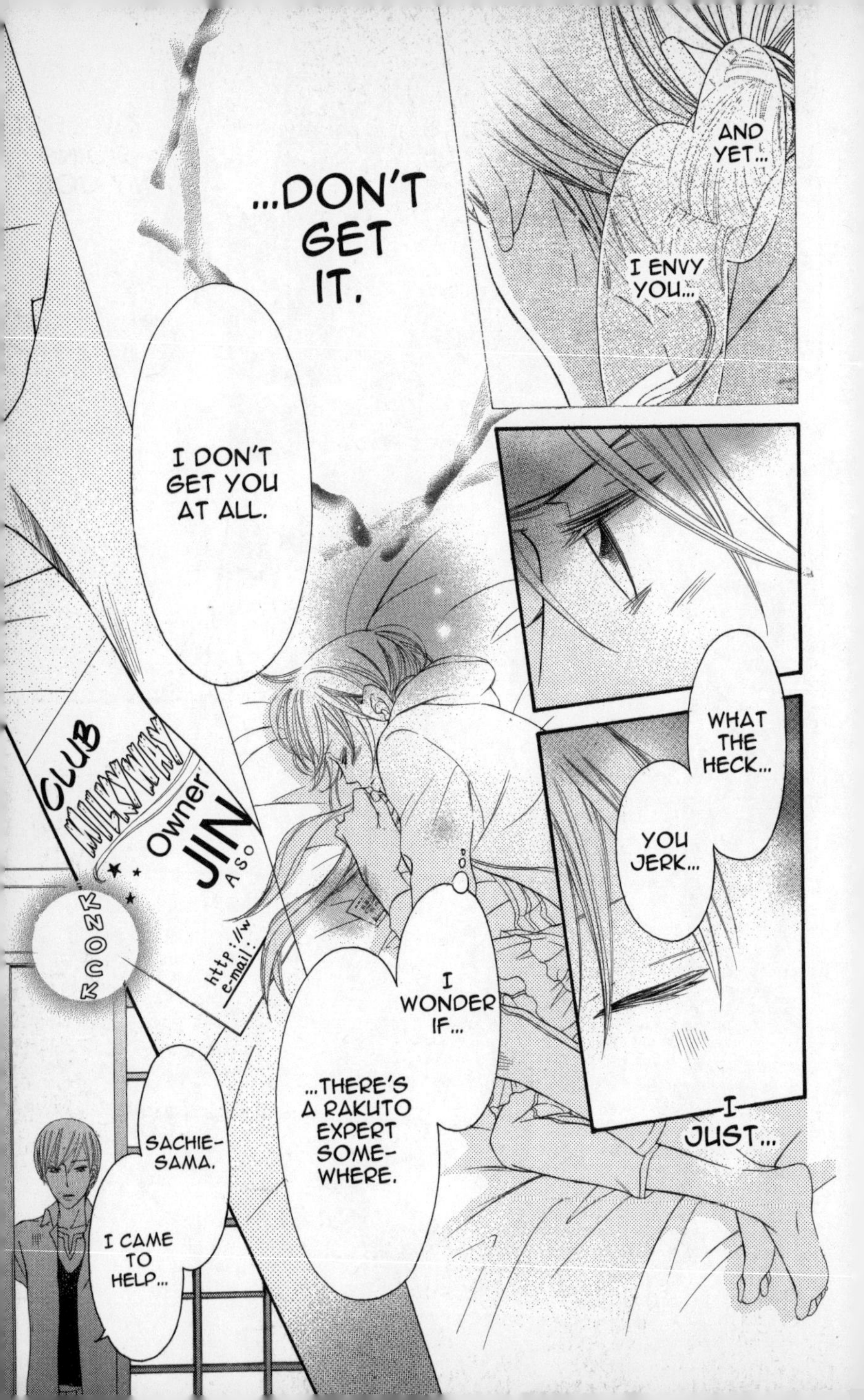
AND YET...
I ENVY YOU...
...DON'T GET IT.
I DON'T GET YOU AT ALL.
WHAT THE HECK...
YOU JERK...
I JUST...
I WONDER IF...
...THERE'S A RAKUTO EXPERT SOME-WHERE.
CLUB
Owner JIN ASO
http://w
e-mail:
KNOCK
SACHIE-SAMA.
I CAME TO HELP...

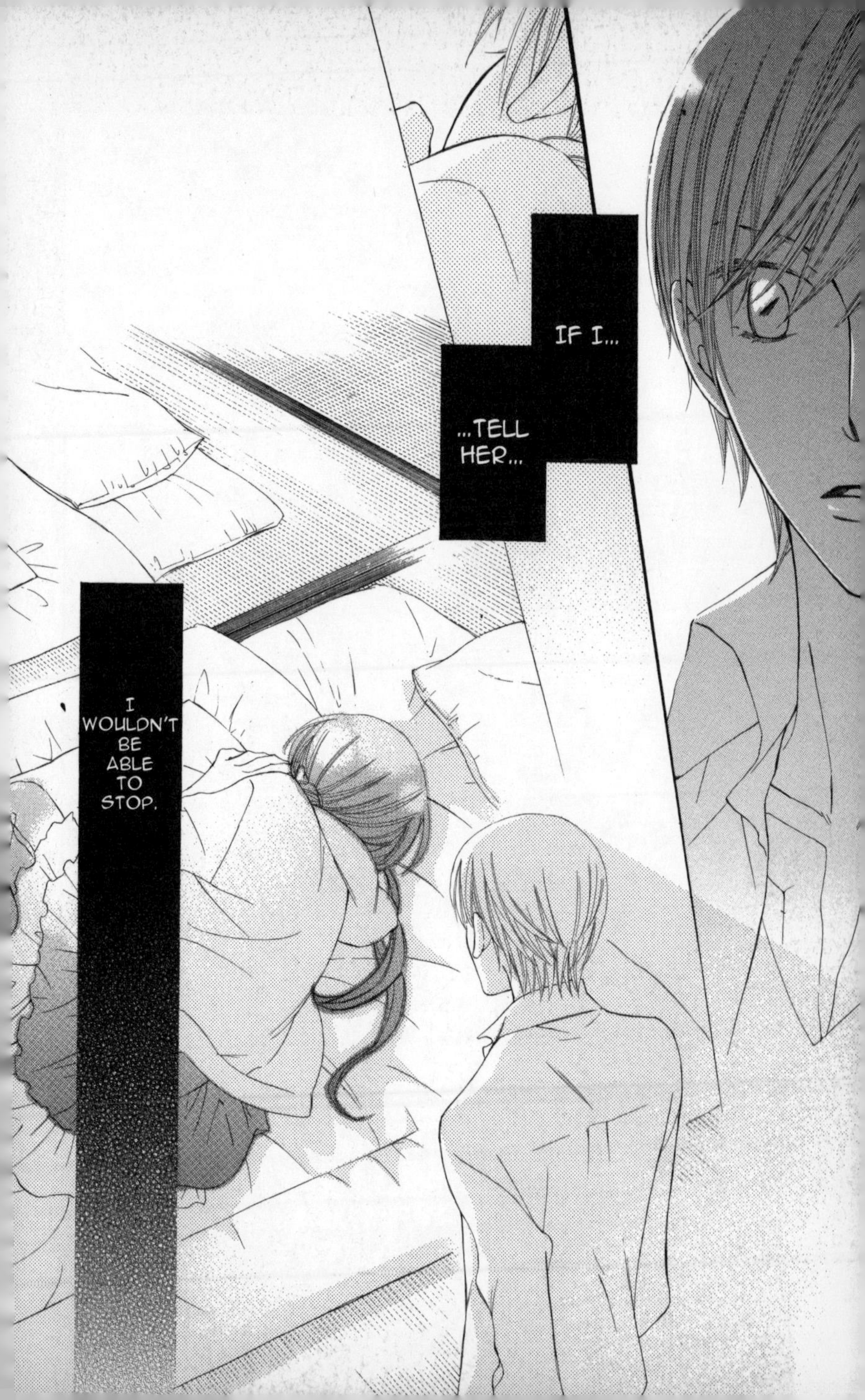
IF I...
...TELL HER...
I WOULDN'T BE ABLE TO STOP.

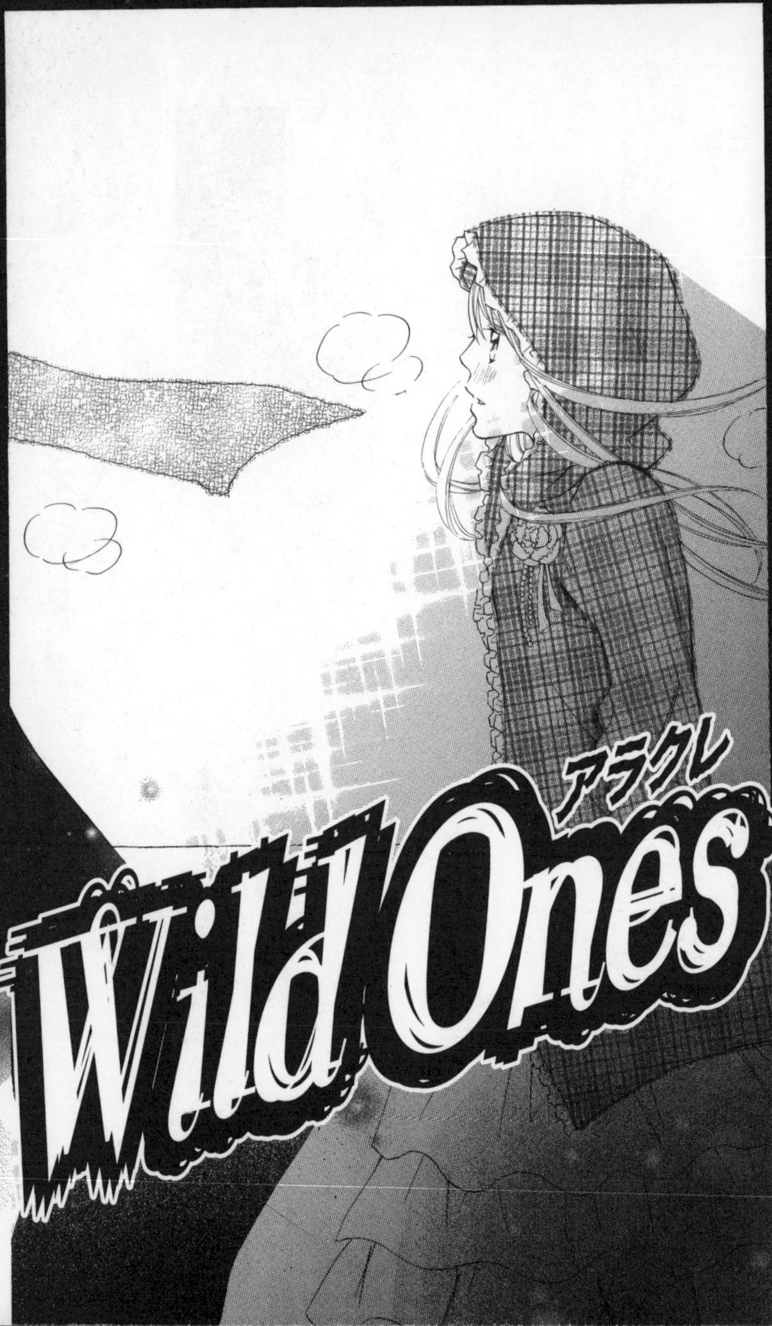
アラクレ
Wild Ones

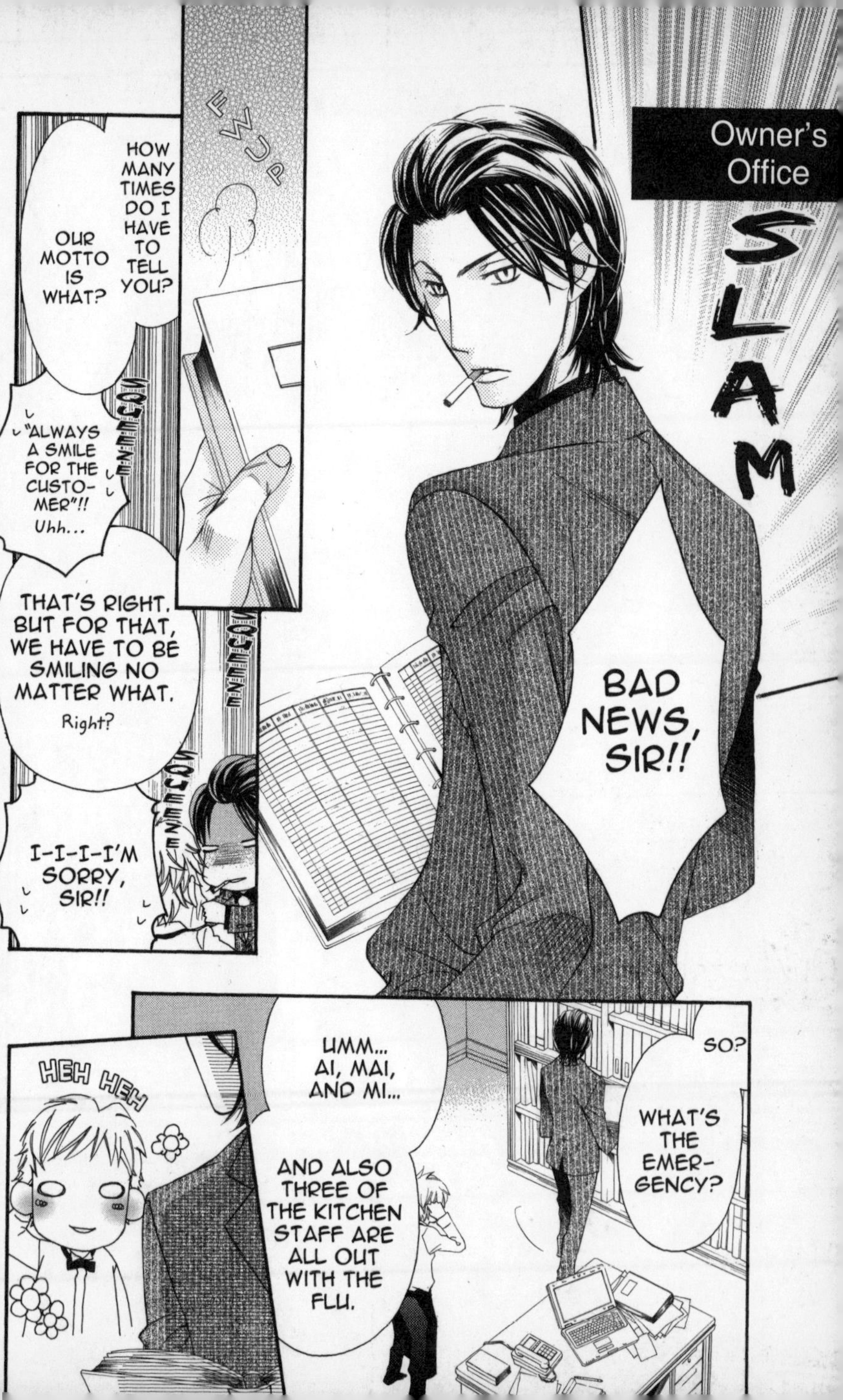
Owner's Office
SLAM
BAD NEWS, SIR!!
FWUP
HOW MANY TIMES DO I HAVE TO TELL YOU?
OUR MOTTO IS WHAT?
SQUEEEEE
"ALWAYS A SMILE FOR THE CUSTO-MER"!! Uhh...
SQUEEEEE
THAT'S RIGHT. BUT FOR THAT, WE HAVE TO BE SMILING NO MATTER WHAT. Right?
SQUEEEEE
I-I-I-I'M SORRY, SIR!!
SO?
WHAT'S THE EMER-GENCY?
UMM... AI, MAI, AND MI...
AND ALSO THREE OF THE KITCHEN STAFF ARE ALL OUT WITH THE FLU.
HEH HEH

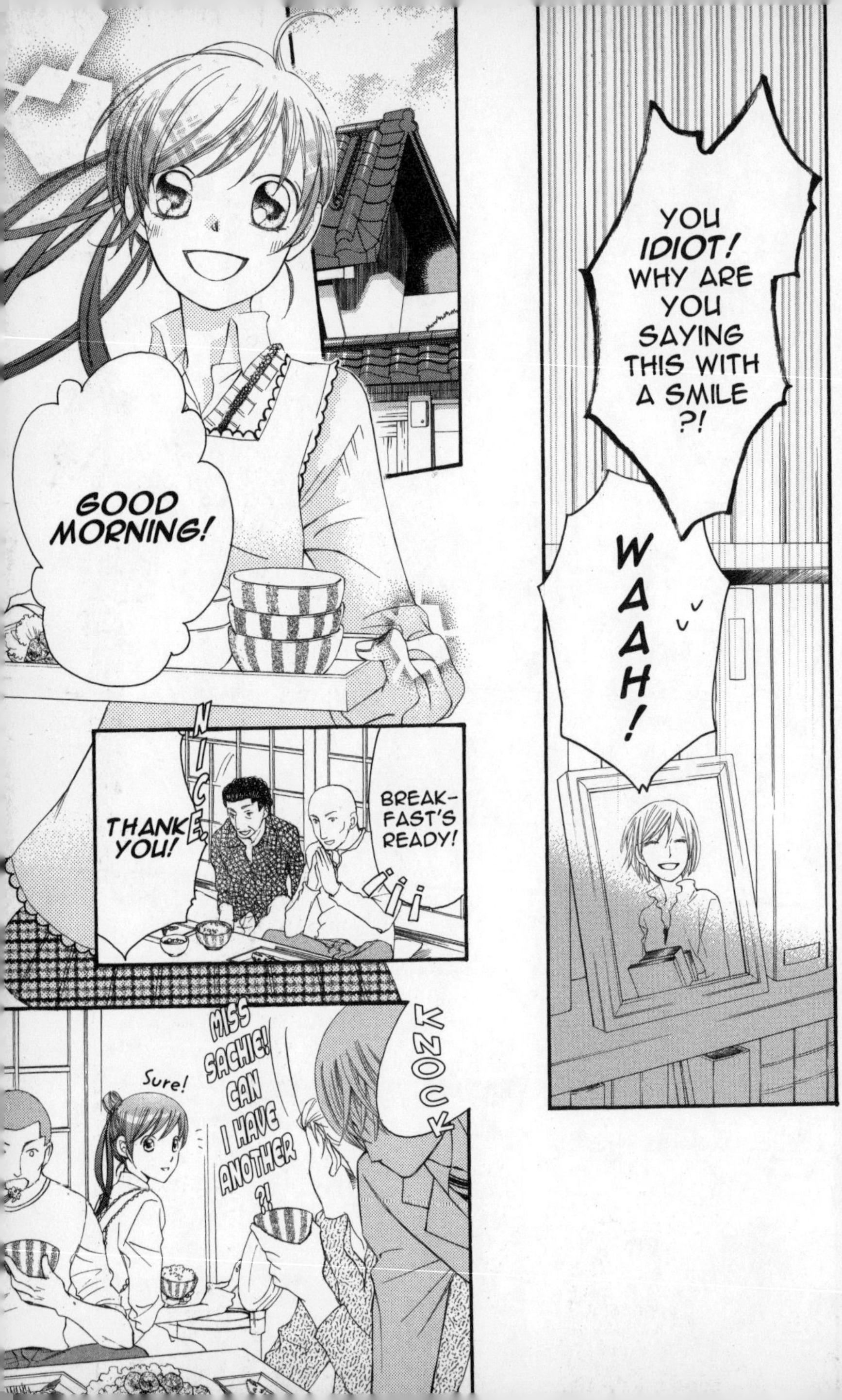
YOU IDIOT! WHY ARE YOU SAYING THIS WITH A SMILE ?!
WAAH!
GOOD MORNING!
BREAK-FAST'S READY!
!!!
NICE.
THANK YOU!
KNOCK
MISS SACHIE! CAN I HAVE ANOTHER ?!
Sure!

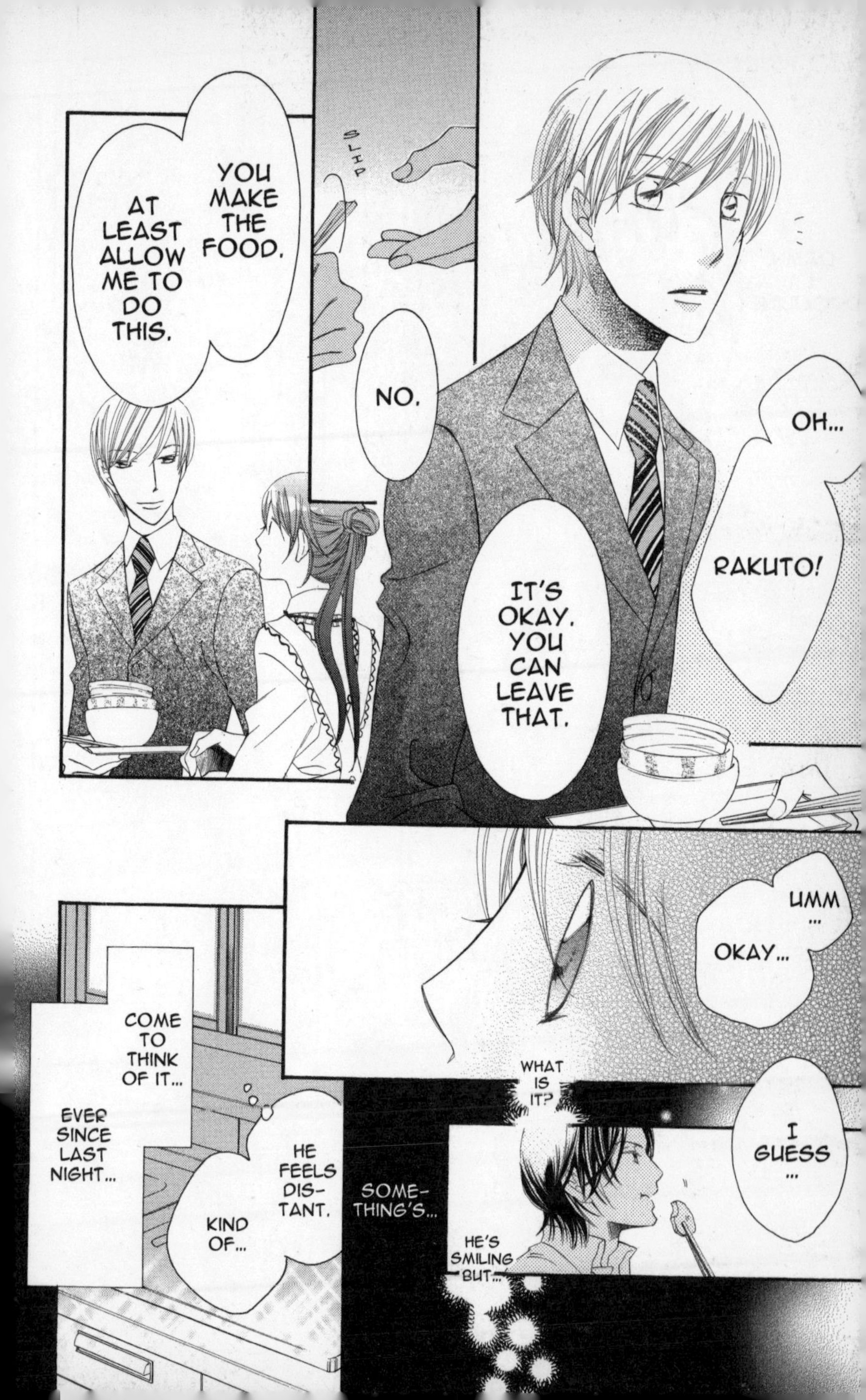
OH...
RAKUTO!
IT'S OKAY. YOU CAN LEAVE THAT.
SLIP
NO.
YOU MAKE THE FOOD.
AT LEAST ALLOW ME TO DO THIS.
UMM... OKAY...
WHAT IS IT?
I GUESS...
HE'S SMILING BUT...
SOME-THING'S...
HE FEELS DIS-TANT.
KIND OF...
COME TO THINK OF IT...
EVER SINCE LAST NIGHT...

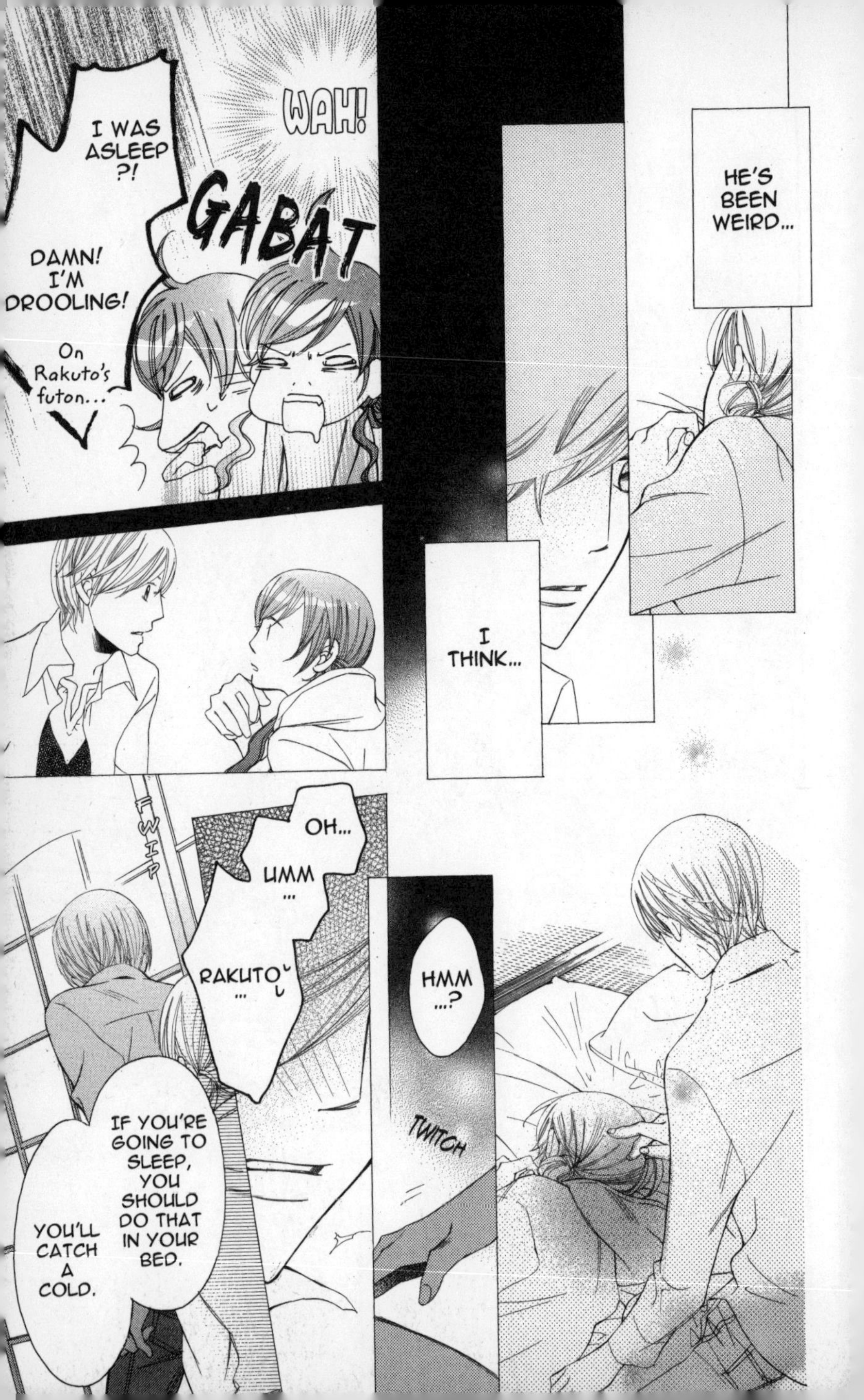
HE'S BEEN WEIRD...
I THINK...
WAH!
I WAS ASLEEP ?!
GABAT
DAMN! I'M DROOLING!
On Rakuto's futon...
HMM ...?
TWITCH
FWIP
OH...
UMM ...
RAKUTO ...
IF YOU'RE GOING TO SLEEP, YOU SHOULD DO THAT IN YOUR BED.
YOU'LL CATCH A COLD.

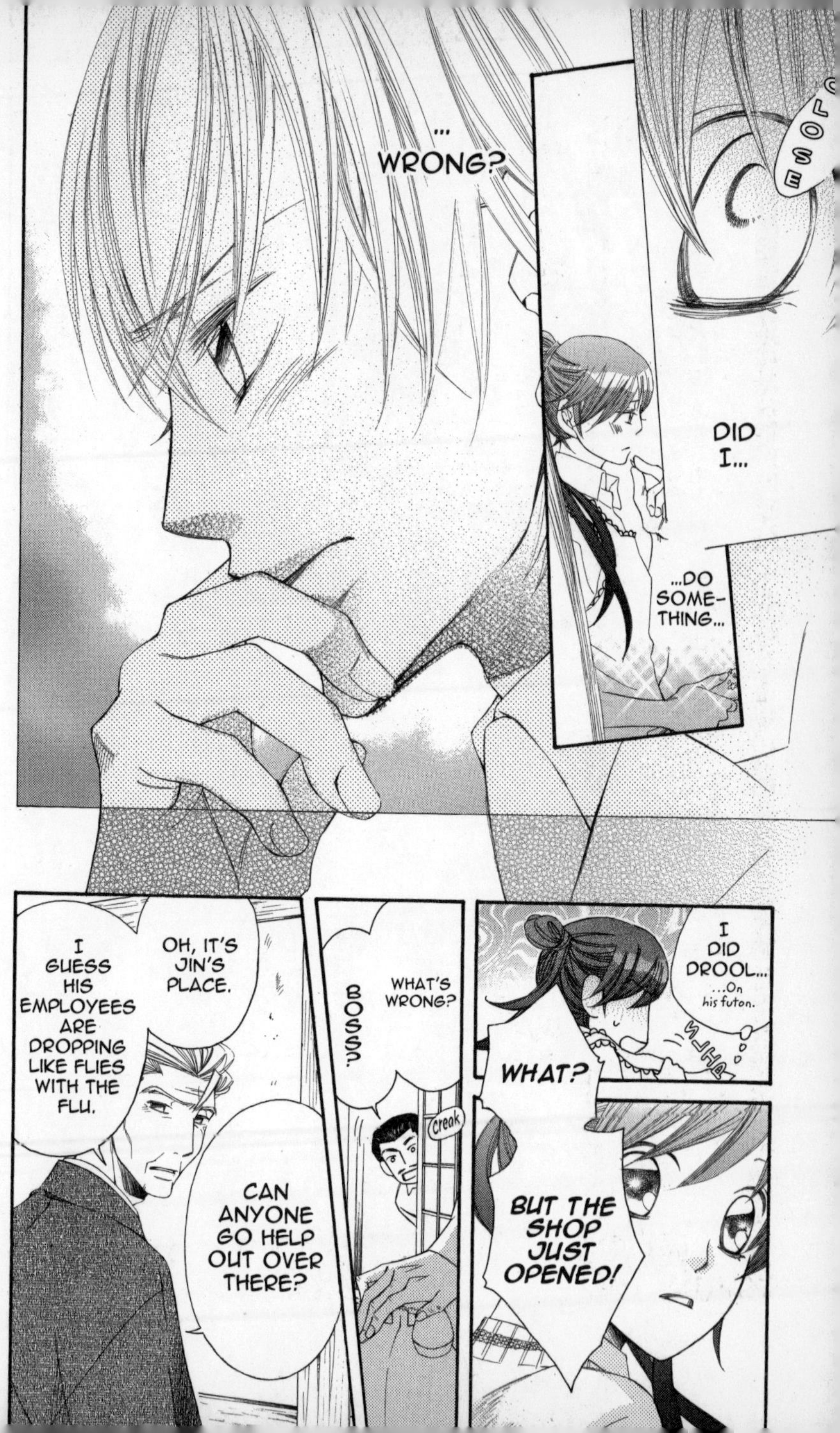
CLOSE
DID I...
...DO SOMETHING...
...WRONG?
I DID DROOL... ...On his futon.
WHAT?
BUT THE SHOP JUST OPENED!
Creak
BOSS?
WHAT'S WRONG?
OH, IT'S JIN'S PLACE.
I GUESS HIS EMPLOYEES ARE DROPPING LIKE FLIES WITH THE FLU.
CAN ANYONE GO HELP OUT OVER THERE?

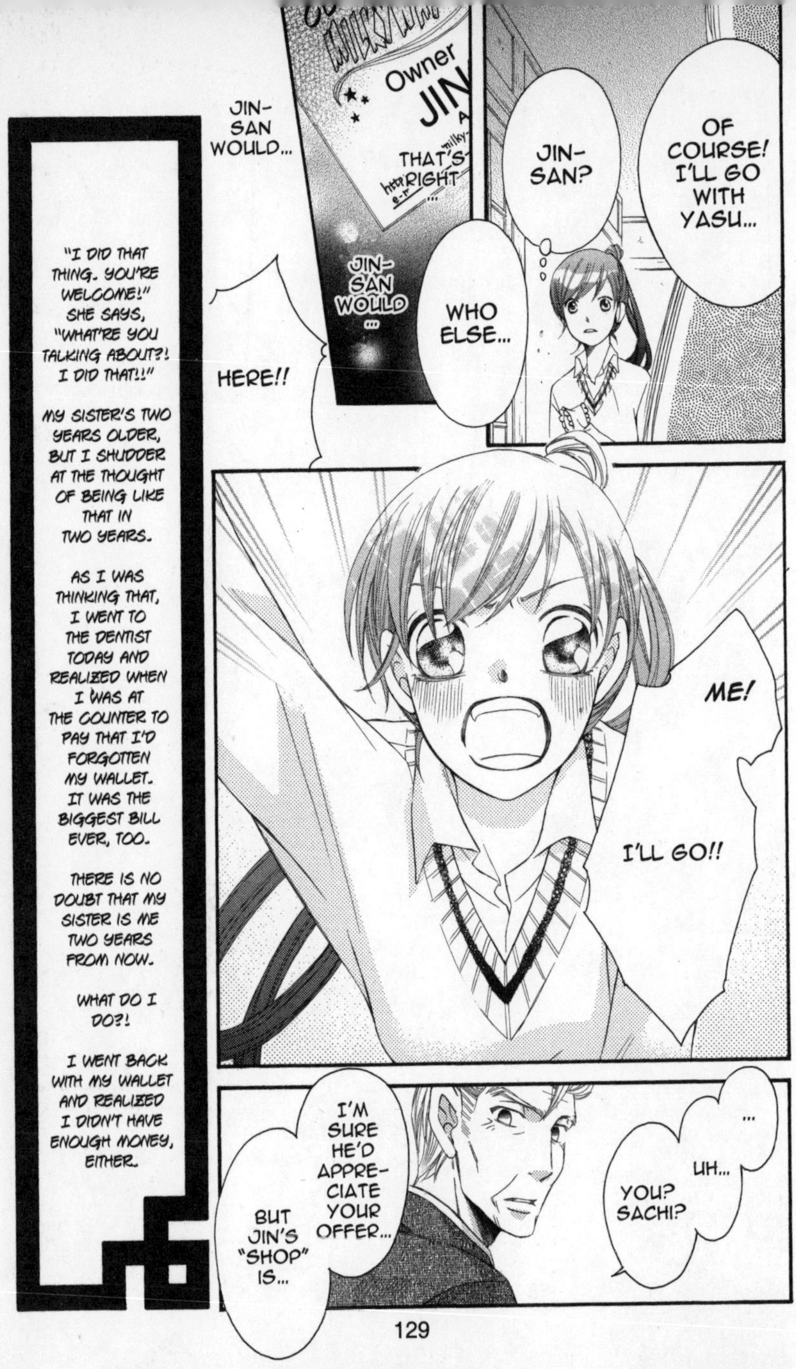
OF COURSE! I'LL GO WITH YASU...
JIN-SAN?
WHO ELSE...
Owner JIN
THAT'S RIGHT ...
JIN-SAN WOULD ...
JIN-SAN WOULD...
HERE!!
ME!
I'LL GO!!
...
UH... YOU? SACHI?
I'M SURE HE'D APPRECIATE YOUR OFFER...
BUT JIN'S "SHOP" IS...

"I DID THAT THING. YOU'RE WELCOME!" SHE SAYS, "WHAT'RE YOU TALKING ABOUT?! I DID THAT!!"

MY SISTER'S TWO YEARS OLDER, BUT I SHUDDER AT THE THOUGHT OF BEING LIKE THAT IN TWO YEARS.

AS I WAS THINKING THAT, I WENT TO THE DENTIST TODAY AND REALIZED WHEN I WAS AT THE COUNTER TO PAY THAT I'D FORGOTTEN MY WALLET. IT WAS THE BIGGEST BILL EVER, TOO.

THERE IS NO DOUBT THAT MY SISTER IS ME TWO YEARS FROM NOW.

WHAT DO I DO?!

I WENT BACK WITH MY WALLET AND REALIZED I DIDN'T HAVE ENOUGH MONEY, EITHER.

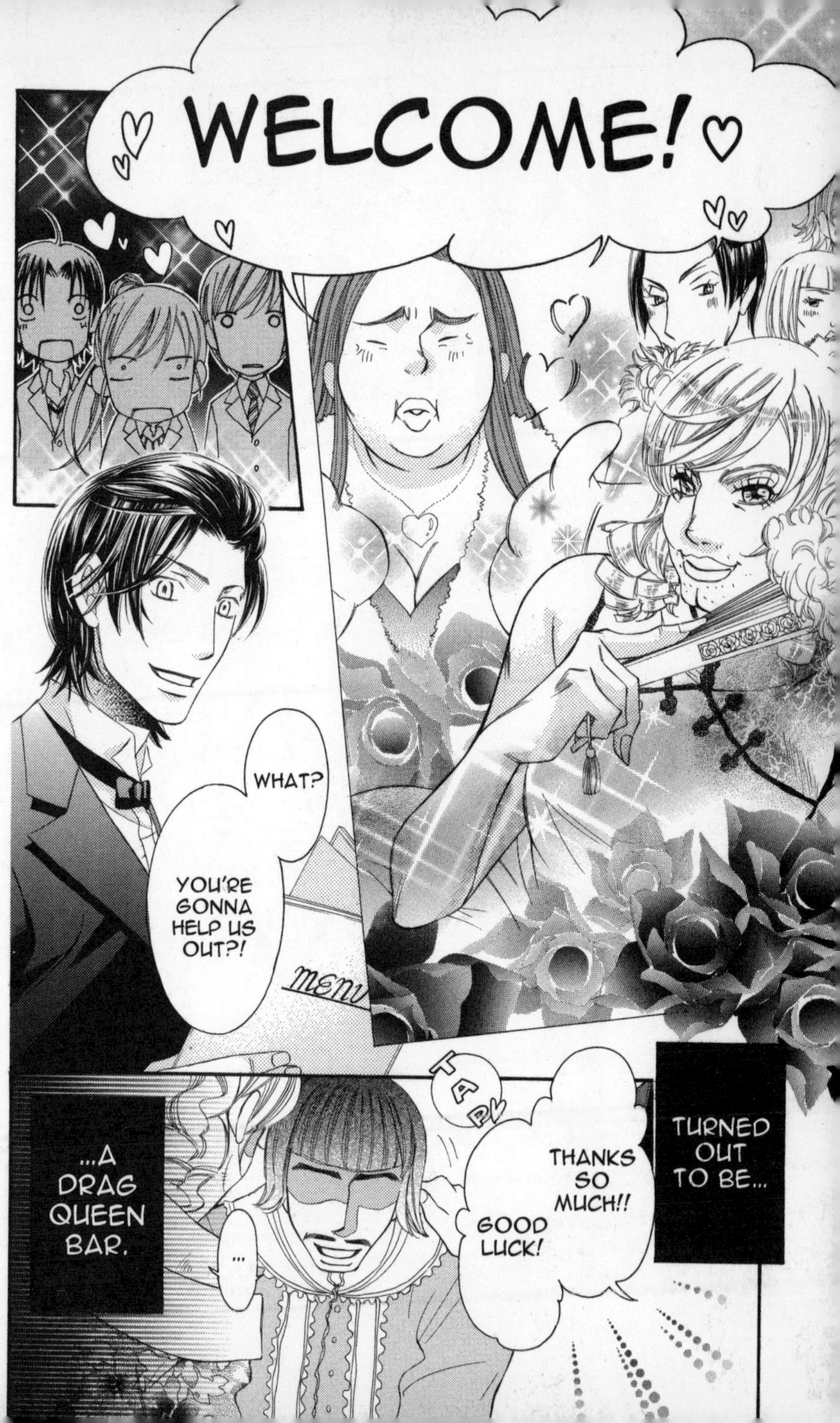
WELCOME!
WHAT?
YOU'RE GONNA HELP US OUT?!
MENU
TURNED OUT TO BE...
TAP
THANKS SO MUCH!!
GOOD LUCK!
...
...A DRAG QUEEN BAR.

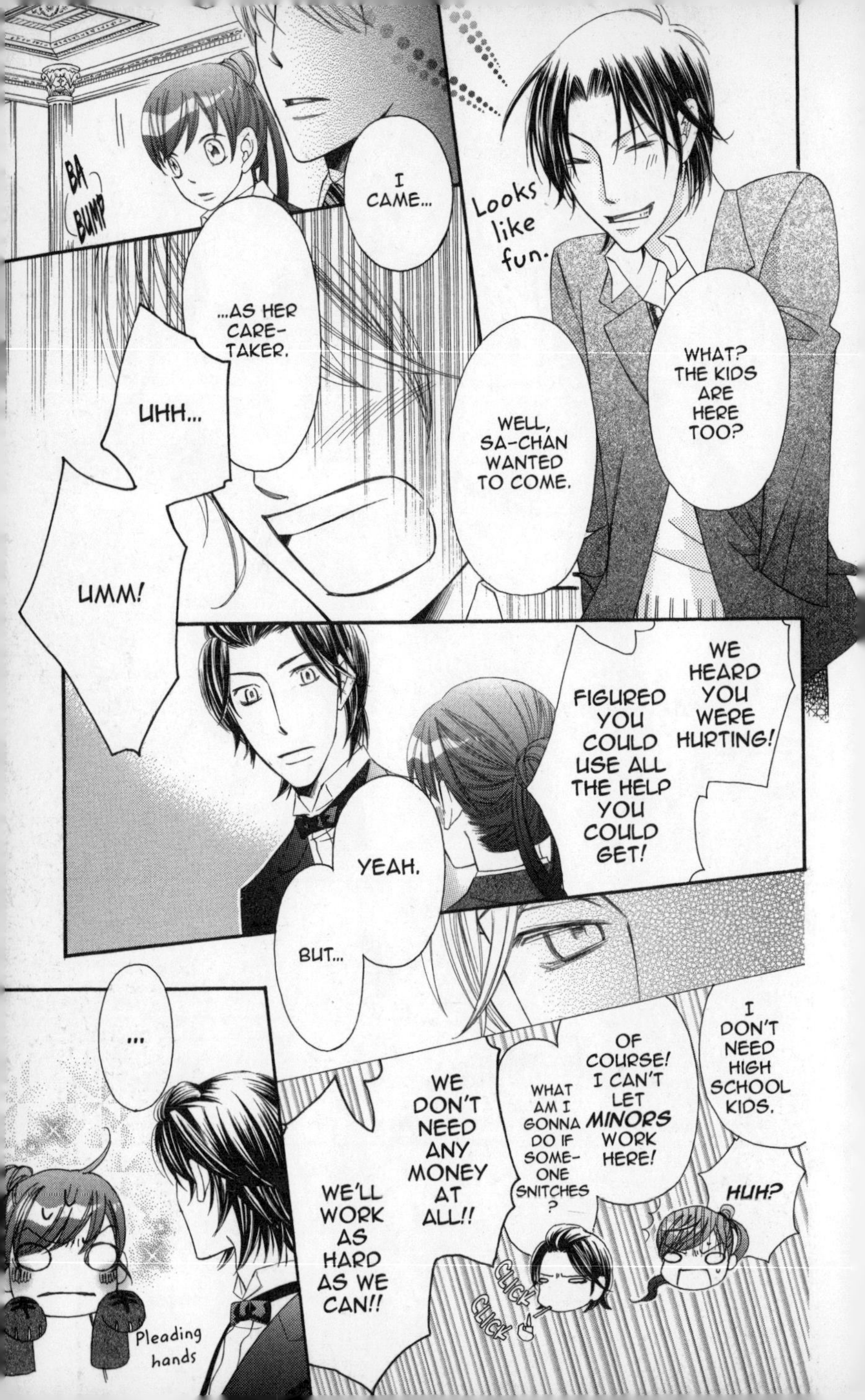
Looks like fun.
WHAT? THE KIDS ARE HERE TOO?
WELL, SA-CHAN WANTED TO COME.
I CAME...
BA BUMP
...AS HER CARE-TAKER.
UHH...
UMM!
WE HEARD YOU WERE HURTING!
FIGURED YOU COULD USE ALL THE HELP YOU COULD GET!
YEAH.
BUT...
I DON'T NEED HIGH SCHOOL KIDS.
OF COURSE! I CAN'T LET MINORS WORK HERE!
WHAT AM I GONNA DO IF SOME-ONE SNITCHES?
HUH?
CLICK CLICK
WE DON'T NEED ANY MONEY AT ALL!!
WE'LL WORK AS HARD AS WE CAN!!
...
Pleading hands

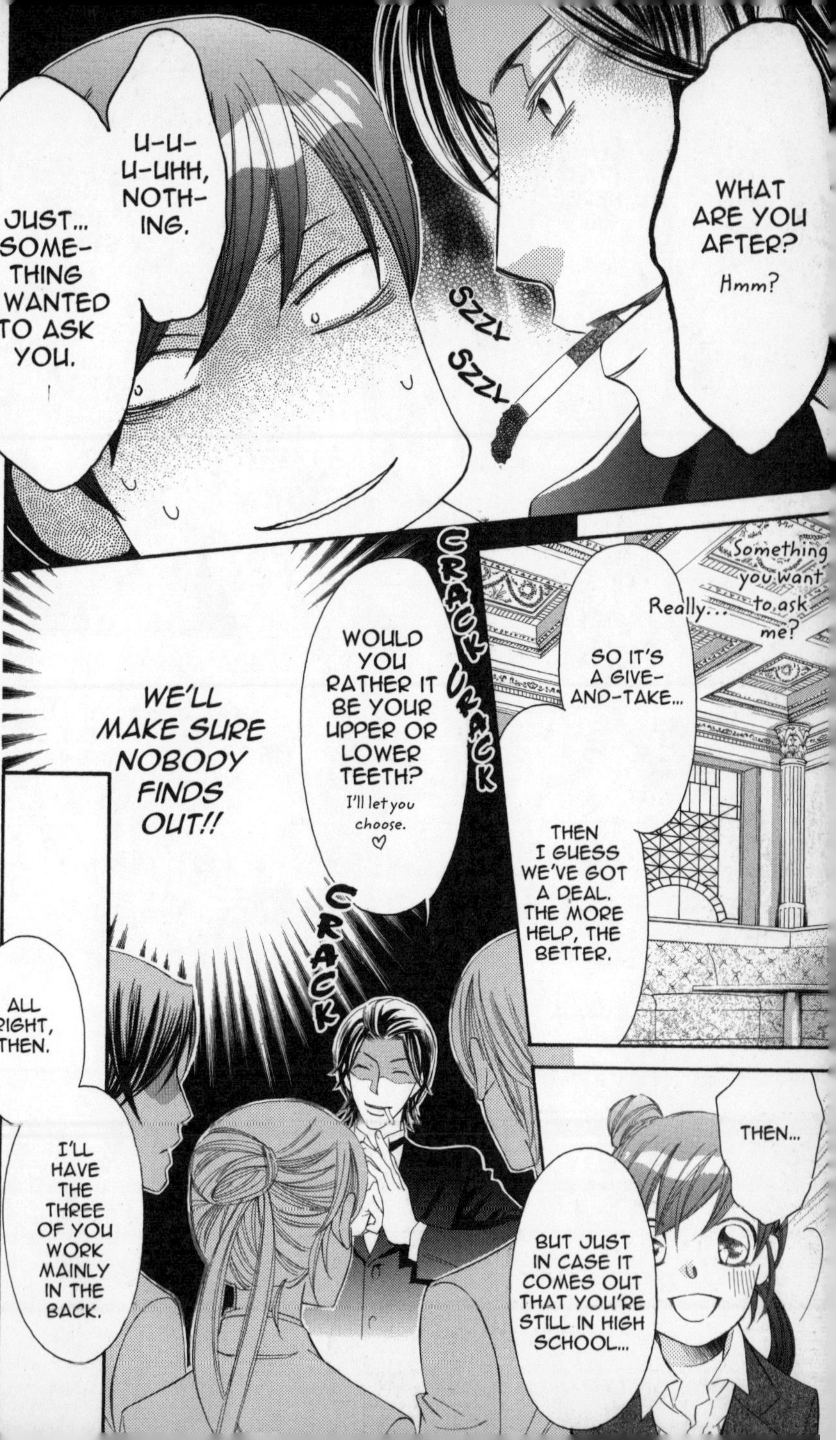
WHAT ARE YOU AFTER?
Hmm?
SZZZ SZZZ
U-U-U-UHH, NOTHING.
JUST... SOMETHING I WANTED TO ASK YOU.
Something you want to ask me?
Really...
SO IT'S A GIVE-AND-TAKE...
THEN I GUESS WE'VE GOT A DEAL. THE MORE HELP, THE BETTER.
CRACK CRACK
WOULD YOU RATHER IT BE YOUR UPPER OR LOWER TEETH?
I'll let you choose. ♡
WE'LL MAKE SURE NOBODY FINDS OUT!!
CRACK
THEN...
BUT JUST IN CASE IT COMES OUT THAT YOU'RE STILL IN HIGH SCHOOL...
ALL RIGHT, THEN.
I'LL HAVE THE THREE OF YOU WORK MAINLY IN THE BACK.

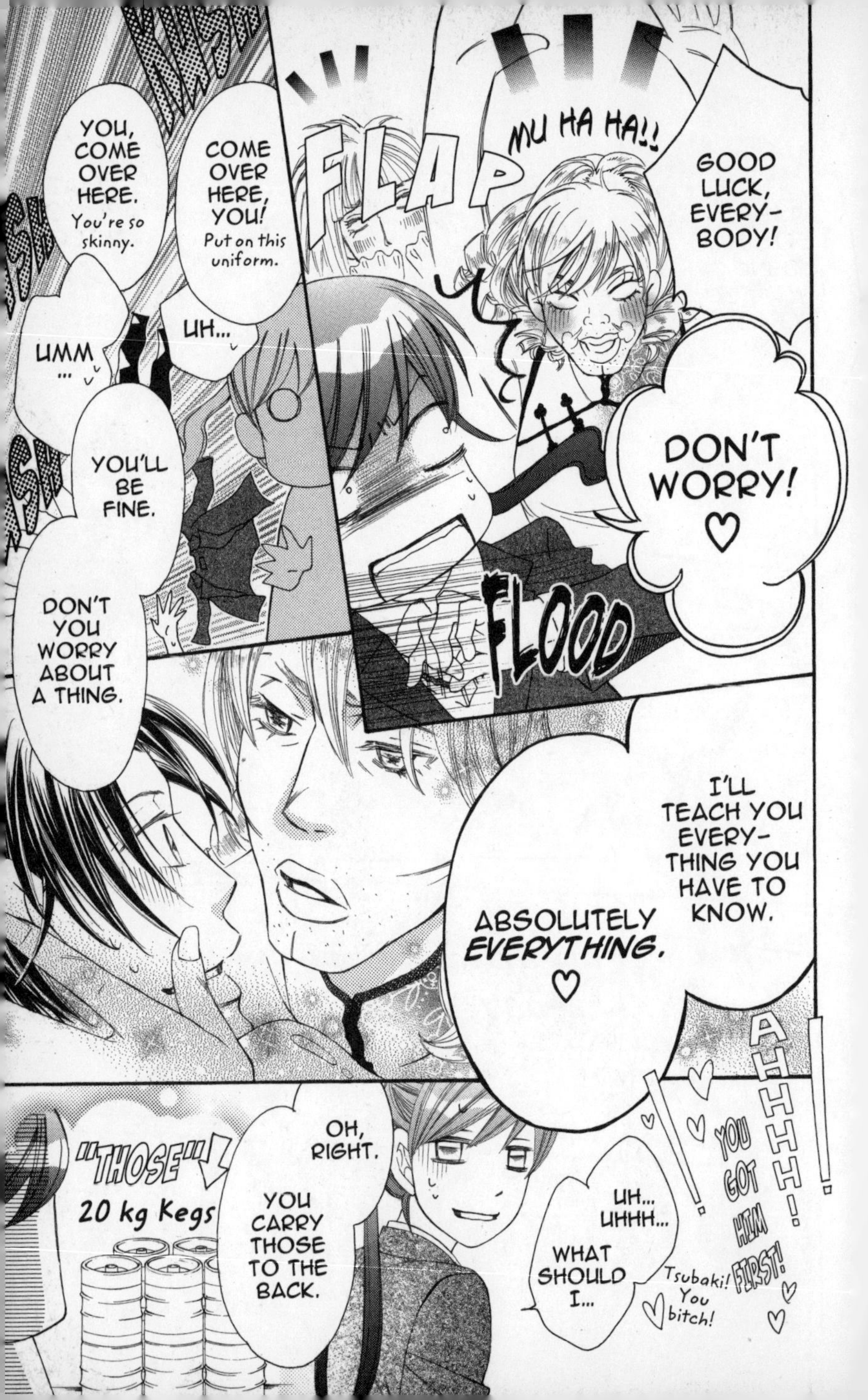
MU HA HA!!
GOOD LUCK, EVERYBODY!
FLAP
DON'T WORRY! ♡
FLOOD
COME OVER HERE, YOU! Put on this uniform.
YOU, COME OVER HERE. You're so skinny.
UH...
UMM...
YOU'LL BE FINE.
DON'T YOU WORRY ABOUT A THING.
I'LL TEACH YOU EVERYTHING YOU HAVE TO KNOW.
ABSOLUTELY EVERYTHING. ♡
AHHHHH!
YOU GOT HIM FIRST!
Tsubaki! You bitch!
UH... UHHH...
WHAT SHOULD I...
OH, RIGHT.
YOU CARRY THOSE TO THE BACK.
"THOSE"
20 kg Kegs

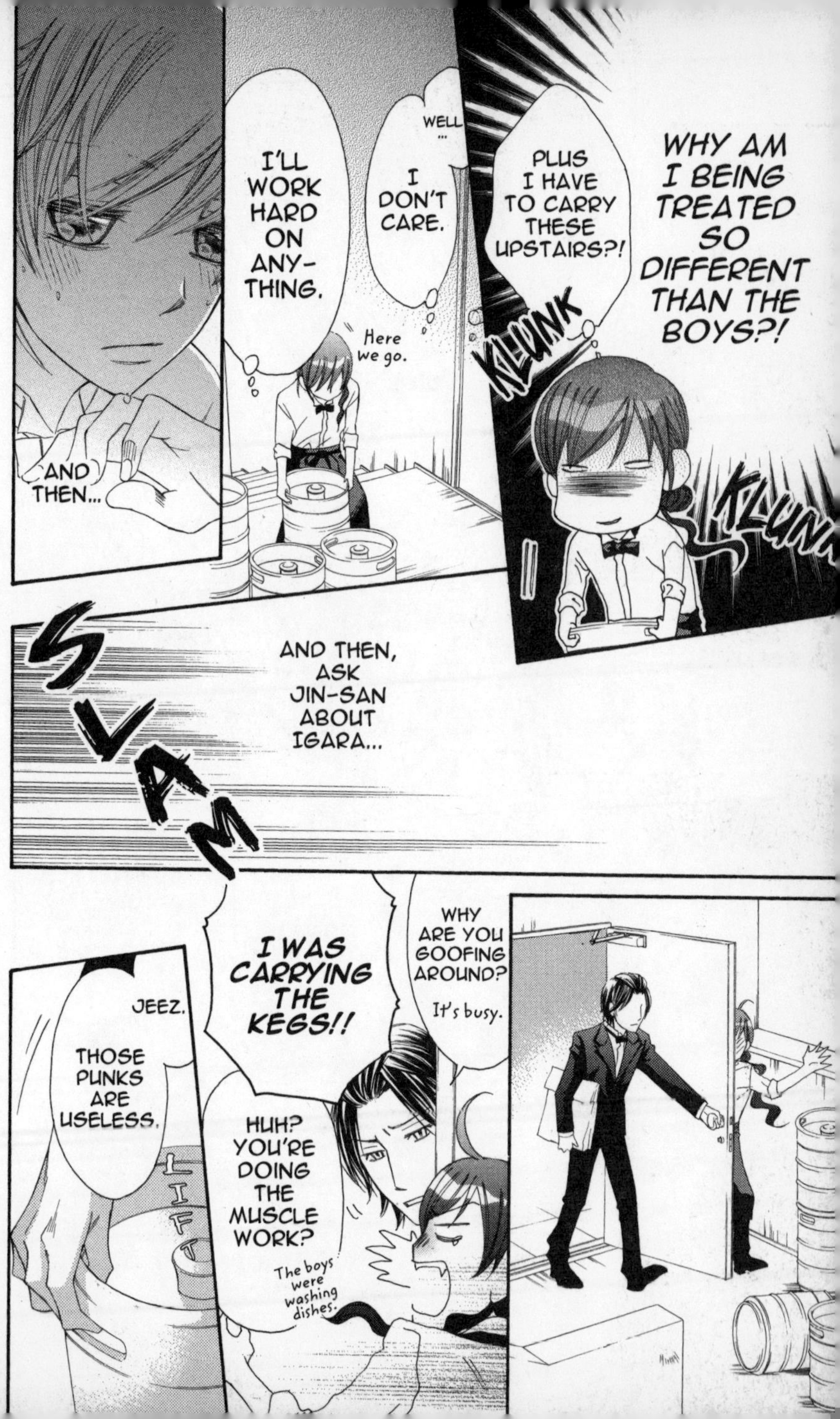
WHY AM I BEING TREATED SO DIFFERENT THAN THE BOYS?!
PLUS I HAVE TO CARRY THESE UPSTAIRS?!
KLUNK
KLUNK
WELL...
I DON'T CARE.
I'LL WORK HARD ON ANY-THING.
Here we go.
AND THEN...
AND THEN, ASK JIN-SAN ABOUT IGARA...
SLAM
WHY ARE YOU GOOFING AROUND?
It's busy.
I WAS CARRYING THE KEGS!!
HUH? YOU'RE DOING THE MUSCLE WORK?
The boys were washing dishes.
JEEZ.
THOSE PUNKS ARE USELESS.
LIFT

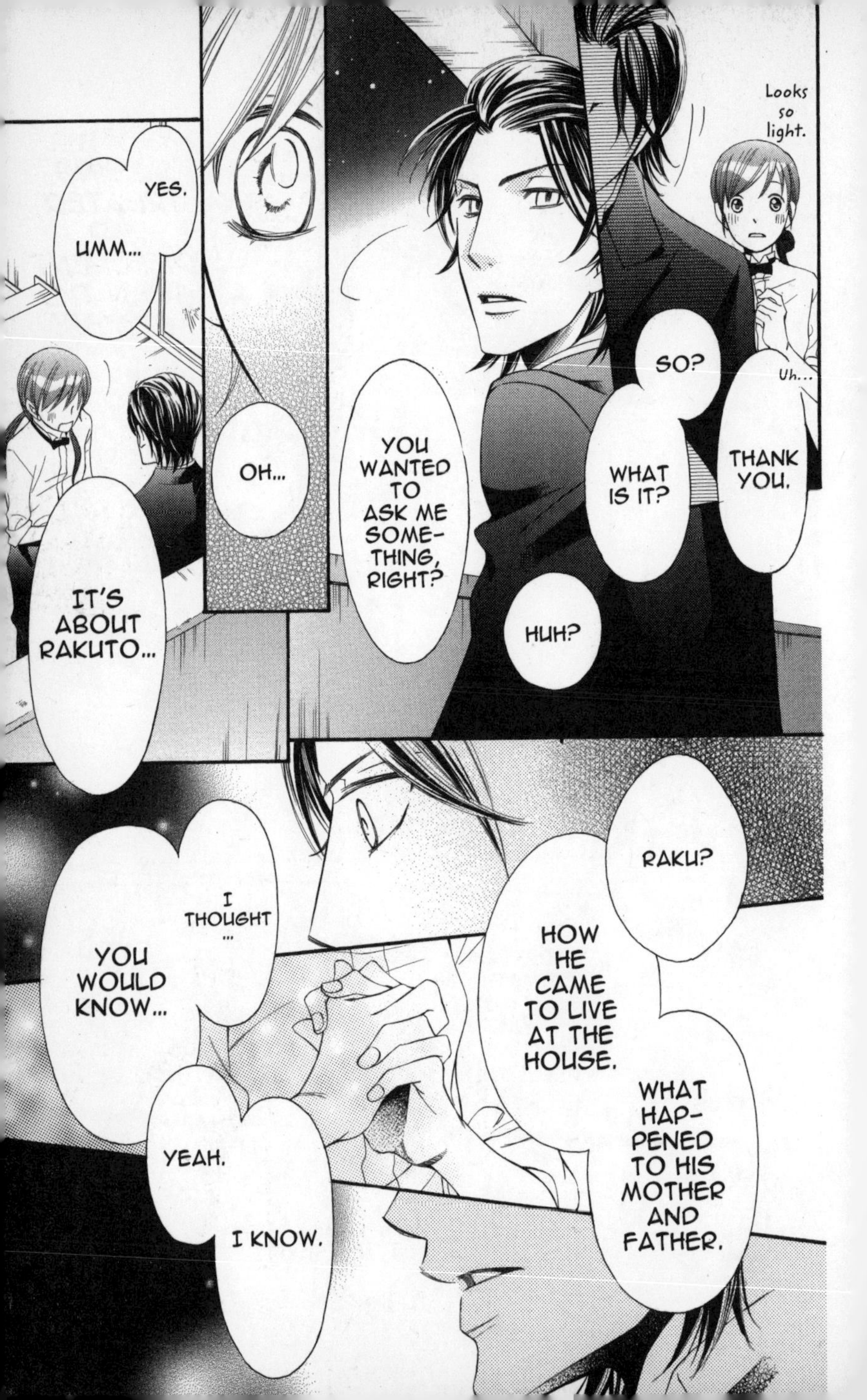
Looks so light.
Uh...
THANK YOU.
SO?
WHAT IS IT?
HUH?
YOU WANTED TO ASK ME SOME-THING, RIGHT?
OH...
YES.
UMM...
IT'S ABOUT RAKUTO...
RAKU?
HOW HE CAME TO LIVE AT THE HOUSE.
WHAT HAP-PENED TO HIS MOTHER AND FATHER.
I THOUGHT...
YOU WOULD KNOW...
YEAH.
I KNOW.

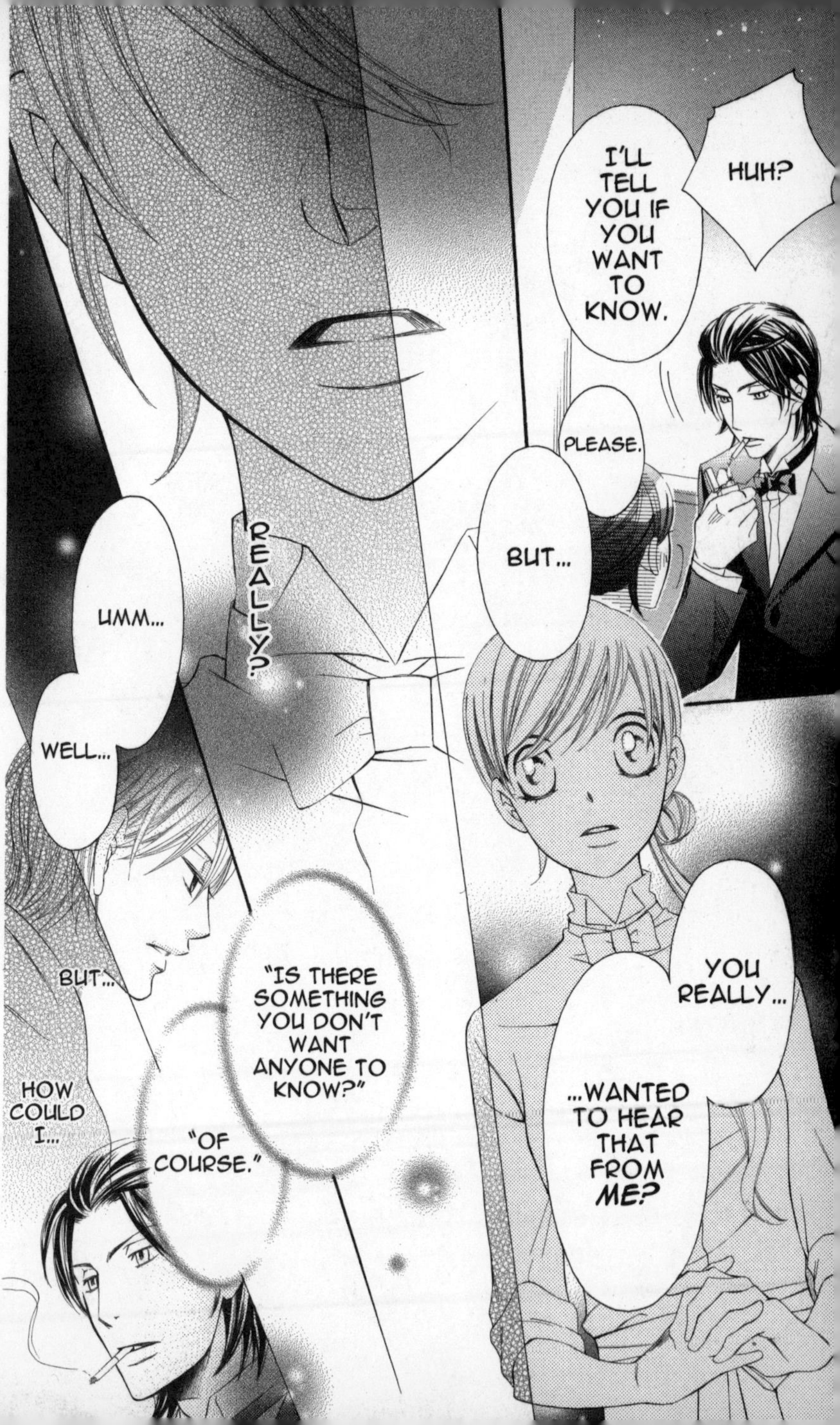
HUH?
I'LL TELL YOU IF YOU WANT TO KNOW.
PLEASE.
BUT...
YOU REALLY...
...WANTED TO HEAR THAT FROM *ME?*
REALLY?
UMM...
WELL...
BUT...
"IS THERE SOMETHING YOU DON'T WANT ANYONE TO KNOW?"
"OF COURSE."
HOW COULD I...

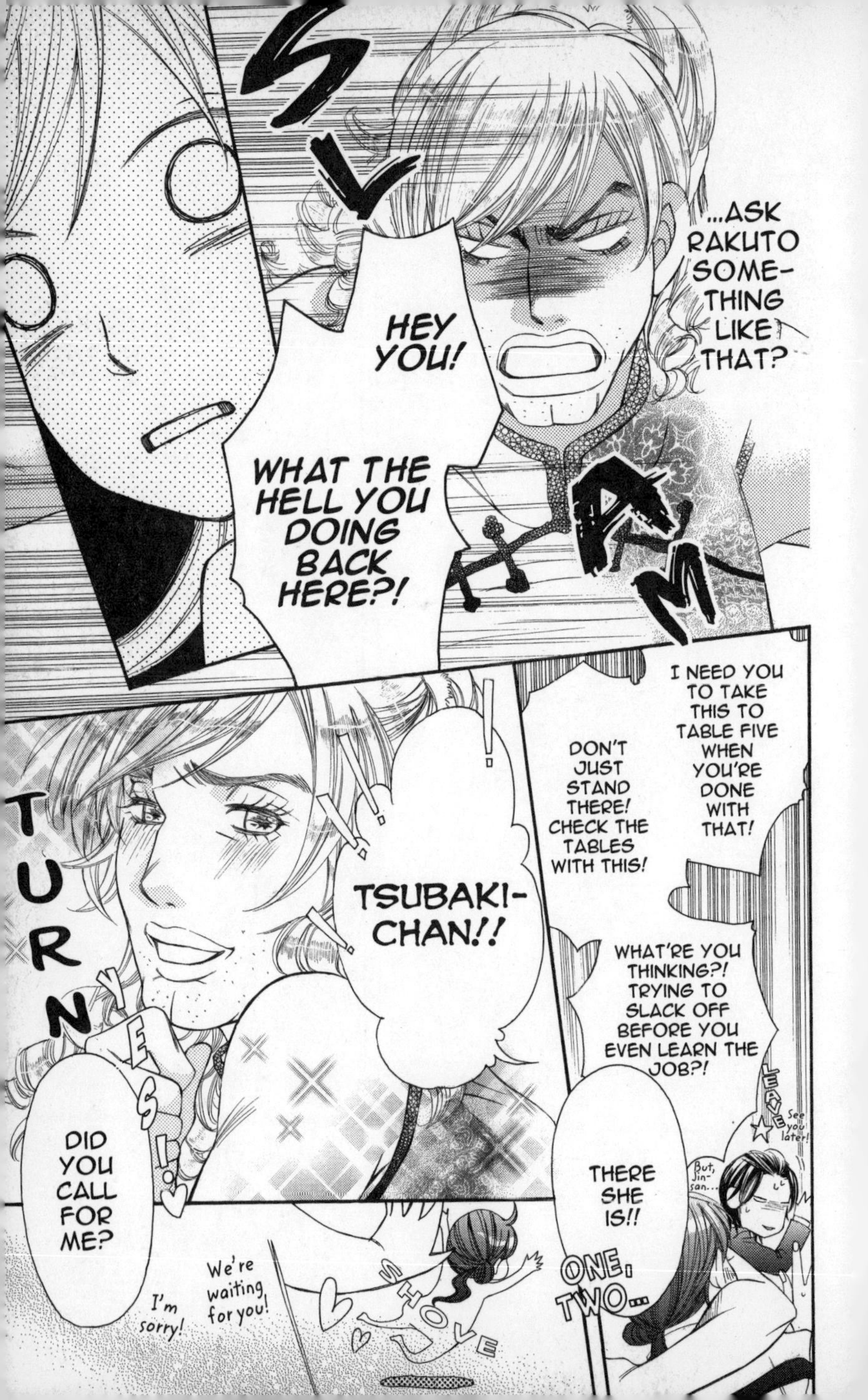
...ASK RAKUTO SOMETHING LIKE THAT?
SLAM
HEY YOU!
WHAT THE HELL YOU DOING BACK HERE?!
I NEED YOU TO TAKE THIS TO TABLE FIVE WHEN YOU'RE DONE WITH THAT!
DON'T JUST STAND THERE! CHECK THE TABLES WITH THIS!
WHAT'RE YOU THINKING?! TRYING TO SLACK OFF BEFORE YOU EVEN LEARN THE JOB?!
LEAVE
See you later!
But, Jin-san...
TSUBAKI-CHAN!!
TURN
YES!
DID YOU CALL FOR ME?
THERE SHE IS!!
ONE, TWO...
SHOVE
We're waiting for you!
I'm sorry!

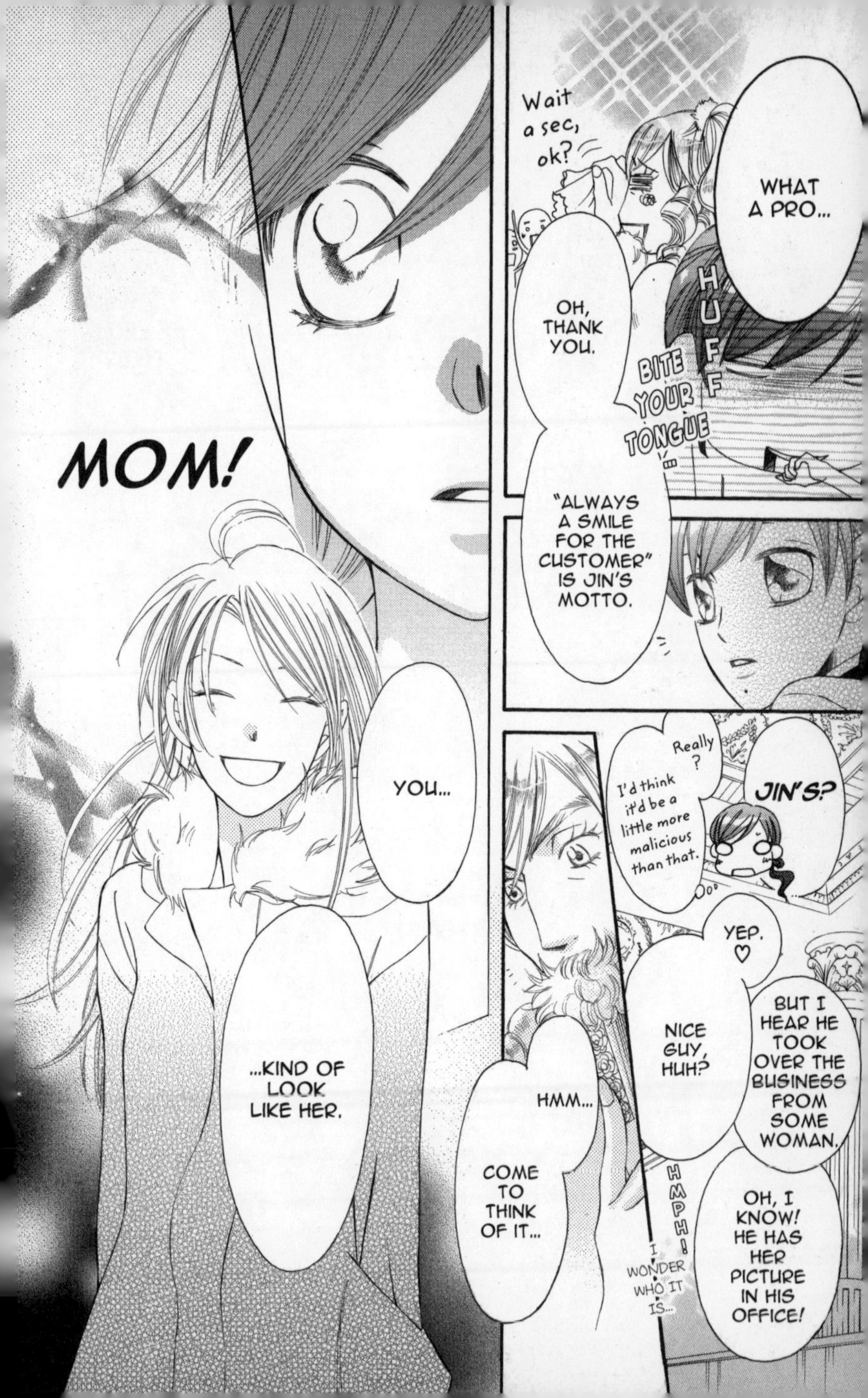
WHAT A PRO...
HUFF
Wait a sec, ok?
OH, THANK YOU.
BITE YOUR TONGUE
"ALWAYS A SMILE FOR THE CUSTOMER" IS JIN'S MOTTO.
JIN'S?
Really?
I'd think it'd be a little more malicious than that.
YEP. ♡
BUT I HEAR HE TOOK OVER THE BUSINESS FROM SOME WOMAN.
NICE GUY, HUH?
HMM...
OH, I KNOW! HE HAS HER PICTURE IN HIS OFFICE!
HMPH!
I WONDER WHO IT IS...
COME TO THINK OF IT...
MOM!
YOU...
...KIND OF LOOK LIKE HER.

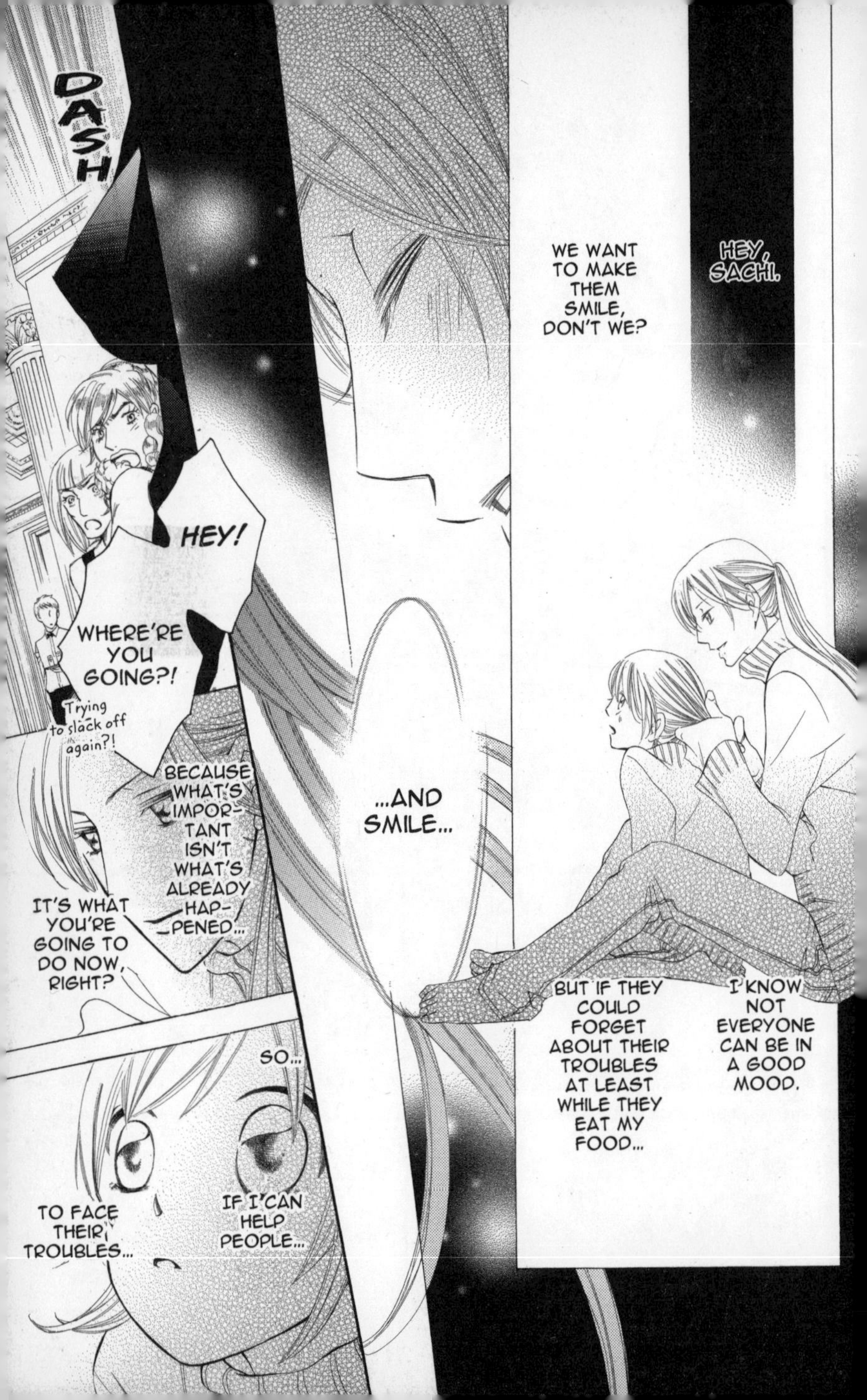
HEY, SACHI.
WE WANT TO MAKE THEM SMILE, DON'T WE?
I KNOW NOT EVERYONE CAN BE IN A GOOD MOOD.
BUT IF THEY COULD FORGET ABOUT THEIR TROUBLES AT LEAST WHILE THEY EAT MY FOOD...
...AND SMILE...
DASH
HEY!
WHERE'RE YOU GOING?!
Trying to slack off again?!
BECAUSE WHAT'S IMPORTANT ISN'T WHAT'S ALREADY HAPPENED...
IT'S WHAT YOU'RE GOING TO DO NOW, RIGHT?
SO...
IF I CAN HELP PEOPLE...
TO FACE THEIR TROUBLES...

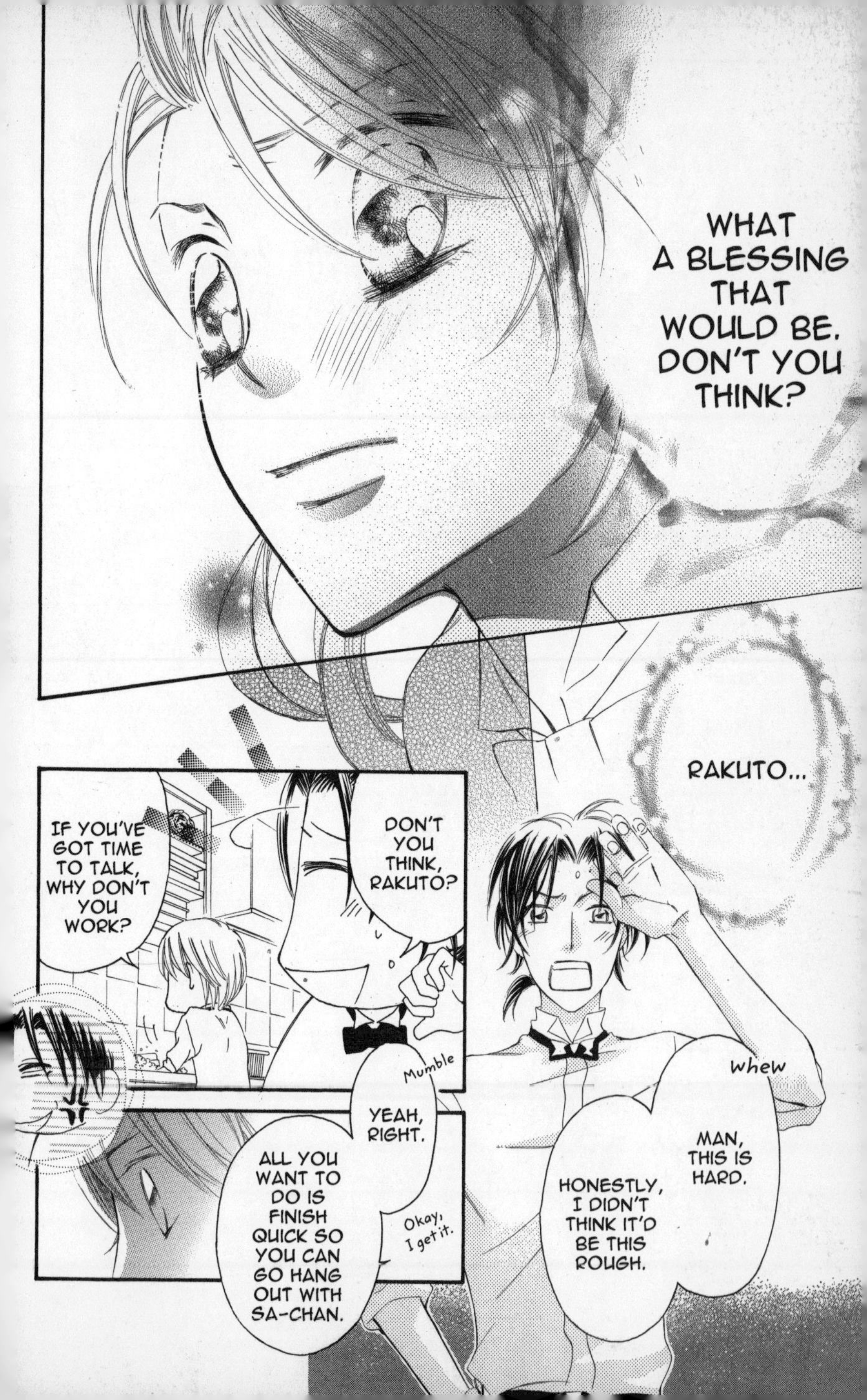
WHAT A BLESSING THAT WOULD BE. DON'T YOU THINK?
RAKUTO...
whew
MAN, THIS IS HARD.
HONESTLY, I DIDN'T THINK IT'D BE THIS ROUGH.
DON'T YOU THINK, RAKUTO?
IF YOU'VE GOT TIME TO TALK, WHY DON'T YOU WORK?
Mumble
YEAH, RIGHT.
ALL YOU WANT TO DO IS FINISH QUICK SO YOU CAN GO HANG OUT WITH SA-CHAN.
Okay, I get it.

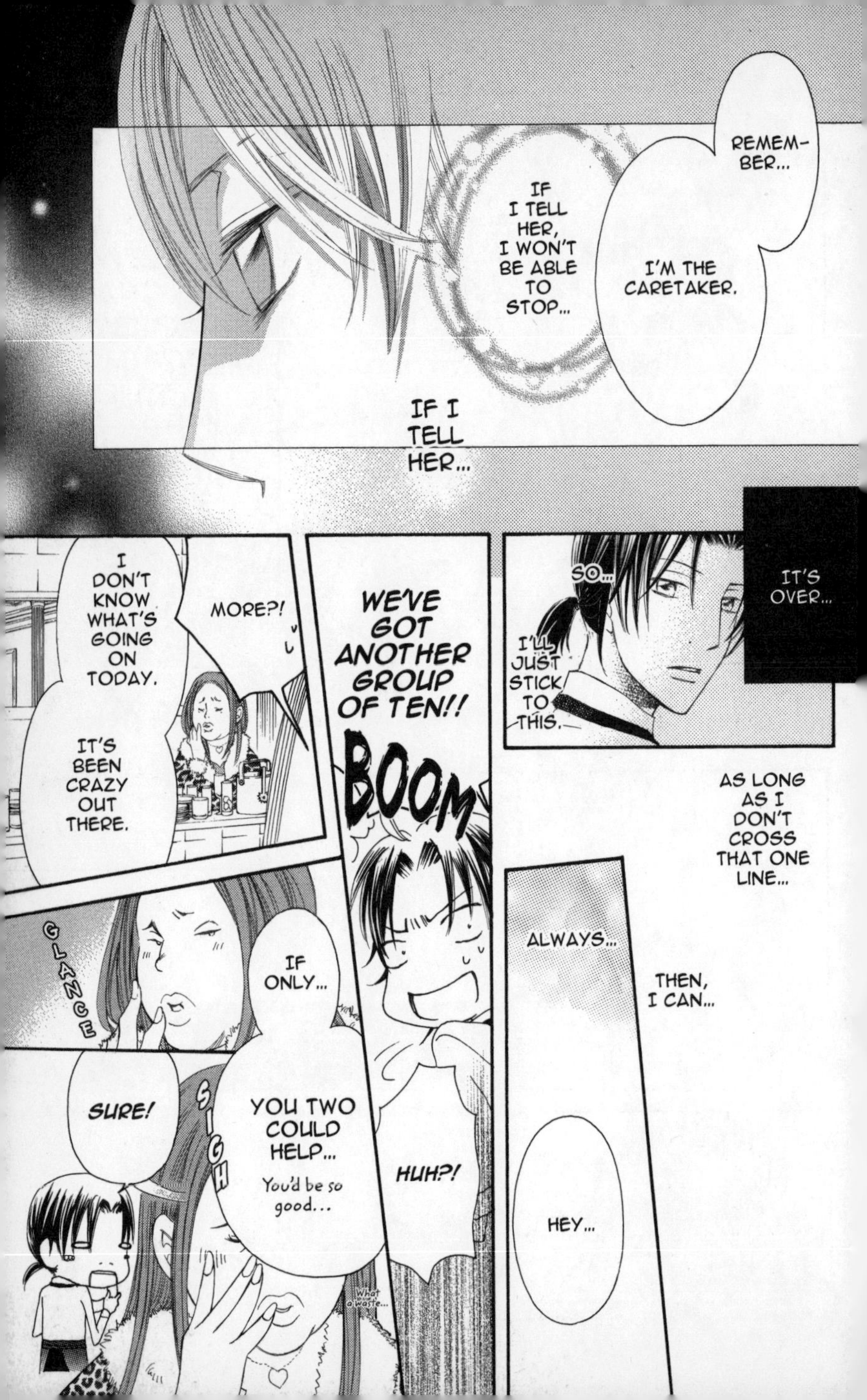
REMEMBER...
I'M THE CARETAKER.
IF I TELL HER, I WON'T BE ABLE TO STOP...
IF I TELL HER...
IT'S OVER...
SO...
I'LL JUST STICK TO THIS.
AS LONG AS I DON'T CROSS THAT ONE LINE...
ALWAYS...
THEN, I CAN...
HEY...
WE'VE GOT ANOTHER GROUP OF TEN!!
BOOM
HUH?!
I DON'T KNOW WHAT'S GOING ON TODAY.
MORE?!
IT'S BEEN CRAZY OUT THERE.
GLANCE
IF ONLY...
YOU TWO COULD HELP...
You'd be so good...
SIGH
SURE!
What a waste...

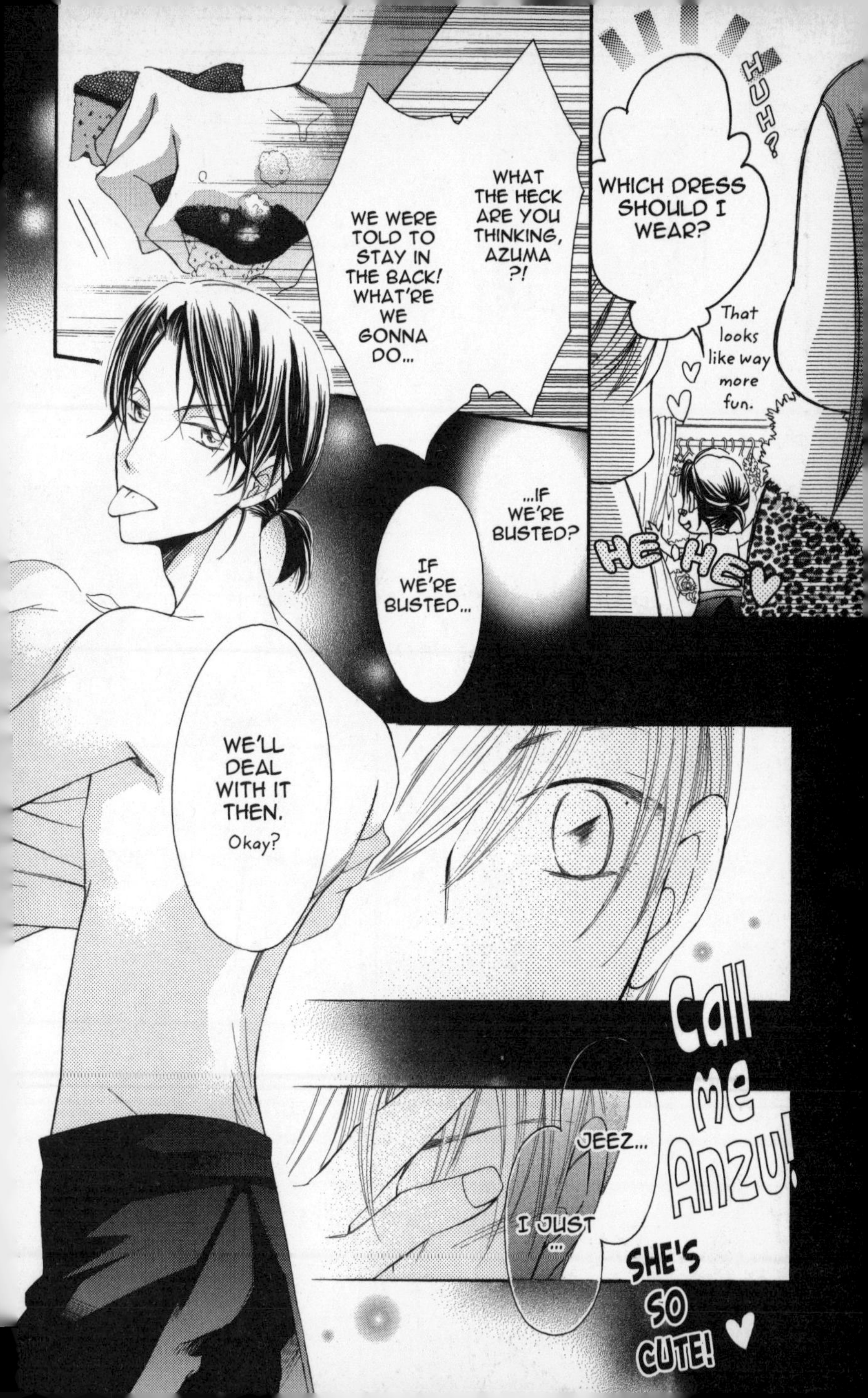
HUH?
WHICH DRESS SHOULD I WEAR?
That looks like way more fun.
HE HE♥
WHAT THE HECK ARE YOU THINKING, AZUMA?!
WE WERE TOLD TO STAY IN THE BACK! WHAT'RE WE GONNA DO...
...IF WE'RE BUSTED?
IF WE'RE BUSTED...
WE'LL DEAL WITH IT THEN.
Okay?
Call me Anzu!
SHE'S SO CUTE! ♥
JEEZ...
I JUST ...

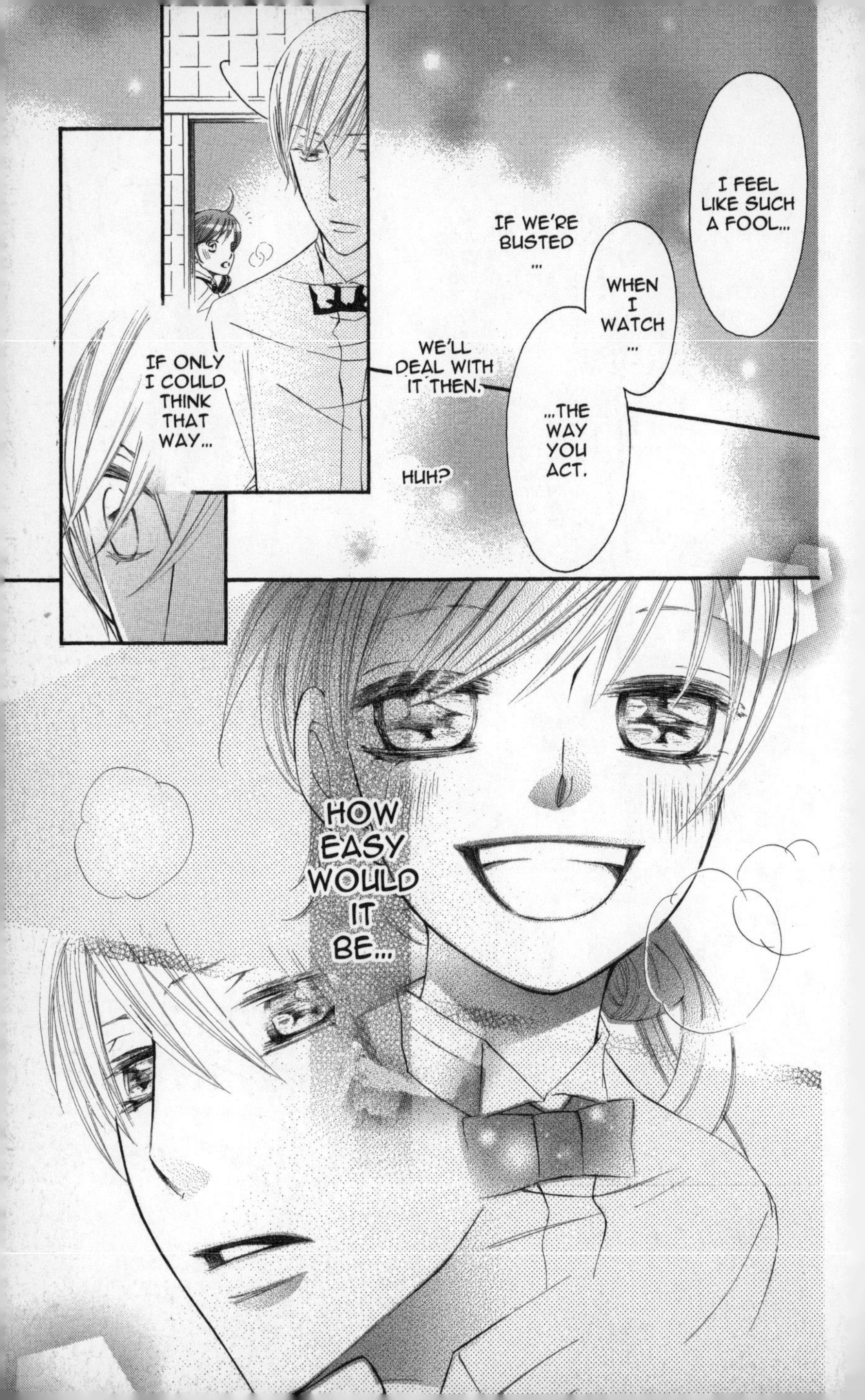
I FEEL LIKE SUCH A FOOL...
WHEN I WATCH ...
...THE WAY YOU ACT.
IF WE'RE BUSTED ...
WE'LL DEAL WITH IT THEN.
HUH?
IF ONLY I COULD THINK THAT WAY...
HOW EASY WOULD IT BE...

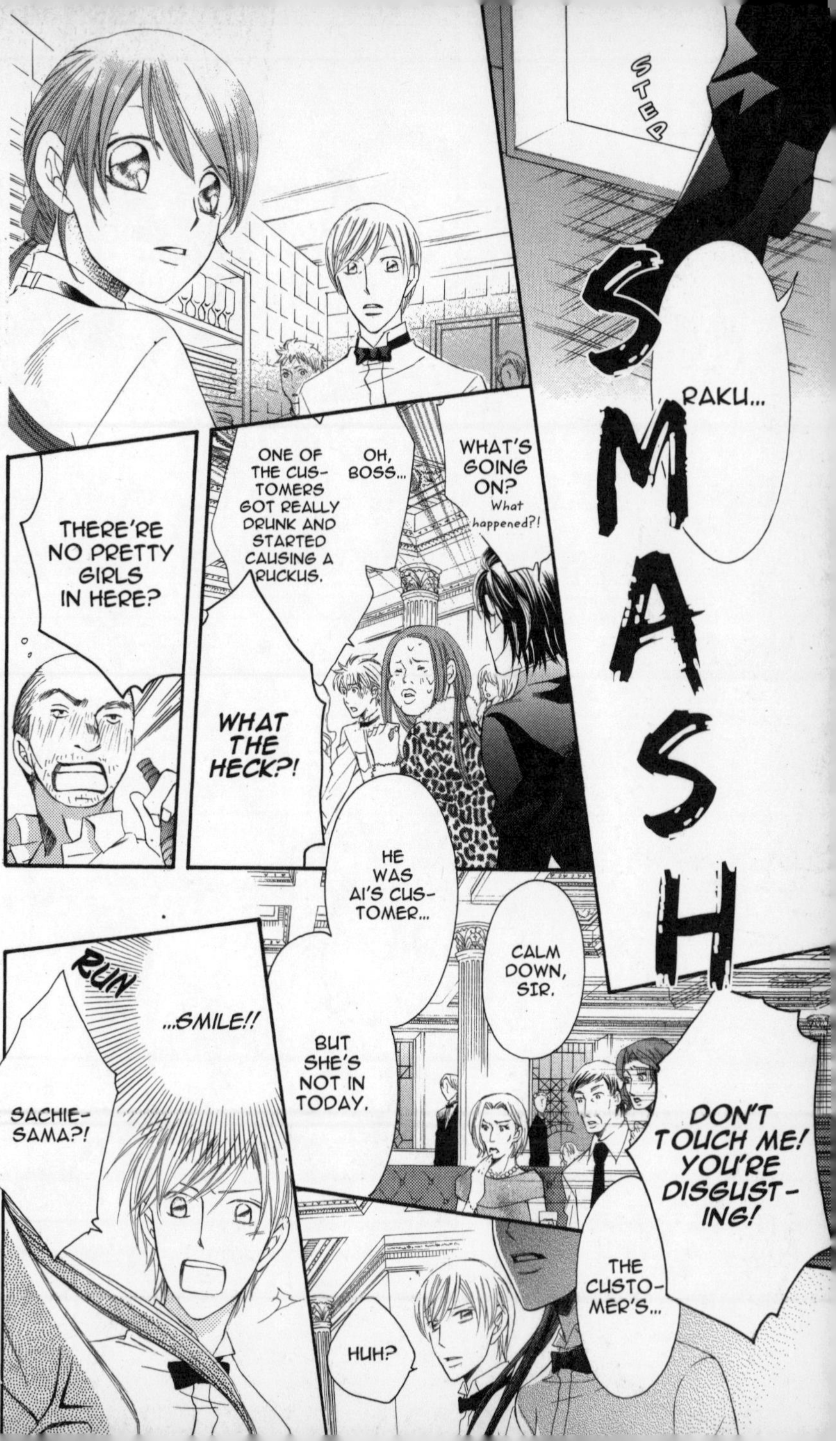
STEP
SMASH
RAKU...
WHAT'S GOING ON?
What happened?!
OH, BOSS...
ONE OF THE CUSTOMERS GOT REALLY DRUNK AND STARTED CAUSING A RUCKUS.
THERE'RE NO PRETTY GIRLS IN HERE?
WHAT THE HECK?!
HE WAS AI'S CUSTOMER...
CALM DOWN, SIR.
BUT SHE'S NOT IN TODAY.
DON'T TOUCH ME! YOU'RE DISGUSTING!
THE CUSTOMER'S...
...SMILE!!
RUN
SACHIE-SAMA?!
HUH?

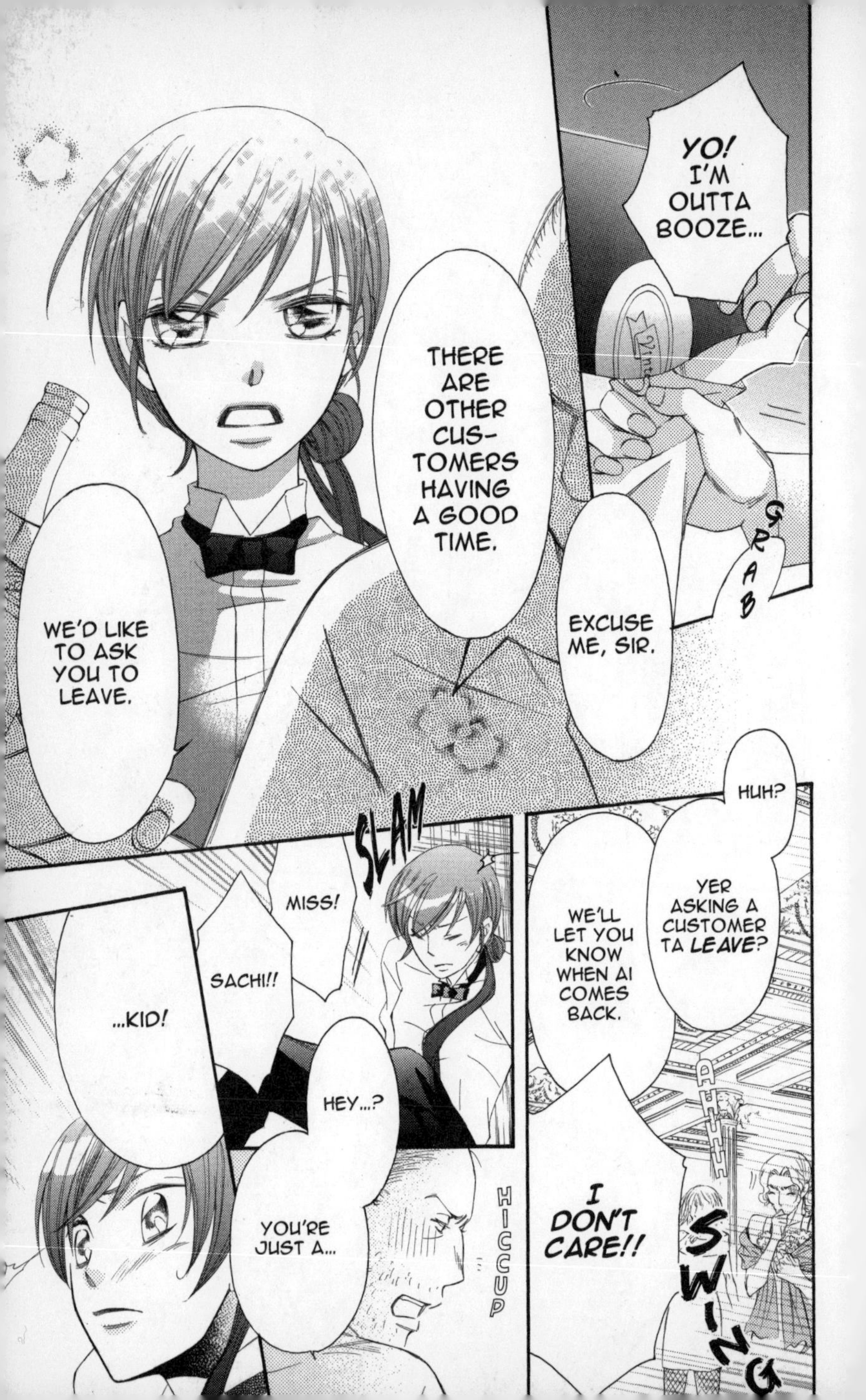
YO! I'M OUTTA BOOZE...
GRAB
EXCUSE ME, SIR.
THERE ARE OTHER CUS-TOMERS HAVING A GOOD TIME.
WE'D LIKE TO ASK YOU TO LEAVE.
SLAM
HUH?
YER ASKING A CUSTOMER TA LEAVE?
WE'LL LET YOU KNOW WHEN AI COMES BACK.
I DON'T CARE!!
SWING
MISS!
SACHI!!
...KID!
HEY...?
HICCUP
YOU'RE JUST A...

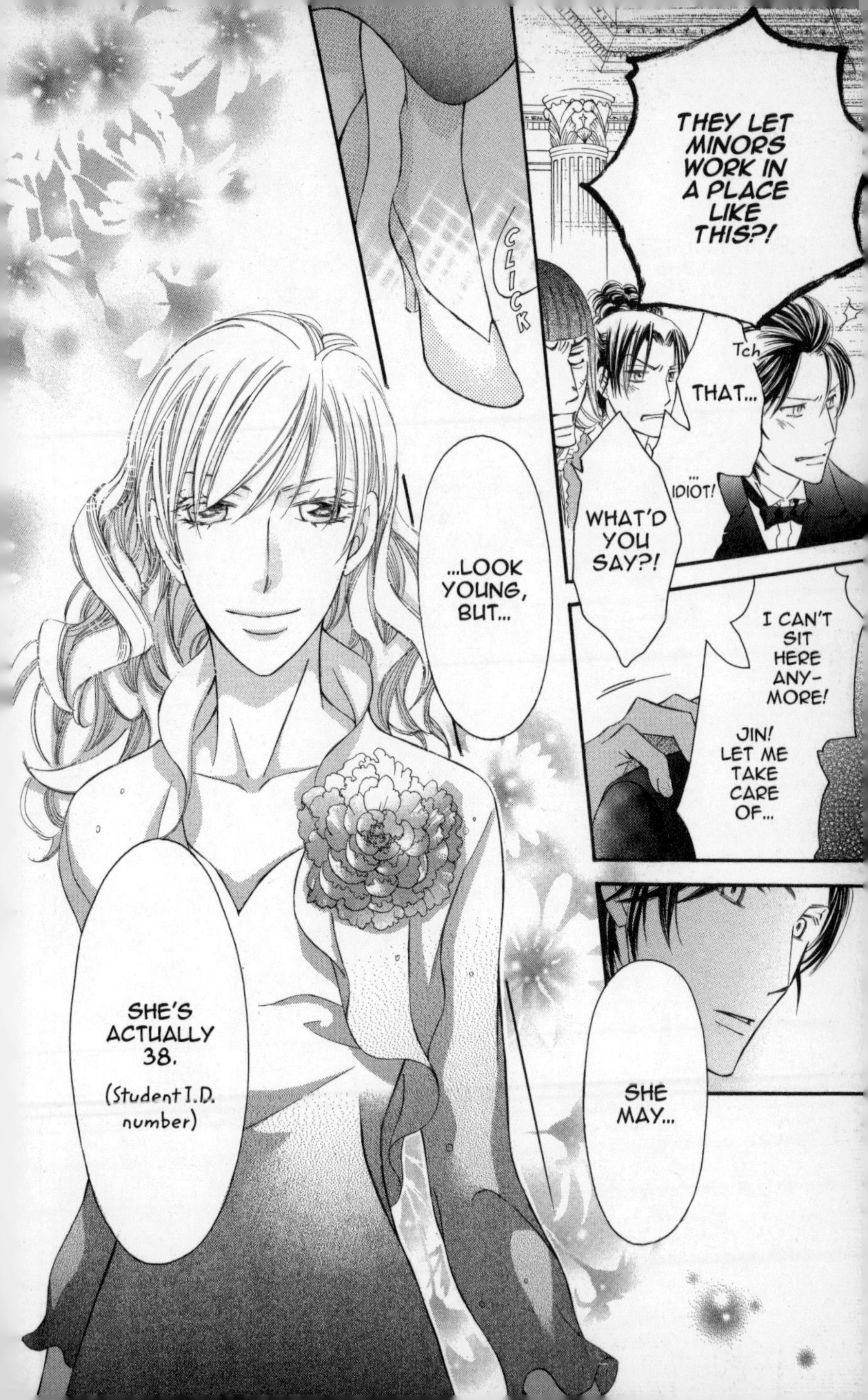
THEY LET MINORS WORK IN A PLACE LIKE THIS?!
Tch
THAT...
...IDIOT!
WHAT'D YOU SAY?!
I CAN'T SIT HERE ANY-MORE!
JIN! LET ME TAKE CARE OF...
SHE MAY...
CLICK
...LOOK YOUNG, BUT...
SHE'S ACTUALLY 38.
(Student I.D. number)

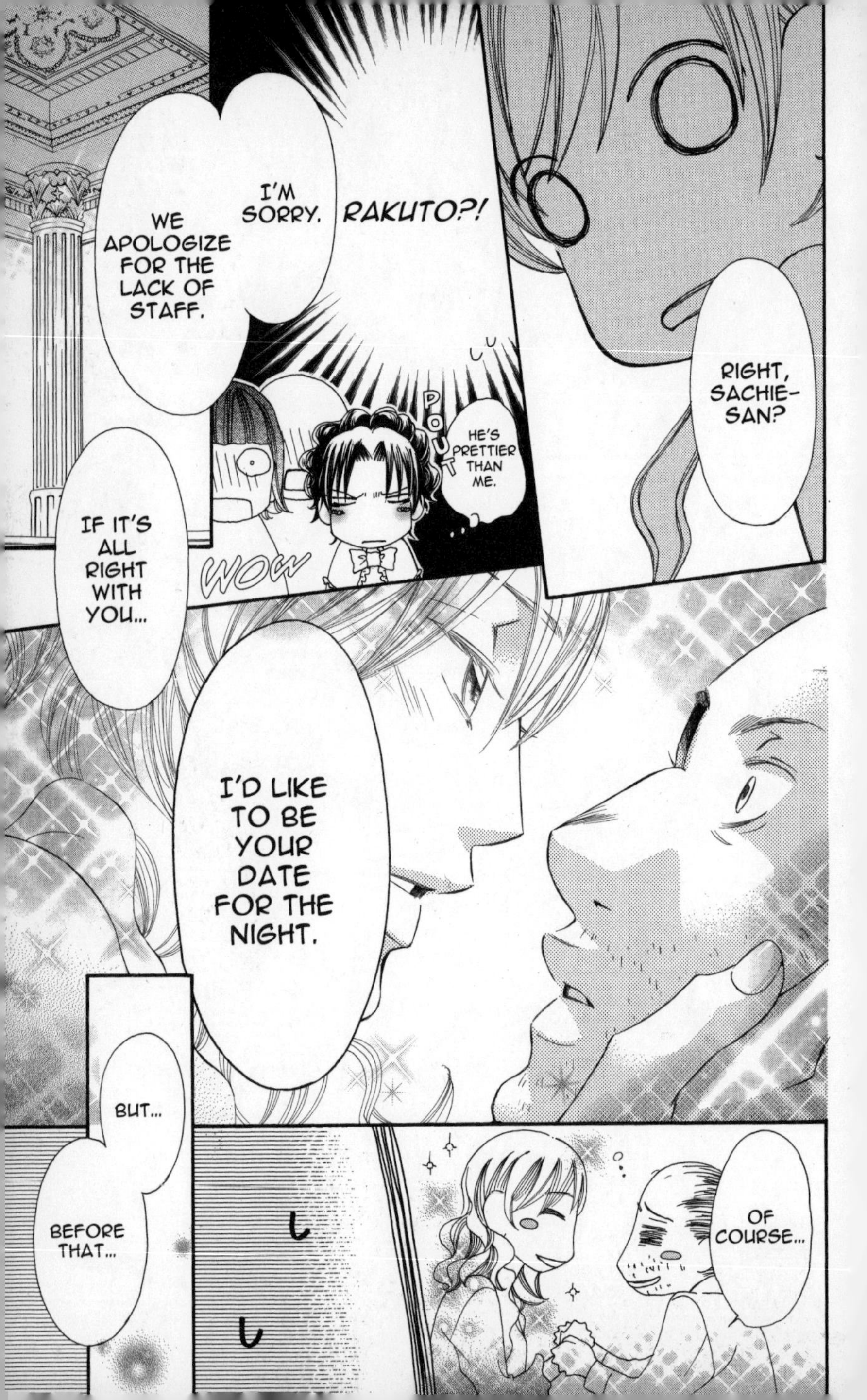

RIGHT, SACHIE-SAN?
RAKUTO?!
I'M SORRY.
WE APOLOGIZE FOR THE LACK OF STAFF.
POUT
HE'S PRETTIER THAN ME.
WOW
IF IT'S ALL RIGHT WITH YOU...
I'D LIKE TO BE YOUR DATE FOR THE NIGHT.
OF COURSE...
BUT...
BEFORE THAT...

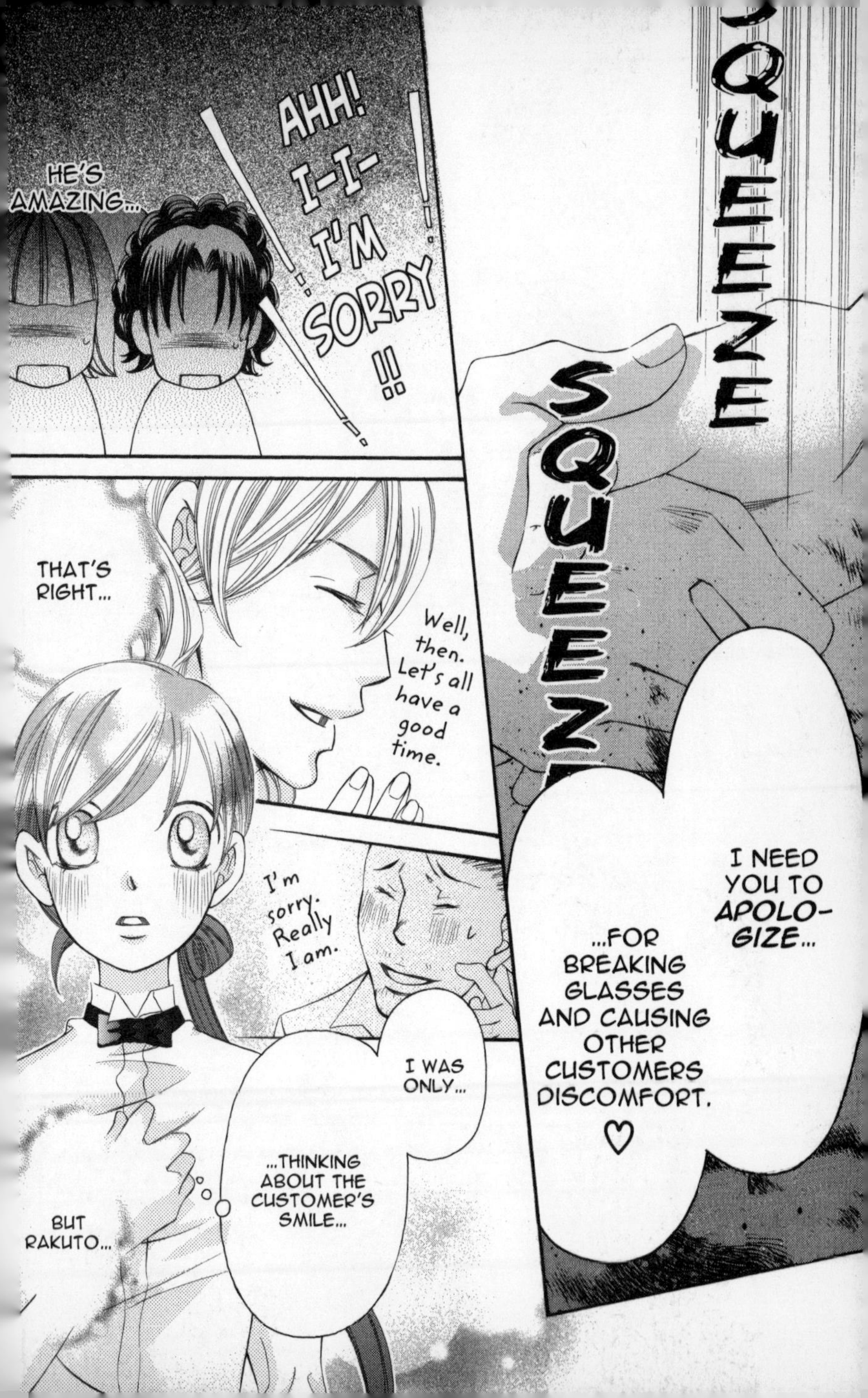
SQUEEZE
SQUEEZE
I NEED YOU TO APOLOGIZE...
...FOR BREAKING GLASSES AND CAUSING OTHER CUSTOMERS DISCOMFORT. ♡
AHH! I-I-I'M SORRY!!
HE'S AMAZING...
Well, then. Let's all have a good time.
THAT'S RIGHT...
I'm sorry. Really I am.
I WAS ONLY...
...THINKING ABOUT THE CUSTOMER'S SMILE...
BUT RAKUTO...

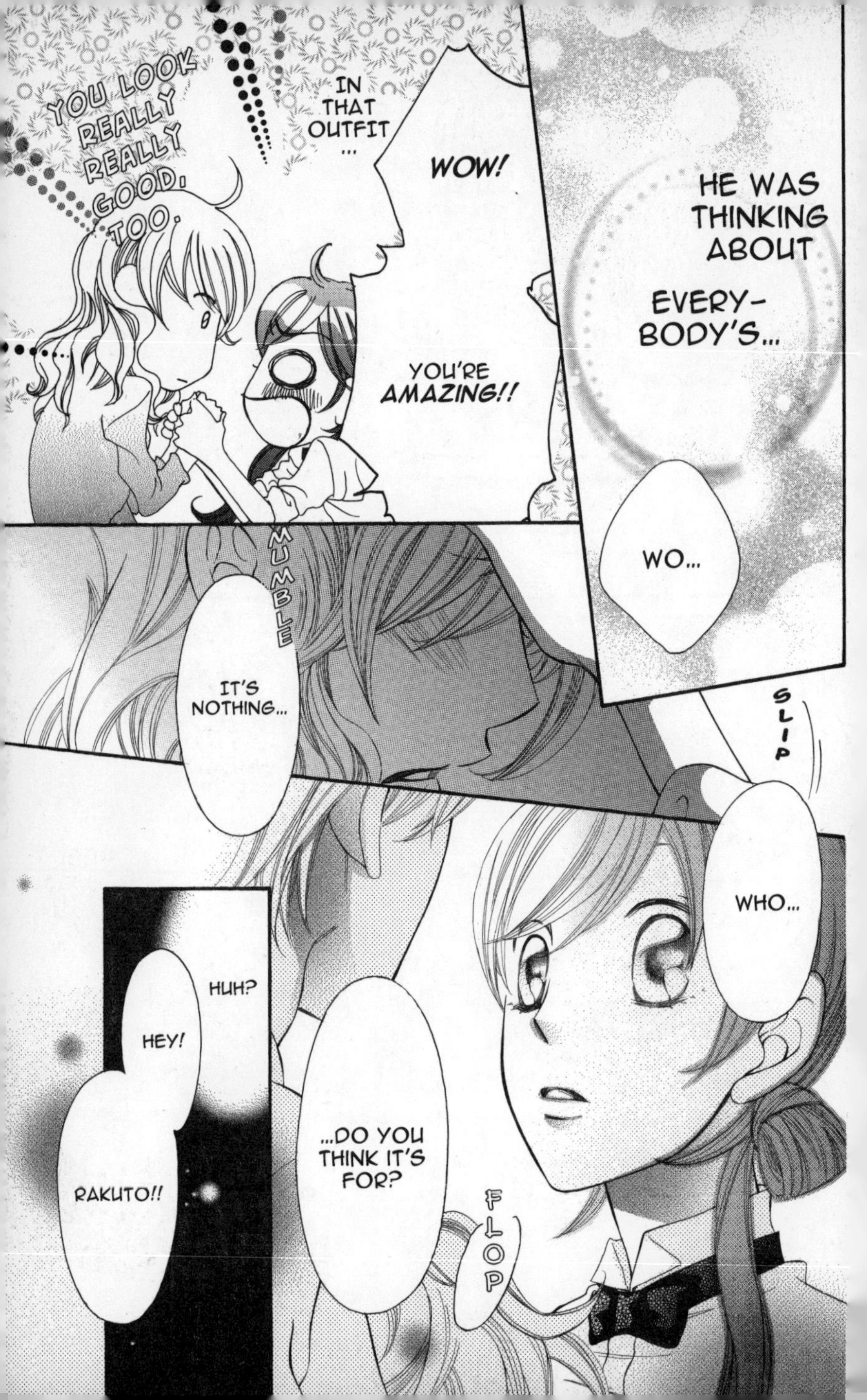
HE WAS THINKING ABOUT
EVERY-BODY'S...
WO...
WOW!
IN THAT OUTFIT ...
YOU'RE AMAZING!!
YOU LOOK REALLY REALLY GOOD, TOO.
MUMBLE
IT'S NOTHING...
SLIP
WHO...
FLOP
...DO YOU THINK IT'S FOR?
RAKUTO!!
HEY!
HUH?

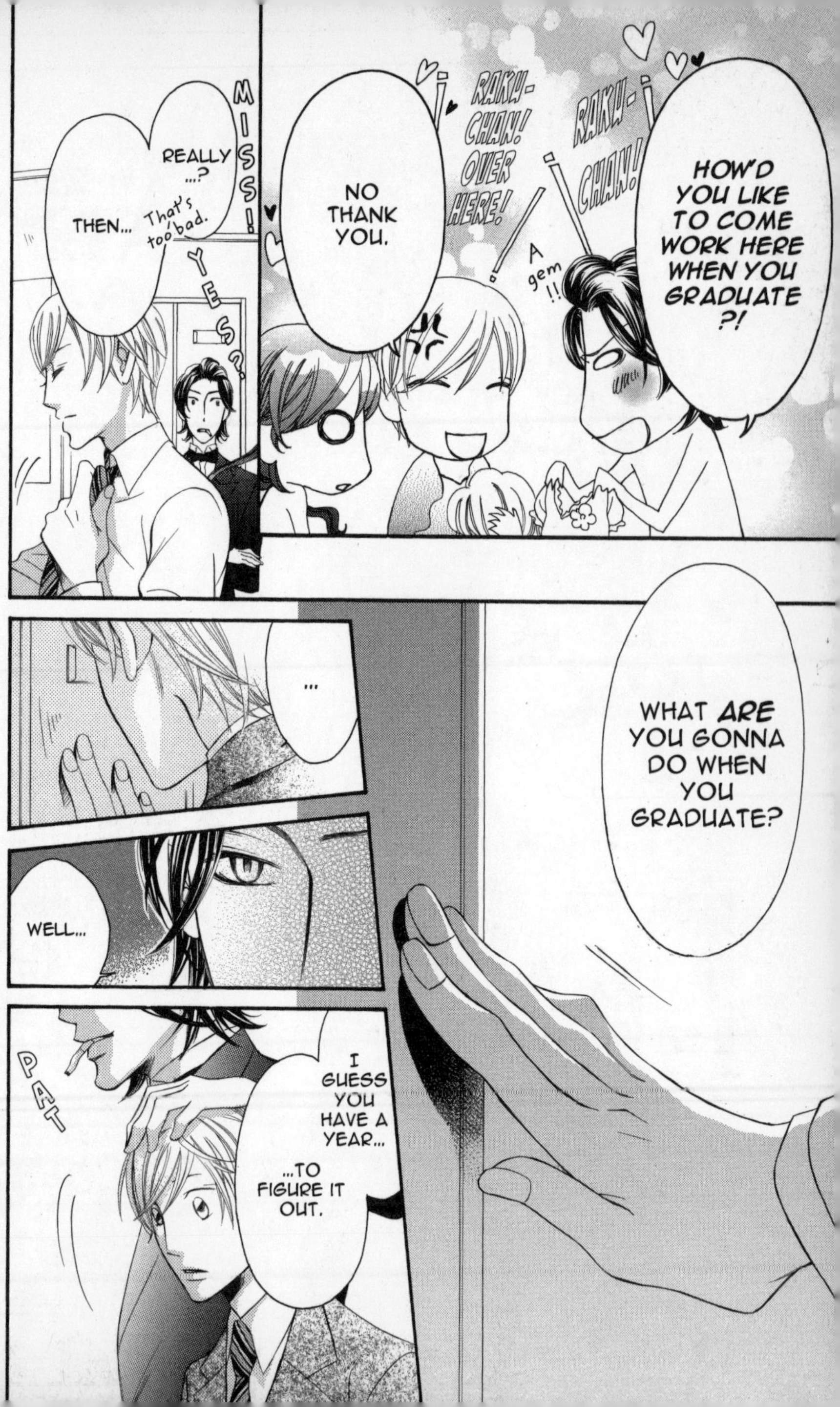
HOW'D YOU LIKE TO COME WORK HERE WHEN YOU GRADUATE ?!
RAKU-CHAN!
A gem !!
RAKU-CHAN! OVER HERE!
NO THANK YOU.
MISS! YES?
REALLY ...?
THEN... That's too bad.
WHAT ARE YOU GONNA DO WHEN YOU GRADUATE?
...
WELL...
PAT
I GUESS YOU HAVE A YEAR...
...TO FIGURE IT OUT.

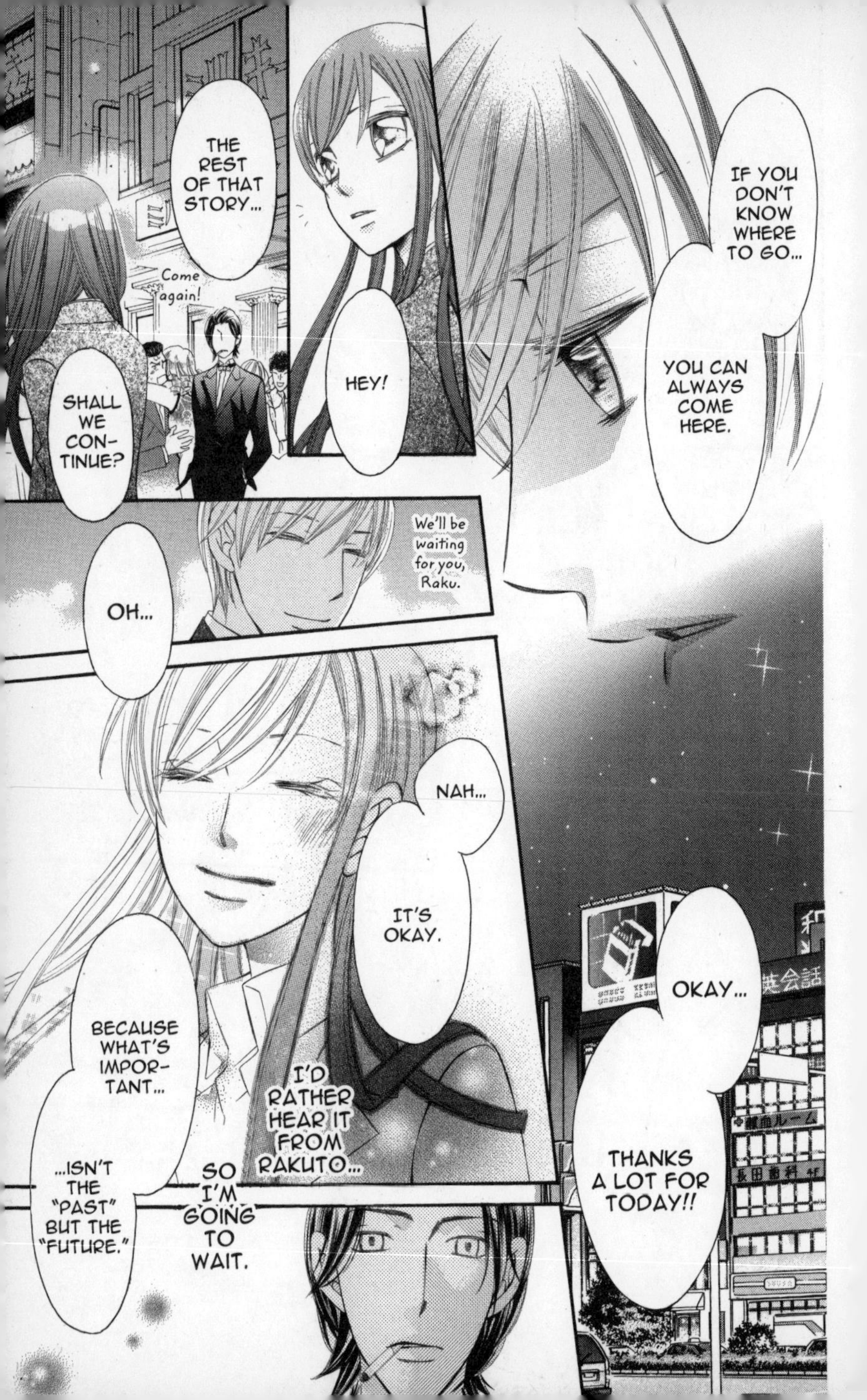
IF YOU DON'T KNOW WHERE TO GO...
YOU CAN ALWAYS COME HERE.
OKAY...
THANKS A LOT FOR TODAY!!
HEY!
THE REST OF THAT STORY...
Come again!
SHALL WE CON-TINUE?
We'll be waiting for you, Raku.
OH...
NAH...
IT'S OKAY.
I'D RATHER HEAR IT FROM RAKUTO...
BECAUSE WHAT'S IMPOR-TANT...
...ISN'T THE "PAST" BUT THE "FUTURE."
SO I'M GOING TO WAIT.

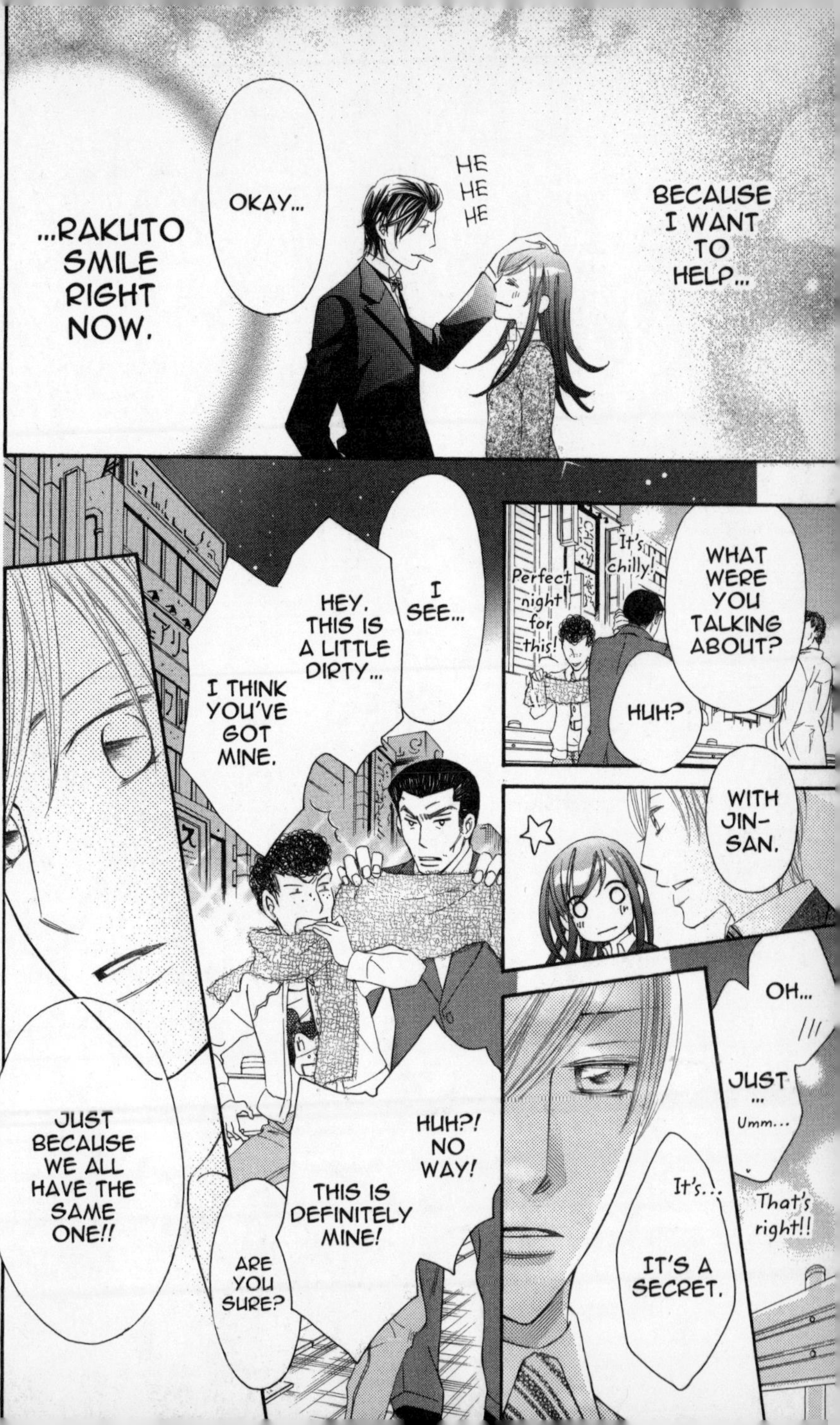
BECAUSE I WANT TO HELP...
HE HE HE
OKAY...
...RAKUTO SMILE RIGHT NOW.
WHAT WERE YOU TALKING ABOUT?
It's chilly!
Perfect night for this!
HUH?
WITH JIN-SAN.
OH...
JUST...
Umm...
That's right!!
It's...
IT'S A SECRET.
I SEE...
HEY. THIS IS A LITTLE DIRTY...
I THINK YOU'VE GOT MINE.
HUH?! NO WAY!
THIS IS DEFINITELY MINE!
ARE YOU SURE?
JUST BECAUSE WE ALL HAVE THE SAME ONE!!

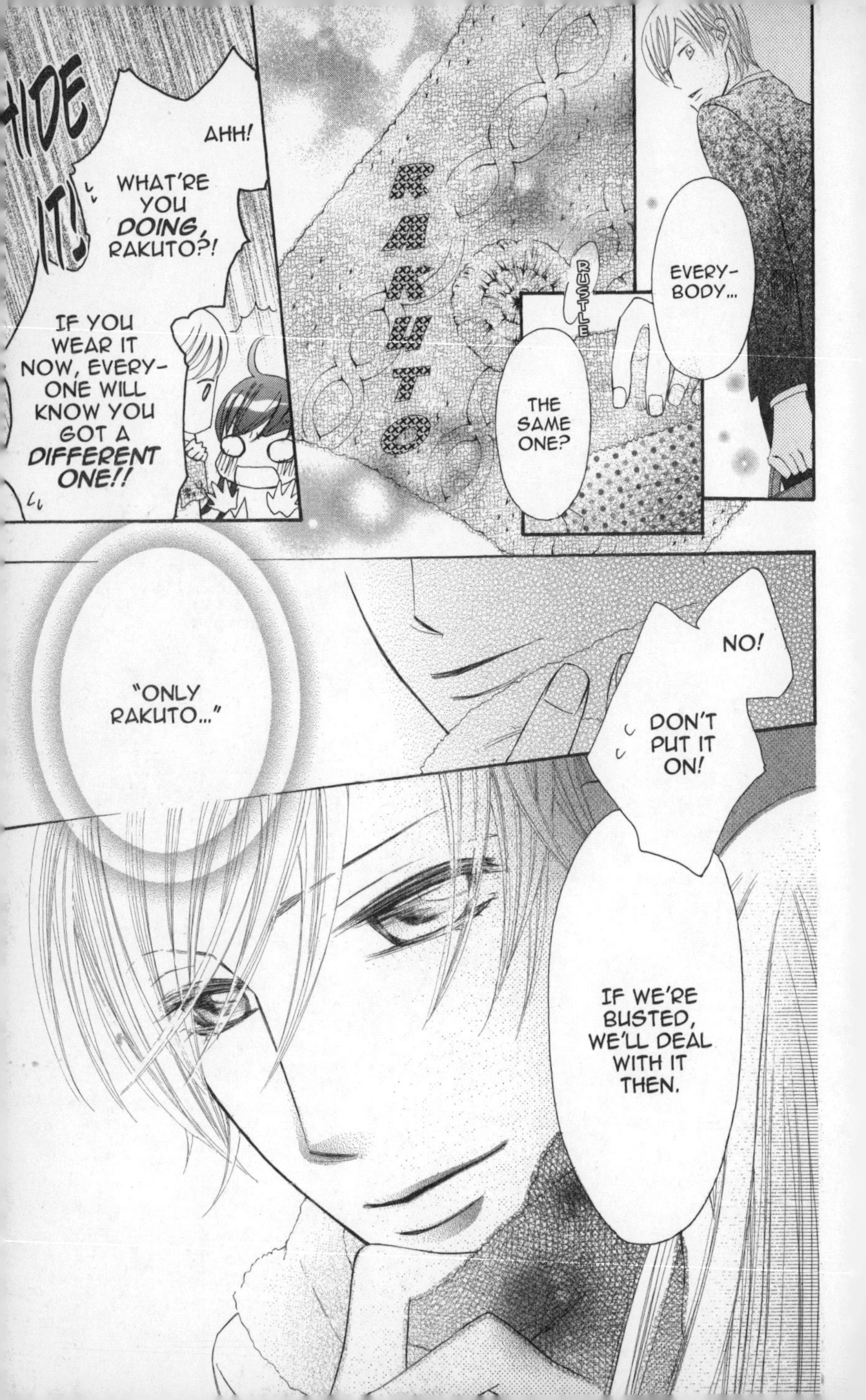
EVERY-BODY...
RUSTLE
THE SAME ONE?
RAKUTO
AHH!
WHAT'RE YOU DOING, RAKUTO?!
HIDE IT!
IF YOU WEAR IT NOW, EVERY-ONE WILL KNOW YOU GOT A DIFFERENT ONE!!
NO!
DON'T PUT IT ON!
"ONLY RAKUTO..."
IF WE'RE BUSTED, WE'LL DEAL WITH IT THEN.

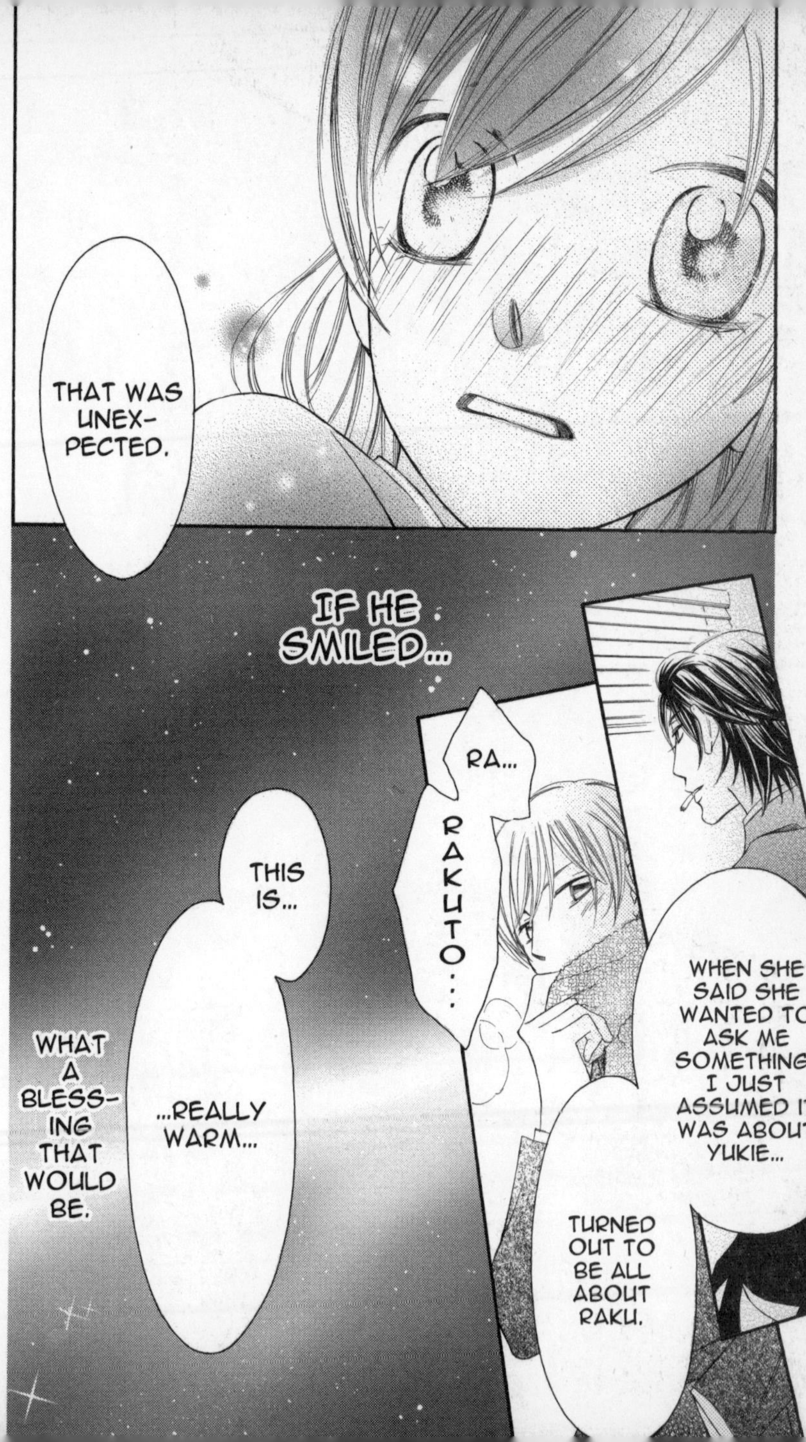
THAT WAS UNEX-PECTED.
WHEN SHE SAID SHE WANTED TO ASK ME SOMETHING, I JUST ASSUMED IT WAS ABOUT YUKIE...
TURNED OUT TO BE ALL ABOUT RAKU.
RA...
RAKUTO...
IF HE SMILED...
THIS IS...
...REALLY WARM...
WHAT A BLESS-ING THAT WOULD BE.

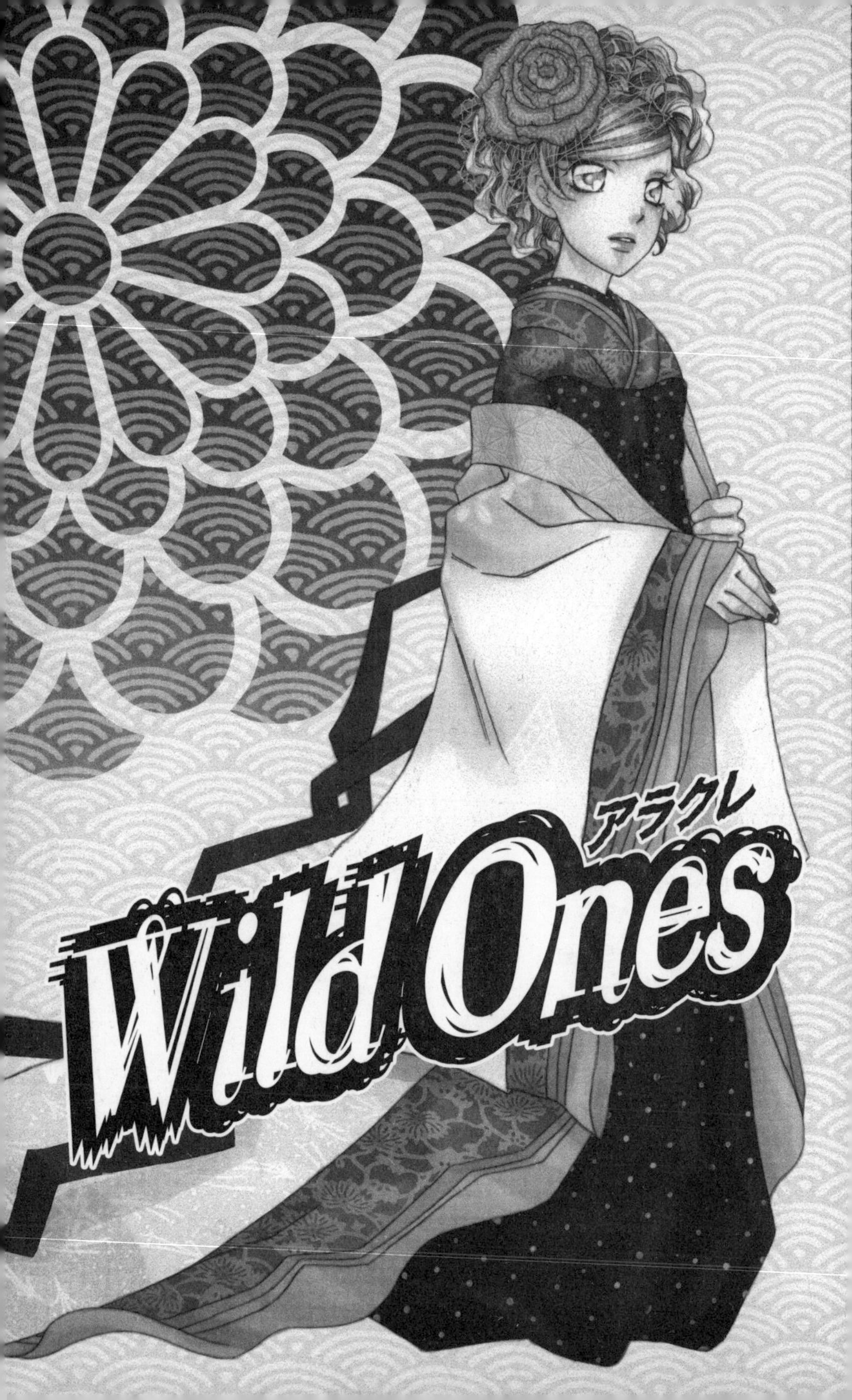
アラクレ
Wild Ones

A botched front page from
Christmas (↑ For the first story)

They said, ever so
uncomfortably…
"Miss Fujiwara…
This is a little…"
And turned it down…

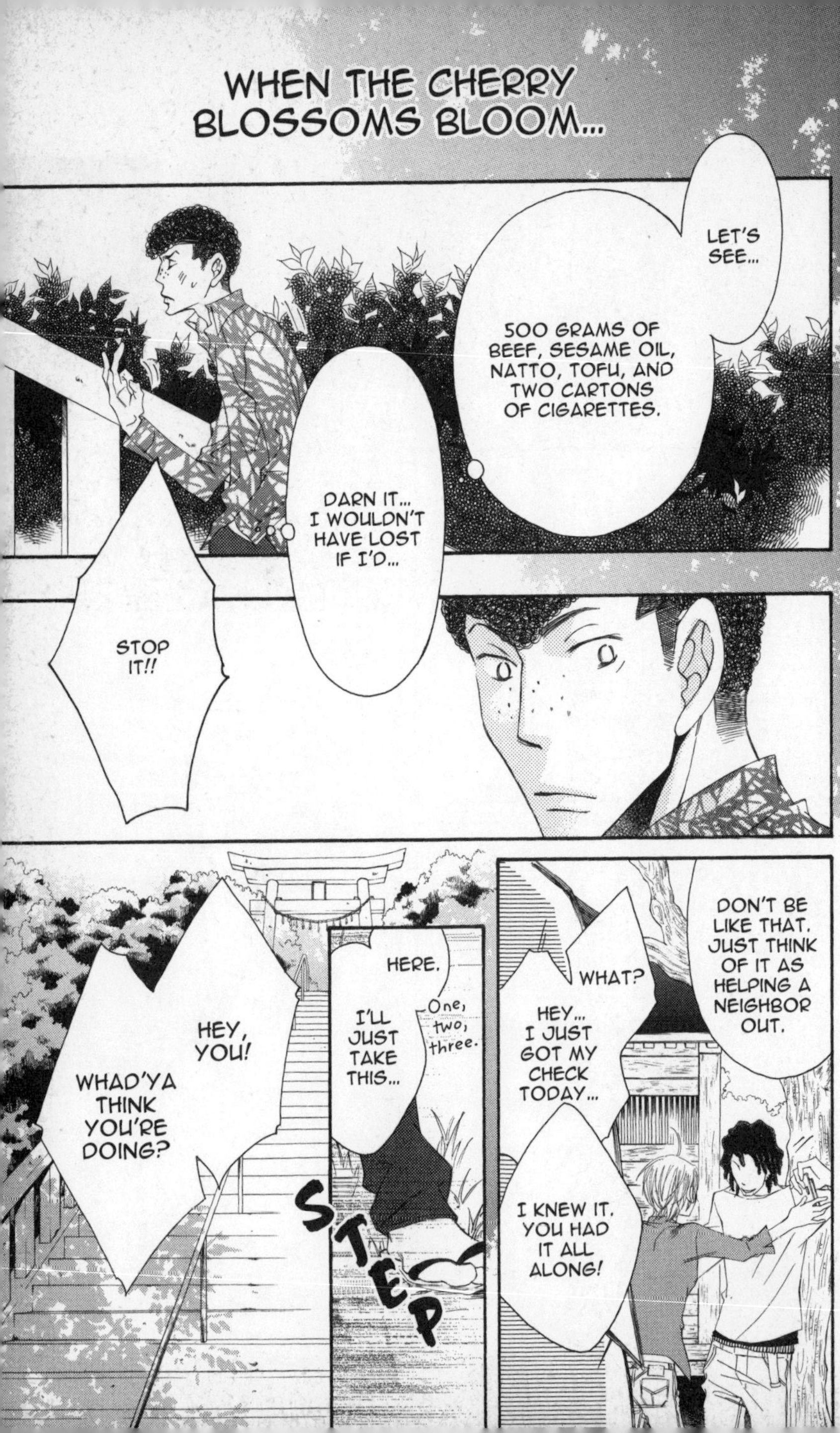
WHEN THE CHERRY BLOSSOMS BLOOM...
LET'S SEE...
500 GRAMS OF BEEF, SESAME OIL, NATTO, TOFU, AND TWO CARTONS OF CIGARETTES.
DARN IT... I WOULDN'T HAVE LOST IF I'D...
STOP IT!!
DON'T BE LIKE THAT. JUST THINK OF IT AS HELPING A NEIGHBOR OUT.
WHAT?
HEY... I JUST GOT MY CHECK TODAY...
I KNEW IT. YOU HAD IT ALL ALONG!
HERE.
One, two, three.
I'LL JUST TAKE THIS...
STEP
HEY, YOU!
WHAD'YA THINK YOU'RE DOING?

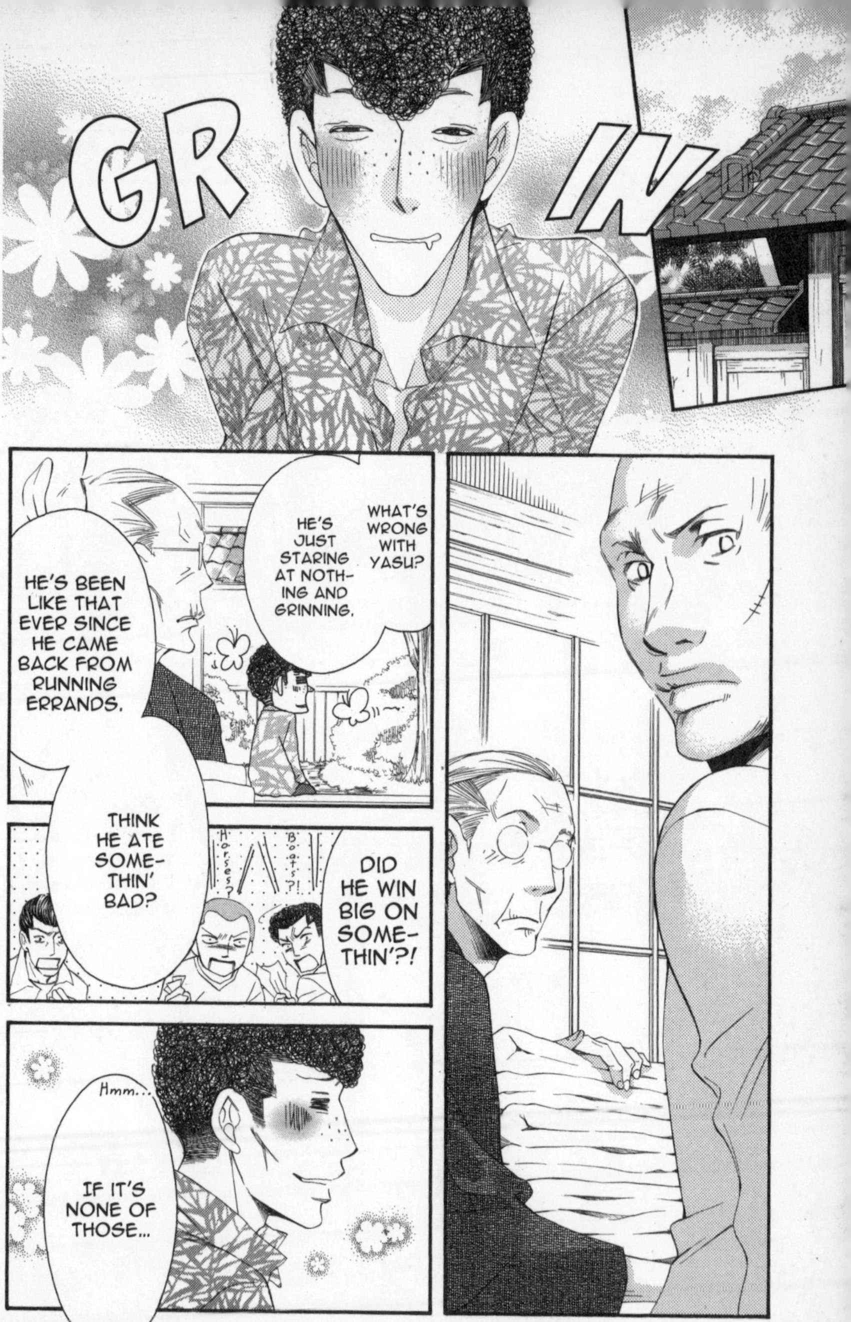
GRIN
WHAT'S WRONG WITH YASU?
HE'S JUST STARING AT NOTHING-ING AND GRINNING.
HE'S BEEN LIKE THAT EVER SINCE HE CAME BACK FROM RUNNING ERRANDS.
DID HE WIN BIG ON SOMETHIN'?!
Boats?!
Horses?
THINK HE ATE SOMETHIN' BAD?
Hmm...
IF IT'S NONE OF THOSE...

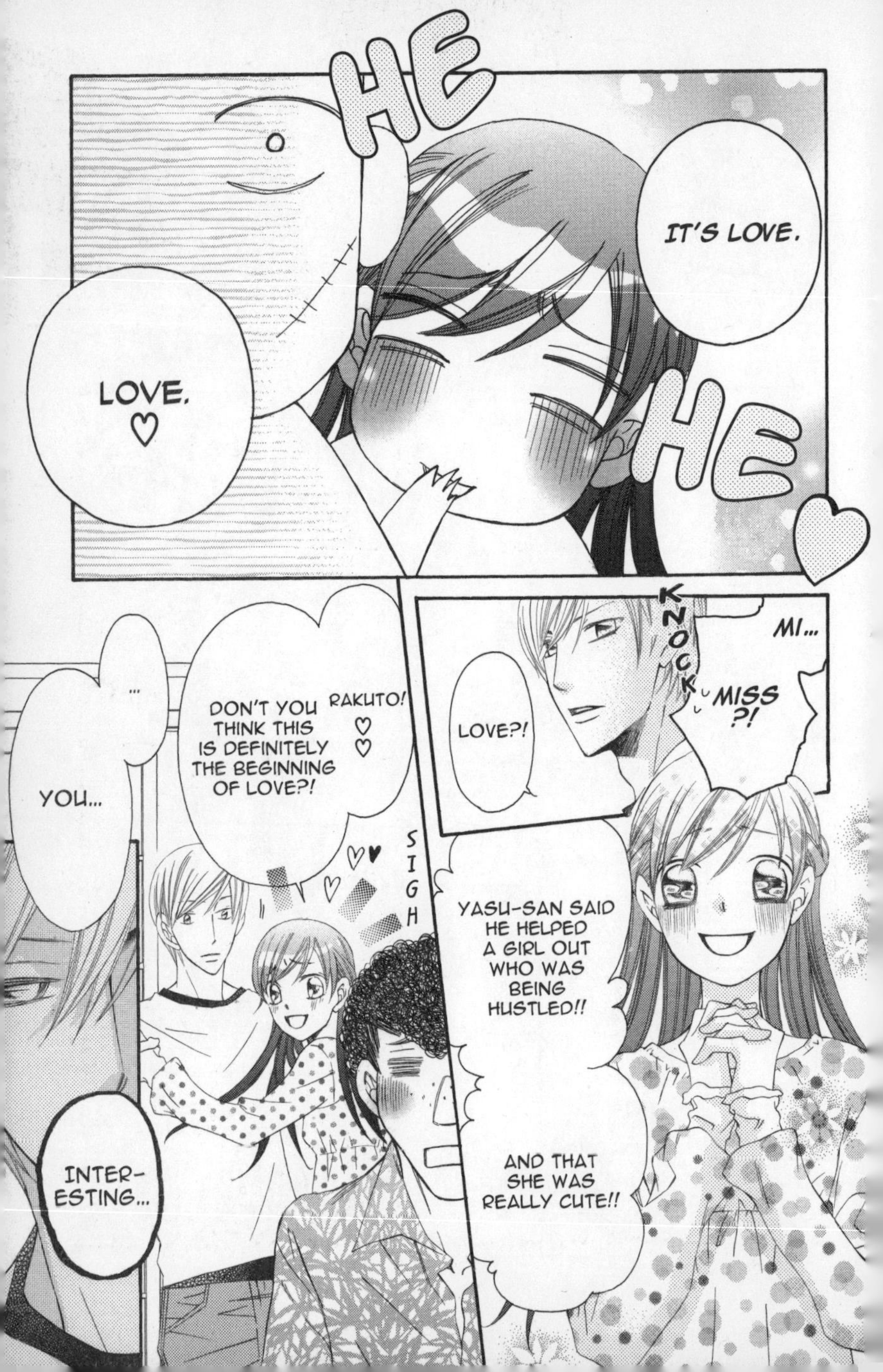

IT'S LOVE.
HE
HE
LOVE. ♡
KNOCK
MI... MISS ?!
LOVE?!
YASU-SAN SAID HE HELPED A GIRL OUT WHO WAS BEING HUSTLED!!
AND THAT SHE WAS REALLY CUTE!!
RAKUTO! ♡ ♡
DON'T YOU THINK THIS IS DEFINITELY THE BEGINNING OF LOVE?!
SIGH
...
YOU...
INTER-ESTING...

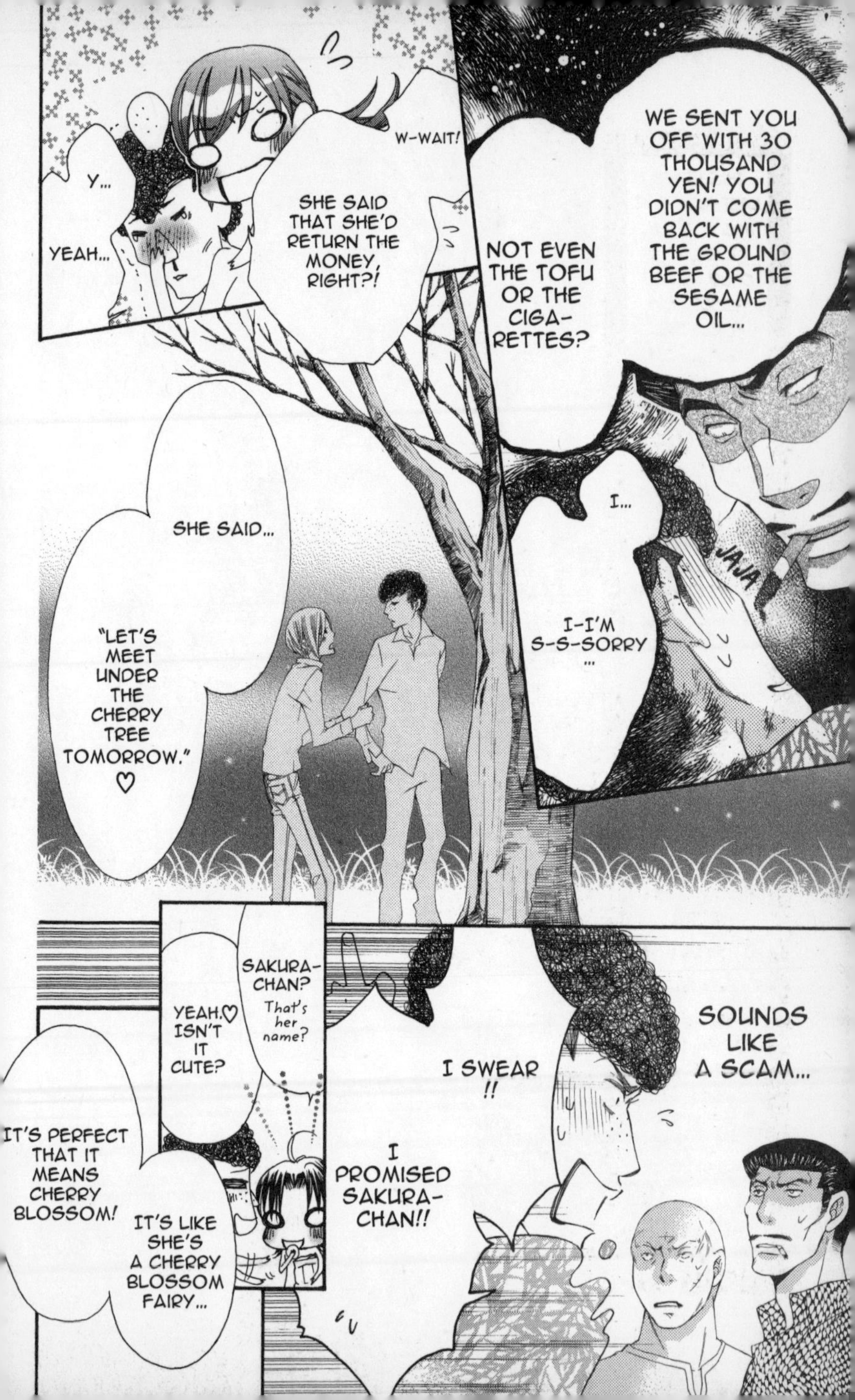
WE SENT YOU OFF WITH 30 THOUSAND YEN! YOU DIDN'T COME BACK WITH THE GROUND BEEF OR THE SESAME OIL...
NOT EVEN THE TOFU OR THE CIGA-RETTES?
I...
JAJA
I-I'M S-S-SORRY ...
W-WAIT!
SHE SAID THAT SHE'D RETURN THE MONEY, RIGHT?!
Y...
YEAH...
SHE SAID...
"LET'S MEET UNDER THE CHERRY TREE TOMORROW." ♡
SOUNDS LIKE A SCAM...
I SWEAR !!
I PROMISED SAKURA-CHAN!!
SAKURA-CHAN? That's her name?
YEAH,♡ ISN'T IT CUTE?
IT'S PERFECT THAT IT MEANS CHERRY BLOSSOM!
IT'S LIKE SHE'S A CHERRY BLOSSOM FAIRY...

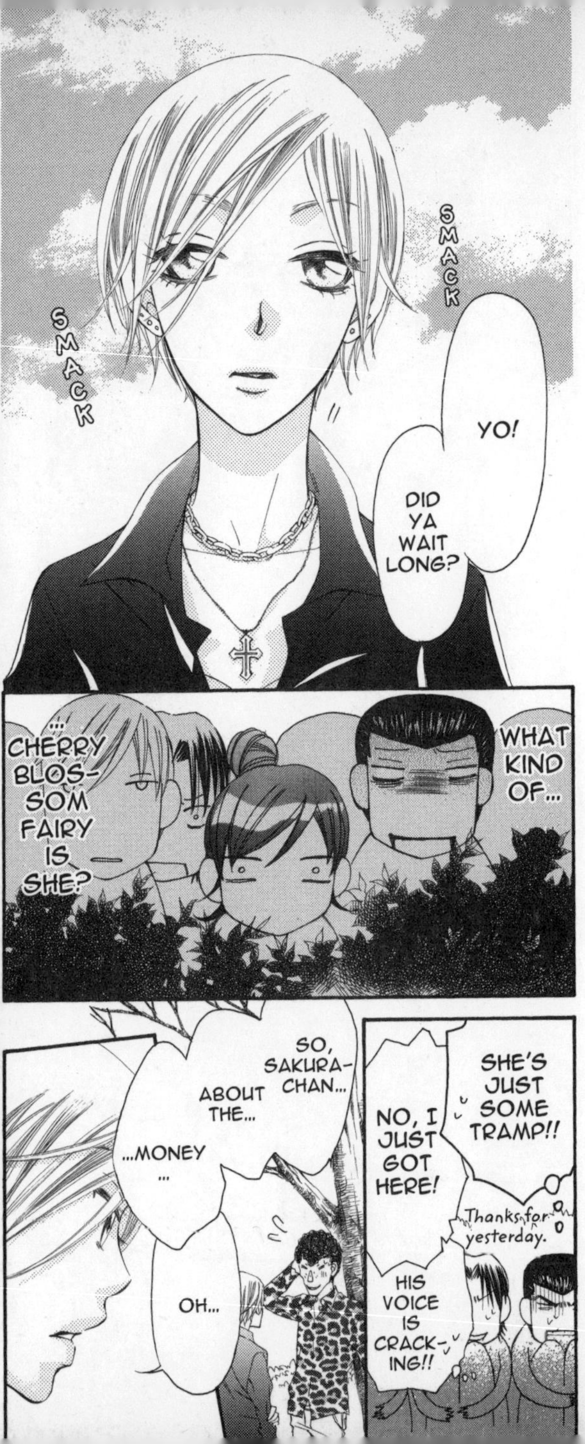
SMACK
SMACK
YO!
DID YA WAIT LONG?
WHAT KIND OF...
...CHERRY BLOS-SOM FAIRY IS SHE?
SHE'S JUST SOME TRAMP!!
NO, I JUST GOT HERE!
Thanks for yesterday.
HIS VOICE IS CRACK-ING!!
SO, SAKURA-CHAN...
ABOUT THE...
...MONEY...
OH...

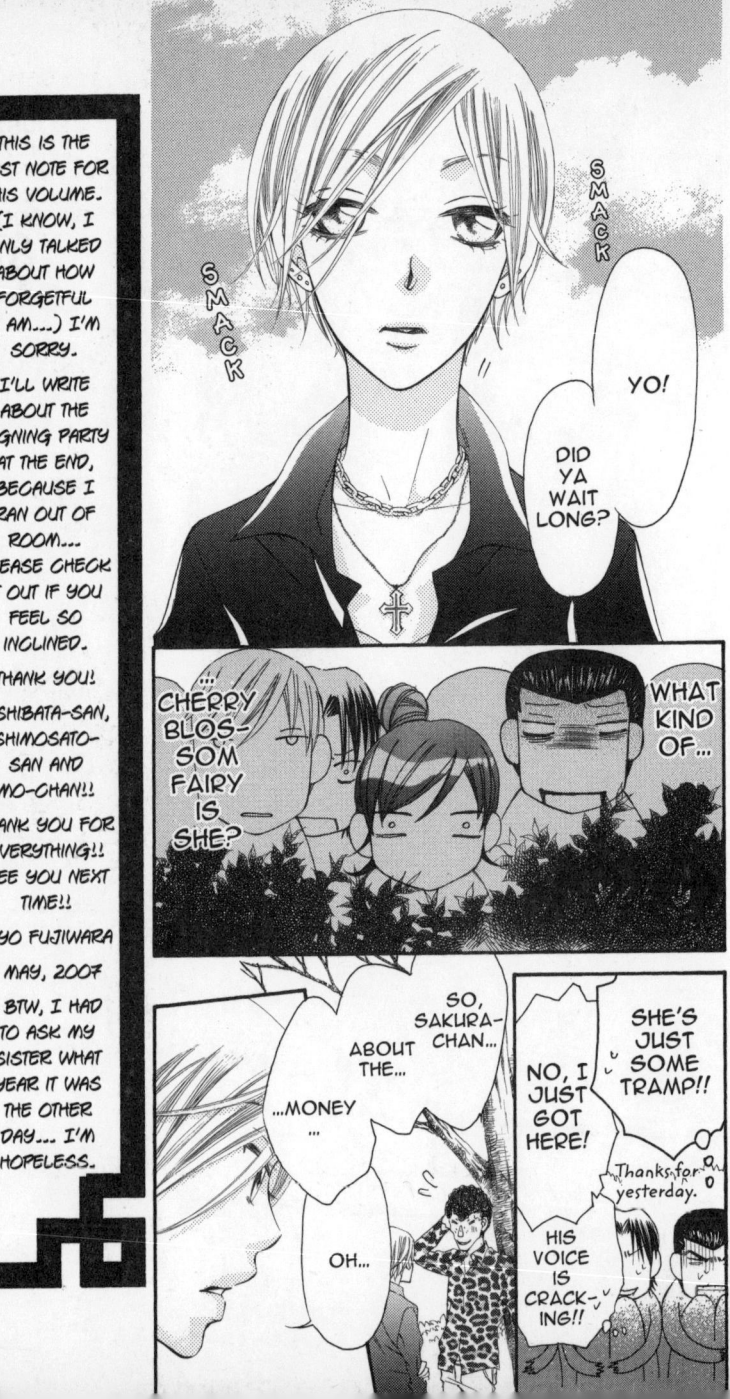

THIS IS THE LAST NOTE FOR THIS VOLUME. (I KNOW, I ONLY TALKED ABOUT HOW FORGETFUL I AM...) I'M SORRY.

I'LL WRITE ABOUT THE SIGNING PARTY AT THE END, BECAUSE I RAN OUT OF ROOM... PLEASE CHECK IT OUT IF YOU FEEL SO INCLINED.

THANK YOU!

SHIBATA-SAN, SHIMOSATO-SAN AND MO-CHAN!!

THANK YOU FOR EVERYTHING!! SEE YOU NEXT TIME!!

KIYO FUJIWARA

MAY, 2007

BTW, I HAD TO ASK MY SISTER WHAT YEAR IT WAS THE OTHER DAY... I'M HOPELESS.

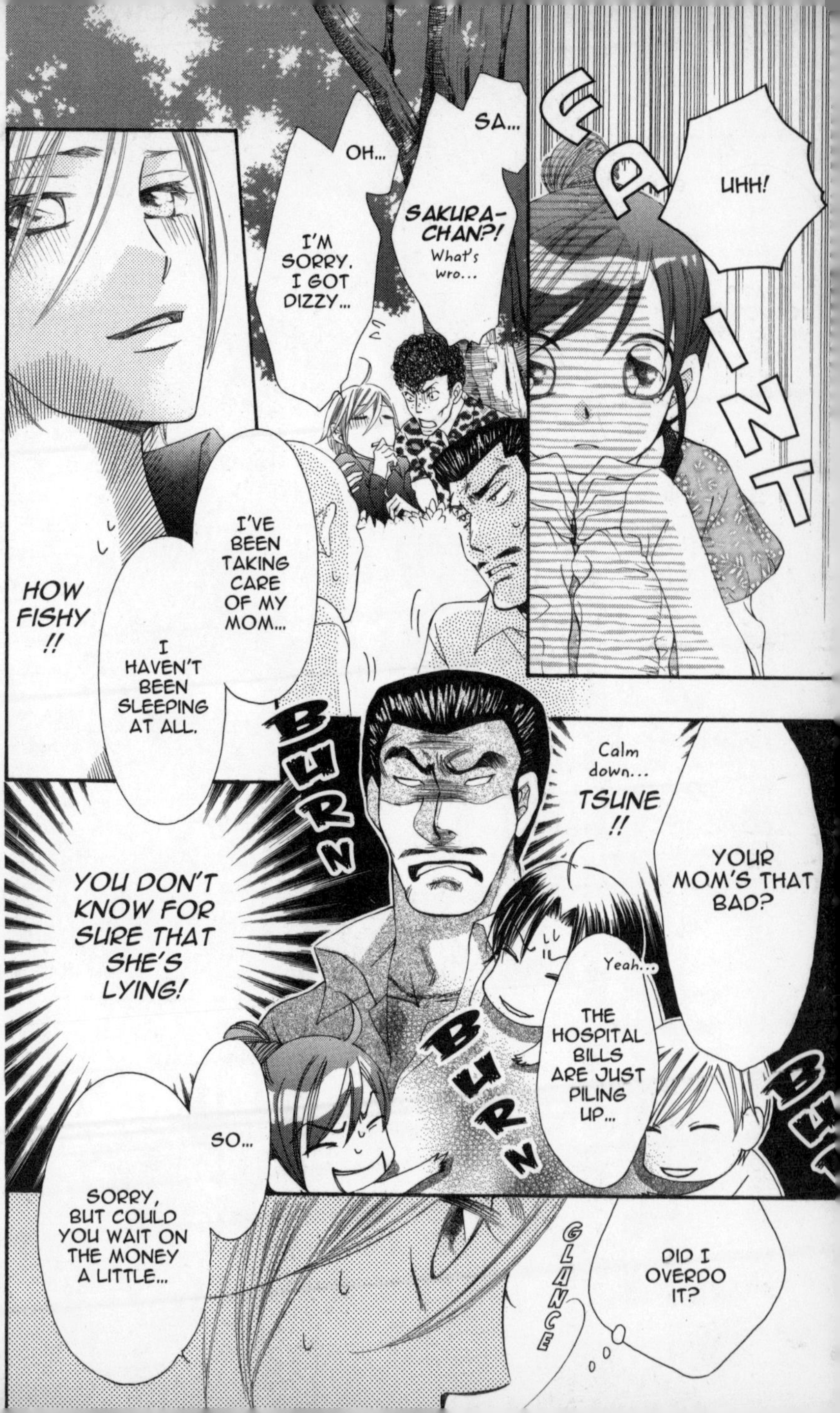
UHH!
FAINT
SA...
SAKURA-CHAN?!
What's wro...
OH...
I'M SORRY. I GOT DIZZY...
I'VE BEEN TAKING CARE OF MY MOM...
I HAVEN'T BEEN SLEEPING AT ALL.
HOW FISHY!!
YOUR MOM'S THAT BAD?
Calm down... TSUNE!!
BURN
YOU DON'T KNOW FOR SURE THAT SHE'S LYING!
Yeah...
THE HOSPITAL BILLS ARE JUST PILING UP...
BURN
SO...
DID I OVERDO IT?
GLANCE
SORRY, BUT COULD YOU WAIT ON THE MONEY A LITTLE...

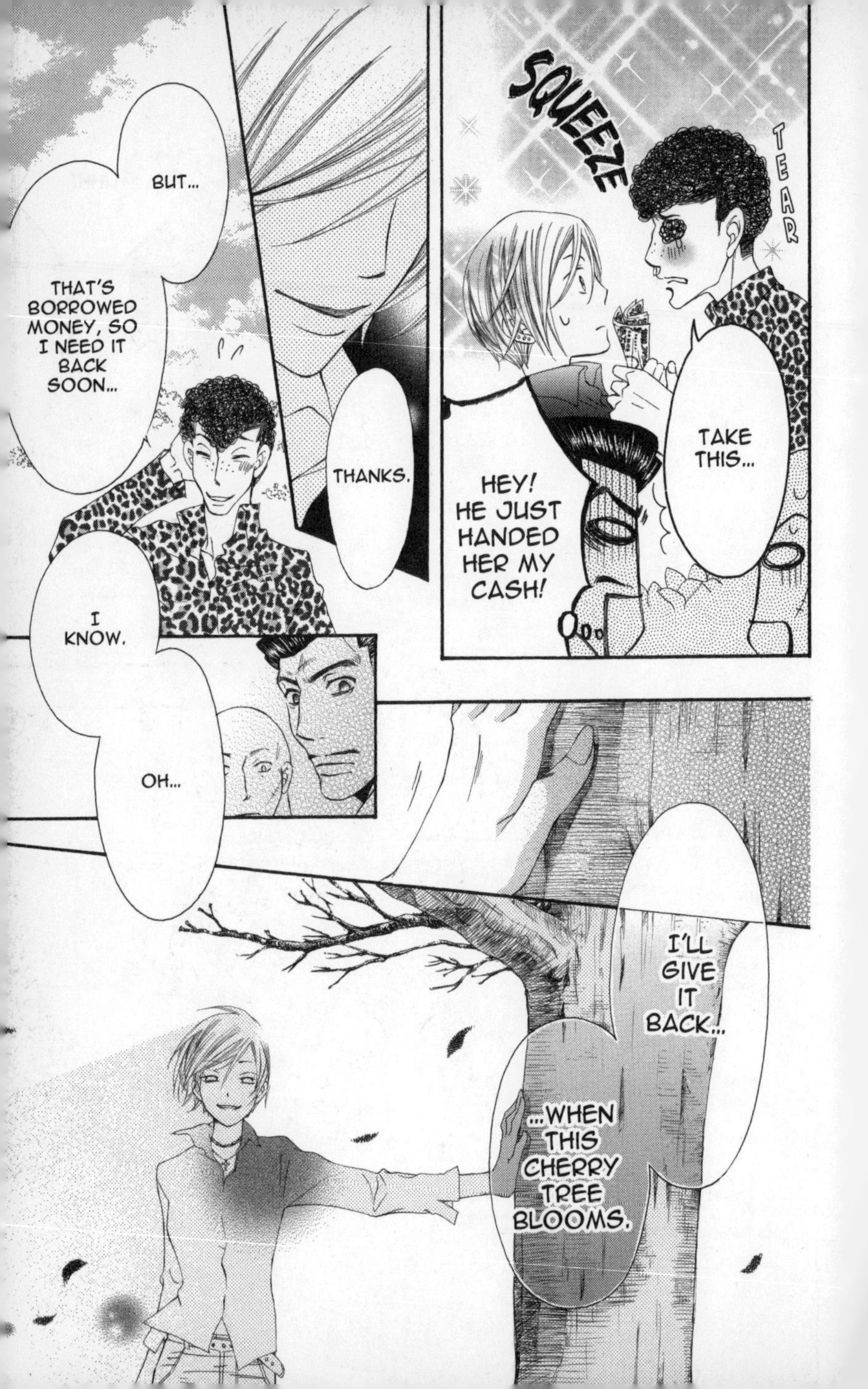
SQUEEZE
TEAR
TAKE THIS...
HEY! HE JUST HANDED HER MY CASH!
THANKS.
BUT...
THAT'S BORROWED MONEY, SO I NEED IT BACK SOON...
I KNOW.
OH...
I'LL GIVE IT BACK...
...WHEN THIS CHERRY TREE BLOOMS.

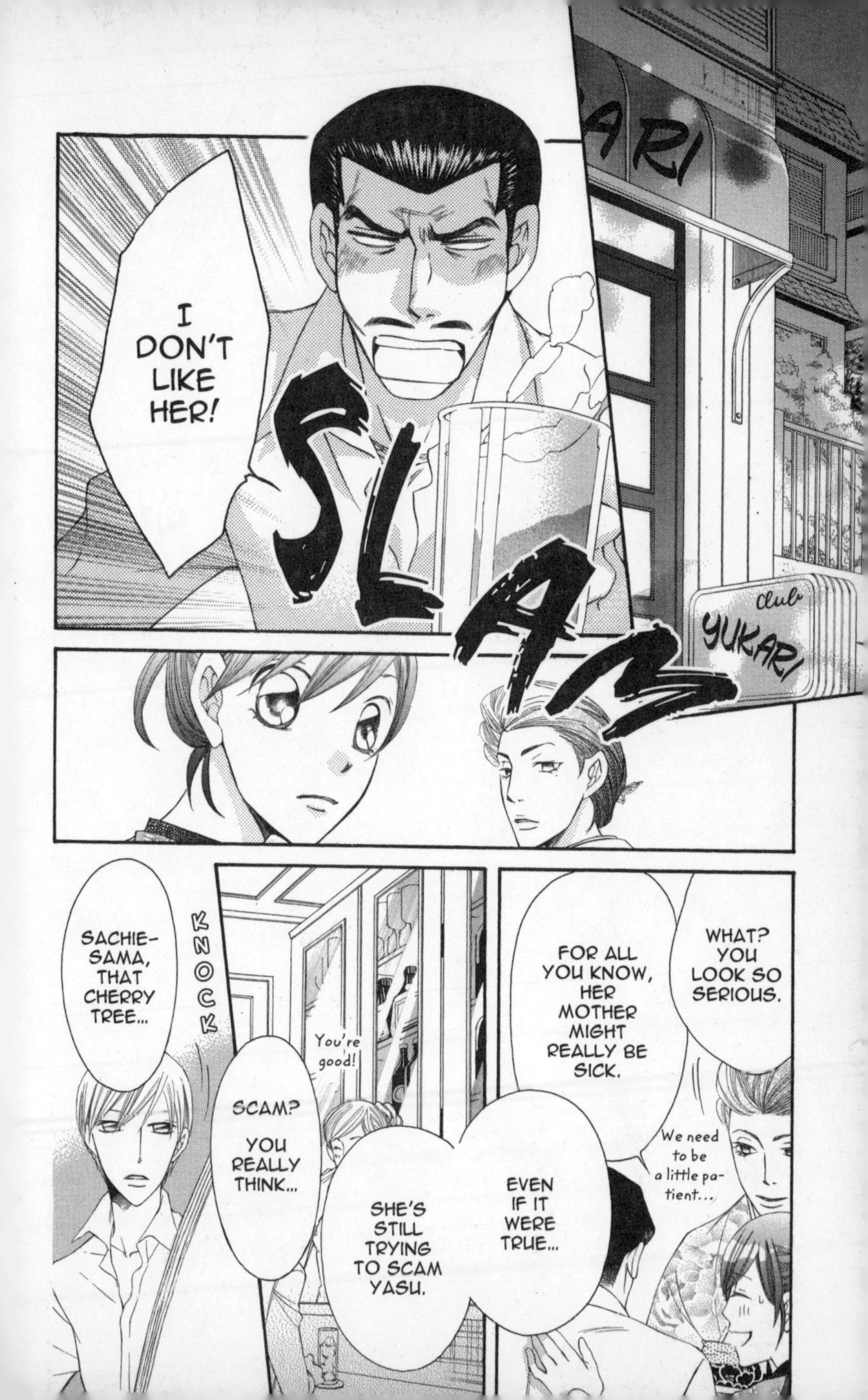

club YUKARI
I DON'T LIKE HER!
SLAM
WHAT? YOU LOOK SO SERIOUS.
FOR ALL YOU KNOW, HER MOTHER MIGHT REALLY BE SICK.
We need to be a little patient...
EVEN IF IT WERE TRUE...
SHE'S STILL TRYING TO SCAM YASU.
SCAM?
YOU REALLY THINK...
You're good!
KNOCK
SACHIE-SAMA, THAT CHERRY TREE...

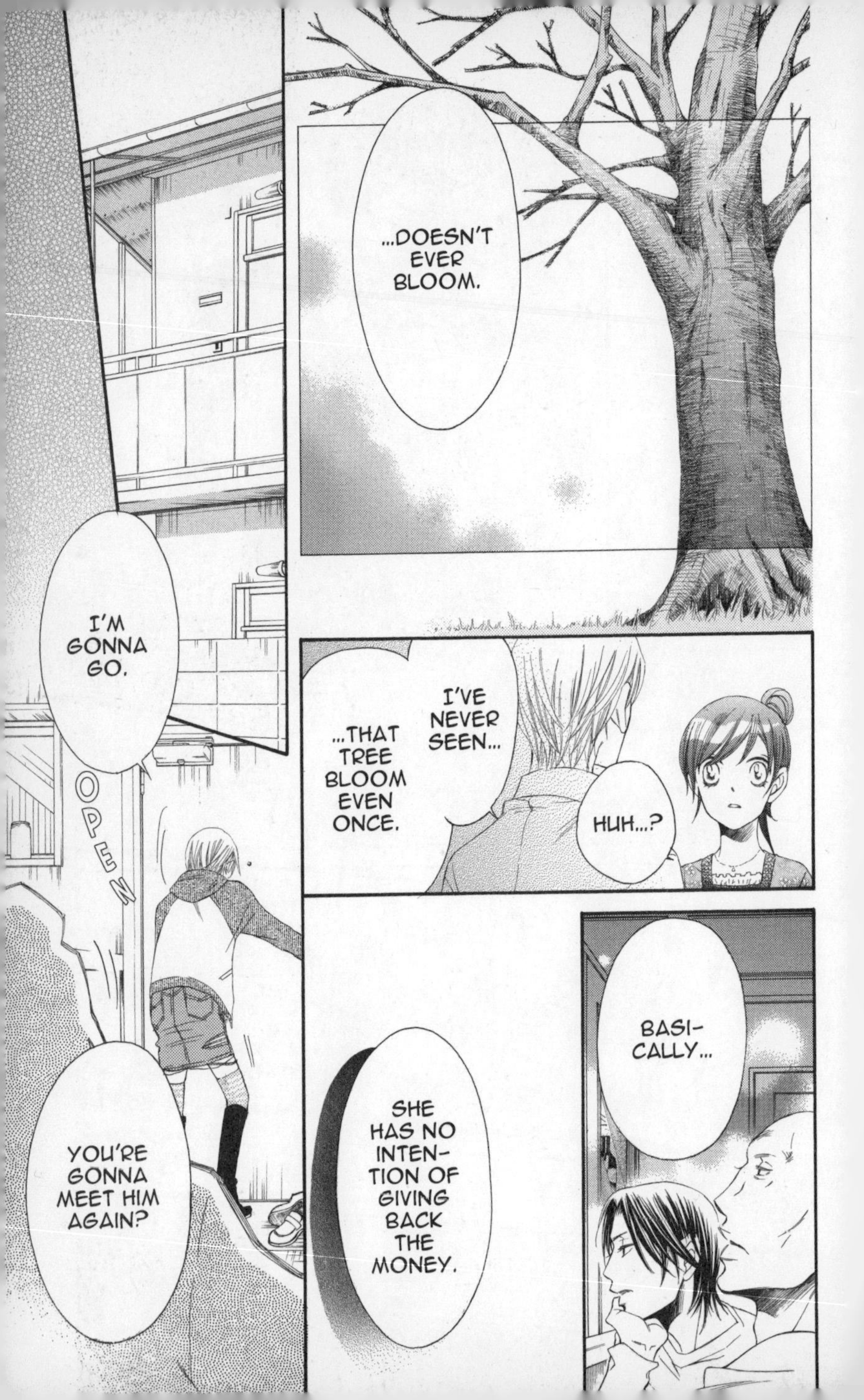
...DOESN'T EVER BLOOM.
I'VE NEVER SEEN...
...THAT TREE BLOOM EVEN ONCE.
HUH...?
BASI-CALLY...
SHE HAS NO INTEN-TION OF GIVING BACK THE MONEY.
I'M GONNA GO.
OPEN
YOU'RE GONNA MEET HIM AGAIN?

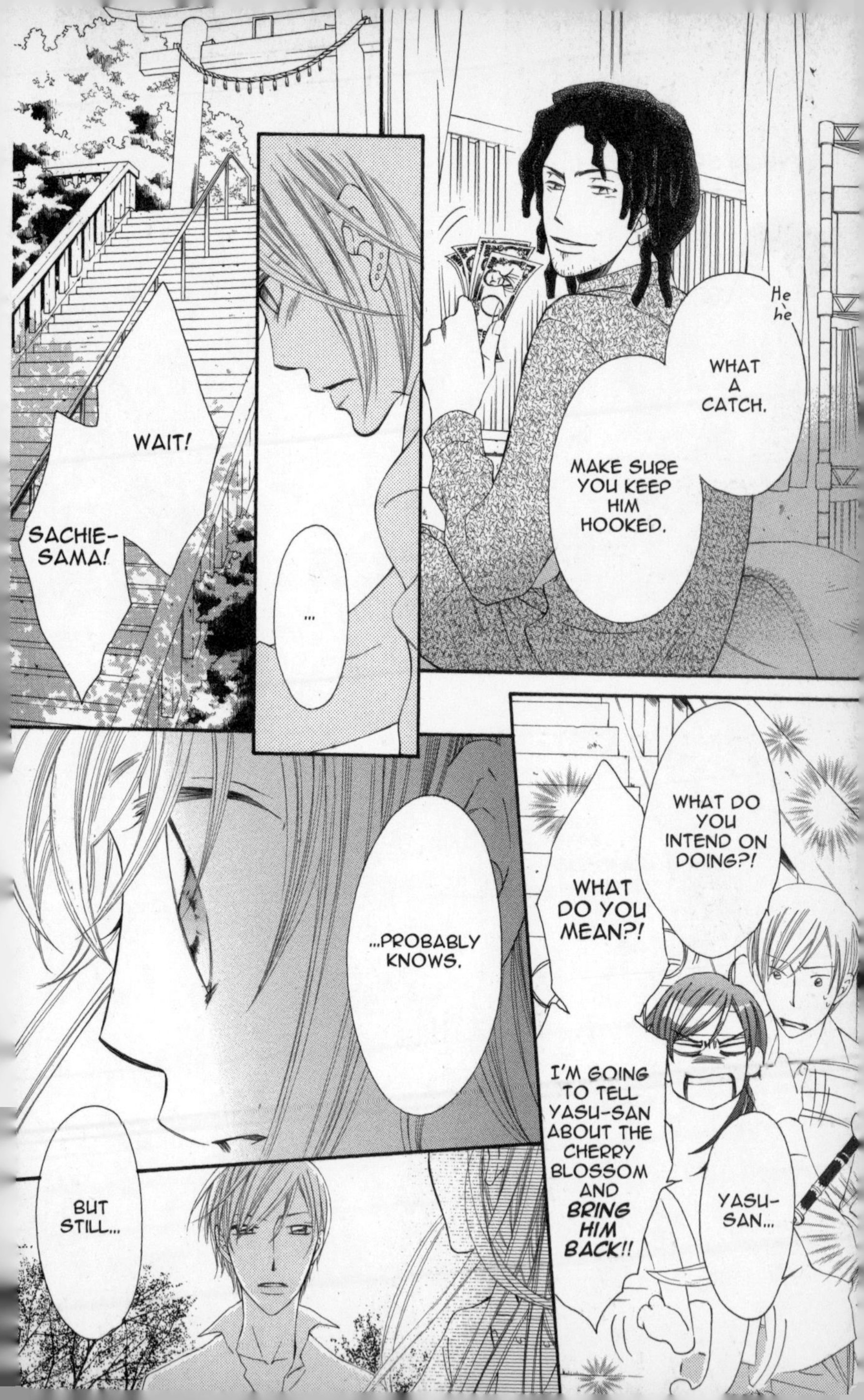
He he
WHAT A CATCH.
MAKE SURE YOU KEEP HIM HOOKED.
...
WAIT!
SACHIE-SAMA!
WHAT DO YOU INTEND ON DOING?!
WHAT DO YOU MEAN?!
YASU-SAN...
I'M GOING TO TELL YASU-SAN ABOUT THE CHERRY BLOSSOM AND BRING HIM BACK!!
...PROBABLY KNOWS.
BUT STILL...

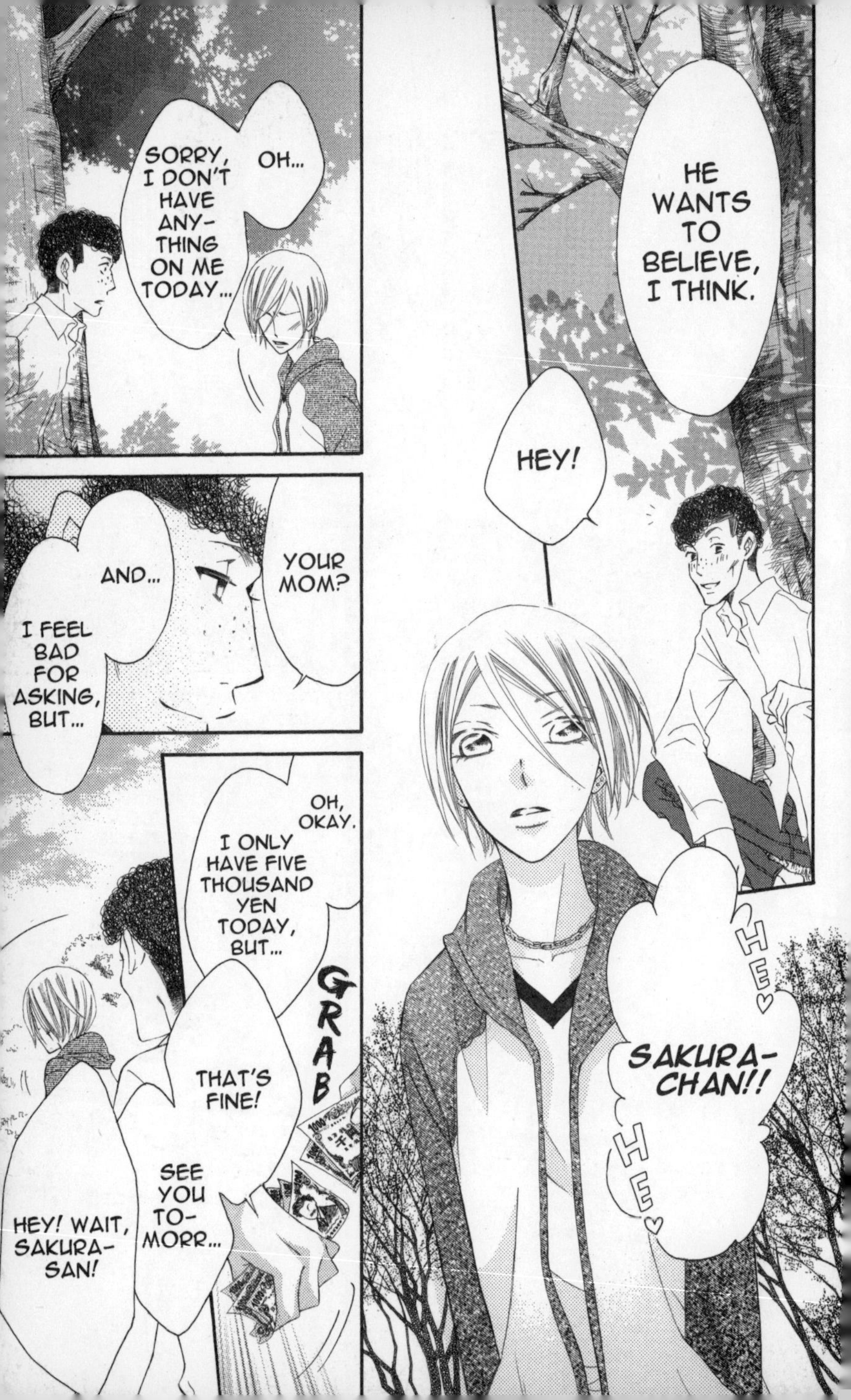
HE WANTS TO BELIEVE, I THINK.
HEY!
HE♥ HE♥ SAKURA-CHAN!!
OH...
SORRY, I DON'T HAVE ANY-THING ON ME TODAY...
YOUR MOM?
AND...
I FEEL BAD FOR ASKING, BUT...
OH, OKAY. I ONLY HAVE FIVE THOUSAND YEN TODAY, BUT...
GRAB
THAT'S FINE!
SEE YOU TO-MORR...
HEY! WAIT, SAKURA-SAN!

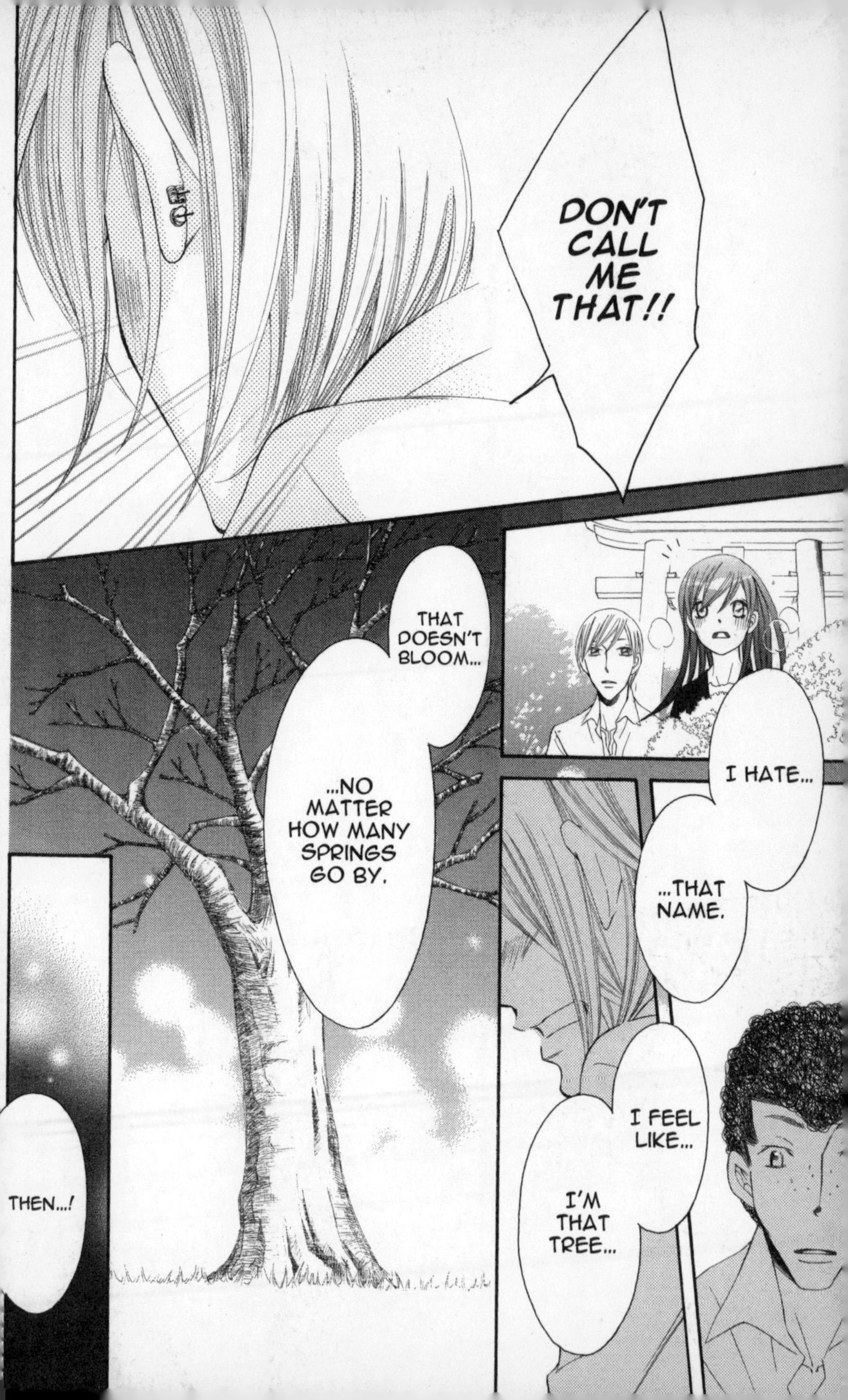
DON'T CALL ME THAT!!
I HATE...
...THAT NAME.
I FEEL LIKE...
I'M THAT TREE...
THAT DOESN'T BLOOM...
...NO MATTER HOW MANY SPRINGS GO BY.
THEN...!

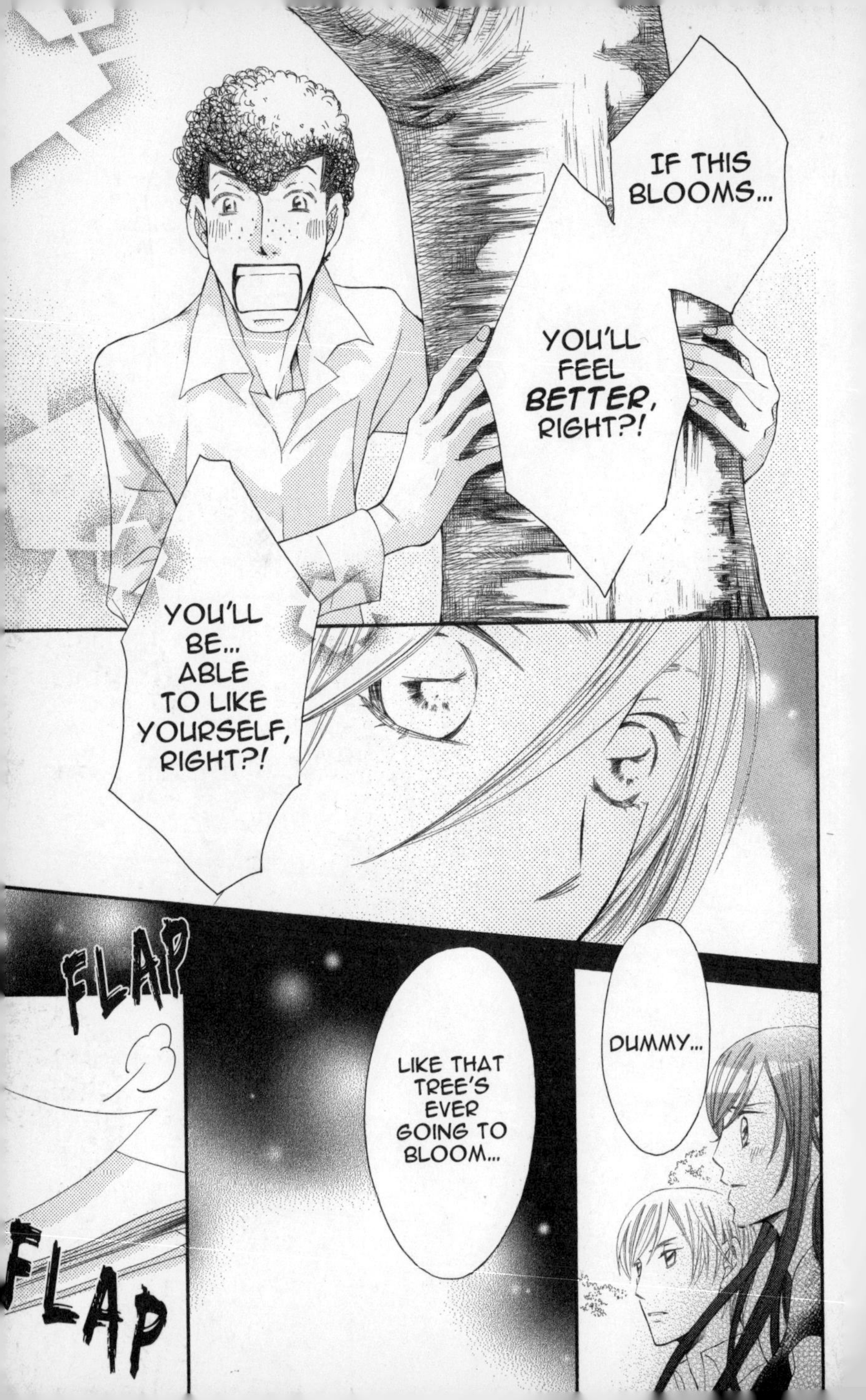
IF THIS BLOOMS...
YOU'LL FEEL **BETTER**, RIGHT?!
YOU'LL BE... ABLE TO LIKE YOURSELF, RIGHT?!
DUMMY...
LIKE THAT TREE'S EVER GOING TO BLOOM...
FLAP
FLAP

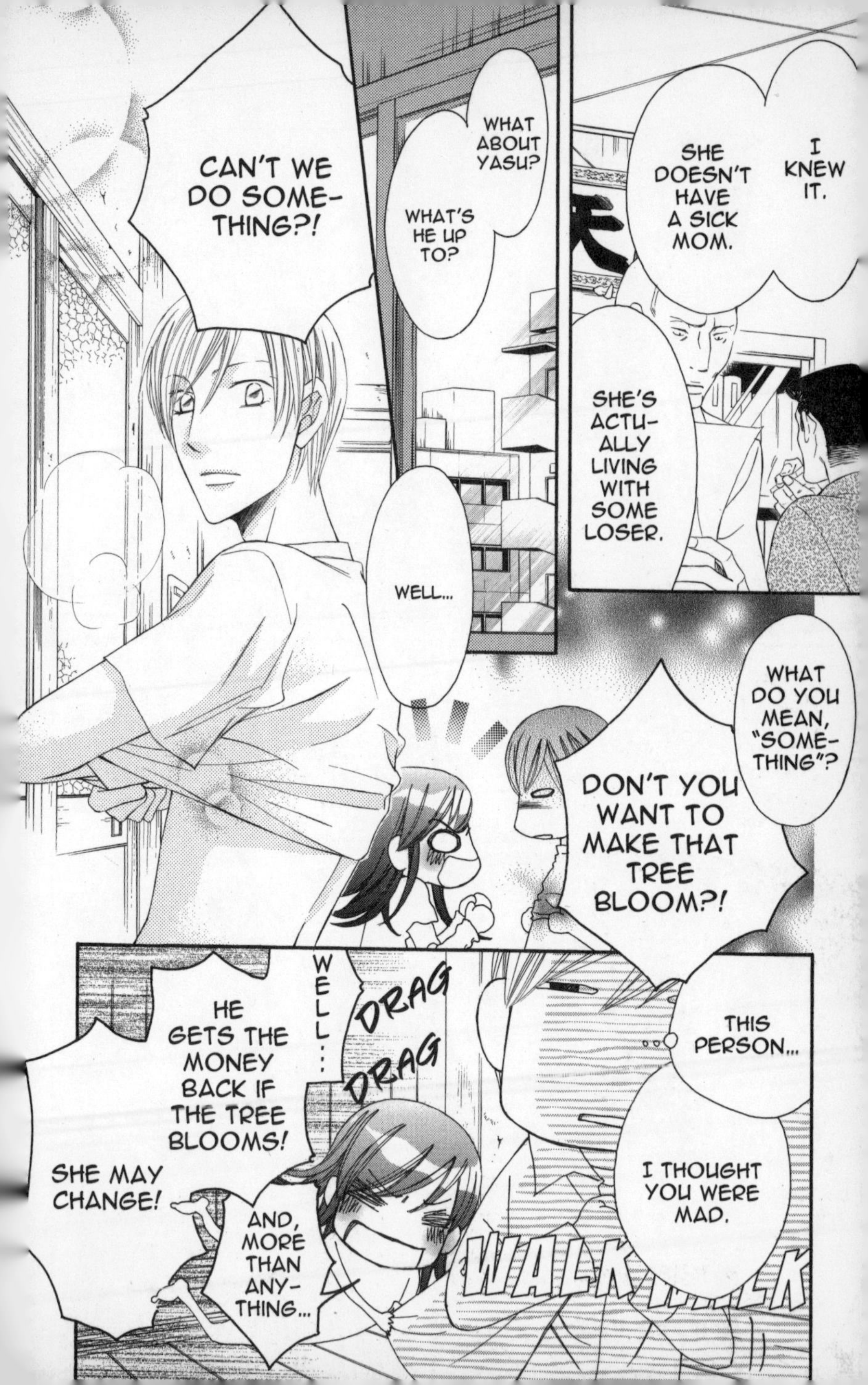
I KNEW IT.
SHE DOESN'T HAVE A SICK MOM.
SHE'S ACTUALLY LIVING WITH SOME LOSER.
WHAT ABOUT YASU?
WHAT'S HE UP TO?
CAN'T WE DO SOMETHING?!
WELL...
WHAT DO YOU MEAN, "SOMETHING"?
DON'T YOU WANT TO MAKE THAT TREE BLOOM?!
THIS PERSON...
I THOUGHT YOU WERE MAD.
WALK WALK
DRAG DRAG
WELL...
HE GETS THE MONEY BACK IF THE TREE BLOOMS!
SHE MAY CHANGE!
AND, MORE THAN ANYTHING...

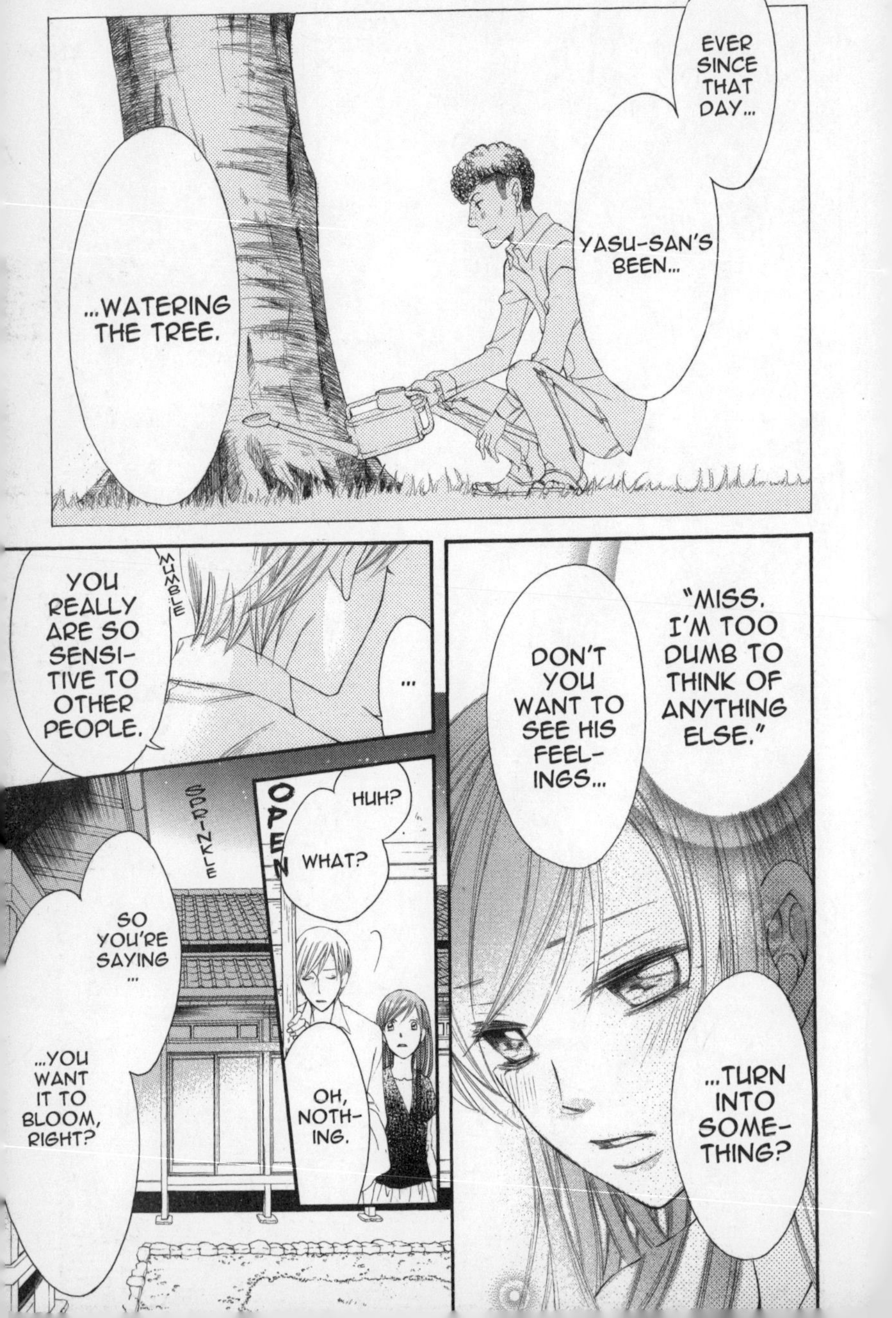
EVER SINCE THAT DAY...
YASU-SAN'S BEEN...
...WATERING THE TREE.
"MISS. I'M TOO DUMB TO THINK OF ANYTHING ELSE."
DON'T YOU WANT TO SEE HIS FEELINGS...
...TURN INTO SOMETHING?
...
MUMBLE
YOU REALLY ARE SO SENSITIVE TO OTHER PEOPLE.
OPEN
HUH?
WHAT?
OH, NOTHING.
SPRINKLE
SO YOU'RE SAYING...
...YOU WANT IT TO BLOOM, RIGHT?

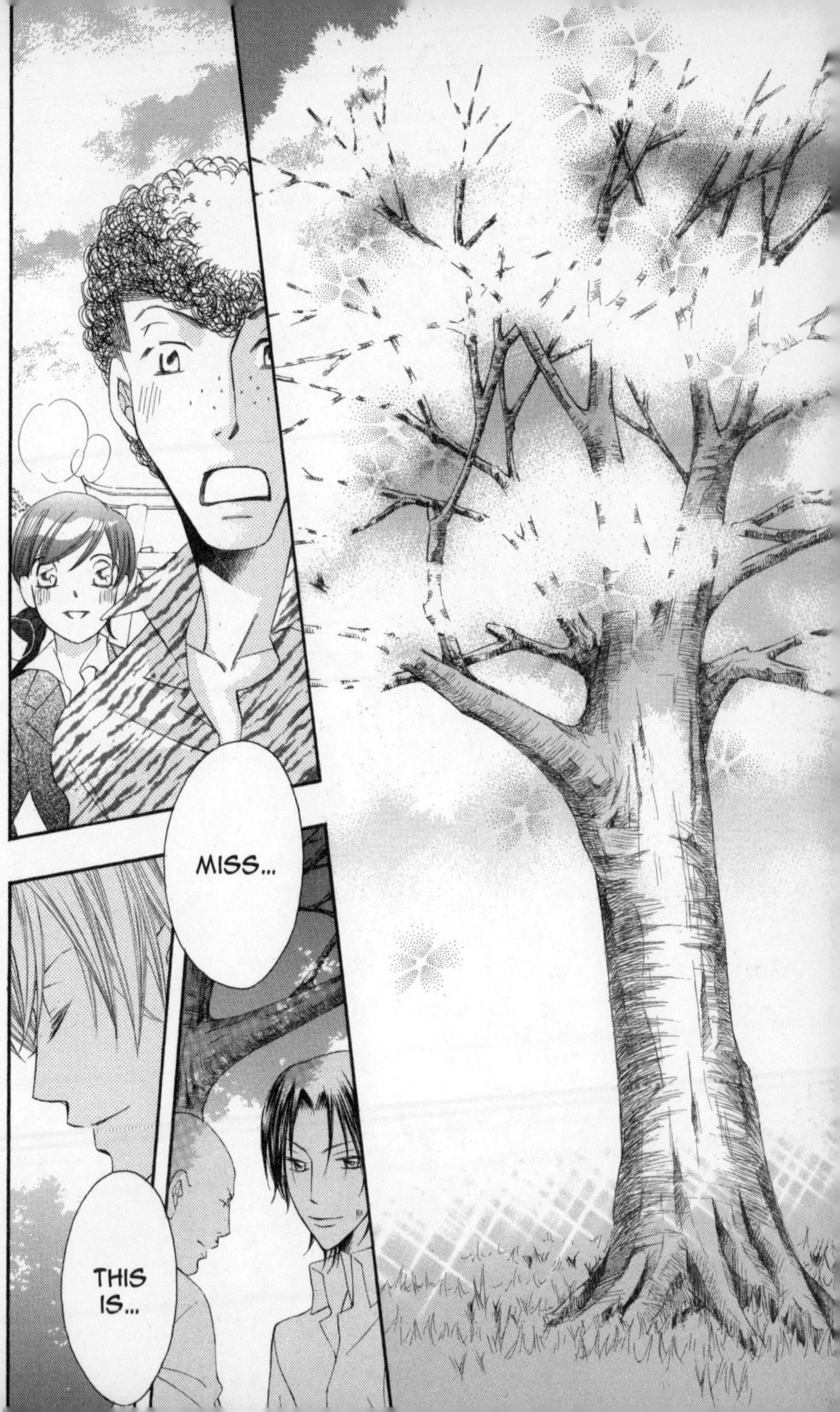
MISS...
THIS IS...

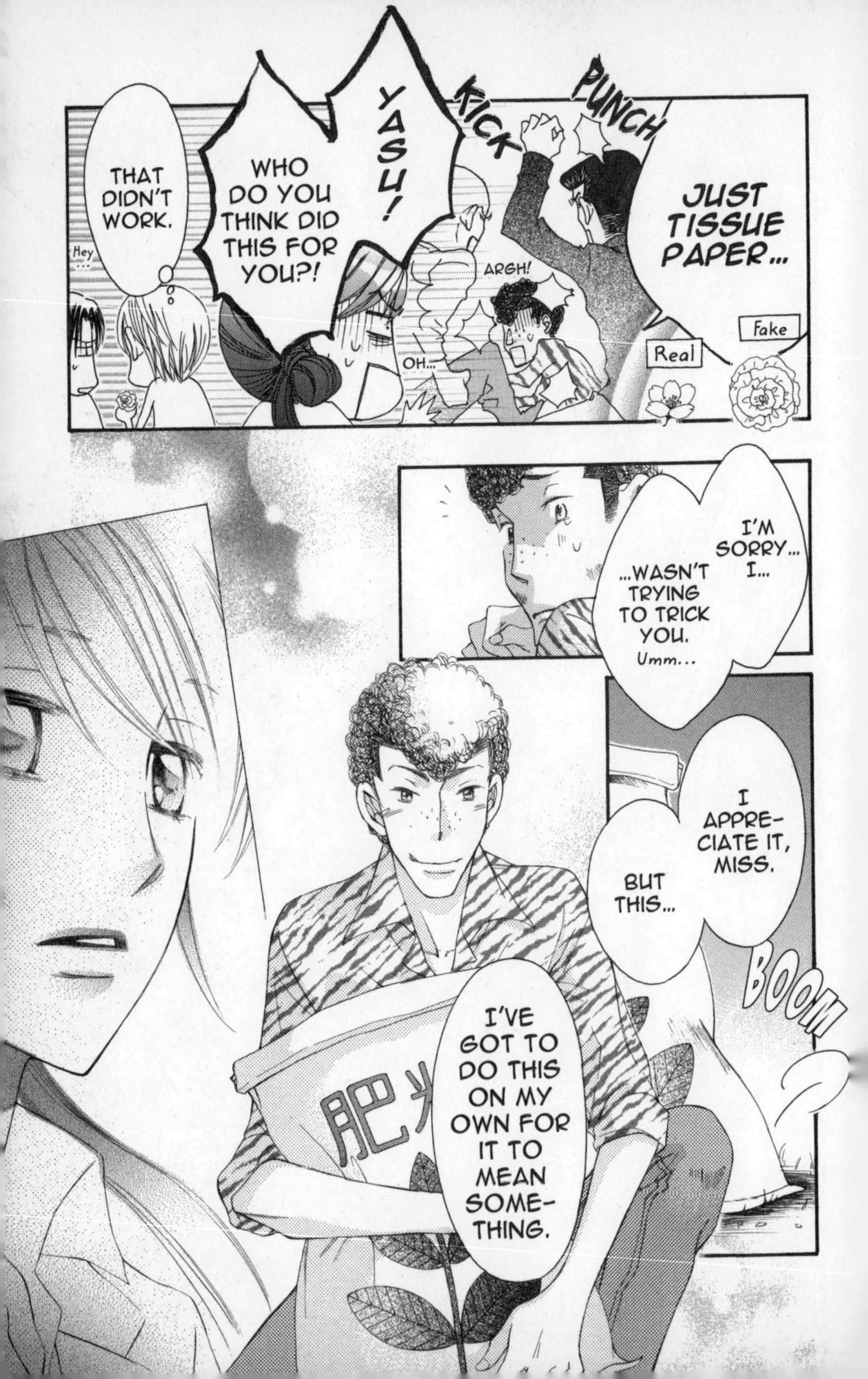
JUST TISSUE PAPER...
Fake
Real
PUNCH
KICK
ARGH!
OH...
YASU!
WHO DO YOU THINK DID THIS FOR YOU?!
THAT DIDN'T WORK.
Hey...
I'M SORRY... I...
...WASN'T TRYING TO TRICK YOU.
Umm...
I APPRECIATE IT, MISS.
BUT THIS...
BOOM
I'VE GOT TO DO THIS ON MY OWN FOR IT TO MEAN SOMETHING.

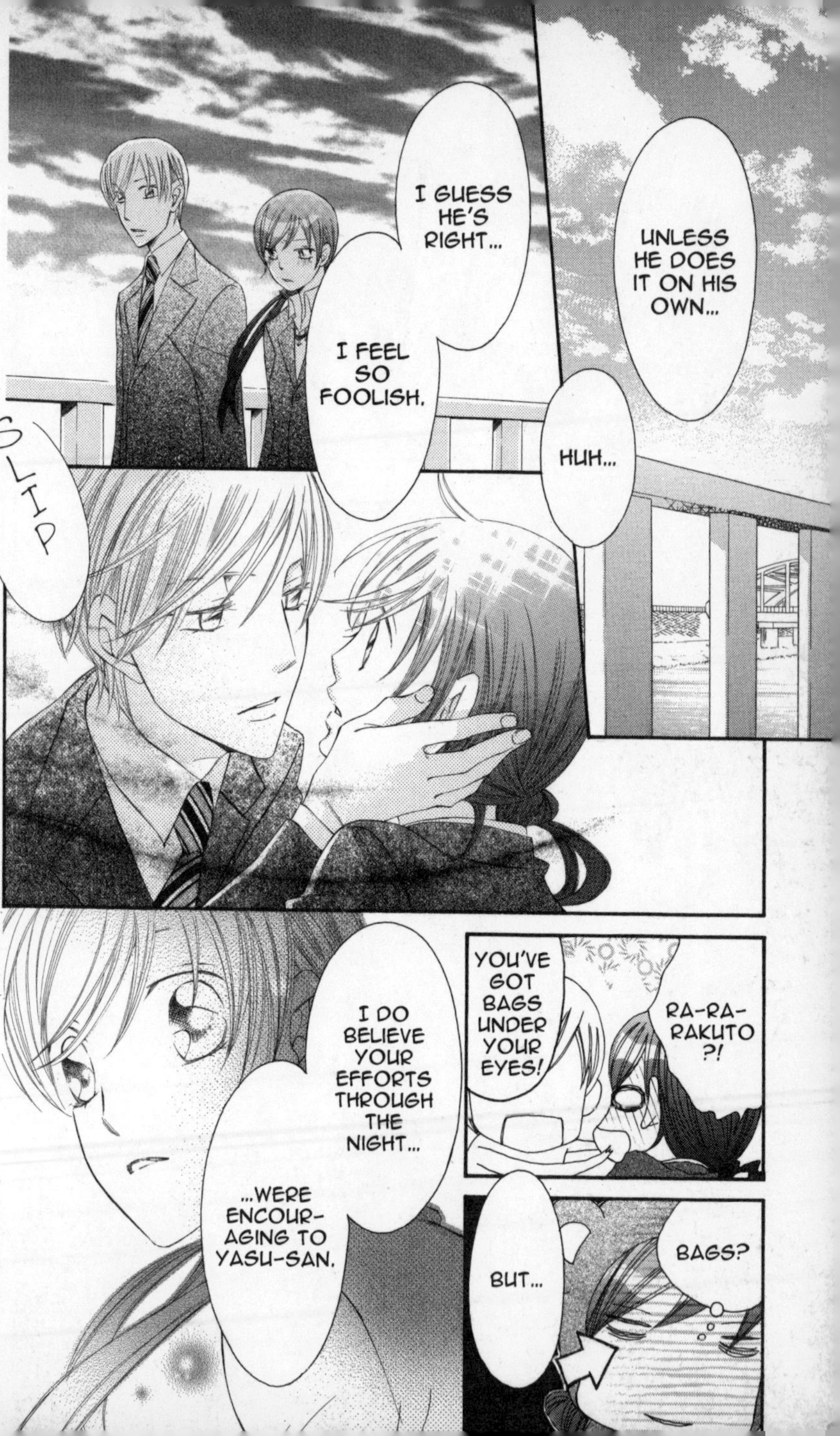
UNLESS HE DOES IT ON HIS OWN...
HUH...
I GUESS HE'S RIGHT...
I FEEL SO FOOLISH.
SLIP
RA-RA-RAKUTO ?!
YOU'VE GOT BAGS UNDER YOUR EYES!
BAGS?
BUT...
I DO BELIEVE YOUR EFFORTS THROUGH THE NIGHT...
...WERE ENCOUR-AGING TO YASU-SAN.

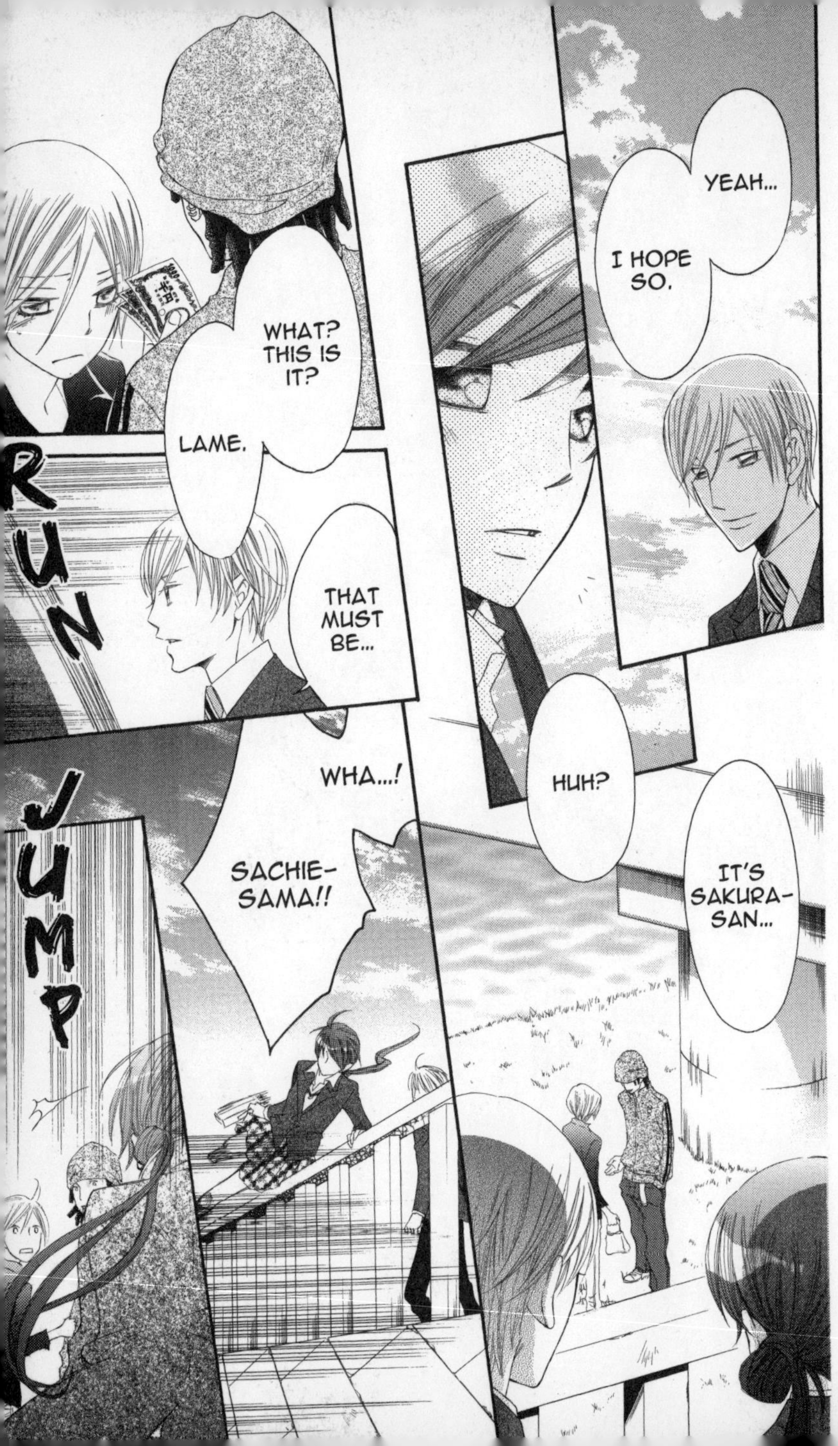
YEAH...
I HOPE SO.
HUH?
WHAT? THIS IS IT?
LAME.
THAT MUST BE...
IT'S SAKURA-SAN...
WHA...!
SACHIE-SAMA!!
RUN
JUMP

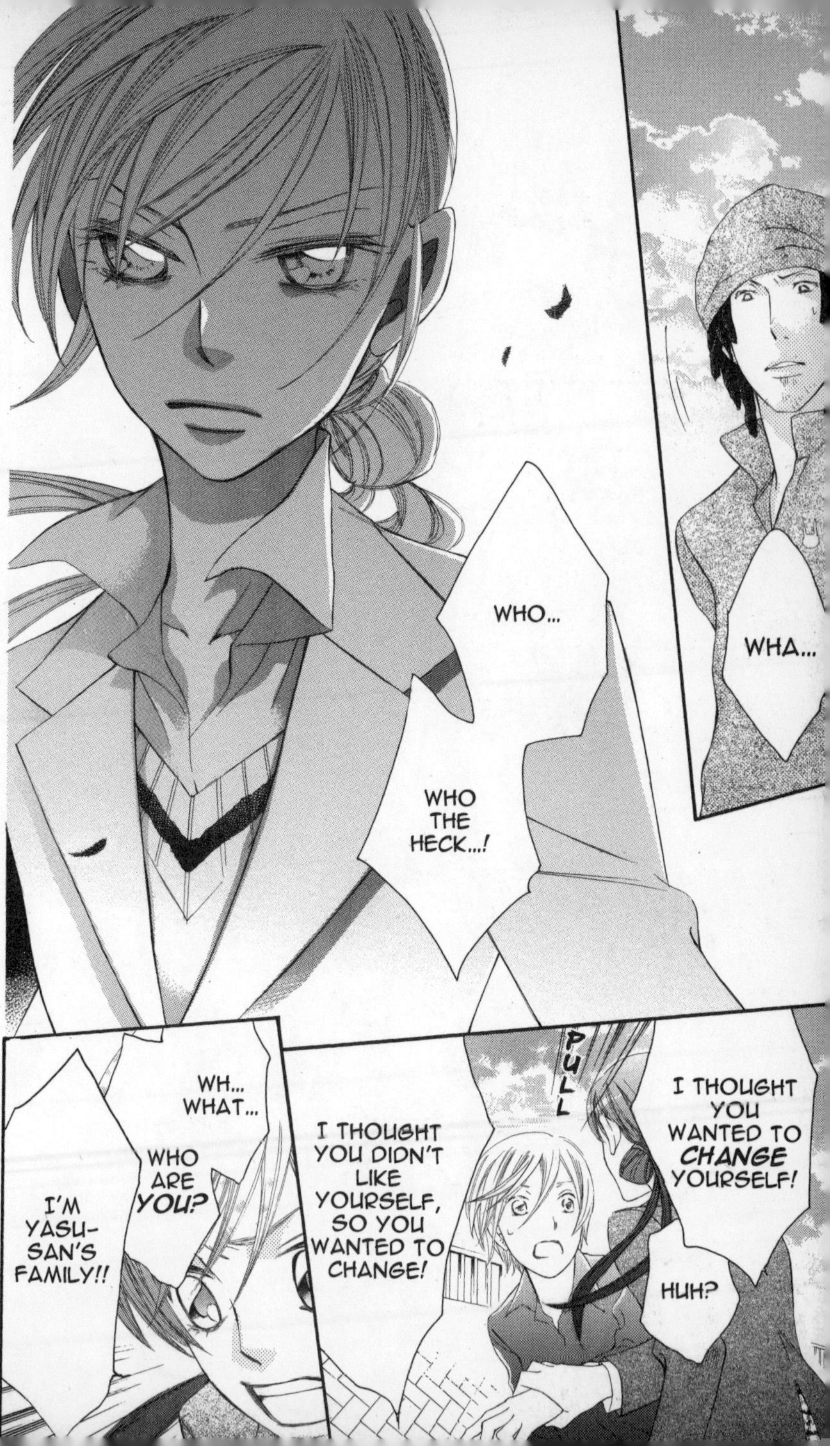
WHA...
WHO...
WHO THE HECK...!
I THOUGHT YOU WANTED TO CHANGE YOURSELF!
HUH?
PULL
I THOUGHT YOU DIDN'T LIKE YOURSELF, SO YOU WANTED TO CHANGE!
WH... WHAT...
WHO ARE YOU?
I'M YASU-SAN'S FAMILY!!

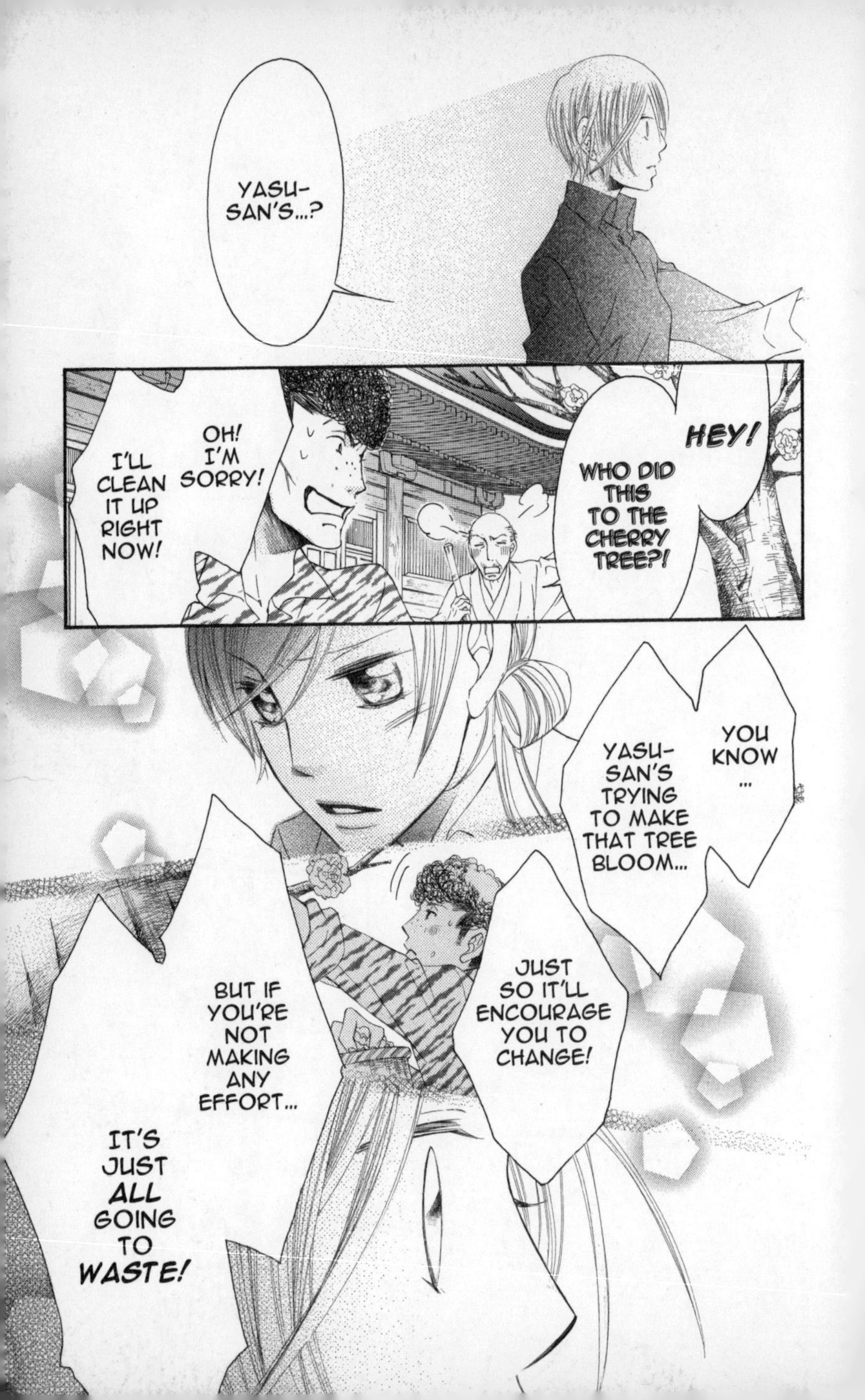
YASU-SAN'S...?
HEY! WHO DID THIS TO THE CHERRY TREE?!
OH! I'M SORRY!
I'LL CLEAN IT UP RIGHT NOW!
YOU KNOW ...
YASU-SAN'S TRYING TO MAKE THAT TREE BLOOM...
JUST SO IT'LL ENCOURAGE YOU TO CHANGE!
BUT IF YOU'RE NOT MAKING ANY EFFORT...
IT'S JUST ALL GOING TO WASTE!

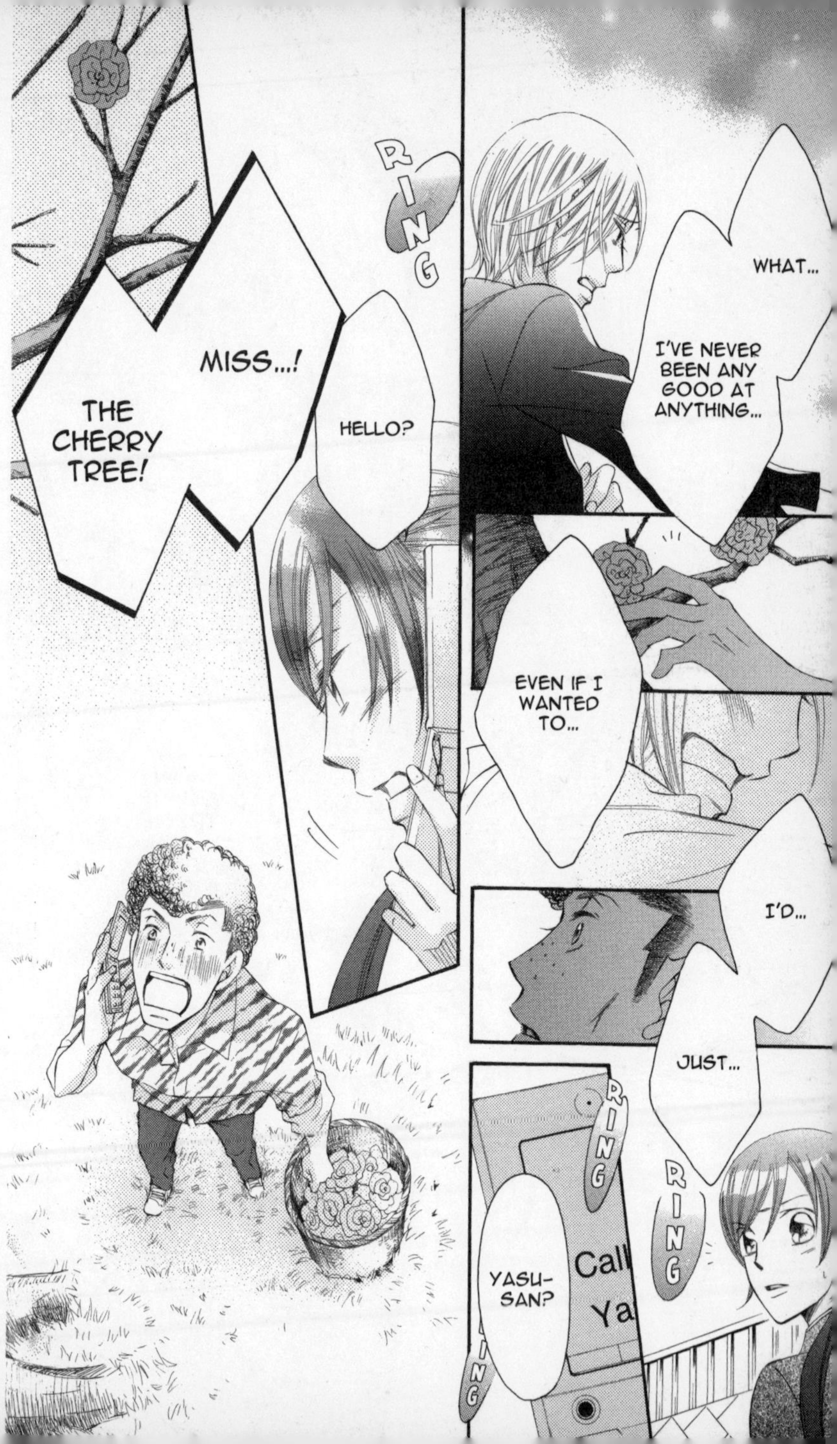
WHAT...
I'VE NEVER BEEN ANY GOOD AT ANYTHING...
EVEN IF I WANTED TO...
I'D...
JUST...
RING
RING
YASU-SAN?
Call
Ya
RING
HELLO?
MISS...!
THE CHERRY TREE!

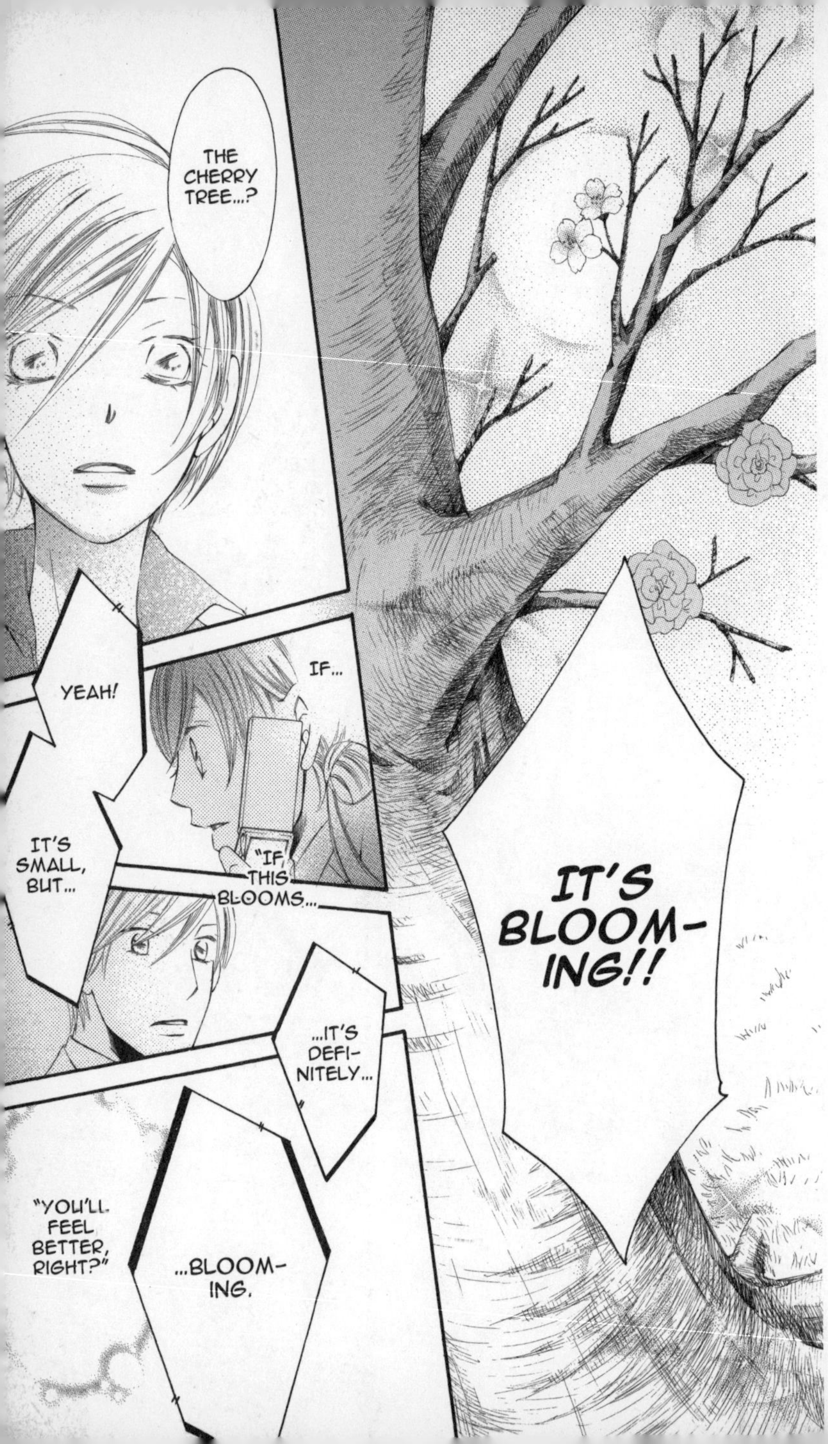
IT'S BLOOMING!!
THE CHERRY TREE...?
YEAH!
IF...
IT'S SMALL, BUT...
"IF, THIS BLOOMS...
...IT'S DEFINITELY...
...BLOOMING.
"YOU'LL FEEL BETTER, RIGHT?"

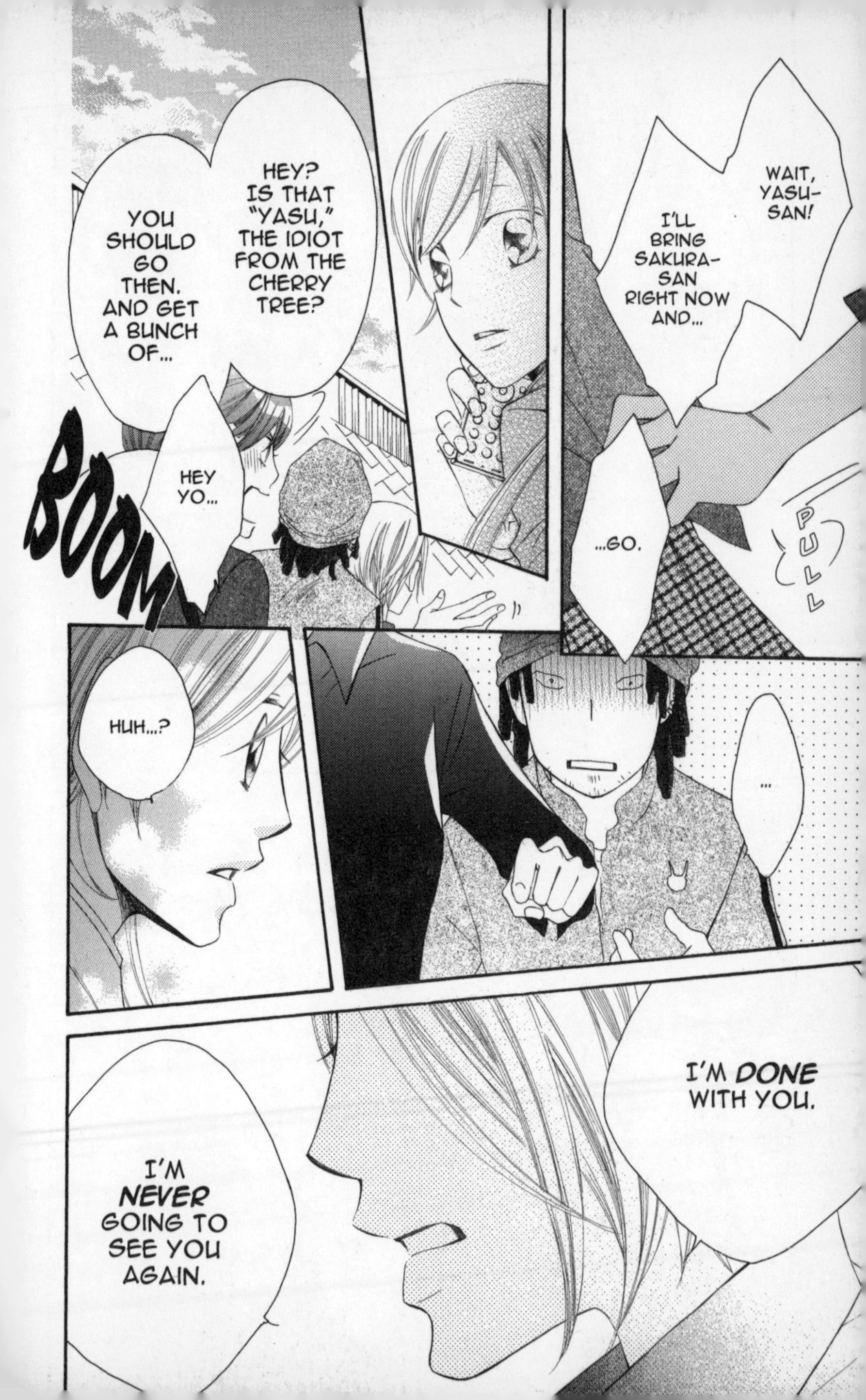
WAIT, YASU-SAN!
I'LL BRING SAKURA-SAN RIGHT NOW AND...
PULL
...GO.
HEY? IS THAT "YASU," THE IDIOT FROM THE CHERRY TREE?
YOU SHOULD GO THEN. AND GET A BUNCH OF...
HEY YO...
BOOM
...
HUH...?
I'M DONE WITH YOU.
I'M NEVER GOING TO SEE YOU AGAIN.

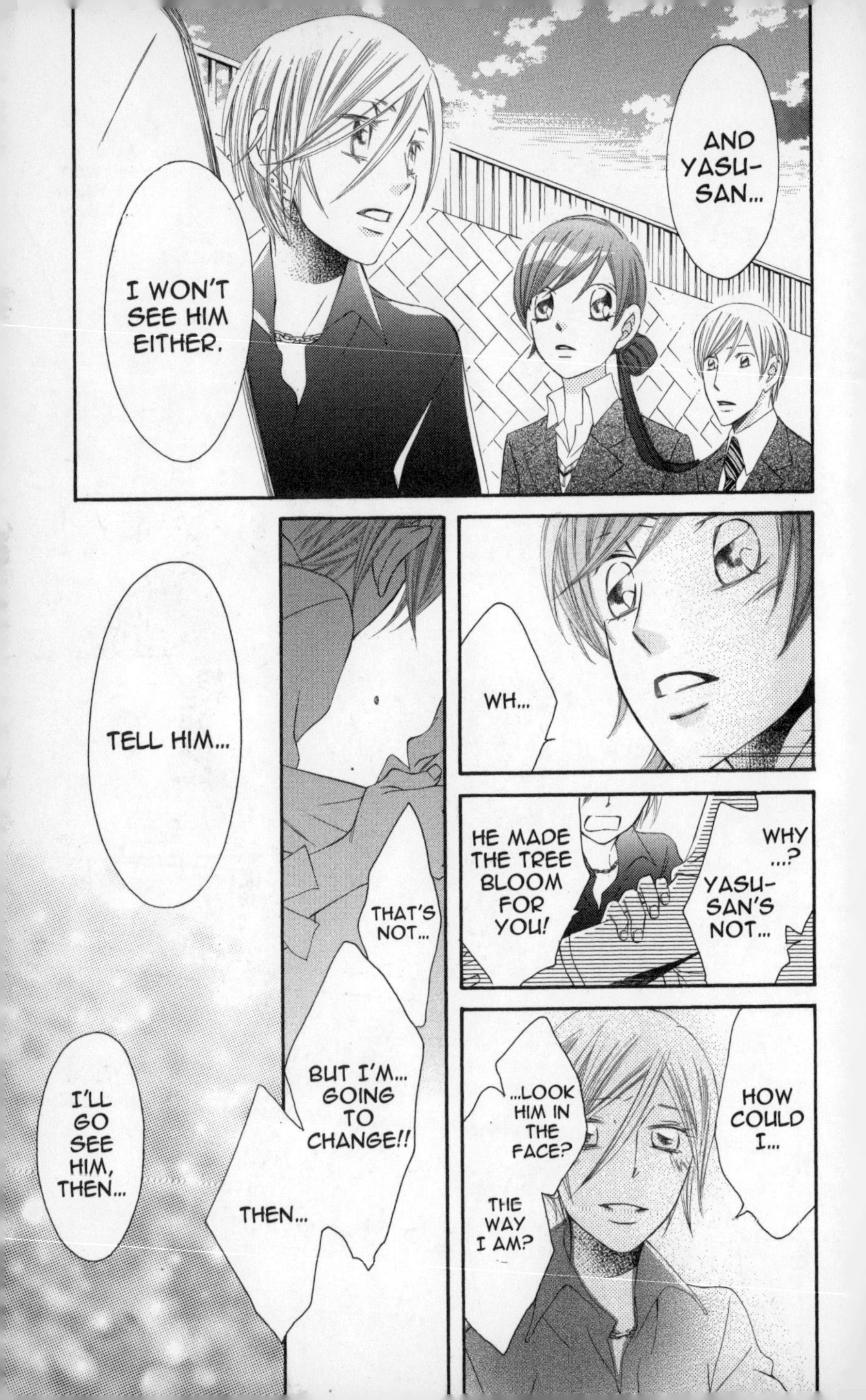
AND YASU-SAN...
I WON'T SEE HIM EITHER.
WH...
WHY ...?
YASU-SAN'S NOT...
HE MADE THE TREE BLOOM FOR YOU!
HOW COULD I...
...LOOK HIM IN THE FACE?
THE WAY I AM?
THAT'S NOT...
BUT I'M... GOING TO CHANGE!!
THEN...
TELL HIM...
I'LL GO SEE HIM, THEN...

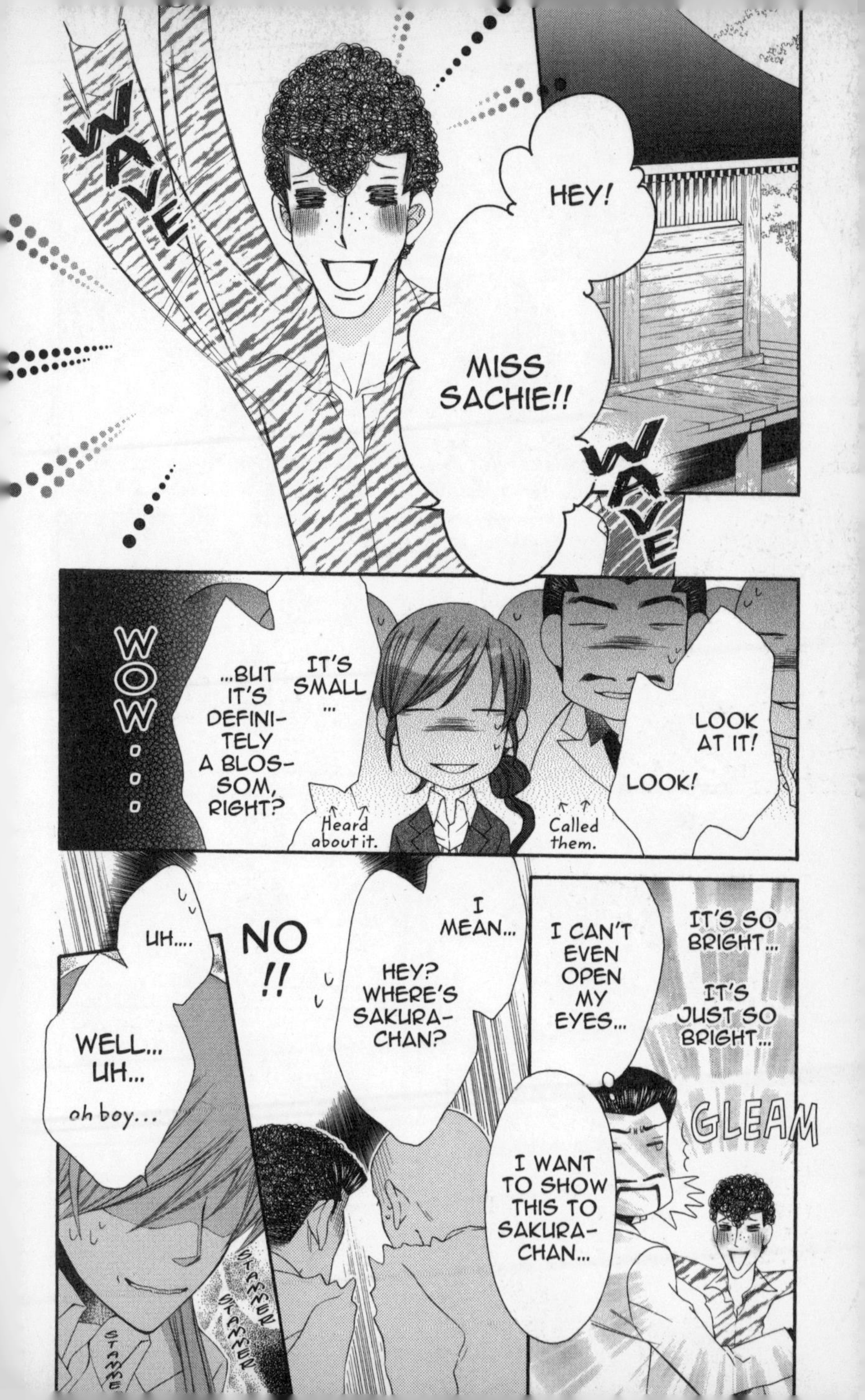
HEY!
MISS SACHIE!!
WAVE
WAVE
LOOK AT IT!
LOOK!
Called them.
IT'S SMALL ...
...BUT IT'S DEFINITELY A BLOSSOM, RIGHT?
Heard about it.
WOW...
IT'S SO BRIGHT...
IT'S JUST SO BRIGHT...
I CAN'T EVEN OPEN MY EYES...
GLEAM
I WANT TO SHOW THIS TO SAKURA-CHAN...
I MEAN...
HEY? WHERE'S SAKURA-CHAN?
NO !!
UH....
WELL... UH...
oh boy...
STAMMER
STAMMER
STAMMER

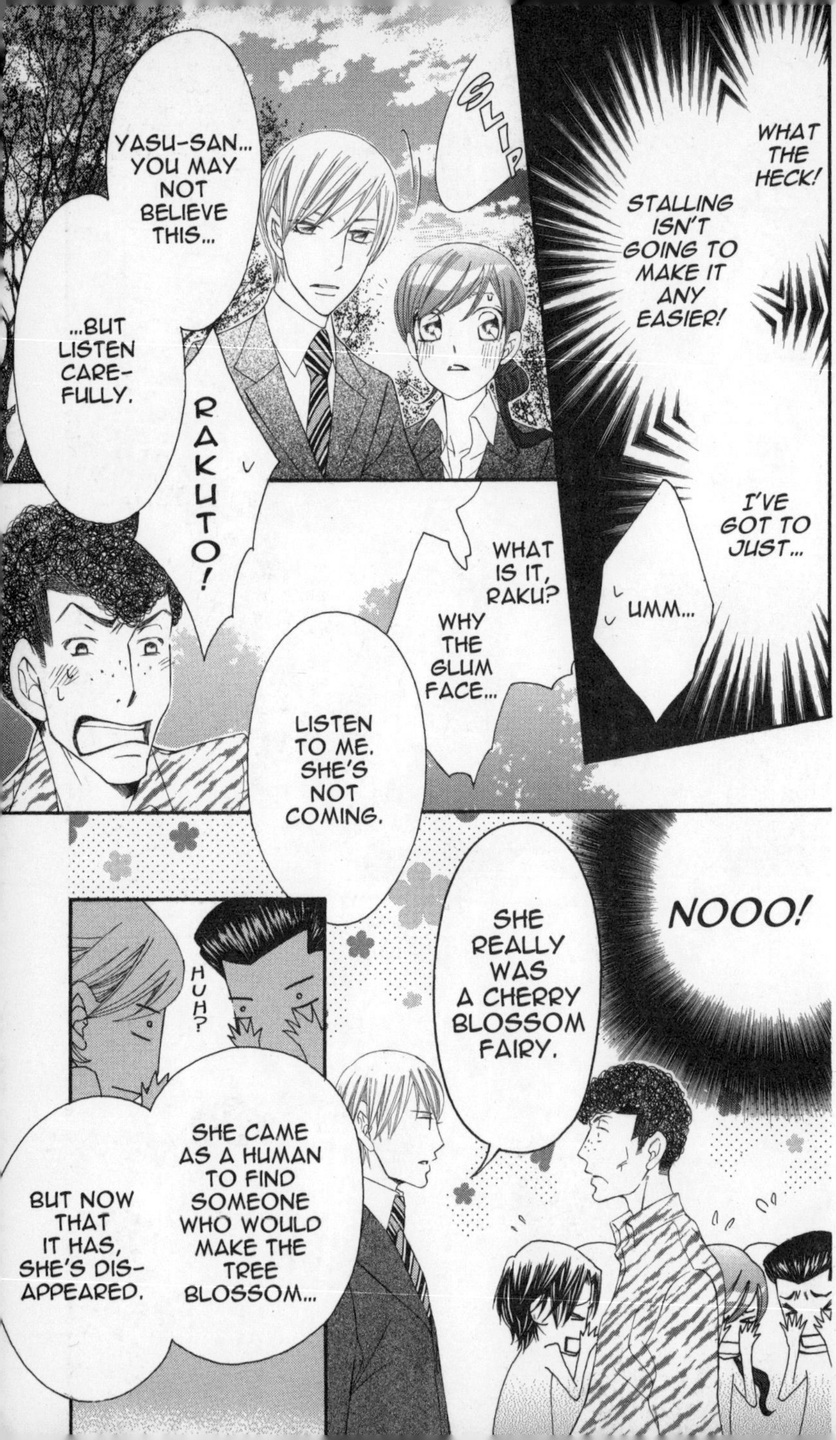
WHAT THE HECK!
STALLING ISN'T GOING TO MAKE IT ANY EASIER!
I'VE GOT TO JUST...
UMM...
SLIP
YASU-SAN... YOU MAY NOT BELIEVE THIS...
...BUT LISTEN CARE-FULLY.
RAKUTO!
WHAT IS IT, RAKU? WHY THE GLUM FACE...
LISTEN TO ME. SHE'S NOT COMING.
NOOO!
SHE REALLY WAS A CHERRY BLOSSOM FAIRY.
HUH?
SHE CAME AS A HUMAN TO FIND SOMEONE WHO WOULD MAKE THE TREE BLOSSOM...
BUT NOW THAT IT HAS, SHE'S DIS-APPEARED.

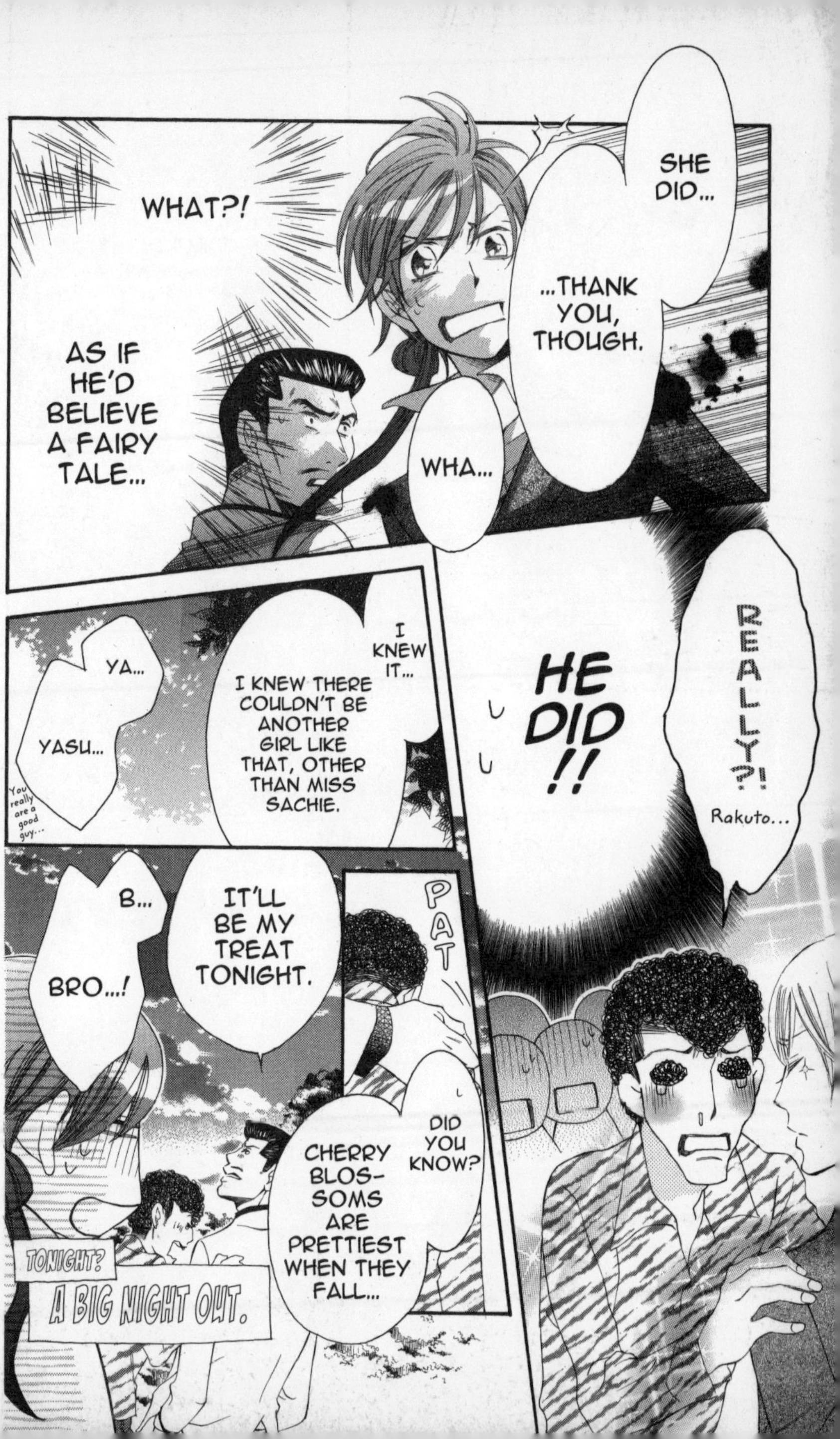
SHE DID...
...THANK YOU, THOUGH.
WHAT?!
WHA...
AS IF HE'D BELIEVE A FAIRY TALE...
REALLY?!
Rakuto...
HE DID!!
I KNEW IT...
I KNEW THERE COULDN'T BE ANOTHER GIRL LIKE THAT, OTHER THAN MISS SACHIE.
YA...
YASU...
You really are a good guy...
PAT
DID YOU KNOW?
CHERRY BLOSSOMS ARE PRETTIEST WHEN THEY FALL...
IT'LL BE MY TREAT TONIGHT.
B...
BRO...!
TONIGHT?
A BIG NIGHT OUT.

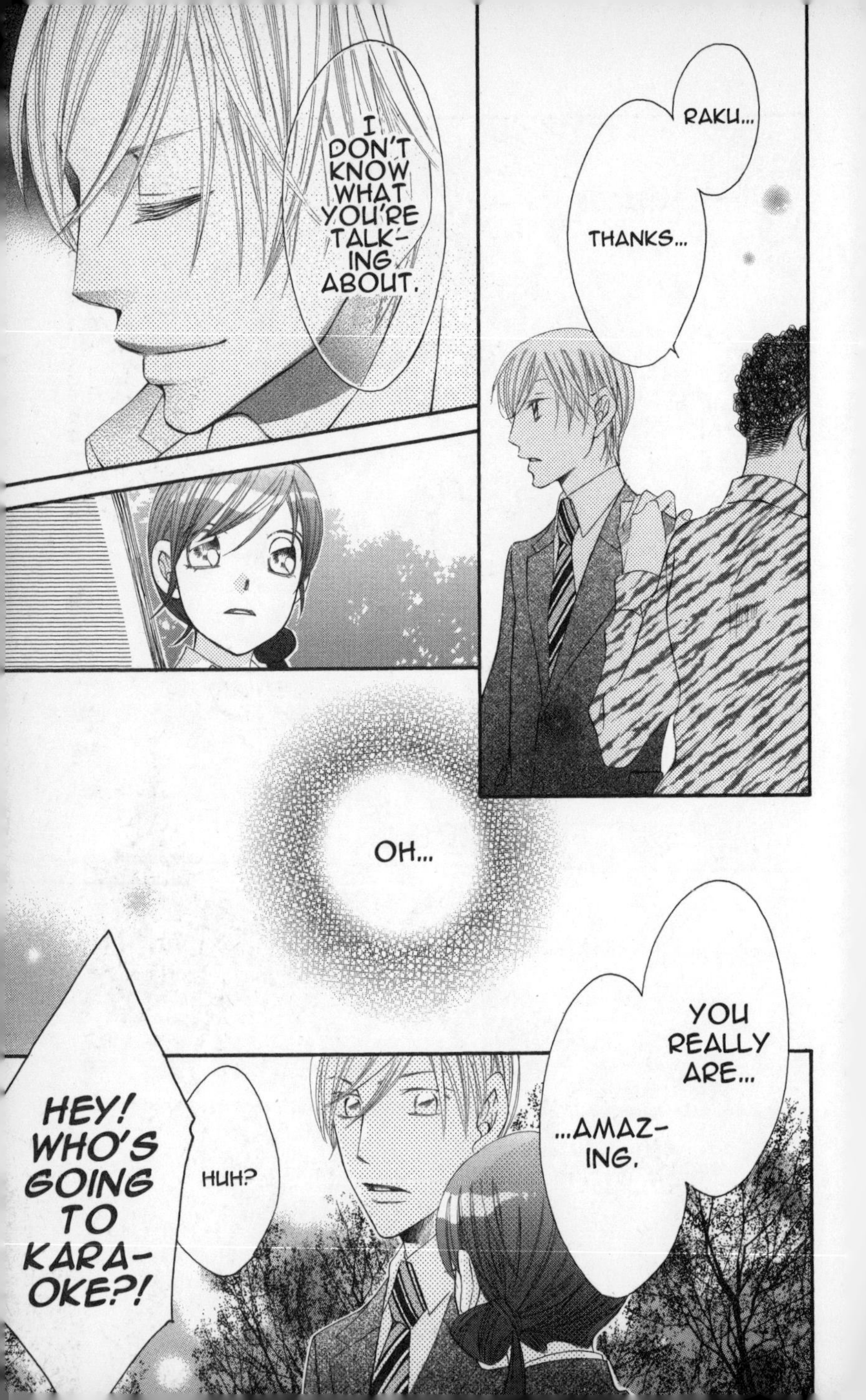
RAKU...
THANKS...
I DON'T KNOW WHAT YOU'RE TALK-ING ABOUT.
OH...
YOU REALLY ARE...
...AMAZ-ING.
HUH?
HEY! WHO'S GOING TO KARA-OKE?!

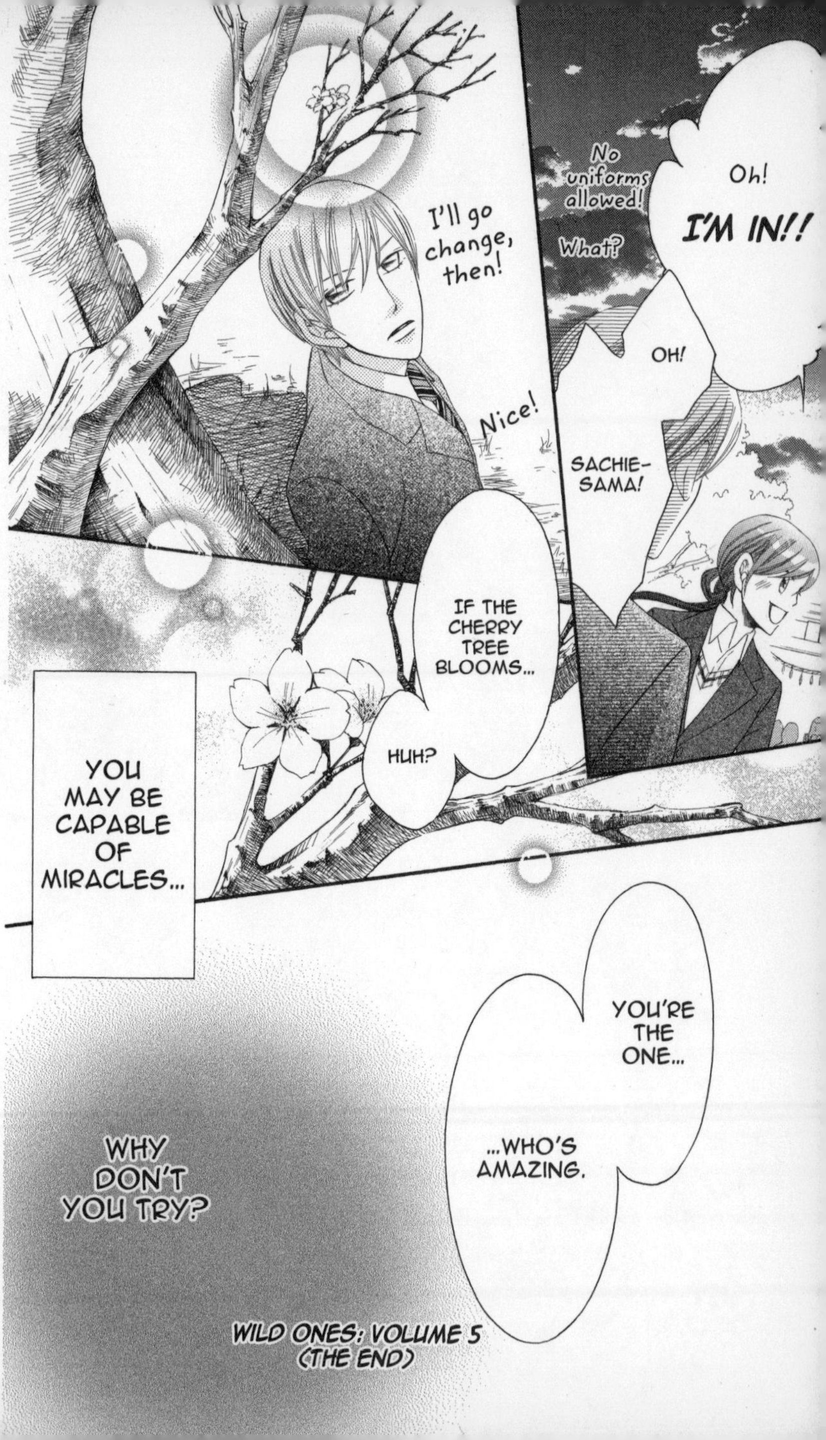
Oh!
I'M IN!!
No uniforms allowed!
What?
OH!
SACHIE-SAMA!
I'll go change, then!
Nice!
IF THE CHERRY TREE BLOOMS...
HUH?
YOU MAY BE CAPABLE OF MIRACLES...
YOU'RE THE ONE...
...WHO'S AMAZING.
WHY DON'T YOU TRY?
WILD ONES: VOLUME 5
(THE END)

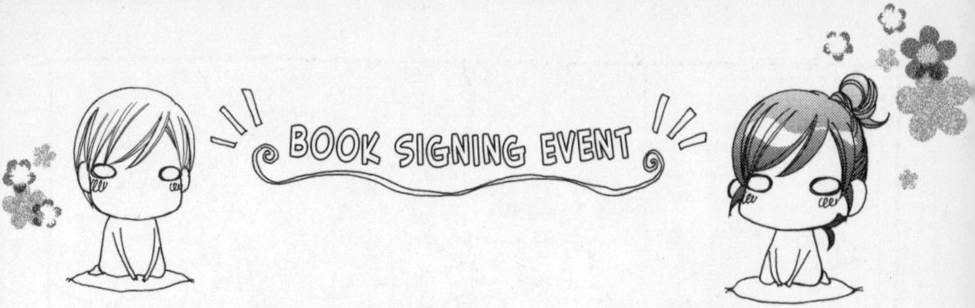
BOOK SIGNING EVENT

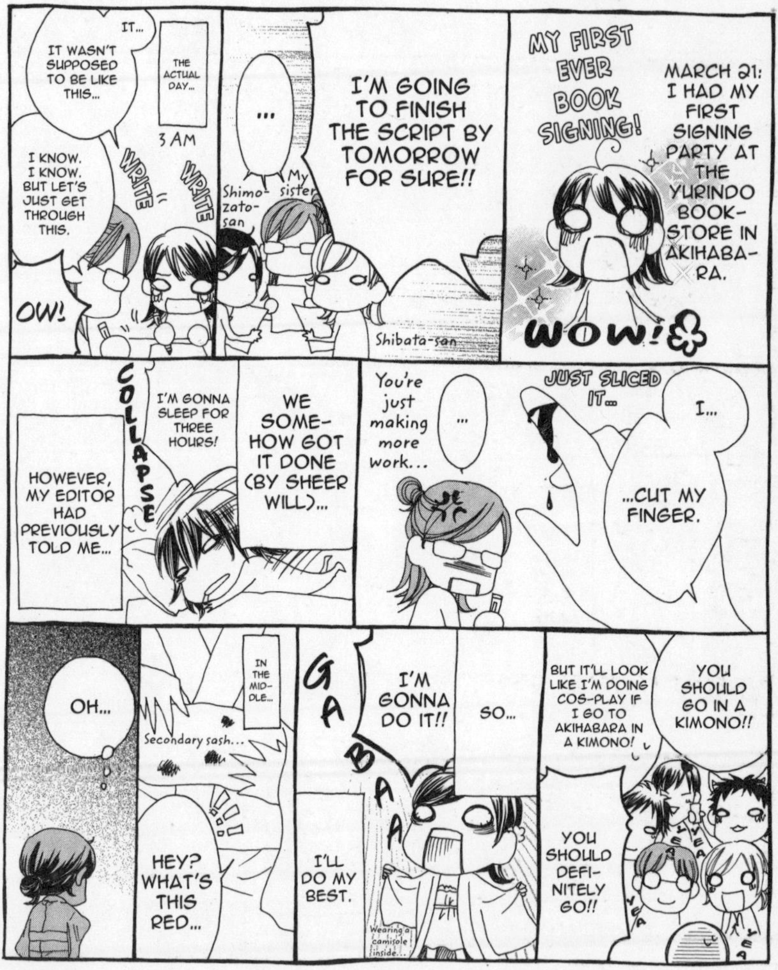
MY FIRST EVER BOOK SIGNING!
MARCH 21: I HAD MY FIRST SIGNING PARTY AT THE YURINDO BOOKSTORE IN AKIHABARA.
WOW!
I'M GOING TO FINISH THE SCRIPT BY TOMORROW FOR SURE!!
...
My sister
Shimozato-san
Shibata-san
THE ACTUAL DAY...
3 AM
IT...
IT WASN'T SUPPOSED TO BE LIKE THIS...
I KNOW. I KNOW. BUT LET'S JUST GET THROUGH THIS.
WRITE
WRITE
OW!
JUST SLICED IT...
I...
...CUT MY FINGER.
You're just making more work...
...
WE SOMEHOW GOT IT DONE (BY SHEER WILL)...
I'M GONNA SLEEP FOR THREE HOURS!
COLLAPSE
HOWEVER, MY EDITOR HAD PREVIOUSLY TOLD ME...
YOU SHOULD GO IN A KIMONO!!
BUT IT'LL LOOK LIKE I'M DOING COS-PLAY IF I GO TO AKIHABARA IN A KIMONO!
YOU SHOULD DEFINITELY GO!!
YEA
YEA
YEA
YEA
SO...
I'M GONNA DO IT!!
GABAA
I'LL DO MY BEST.
Wearing a camisole inside...
IN THE MIDDLE...
Secondary sash...
HEY? WHAT'S THIS RED...
OH...

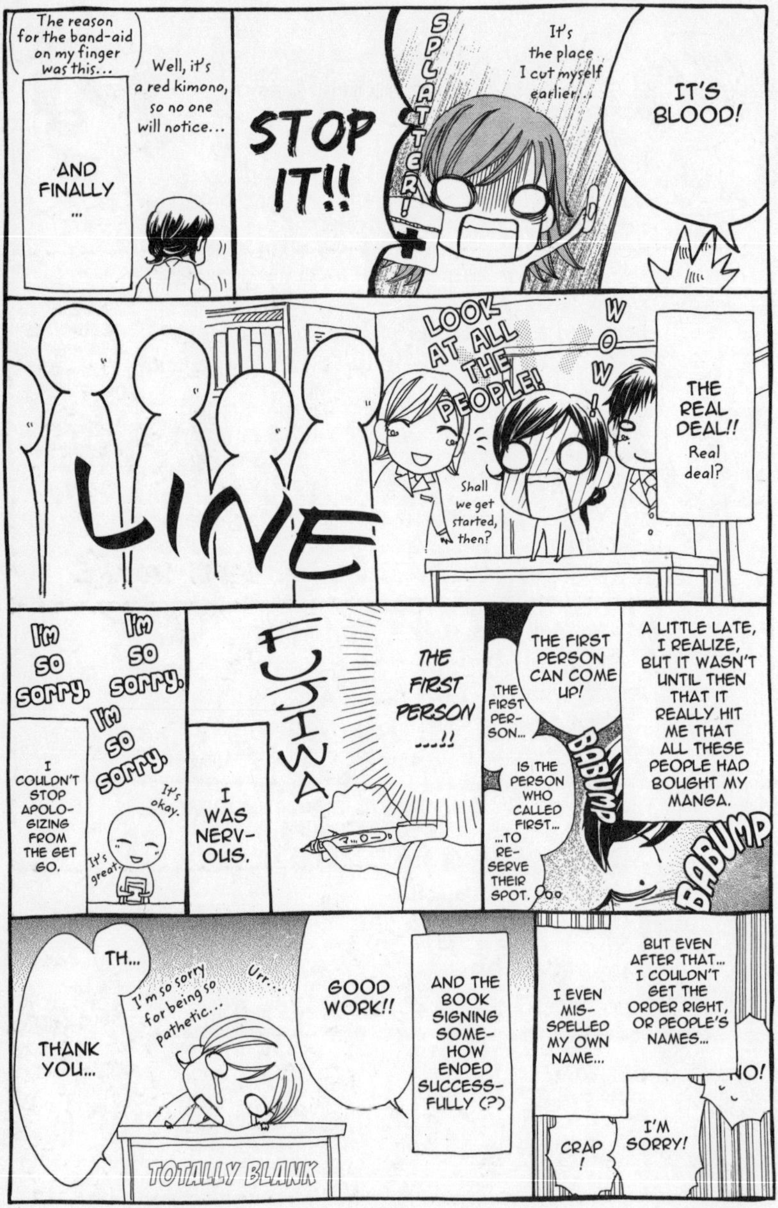
IT'S BLOOD!
It's the place I cut myself earlier...
SPLATTER!
STOP IT!!
Well, it's a red kimono, so no one will notice...
The reason for the band-aid on my finger was this...
AND FINALLY ...
THE REAL DEAL!!
Real deal?
WOW!
LOOK AT ALL THE PEOPLE!
Shall we get started, then?
LINE
A LITTLE LATE, I REALIZE, BUT IT WASN'T UNTIL THEN THAT IT REALLY HIT ME THAT ALL THESE PEOPLE HAD BOUGHT MY MANGA.
BABUMP
BABUMP
THE FIRST PERSON CAN COME UP!
THE FIRST PERSON...
IS THE PERSON WHO CALLED FIRST...
...TO RESERVE THEIR SPOT.
THE FIRST PERSON ...!!
FUJIWA
I WAS NERVOUS.
I'm so sorry.
I'm so sorry.
I'm so sorry.
It's okay.
It's great.
I COULDN'T STOP APOLOGIZING FROM THE GET GO.
BUT EVEN AFTER THAT... I COULDN'T GET THE ORDER RIGHT, OR PEOPLE'S NAMES...
NO!
I'M SORRY!
CRAP!
I EVEN MISSPELLED MY OWN NAME...
AND THE BOOK SIGNING SOMEHOW ENDED SUCCESSFULLY (?)
GOOD WORK!!
Urr...
I'm so sorry for being so pathetic...
TH... THANK YOU...
TOTALLY BLANK

I RECEIVED A LOT OF FLOWERS AND PRESENTS. I DON'T THINK I'LL EVER RECEIVE THIS MANY GIFTS FOR THE REST OF MY LIFE. (HEH) IT WAS AMAZING!

BUT, MORE THAN THE GIFTS, HAVING PEOPLE SHOW UP MADE ME THE HAPPIEST. I REALLY APPRECIATED PEOPLE TAKING TIME OUT OF THEIR BUSY SCHEDULES TO COME SEE ME.

I HAD MY SISTER TAKE A NOTEBOOK AROUND WHILE PEOPLE WERE WAITING IN LINE, AND SHE TOLD ME LATER THAT PEOPLE WERE REALLY SELECTIVE ABOUT THEIR WORDS AND SPENT TIME THINKING ABOUT WHAT TO WRITE, NO MATTER HOW SHORT THEIR NOTE ENDED UP BEING. I'VE READ THEM ALL. IT'S MY TREASURE.

IT REALLY WAS THE HAPPIEST DAY OF MY LIFE AND HAS BECOME A GREAT SOURCE OF ENCOURAGEMENT FOR ME.

I'D LIKE TO THANK YURINDO, THE EDITORIAL STAFF, AND THE SALES STAFF FOR GIVING ME THIS GREAT OPPORTUNITY.

AND TO THOSE THAT CAME AND VISITED...

THE PEOPLE WHO CAME FROM HIROSHIMA, THE MOTHER WHO CAME FOR HER DAUGHTER AWAITING SURGERY, THE SHY-LOOKING FATHER WHO CAME FOR THE MOTHER... MEN, WOMEN, BOYS, GIRLS... I REALIZED HOW MANY PEOPLE ARE SUPPORTING ME.

THANK YOU SO MUCH.

I AM SO BLESSED.

I AM SO GLAD THAT I DO MANGA.

I ASK FOR YOUR SUPPORT IN MY FUTURE ENDEAVORS.

MAY 2007

KIYO FUJIWARA

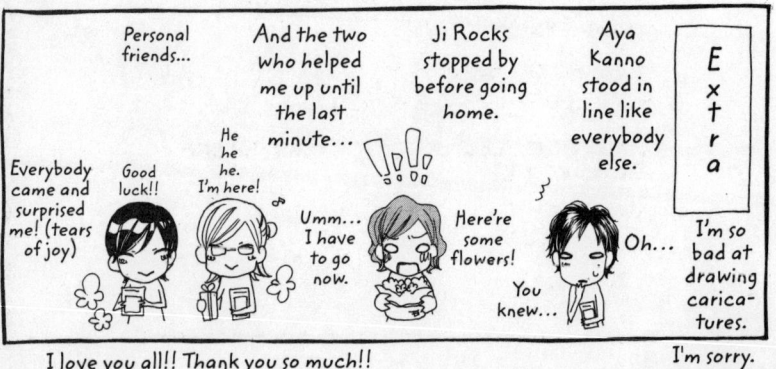

Extra
I'm so bad at drawing carica-tures.
Aya Kanno stood in line like everybody else.
Oh...
You knew...
Ji Rocks stopped by before going home.
Here're some flowers!
And the two who helped me up until the last minute...
Umm... I have to go now.
He he he. I'm here!
Personal friends...
Good luck!!
Everybody came and surprised me! (tears of joy)

I'm sorry.

I love you all!! Thank you so much!!

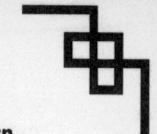

Wanna be part of the *Wild Ones* gang? Then you gotta learn the lingo! Here are some cultural notes to help you out!

HONORIFICS

San – the most common honorific title; it is used to address people outside one's immediate family and close friends. (On page 22, Takaya refers to Sachie as "-san.")

Sama – the formal version of san; this honorific title is used primarily in addressing persons much higher in rank than oneself. Sama is also used when the speaker wants to show great respect or deference. (For most of the series, Rakuto calls Sachie "Sachie-sama" in addition to "princess.")

Chan – an informal version of san used to address children and females. Chan can be used as a term of endearment between women who are good friends. (Azuma refers to Sachie as "Sa-chan.")

Senpai – honorific title used to address upperclassmen, elders and seniors in the same club or school the speaker belongs to. (The girls in Sachie's second year class call Rakuto, a third year, "Igarashi-senpai.")

NOTES

Page 22, panel 1 – Odd or Even (dice gambling)
"Odd or Even" is a traditional dice gambling game run by the yakuza. Two dice are shaken in a cup, which is placed upside down on the floor. The players bet whether the roll will come up odd or even, and then the dice roller lifts the cup to show the result.

Page 24, panel 3 – The New Year's Ogre
In northern Japan, local men dress up as ogres on New Year's Eve and go from house to house shouting, "Where are the naughty children?!" They then come into the house and warn the children to behave and obey their parents.

Page 38, panel 1 – Yakuza introduction
In traditional yazuka culture, when one gang member introduces himself to a different gang, he uses a specific formula in archaic language where he lists his first and last names and the place he was born, and expresses his honor at making the new acquaintance. Raizo uses this formula when speaking to Takaya's father.

Page 64, panel 2 – New Year's shrine visit
Japanese people visit local Shinto shrines on New Year's Day to pray for luck and health in the coming year.

Page 67, panel 2 – First dream of the year
The first dream one has in the new year is considered to hold special meaning and will predict one's fortune or fate for the coming year.

Page 73, panel 1 – Sweet Sake
A special sweet sake with rice pulp is served at shrines at New Year's and is believed to bestow health and good fortune.

Kiyo Fujiwara made her manga debut in 2000 in *Hana to Yume* magazine with *Bokuwane*. Her other works include *Hard Romantic-ker*, *Help!!* and *Gold Rush 21*. She comes from Akashi-shi in Hyogo Prefecture but currently lives in Tokyo. Her hobbies include playing drums and bass guitar and wearing kimono.

WILD ONES
VOL. 5
The Shojo Beat Manga Edition

STORY AND ART BY
KIYO FUJIWARA

Translation & Adaptation/Mai Ihara
Touch-up Art & Lettering/HudsonYards
Cover Design/Hidemi Dunn
Interior Design/Yuki Ameda
Editor/Jonathan Tarbox

Editor in Chief, Books/Alvin Lu
Editor in Chief, Magazines/Marc Weidenbaum
VP, Publishing Licensing/Rika Inouye
VP, Sales & Product Marketing/Gonzalo Ferreyra
VP, Creative/Linda Espinosa
Publisher/Hyoe Narita

Arakure by Kiyo Fujiwara
© Kiyo Fujiwara 2007
All rights reserved.
First published in Japan in 2007 by HAKUSENSHA, Inc., Tokyo.
English language translation rights arranged with HAKUSENSHA, Inc., Tokyo. The
stories, characters and incidents mentioned in this publication are entirely fictional.

Printed in Canada

Published by VIZ Media, LLC
P.O. Box 77010
San Francisco, CA 94107

Shojo Beat Manga Edition
10 9 8 7 6 5 4 3 2 1
First printing, December 2008

www.viz.com

store.viz.com

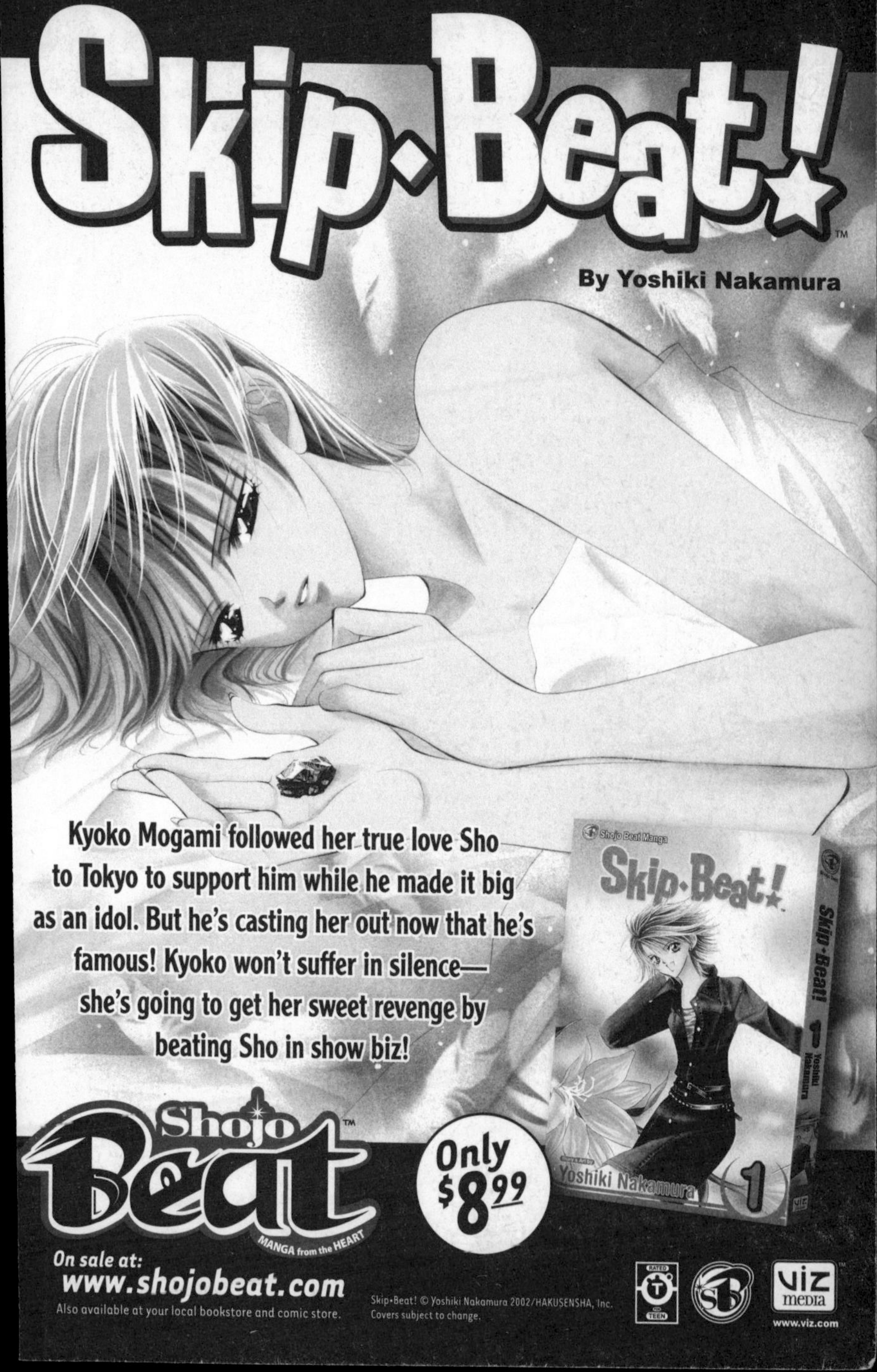
Skip·Beat!™
By Yoshiki Nakamura
Kyoko Mogami followed her true love Sho to Tokyo to support him while he made it big as an idol. But he's casting her out now that he's famous! Kyoko won't suffer in silence—she's going to get her sweet revenge by beating Sho in show biz!
Shojo Beat Manga
Skip·Beat!
Yoshiki Nakamura
1
Shojo Beat™
MANGA from the HEART
Only $8.99
On sale at:
www.shojobeat.com
Also available at your local bookstore and comic store.
Skip•Beat! © Yoshiki Nakamura 2002/HAKUSENSHA, Inc.
Covers subject to change.
RATED T TEEN
VIZ media
www.viz.com

changed significantly in the small population but not in the large population. This can be seen by tabulating the gene frequencies as follows:

For the small population, the genotype distribution after the trauma will be:

$$\frac{p^2}{36} + \frac{2pq}{48} + \frac{q^2}{8} = 92$$

The gene frequency of $t\,(q)$ after the trauma is calculated from equation (3) as:

$$q = \frac{8 \times 2 + 48 \times 1}{92 \times 2} = \frac{16 + 48}{184} = 0.348$$

The corresponding frequency of $T\,(p)$ is

$$p = 1 - q = 1. - 0.348 = 0.652$$

By the same token, the gene frequencies of t and T in the large population after the trauma will be 0.3995 and 0.6005. Thus, only the small population experiences a significant change in gene frequencies caused by the chance event.

Genetic drift can also be caused by inbreeding in a small population that can be represented by the *founder effect.* If a population is founded by a few individuals being isolated from the rest of the outbreeding population, it is possible that the isolated individuals may have unusually high frequencies of one or more harmful alleles. These alleles presumably result from previous inbreeding. Founder effect may plague also the surviving members of a population that suffers a famine or other catastrophes. The expansion of such a small population could lead to the establishment of harmful genes, the so-called *bottle neck* effect.

Examples of genetic drift can be found in laboratory and natural populations (21). It has been shown that the variability of chromosome arrangement of experimental populations of *Drosophila pseudoobscura* raised in isolated conditions depends on the number of founding individuals carrying different chromosome gene arrangements. The genetic homogeneity of certain human populations can also be traced to the few founders. For example, the Ramah Navaho Indian tribe began their population after isolation from an outbreeding population.

Finally, one must consider the interplay of neutral mutations and genetic drift resulting in gene frequency change. Mutations that are neither beneficial nor harmful to organisms are termed neutral and are the source of new genes that will be established eventually in the population by

random drift. In other words, there is no selection
tions by the environment or from intrinsic factors wi

Recently it has been hypothesized that a large am
bility may be attributed to genetic drift acting on ne
produced by a substantial number of neutral mutat
hypothesis will be explored in I.3.3.2.a.1.

References 2.6

1. Griffith, F. J. Hyg. Camb. 27:113; 1928.
2. Avery, O. T.; MacLeod, C. M.; McCarty, M. J. 1944.
3. Watson, J. D.; Crick, F. H. C. Cold Spring Ha Biol. 18:123; 1953.
4. Watson, J. D.; Crick, F. H. C. Nature. 171:464;
5. Nirenberg, M. W.; Mataei, J. H. Proc. Natl 47:1588; 1961.
6. Nishimura, S.; Jones, D. S.; Khorana; H. G. J. 1965.
7. Watson, J. D. Molecular biology of the gene. Me jamin; 1976: 374.
8. Lane, C. D.; Marbaix, G.; Gurdon, J. B. J. Mol.
9. Watson, J. D. Molecular biology of the gene. 482
10. Jacob, F.; Monod, J. J. Mol. Biol. 2:318; 1961.
11. Bachmann, B. J.; Low, K. B.; Taylor, A. L. Bact 1976.
12. Davidson, E. H.; Britten, R. J. Q. Rev. Biol. 48:
13. Soyfer, V. N. In: Evolutionary biology. Dobzhans K.; Steere, W. C. eds. Vol. 8. New York: Plenum
14. Stanier, R. Y.; Adelberg, E. A.; Ingraham, J. The 4th ed. Englewood Cliffs, NJ: Prentice Hall; 1976
15. Hall, Z. W.; Lehman, I. R. J. Mol. Biol. 36:1321;
16. Springgate, C. F.; Loeb, L. A. Proc. Natl. Acad. 1973.
17. Green, M. M. Mutat. Res. 10:353; 1970.
18. Green, M. M. J. Genet. (Suppl.). 73:187; 1973.
19. Dobzhansky, T. Genetics of the evolutionary pro Columbia Univ. Press; 1970: 44.
20. Goldschmidt, R. The material basis of evolution. Yale Univ. Press; 1940.
21. Strickberger, M. W. J. Genet. 2nd ed. New York: 777–79.

3.1 C

In
some
ary,
with
men
How
scie
Th
posi
(posi
know
the
pen
scie
mod
are
obje
so-c
base
T
by
play
Alth
star

changing, with the result that its ability to describe reality is increasing. Therefore, the empirical method is one of the most important tools in the search for consistent and verifiable explanations of reality.

Scientific methodology consists of careful observation and experimentation with suitable controls. Therefore, the scientist must minimize personal bias during collection and interpretation of data. Sometimes the bias of one influential individual can lead to much wasted effort. This was the case when the powerful Russian agronomist T. D. Lysenko advocated the Lamarckian mode of inheritance, regardless of the overwhelming evidence against it (see Sec. I.1.3.). His opinions controlled scientific research in genetics and agriculture for more than 35 years in the Soviet Union. Not until the serious failure of Soviet agriculture in 1964 did the Russian political authorities withdraw their support from Lysenko (2). However, in the absence of political totalitarianism, science is generally a self-corrective enterprise.

For a scientific theory to be established, it must be a generalization supported by a large body of different types of observations and experiments that are reproducible. In addition, it must have discrete parameters and well-defined concepts so that it is *falsifiable* (i.e., the parameters and concepts involved must be subject to empirical scrutiny such that their validity can be established or discredited [3]).

Two conditions are inherent in a good scientific theory, *empirical adequacy* and *rational coherency* (4). Empirical adequacy pertains to the testability of the theory; it must be amenable to empirical verification. Rational coherency demands that the concept under question be internally consistent as well as consistent with other concepts that are arrived at rationally.

Newton's theory of universal gravitation is a good example of a theory that is both empirically adequate and rationally coherent. It is subjected to empirical verification by every intelligent person who observes the fall of an apple toward the earth, and the calculation of the gravitational constant can be determined experimentally by the Cavendish balance. It is also rationally coherent because it has definable and measurable parameters. In addition, it is consistent with Newton's second law of motion (5).

A theory can be supported by two types of evidence, namely, empirical and circumstantial. Empirical evidence is the data collected by experimental observations and reproducible experience. Circumstantial evidence is data that is proposed as factual, based on reasonable inferences from other accepted facts (e.g., empirical facts). However, the latter can often be interpreted in many different ways, sometimes, resulting in

175

opposing positions. Therefore, empirical evidence is more powerful in the verification or falsification of a theory.

The controversy over the theory of spontaneous generation illustrates the importance of empirical evidence. During medieval times a popular theory stated that life arose continually from the nonliving. This belief was based on circumstantial evidence. People observed worms creeping from mud, maggots crawling from decaying meat, microbes coming from refuse of various kinds and they concluded that this was new life appearing. It was believed also that microorganisms found in spoiled meat broth arose spontaneously from nonliving materials (*see* I.3.3.1).

It was not until the nineteenth century that Louis Pasteur gathered empirical evidence to demonstrate that microorganisms in the air cause meat broth contamination. He filtered air and identified microscopically the microorganisms trapped in the air filter. He showed also that the trapped microorganisms contaminated boiled sterile broth. Thus, the theory of spontaneous generation under present earth conditions was discredited (*see* I.3.3.1.a).

The strengths and weaknesses of the Neo-Darwinian evolutionary theory can be evaluated, using the criteria listed above. This author submits that the strengths of the theory lie in *microevolution* (the special theory of evolution); however, *macroevolution* (the general theory of organic evolution) has serious difficulties in meeting the above criteria. The validity of microevolution will be evaluated in 3.2 and macroevolution in 3.3.

References 3.1

1. Bube, R. The human quest. Waco, TX: Word; 1971: 50–66.
2. Lerner, M. I.; Libby, W. J. Heredity, evolution and society. San Francisco: Freeman; 1976: 389–94.
3. Popper, F. R. The logic of scientific discovery. London: Hutchinson; 1959.
4. Holmes, A. Chairman, Department of Philosophy, Wheaton College. Personal communication. Faith and Learning Seminar. Wheaton, IL: Summer, 1976.
5. Sears, F. W.; Zemansky, M. W. University physics. London: Addison-Wesley; 1963: 93–108.

3.2 Evaluation of Microevolution (The Special Theory of Evolution)

3.2.1 *Empirical Adequacy.* The mechanism of the Neo-Darwinian concepts of microevolution can be documented empirically.

a) *Mutation as the Raw Material of Evolution.* As described in I.2.6,

Sterile
nutrient
Control
valve
Sterile
cotton
filter
Air inlet
for
aeration
and
agitation
Opening for bacterial inoculation
and air outlet
Siphon
overflow
Growth chamber

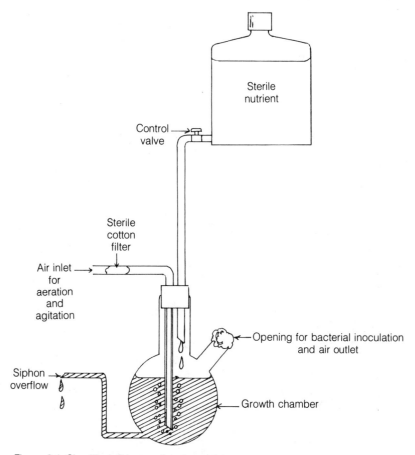

Figure 3.1. Simplified diagram of a chemostat.

spontaneous mutations, especially those caused by nucleotide substitution, may not necessarily be harmful to an organism. They can also be either neutral or advantageous. The beneficial effects of mutations have been documented best in microorganisms. For example, certain spontaneous mutants of *Bacillus subtilis*, a commonly found soil bacterium, show an increased growth rate even in the absence of selection. Mutants grew faster than the normal (wild type) bacteria at 31°C, 34°C, 37°C, 45°C, and 48°C in a defined culture medium that provided only minimum essential nutrients (1).

Behavior of bacterial mutants like those above is studied in a chemostat (Figure 3.1). The device allows the continuous growth of bacterial culture. The design of the apparatus ensures the constant supply of nutrients and oxygen to the growth chamber as well as the continuous washout of excess bacteria that, if allowed to remain in the chamber, would slow the overall bacterial growth rate. Optimal temperature and oxygen levels for growth are maintained. Theoretically, a pure bacterial culture in the growth chamber could grow for an indefinite period of time if contamination from other microorganisms is avoided. Therefore, the effects of mutation in the pure culture can be followed for many generations. A bacterial strain growing in the chemostat for 10 days at 37°C at a generation time of two hours and at an original density of 5×10^8/ml was replaced by a new bacterial strain that arose from spontaneous mutation. The growth rate of the mutant was five times the rate of the original strain (2).

The cumulative effect of several sequential nucleotide replacement mutations was shown to be harmless or beneficial in the human colon bacterium *Escherichia coli*. The strain selected contained a mutant locus in the mutator gene (*see* I.2.6.3.a.3). It was grown in a chemostat for 1400 generations, and during this time a nucleotide replacement rate of about seven transversions per bacterium per generation was calculated. At the end of the growth period approximately 10 000 nucleotide pairs were replaced in the bacterial strains found in the chemostat. It was found that this drastically mutated bacterial strain grew at the same rate as the original bacterial culture in the chemostat (3).

In another experiment that involved the study of competition of a normal strain of bacteria with a bacterial strain mutated in its mutator gene, equal numbers of each strain were introduced into the chemostat at the beginning. The mutant strain was observed to outgrow the wild-type strain 23- to 102-fold in periods ranging from 99 to 777 elapsed generations. Comparable ratios were also observed if initial mutant populations were less than the normal strain. These experiments suggest that the mutant strain that underwent extensive nucleotide substitutions in its own DNA, presumably as a result of a mutated form of DNA polymerase, actually grew faster than the nonmutated strain (4). The cumulative effect of several nucleotide substitutions appeared to be *beneficial* under the conditions of the experiment.

Irradiation-induced mutations also may be favorable to an organism. A study was made of the effects of x-irradiation on the fruit fly *Drosophila birchii*. Two identical populations were established from a natural population. One population served as a control while the other population was given 1000 R (Roentgens) of x-ray during each of the first three generations. This dosage of irradiation was enough to induce a large number of mutations. During the initial generations, the number of flies in the irradiated population was smaller than the control population, presuma-

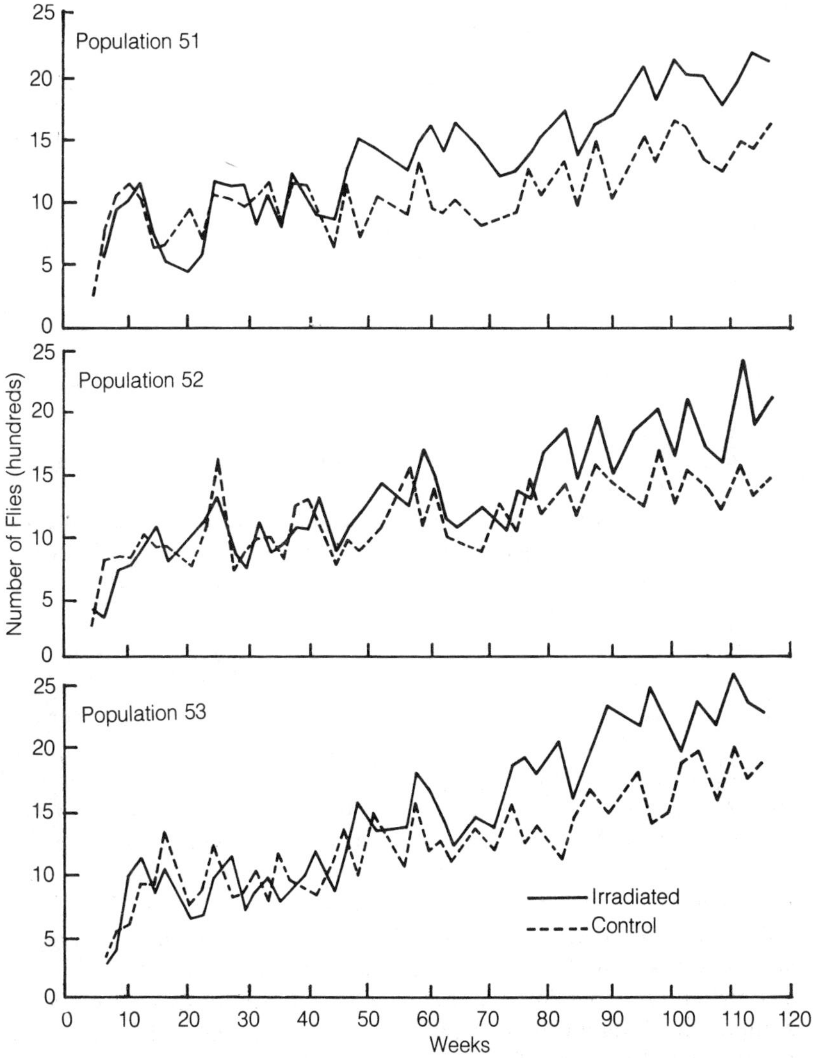
Population 51
Population 52
Population 53
Number of Flies (hundreds)
Weeks
0
5
10
15
20
25
0
10
20
30
40
50
60
70
80
90
100
110
120
Irradiated
Control

Figure 3.2. Rate of evolution in irradiated and nonirradiated experimental populations of *Drosophila birchii*. Each of three large populations was divided into two: one was subject to irradiation for three generations, the other was the control. All populations became increasingly adapted to the experimental environment, as reflected in the gradual increase in size. The irradiated populations, however, increased at a faster rate than the controls, evincing that some mutations induced by radiation may be favorable to their carriers. Reprinted, with permission, from Dobzhansky, T. et al. Evolution. San Francisco: W. H. Freeman and Co.; 1977. © 1977 by W. H. Freeman and Co.

Table 3.1. Rate of evolution of irradiated and nonirradiated populations of *Drosophila birchii* in the experiment in Figure 3.2.*

Population		Mean number of flies in population	Increase in number of flies per week
51	Control	1093 ± 47	6.9 ± 2.0
	Irradiated	1337 ± 73	11.5 ± 3.0
52	Control	1106 ± 53	8.3 ± 2.0
	Irradiated	1283 ± 86	15.2 ± 3.2
53	Control	1121 ± 70	6.4 ± 2.0
	Irradiated	1334 ± 103	12.9 ± 3.2

*NOTE: From Proceedings of National Academy of Science, Washington, D.C. 63(3)790–93; 1969.

bly due to flies dying from harmful mutations caused by radiation. However, in succeeding generations the irradiated populations recovered, and they outgrew the control populations in approximately two years, during which time 30 to 40 generations passed (Figure 3.2, Table 3.1). In the experiment, radiation-induced mutations permit the flies to better exploit the experimental conditions (Table 3.1).

b) *Selection as the Driving Force for Evolution.* The principle of selective medium has been widely used in microbiological laboratories to isolate rare bacterial mutants. When this principle is used, a certain nutrient necessary for the growth of unmutated bacteria is withheld from the selected agar medium; therefore, the only bacteria that grow on this agar plate are strains that are mutated to become independent of the missing nutrient. By the same token, when a drug such as an antibiotic that kills normal unmutated bacteria is added to the agar medium, the only bacteria that survive in the drug-supplemented medium is a strain mutated to acquire drug resistance. By this principle, mutation as rare as one mutant per one billion wild-type bacteria can be detected. When a bacterial culture containing a mutant is introduced into a selective agar medium, the mutant will grow and form a visible colony at the expense of the unmutated bacteria after an appropriate time of incubation. Experimental work with the many bacterial mutants that were originally isolated by using the principle of selective medium has contributed greatly to advances in molecular genetics (1,5).

With the discovery and use of antibiotics to fight bacterial infection, several drug-resistant strains of bacteria have increased in occurrence and are of medical concern. For example, the widespread use of penicillin has fostered an increase in populations of penicillin-resistant *Staphylolococ-*